FEMALE "CIRCUMCISION" IN AFRICA

Directions in Applied Anthropology:
Adaptations and Innovations

FEMALE "CIRCUMCISION" IN AFRICA

CULTURE, CONTROVERSY, AND CHANGE

edited by
Bettina Shell-Duncan
Ylva Hernlund

LYNNE
RIENNER
PUBLISHERS

BOULDER
LONDON

First published in the United States of America in 2000 by
Lynne Rienner Publishers, Inc.
1800 30th Street, Boulder, Colorado 80301
www.rienner.com

and in the United Kingdom by
Lynne Rienner Publishers, Inc.
3 Henrietta Street, Covent Garden, London WC2E 8LU

Paperback edition published in 2001

Library of Congress Cataloging-in-Publication Data
Female "circumcision" in Africa : culture, controversy, and change / edited by Bettina
Shell-Duncan, Ylva Hernlund.
    p.   cm. — (Directions in applied anthropology)
    Includes bibliographical references and index.
    1. Female circumcision—Africa.   I. Shell-Duncan, Bettina, 1963–   . II. Hernlund, Ylva,
1962– .   III. Series.
GN484.F443 2000
392.1'4'096—dc21

00-023511

British Cataloguing in Publication Data
A Cataloguing in Publication record for this book
is available from the British Library.

ISBN 1-55587-871-7 (hc. : alk. paper)
ISBN 1-55587-995-0 (pbk. : alk. paper)

Printed and bound in the United States of America

5   4   3

Contents

Preface

In 1997 we participated in a panel on "female genital mutilation" at the annual meeting of the Society for Applied Anthropology. Although we are both in the Department of Anthropology at the University of Washington, we were at that time completely unacquainted with one another's work: Ylva Hernlund focuses on sociocultural anthropology and Bettina Shell-Duncan on biocultural anthropology. Minor as this division may seem, it was enough to cause each of us to be unfamiliar with the particular body of knowledge on which the other based her research. As we furthered our interactions, we were struck by the different perspectives we each brought to issues relating to female "circumcision." It was this realization that inspired us to examine the topic in a multidisciplinary manner by compiling an edited volume.

We started with a simple process, each writing a "wish list" of people whose work we admired. Then, as we contacted these people, we asked them for further suggestions of scholars whose work they respected. It was primarily through this process that we expanded our list (although other linkages were made in more unorthodox ways—Ylva Hernlund and Fuambai Ahmadu struck up a casual conversation in a market café in the Gambia and soon came to realize the complementary nature of each other's work!).

Completion of this volume has been much more than an administrative task of assembling chapters encompassing a broad range of scholarly perspectives. It has been an extraordinary learning experience in which we, as editors and authors, deepened our appreciation and understanding of diverse approaches. Our hard-working contributors eagerly exchanged drafts of manuscripts and participated in discussions that expanded debates and sharpened the focus of each of the contributed chapters.

We wish to extend our gratitude to each of the contributors for their willingness to participate in this process, for the great deal of effort and thought that each one of them contributed to this project, and for the insights they brought to this manuscript. Specifically, we wish to thank Lynn Thomas, who read and commented on an early version of Chapter 1 and contributed several of its subheadings; Claudie Gosselin, who shared with us the unpublished paper that gave us the subheading "The Trivialization of Culture"; Fuambai

Ahmadu, who took on the task of concluding the volume with her chapter; and Gerry Mackie, who updated us on ongoing events and directed us to several critical references. Several people generously supplied us with key information: Molly Melching described the Senegalese Tostan campaign; Asha Mohamed, the PATH/MYWO alternative ritual campaign in Kenya; Pia Grassivaro-Gallo, the Somali "Water for Life" experiment; and staff at the U.S. State Department, U.S. aid policy with regard to FGC. We wish to thank Carl Lipo, who kindly created the preliminary version of the map that appears in Chapter 1.

We also wish to thank Stevan Harrell and Soloman Katz, who gave us advice on how to create an edited volume and encouraged us not to shy away from a controversial topic. We are also profoundly grateful to our editor at Lynne Rienner Publishers, Bridget Julian, who has been consistently supportive, creative, and insightful and whose suggestions were always right on target; and to Carolyn Sargent, who reviewed this volume and provided detailed and thoughtful comments that contributed to significant improvement of the final manuscript.

Finally, we wish to thank our endlessly supportive families—Bettina's Tim, Jack, and Luke and Ylva's Ron and Maya—who for two years gave us encouragement, endured our late-night planning sessions, and generously shared us with this project.

Bettina Shell-Duncan
Ylva Hernlund

1

Female "Circumcision" in Africa: Dimensions of the Practice and Debates

Bettina Shell-Duncan & Ylva Hernlund

Having little parallel in its ability to arouse an emotional response, the practice of female "circumcision" has come under increasingly intense international scrutiny from news media, feminist and human rights organizations, health practitioners, and legislators. Although opposition to female "circumcision" has been articulated throughout the twentieth century, starting with missionaries and colonial administrators, the current resurgence of indignation was ignited in part by activists at conferences honoring the United Nations Decade for Women (1975–1985). A practice initially challenged as a moral shortfall has gradually been recast in discourses on women's health and empowerment and international human rights.

A reclassification has taken place: the local has become a global concern, "female circumcision" has become "female genital mutilation" (FGM), and a "traditional practice" has become a "human rights violation." Under the gaze of international attention, the issue of female "circumcision" has come to constitute a site for a number of emotionally charged debates around cultural relativism, international human rights, racism and Western imperialism, medicalization, sexuality, and patriarchal oppression of women, resulting in an onslaught of discussion and writing on the topic. Yet misunderstanding, confusion, and controversy over the complex dimensions of this issue have not been resolved. Indeed, the body of literature on female "circumcision" is quite scattered and disparate, falling into diverse fields such as anthropology, demography, epidemiology, history, public health policy, law, social work, psychology, women's studies, and political science. One of our goals in compiling this volume is to bridge some of these conceptual boundaries by bringing together contributors from varied disciplinary, geographic, and ideological backgrounds and thus highlighting emerging perspectives and related dimensions of the current debates.

The practice of female "circumcision" forces observers, inside and outside academia, to confront broader philosophical and ethical issues. As noted by one anthropologist, "the very decision to write (or not) about the topic has become a political statement, and so is one's choice of tone and terminology" (Gosselin 1996:1). Critics have argued that the discussion of female "circumcision" by Westerners has been excessive, essentializing, and paternalistic. We agree, and seek through this volume to reexamine the role that scholars can and should play in approaching this issue not only by illuminating the wider contexts of the practice but by examining, as well, the way in which the attentions and actions of outsiders are inevitably affecting the process of change.

The intervention of Westerners has been sharply criticized by both African and Western scholars. It has been argued that African people affected by this practice ought to be allowed to "argue this one out for themselves" (Scheper-Hughes 1991:26). Yet, it is important to bear in mind that many people in Africa are already aware that their "traditions" have come under intense scrutiny. The debate over female "circumcision" has throughout much of Africa become impossible to escape and is not likely to fade away but only continue to increase in intensity. Knowing that African traditions have fallen under attack, many Africans have a growing awareness that the practice of female "circumcision" will—for better or worse—be talked about worldwide and are thus eager to have their own voices heard. This volume attempts to provide such a forum for a wide range of voices to speak, revealing the often complex and multifaceted processes through which individuals arrive at their positions of "supporting" or "opposing" the practice. Thus we seek with this collection to create a more balanced perspective than the current polarized debate, which one contributor describes as a "war of visions" (see Rogaia Mustafa Abusharaf in Chapter 8 in this volume).

Just as the debate over female "circumcision" will not simply go away, the increasing pressure being put on African governments, communities, and individuals to eliminate what has come to be perceived as a "harmful tradition" is not likely to be reversed. In many African countries local initiatives opposing the practice are well established and often inextricably linked with international projects. Several of the essays in this volume examine such campaigns, again providing a wide range of perspectives. Contributor Fuambai Ahmadu has argued that although protecting the rights of "a minority of women who oppose the practice is a legitimate and noble cause . . . mounting an international campaign to coerce 80 million adult African women to give up their tradition is unjustified" (Ahmadu 1995:45). Others do not object to such a campaign per se but stress that any action taken to prevent female "circumcision" must originate with the women and communities among whom it is practiced and be grounded in an understanding of the cultural and political contexts in which the practice is situated.

On the levels of both action and discourse, the practice of female "circumcision" is currently undergoing rapid and dramatic change. This change, we argue, is irreversible. As one of us was once told in a discussion about attitudes toward the international campaign against FGM: "It is like when you mix water and sand and you get mud. You can never separate them into sand and water again." On the level of practice, there remains a diminishing amount of choice for communities and individuals whose traditions have become irrevocably situated in the public arena. On the level of discourse, silence on the topic no longer seems to be an option, and the choice that remains is between informed and noninformed discussion. It is with this realization that we have sought to compile a volume that speaks with a wide range of voices to current debates and developments surrounding the practice of female genital cutting in Africa.

Defining the Practice

Female "circumcision" includes a range of practices involving the complete or partial removal or alteration of the external genitalia for nonmedical reasons and appears in widely varied cultural contexts in African and other populations. Gerry Mackie writes in Chapter 13 of the heterogeneity of these practices: "a group may perform it at infancy, before puberty, at puberty, with or without initiation rites, upon contracting marriage, in the seventh month of the first pregnancy, after the birth of the first child."

A number of assumptions are usually associated with the practice: that it is an "ancient" and deeply entrenched practice, that it is associated with initiation, with Islam, and with patriarchy. The essays in this volume wrestle with many of these assumptions, often unearthing unexpected paradoxes. From the sheer volume of literature focused on the topic of female "circumcision," one might surmise that the nature and meaning of the practice are well understood. In even a cursory review of the literature, however, the lack of consensus in terminology and understanding becomes readily apparent. Therefore, we begin by defining the practice of female "circumcision," followed by a discussion of strategies and debates surrounding efforts to eliminate the practice.

Contentious Terminologies

The term "female circumcision" is a euphemistic description of what is really a variety of procedures for altering the female genitalia. A number of terms have been used to describe a wide range of procedures, with one scholar claiming to have identified a staggering eight types of genital cutting (Bryk, quoted in van der Kwaak 1992:778). Although these variations constitute a continuum rather than discretely bounded categories, four major types are generally recognized. The least extensive type, and the only one that can be construed as analogous to male circumcision, is commonly referred to as *sunna,* which is Arabic for "tradition" or "duty" and involves only the cutting of the prepuce or hood of the clitoris. N. Toubia and S. Izett (1998) claim that, in actuality, no medical reports document the existence of this procedure.

Rather, in the majority of cases categorized as *sunna,* all or part of the clitoris is removed along with the clitoral prepuce. Hanny Lightfoot-Klein gives an example from Sudan where *sunna kashfa* (uncovered *sunna*) involves the cutting of "only top or half of the clitoris" (Lightfoot-Klein 1989:33). Procedures involving the removal of all or part of the clitoris are often referred to in the medical literature as *clitoridectomy* (Toubia 1994), and the World Health Organization (WHO) classifies this form as Type I. The second type, often referred to as *excision* and by the WHO as Type II, entails the partial or complete removal of the clitoris, along with part or all of the labia minora. A sharp distinction between clitoridectomy and excision is difficult to draw since one grades into the other. Consequently, attempts to differentiate the two in survey research have proven to be difficult, and commonly the two become collapsed into a single category.

The most radical form of female "circumcision" is known as *infibulation,* or pharaonic circumcision. The former term is Latin and is thought to refer to the ancient Roman practice of fastening a *fibula,* or clasp, through the labia majora to prevent women from having extramarital sex (Dualeh 1982:10). The latter refers to the probable origins of the practice in ancient Egypt, although it has been pointed out that in Egypt infibulation is referred to as "Sudanese circumcision" (e.g., Dorkenoo 1994:33). This procedure involves the complete removal of the clitoris and labia minora as well as most or all of the labia majora. The cut edges are stitched together so as to cover the urethra and vaginal opening, leaving only a minimal opening for the passage of urine and menstrual blood. A small stick is commonly inserted to maintain the opening, and the legs of the girl are bound together to promote healing. In areas where some degree of medicalization of the practice has taken place, antibiotics and anesthesia may be used, and the opening may be sutured with catgut or silk rather than with thorns. The suture that remains following this procedure must be opened for intercourse and childbirth, a procedure known as de-infibulation. This is generally followed by re-infibulation after each birth and often when a woman is widowed or divorced.

In the Sudan, there is a variation known as *matwasat,* or "intermediate circumcision," which is a modified form of infibulation that usually involves a similar amount of cutting but the stitching together of only the anterior two-thirds of the outer labia, leaving a larger posterior opening. This procedure is believed to have evolved as a compromise by circumcisers reacting to the

1946 ban on infibulation in the Sudan, although in a recent survey less than 2 percent of Sudanese women reported having had an intermediate circumcision. Both *matwasat* and infibulation are classified by the WHO as Type III. Another modified form of infibulation, known as "sealing," is practiced in West Africa, although not with the same frequency as other variations. This procedure involves excision and the subsequent sealing of the vagina, not by stitching but by allowing blood to coagulate to form what amounts to an artificial hymen (see Singateh 1985; and Chapters 12 and 13 in this volume).

Apart from these four main types of genital cutting, some lesser-known variations have been reported (collectively referred to as Type IV by the WHO). Nigerian physician Mairo Usman Mandara (see Chapter 5 in this volume) describes several procedures involving *introcision*, the cutting of the internal genitalia. These include *hymenectomy; zur-zur* cuts of the cervix, which are intended to remedy obstructed labor; and *gishiri* cuts, which involve the cutting of the vaginal wall. The latter procedure, it is alleged by Fran Hosken, is intended to facilitate sexual penetration in communities where child marriage is widely practiced (quoted in *Harvard Law Review* 1993:1947).

Finally, there are reports of "symbolic circumcision." Hosken (1993) describes a procedure said to occur in Indonesia and Malaysia, which involves nicking the clitoris with a sharp instrument to cause bleeding but no permanent alteration of the external genitalia. Leslye Obiora (1997:228) also refers to "ritualized marking" in Africa but without giving specific examples. One circumciser in Guinea-Bissau is reported to have performed a simulacrum involving the smearing of red disinfectant over the genital area after pretending to cut the clitoris (*Awaken* newsletter, June 1997: 7). And, according to recent reports from the "Water for Life" project in Somalia, up to 1,000 girls there have in 1996–1998 undergone a "symbolic infibulation" in which members of a medical team administer anesthesia and make a small nick in the clitoris to produce a few drops of blood, after which the girls lie with their legs bound to simulate infibulation (Pia Gallo, personal communication[1]).

In recent years, symbolic cutting has been proposed in a few scattered cases in the West, as well, as part of an effort to eliminate more extensive cutting. An anaesthetized pricking of the clitoris was at one point proposed to be performed by healthcare providers in the Netherlands as an alternative to infibulation among Somali immigrant women (Obiora 1997:285). This proposal provoked strong protest and was never implemented. Likewise, in 1996 a U.S. hospital considered performing a symbolic procedure requested by members of the Somali immigrant community who were willing to let such a transitional measure replace having their daughters infibulated either on a return trip to Somalia or by Somali midwives in the United States (Ostrom 1996a; Coleman 1998). Although the so-called Seattle compromise would have involved no removal of tissue and would have been performed under

anesthesia on girls having given consent, the plan was blocked by intense lobbying from anti-FGM activists as well as by an outpouring of negative public
opinion (e.g., Ostrom 1996b; Paulson 1996).[2] New federal anti-FGM legislation, it was argued, would render the practice unlawful, as would state child
abuse law. Legal scholar Doriane Coleman argues, however, that when the
nonmutilating nature of the proposed procedure is weighed against the harm
inherent in the alternative of infibulation, it cannot legally be argued that the
symbolic act would have "sanctioned medically-unnecessary physical injury
to children" (Coleman 1998:767). She also points to the intellectual dishonesty in allowing hospitals to perform far more intrusive male circumcision,
asking how we can justify "abusing boys but not girls" (Coleman 1998:770).

The choice of terminology in describing these practices is fraught with
political land mines. The general term "female circumcision" has often been
used to refer collectively to all these procedures. With the spread of feminist
consciousness and the development of international women's health movements, however, objection to this term has grown, as it de-emphasizes the
severity of most forms of the practice by comparing it to the removal of the
foreskin in males. The term "genital surgeries" was proposed by Isabelle
Gunning (1992, see also Lewis 1995; Obermeyer 1999) as a value-neutral alternative, but Gifford argues that this term "lends the practice an air of legitimacy, or medical necessity, that is at best suspect" (1994:333).

Increasingly widespread is the term "female genital mutilation," or
"FGM," which is generally promoted by activists as a more accurate term.
Representatives of the anticircumcision organization Foundation for
Women's Health Research and Development (FORWARD) maintain that
"any definitive and irremediable removal of a healthy organ is mutilation"
(Dorkenoo 1994:4). In the same vein, the "London Declaration" adopted in
1992 by the First Study Conference on Genital Mutilation of Girls in Europe
defines "female genital mutilation" as "the removal of, or injury to, any part
of the female organ" (Dorkenoo 1994:4). Many African commentators who
oppose the practice have thus adopted the term, as did the Inter-African Committee (IAC) at its 1990 meeting in Addis Ababa. Objections have been
raised, however, and the use of the word "mutilation" has been criticized because it is "thought to imply excessive judgment by outsiders and insensitiv-
ity toward individuals who have undergone the procedure" (Eliah 1996:13).

In Uganda, an elder was quoted as denouncing "foreigners...who call us
bad names, call us primitive and call our circumcision rites genital mutilation.
It makes us want to do more" (*Newsweek* int. ed., July 5, 1999:46). Members
of the Uganda-based initiative Reproductive, Educative, and Community
Health Programme (REACH) have proposed instead the term "female genital
cutting" (FGC) as a more precise but less value-laden term (*Newsweek* int.
ed., July 5, 1999:46).[3] We agree that the term "mutilation" denotes condemnation and will use "FGM" only in the context of discourses employing that

term. In all other contexts we will instead use "female genital cutting," female "circumcision" (with quotations to acknowledge the imprecision of this term), or the more precise descriptive terms for each procedure: clitoridectomy, excision, and infibulation.

Fragmentary Knowledge

Although female "circumcision" is often referred to as "entrenched" or as a "deeply rooted tradition" practiced for thousands of years in parts of Africa, it is in some places a custom adopted only very recently (see Lori Leonard in Chapter 9 in this volume). Currently, female genital cutting is a widespread practice, having been documented across a broad region of Africa, extending in West Africa from Mauritania to Cameroon, across central Africa, and in the east reaching from Tanzania to Ethiopia. Current global estimates of the prevalence of female "circumcision" are tentative, since nationally representative data do not exist for many countries. National boundaries are not all-important, however, as the distribution of genital cutting is better understood by ethnic groups, and groups practicing genital cutting often straddle national boundaries. Those close together geographically do not necessarily share the practice; for example, in Kenya the Kikuyu historically practiced excision, whereas the Luo did not; in Gambia the Wolof did not practice any form of female genital cutting, whereas most other ethnic groups did. Moreover, as illustrated in a number of contributions to this volume, FGC has become important in drawing boundaries between socioeconomic classes within ethnic groups.

Most accounts of the geographic distribution and prevalence of female genital cutting draw on the work of anticircumcision activist Fran Hosken, who first created a map for the 1979 World Health Organization seminar that has been published in five editions of *The Hosken Report* (most recently 1993) as well as in various papers. Hosken states that her estimates are based on extensive research in Africa; on interviews with medical personnel, midwives, and government officials; and on a search of the medical and ethnographic literature. The inability of other researchers to replicate these findings is, however, cause for caution. Additionally, it is not clear how the patchwork information on geographic distribution has been used to estimate the prevalence of female genital cutting within each country. Nonetheless, Hosken's estimates represent the first attempt to measure the extent of female genital cutting on a country by country basis and have motivated systematic data collection in several nations.

Map 1.1 highlights African countries in which the practice of female genital cutting has been reported since 1979. It is also practiced outside Africa in places including Indonesia, Malaysia, and the Arab peninsula, as well as among immigrant communities worldwide. We will not be examining these

Map 1.1   African countries in which female genital cutting has been reported since 1979

contexts in this volume, however, for the sake of scope.[4] We wish to caution interpretation of this map by noting two points: first, the prevalence of female "circumcision" in countries where some form of the practice is reportedly found varies widely from one ethnic group to another; second, for some countries reliable figures on prevalence are not available, and reports of the existence of the practice are based on anecdotal information. We cautiously include Botswana, Lesotho, and Mozambique (reported by Koso-Thomas 1987) as well as Algeria (where there are "some reported cases," according to the Minority Rights Group 1980), but we could find no corroborating evidence. The 1980 Minority Rights Group report of scattered cases of female "circumcision" in Libya and Malawi is confirmed by the U.S. Department of State 1997 Human Rights Report, although the source of information in either report is unclear.

Reliable estimates of the prevalence of female genital cutting are available for only select countries, and these are presented in Table 1.1. In some cases the data are not nationally representative but refer only to certain regions. Toubia and Izett (1998) have recently reviewed published and unpublished studies of the prevalence of FGC in Africa and presented the most comprehensive overview to date; we have updated their figures with the most recent Demographic and Health Survey (DHS) figures for Tanzania.[5] Additionally, we have chosen not to reproduce Hosken's estimates of prevalence for countries where only anecdotal information is available, since they involve, in our opinion, too much guesswork. We also cautiously report global estimates on the prevalence and types of female genital cutting, since estimates are tentative at best. According to Toubia and Izett (1998), over 132 million women have experienced some form of female genital cutting. "Excision," undifferentiated from clitoridectomy, is the most commonly practiced form, predominating in two-thirds of all countries where female genital cutting exists, and accounting for an estimated 85 percent of all reported cases (Toubia, 1993). Infibulation is largely confined to Sudan, Somalia, northeastern Kenya, Eritrea, parts of Mali, and a very small area in northern Nigeria.[6]

The degree to which the map and figures reflect *current* distribution is not at all clear. Equally difficult to document is the rate at which the practice of female genital cutting is spreading or declining in different populations. Scattered reports indicate that in some areas in which female "circumcision" was formerly universally practiced, it is gradually falling from favor. In other groups where female genital cutting has not historically been practiced or had been abandoned, it is being introduced or revived. Some of these cases involve the constantly evolving borrowing and influence from one ethnic group to another (see, for example, Lightfoot-Klein 1989; in this volume, Chapters 9 and 12 and, for a general discussion of diffusion of the practice, Chapter 13); others involve the resurgence of previously discarded traditions

Table 1.1   Prevalence of Female Genital Cutting in Selected African
            Countries

Country	Estimated Prevalence (%)	Source of Prevalence Rate
Benin	50	A 1993 study by the National Committee on Harmful Traditional Practices found FGC mainly in the northern region. Excision is the most common form.
Burkina Faso	70	Report of the National Committee (Lamizana 1995). The main form of FGC reported is excision.
Cameroon	20	Estimated prevalence based on a study (Njock et al. 1994, cited in Toubia and Izett 1998) in southwestern and far northern provinces by the IAC Cameroon section. Clitoridectomy and excision were reported.
Central African Republic	43	A 1994–1995 National Demographic and Health Survey (Carr 1997) revealed large differences in prevalence based on region of residence and ethnicity.
Chad	60	1990 and 1991 UNICEF-sponsored studies in three regions.
Côte d'Ivoire	43	A 1994 National Demographic Health Survey (Carr 1997) found high prevalence in three regions, the west (79 percent), northwest (88 percent), and north (85 percent).
Djibouti	98	No official studies have been conducted, but the Ministry of Health and the national women's union (Union National des Femmes de Djibouti) have reported that FGC, mainly infibulation, is nearly universal.
Egypt	97	A 1997 National Demographic and Health Survey (Carr 1997) found high rates in all regions of the country. The most commonly reported form of FGC is clitoridectomy.
Eritrea	95	A 1995 National Demographic and Health Survey (Carr 1997) reported little variation by ethnic group or residence location in the country.
Ethiopia	85	A 1995 UNICEF-sponsored study in five regions and an IAC survey in twenty administration regions found clitoridectomy and excision to be the most commonly reported forms of FGC.

(continues)

Table 1.1 (continued)

Country	Estimated Prevalence (%)	Source of Prevalence Rate
Gambia	80	A limited study (Singateh 1985), not nationally representative, reported excision and clitoridectomy as well as a smaller number of infibulations.
Ghana	30	A study in the upper eastern region (Kadri 1986, cited in Toubia and Izett 1998) found a prevalence of 75–100 percent, but a study by the Ghana Association of Women's Welfare (Twumasi 1987, cited in Toubia and Izett 1998) in the southern region found FGC only among migrants from northern Ghana and neighboring countries.
Guinea-Bissau	50	Limited 1990 survey by the Union Democratique des Femmes de la Guinee-Bissau reported that excision is universal among the Muslim population.
Kenya	50	A 1992 Maendeleo Ya Wanawake survey in four regions reports a prevalence of 89.6 percent. However, since several large ethnic groups not included in the survey do not practice FGC, national figures are assumed to be lower.
Liberia	60	According to a 1986 IAC report (Marshall et al. 1986, cited in Toubia and Izett 1998), FGC (mainly excision) is widespread, practiced by all but three ethnic groups.
Mali	94	A 1995–1996 National Demographic and Health Survey (Carr 1997) found high rates of FGC in all ethnic groups except Sonorai and Tamachek women living in isolated desert cities (Timbuktu and Gao).
Mauritania	25	Figures are from a 1987 unpublished study cited by the director of social affairs of the Ministry of Health.
Niger	20	No national studies have been conducted, although excision and clitoridectomy have been reported (according to Toubia and Izett 1998) in studies in three provinces: Diffa, Niamey, and Tillabery.

(continues)

Table 1.1   (continued)

Country	Estimated Prevalence (%)	Source of Prevalence Rate
Nigeria	50	A 1997 Nigerian Inter-African Committee report synthesized the findings of nine IAC-sponsored studies as well as a number of regional studies. Estimates include figures on introcision (hymenectomy, *gishiri* cuts, and *zur-zur* cuts).
Senegal	20	Report of a national study by Environment et Dévelopment du Tiers-Monde (Mottin-Sylla 1990, cited in Toubia and Izett 1998).
Sierra Leone	90	All ethnic groups practice FGC (mostly excision) except for Christian Krios in the western region and in the capital, Freetown (Koso-Thomas 1987).
Somalia	98	According to two reports (Abdulla 1982; Proceedings of the 1988 Seminar in Mogadishu, cited in Toubia and Izett 1998), approximately 80 percent of the operations are infibulation, and the remainder are clitoridectomies.
Sudan	89	A 1989–1990 National Demographic and Health Survey (Carr 1997) found the predominant form of FGC is infibulation, found throughout most of the northern, northeastern, and north-western regions.
Tanzania	18	A 1996 National Demographic and Health Survey (Bureau of Statistics [Tanzania] and Macro International 1997) found that excision and clitoridectomy are the predominant forms of FGC (93 percent of cases).
Togo	0–98	Thérése Locoh (1998) summarizes a 1996 national survey that found that excision varies extensively by ethnic group, with excision found among 98 percent of Tchama women but absent among the Adja Ewe.

Source: Adapted from WHO (1996) and Toubia and Izett (1998).

(see, for example, Astrid Nypan's 1991 article discussing "neotraditionalism" among the Meru of Tanzania). In general, more accurate and detailed information is expected to be available in the near future since questions on female genital cutting developed for the Sudan Demographic and Health Survey (DHS) will likely be included in the next round of DHS surveys in various African countries.

Origins: Recasting the Object of Analysis

There have been a number of attempts to trace the origins of female "circumcision" (see, for example, van der Kwaak 1992; Meinardus 1967; Hicks 1996) although scholars differ in their views regarding the importance of such an analysis. Some maintain that the conditions that led to the initial adoption of female "circumcision" are not static and knowing them will not enhance understanding of the perpetuation of the practice. For instance, Janice Boddy has argued that knowledge of this "custom's remote historical origins [does not] . . . contribute to our understanding of its present significance" (Boddy 1982:685). Ellen Gruenbaum adds that "the persistence of a practice that has negative consequences must be explained in terms of the present circumstances that encourage or discourage its continuation" (Gruenbaum 1996:460).

The attempt to theoretically reconstruct the origins of the practice does present a formidable challenge that to many may seem an exercise in futility, leading one scholar to caution that "even retroactive reconstruction via circumstantial extrapolation is problematic" (Obiora 1997:301). To others, however, this is an essential endeavor. As Ahmadu argues in Chapter 14, "the question of origin is becoming increasingly important, particularly to African women who uphold the tradition and are continually finding themselves in a position to justify the practice to outsiders, and perhaps more so, to themselves."

Arguing from a different angle, political scientist Gerry Mackie insists that the origins of the practice cannot be conceptually separated from its continuation or from any strategies for its elimination (1996 and Chapter 13 in this volume). Although he agrees that the reasons for the origin of the practice are distinct from the reasons for its maintenance, Mackie presents a single-source diffusion theory of FGC that locates its genesis in ancient Meroe (in present-day Sudan), where infibulation was practiced in the context of fidelity control and paternity confidence mechanisms under conditions of "imperial female slavery."

Others have suggested the possibility of a dual source of origins: although infibulation may indeed have spread outward from a core area, it then encountered and merged with preexisting practices of genital cutting of both males and females (e.g., Report of the UN Special Working Group on Traditional Practices, henceforth UN 1986). "Female genital mutilation must have developed independently among certain ethnic groups in sub-Saharan Africa as part of puberty rites" writes Dorkenoo (Dorkenoo 1994:34). Lightfoot-Klein adds that "excision practices can be assumed to date back thousands of years," but that at some point these "came into conjunction with the obsessive preoccupation with virginity and chastity that today still characterizes Islamic-Arabic cultures" (Lightfoot-Klein 1989:27). Mackie argues instead that genital cutting, originating from a single source, met and in some cases became incorporated into noncutting initiation ritual.

Establishing the Medical "Facts"

Typically, anti-FGM literature not only describes the nature and likely origins of female "circumcision" but also establishes the medical "facts" about the practice.[7] This discussion is often divided into a recitation of short-term, long-term, and obstetrical complications. *Short-term complications* include hemorrhage, severe pain, local and systemic infection, shock from blood loss, and potentially death. Infection is associated with delayed healing and the formation of keloid scars. In addition, pain and fear following the procedure can lead to acute urinary retention. *Long-term complications* are said to be associated more often with infibulation than with excision or clitoridectomy (Toubia 1993), although this has been poorly researched. Possible long-term complications include genito-urinary problems, such as difficulties with menstruation and urination that result from a nearly complete sealing off of the vagina and urethra. Untreated lower urinary tract infections can ascend to the bladder and kidneys, potentially resulting in renal failure, septicemia, and death. Chronic pelvic infections can cause back pain, dysmenorrhea (painful menstruation), and infertility. Another frequently mentioned complication is the formation of dermoid cysts, resulting from embedding epithelial cells and sebaceous glands in the stitched area. Additionally, if the clitoral nerve is trapped in a stitch or in the scar tissue, a painful neuroma (tumor of neural tissue) can develop. All forms of female genital cutting are alleged to be potentially associated with diminished sexual pleasure and, in certain cases, inability to experience a clitoral orgasm. Infibulated women may experience painful intercourse and often have to be cut open for penetration to occur at all. *Obstetrical complications* are most often reported in association with infibulation, including obstructed labor and excessive bleeding from tearing and de-infibulation during childbirth. Obstructed labor may lead to the formation of vesico-vaginal and recto-vaginal fistulae (openings between the vagina and the urethra or rectum, allowing for urine or feces to pass through the vagina). Toubia and Izett (1998) point out, however, that fistulae in Africa also result from pregnancy in young girls whose pelvises are not well developed and that the contribution of FGC to the development of fistulae has not been adequately documented. Some researchers have suggested that increased obstetrical risk exists for excised women as well (e.g., Epelboin and

Epelboin 1981). Scar tissue may contribute to obstructed labor, since fibrous vulvar tissue fails to dilate during contractions. Furthermore, hemorrhage may result from tearing through scar tissue.

This laundry list of adverse health outcomes, the "medical sequelae," is repeated in the introduction of nearly all papers in the voluminous literature on female "circumcision" because allegations of health hazards form the cornerstone of opposition to the practice. Surprisingly little attention is devoted to considering the original source of this information—often medical observations published by British colonial surgeons and gynecologists in the 1930s and 1940s—or the incidence of various complications arising from different types of genital cutting (see also Obiora 1997). Instead, noteworthy case studies on infibulation are generalized to describe the health risks of *all* forms of genital cutting and to support the view that genital mutilation should be treated as a public health problem.

Attempts have been made to quantify the range and frequency of "circumcision"-related medical complications from clinic and hospital records (e.g., Aziz 1980; Rushwan 1980; De Silva 1989). Because these data suffer from selection bias, they need to be interpreted with caution. Women are often reluctant to seek medical attention because of modesty and, especially in rural settings, inaccessibility of health services. Consequently, complications tend to be reported only if they are severe and prolonged (El Dareer 1982). Furthermore, in some countries such as the Sudan, certain types of genital cutting have been made illegal, and women may hide medical complications for fear of legal repercussions (El Dareer 1982; Toubia 1993).

The best information available on the incidence of various complications attributable to genital cutting comes from several large-scale population-based surveys, the first of which was conducted by Asma El Dareer in northern Sudan (El Dareer 1982). Self-reported retrospective survey data, however, also suffer from a number of limitations such as recall bias; and the results of different surveys are not in all aspects directly comparable because of differences in classifying morbidity and different question construction and probing techniques. For example, the broad range of women reporting hemorrhage following clitoridectomy (as low as 6 percent in the Sudan, according to El Dareer 1982, and as high as 41 percent in central and southern Kenya, according to MYWO 1991) likely reflects variation in the type of cutting, sanitation, and training of the circumciser as well as survey methodology. This broad range of estimated incidence suggests that when evaluating risk factors of genital cutting, it is important to control for factors that may contribute to this range in variation, such as training of the circumciser, location of the operation, and medical support (see Bettina Shell-Duncan, Walter Obungu Obiero, and Leunita Auko Muruli in Chapter 6 in this volume; Obiora 1997:291). Additionally, it highlights the need to cautiously interpret self-reported retrospective data (see also Parker 1995).

Clearly, better information is needed in order to assess the magnitude of "circumcision"-related morbidity as a public health problem. This need is driven, in part, by the fact that strategies to eliminate female "circumcision" are, in most instances, rooted primarily in a health approach (see section below, Strategies to Eliminate Female Genital Cutting: "Eradication" Efforts). Yet when communities practicing clitoridectomy and excision become targeted by anti-FGM campaigns, medical "facts" derived from reports on infibulation are often not supported by the experience of community members, and the incongruity between propaganda and lived experience has the potential to undermine the credibility of anticircumcision campaigns, as is illustrated in several contributions to this volume (see Chapters 6, 10, 11, 12, and 14; see also Obermeyer 1999; Obiora 1997).

Another issue that is evaluated differently in international discourses on FGM than in at least some local perceptions of the practice concerns the pain that, although perhaps exaggerated and sensationalized in the literature, clearly accompanies unanaesthesized genital cutting procedures. Claudie Gosselin notes that "for most Westerners, generally encultured in a society where bodies are managed by medicine and where pain is considered something to be avoided, the descriptions of the various surgeries, usually performed in non-medical settings, evoke strong feelings of horror" (Gosselin, in press). Nancy Scheper-Hughes evaluates this type of reaction as "moral outrage [over a] practice that is alien to our culture" and points out that we do not, with equal vehemence, denounce our own practice of "sexually mutilating" baby boys by circumcising them without anesthesia (Scheper-Hughes 1991:26–27). Indeed, there appears to exist in the West a tolerance of, and perhaps appreciation for, the assumption that masculine ideals are honed through painful initiations that respond to group needs. In *Manhood in the Making*, David Gilmore argues that fear of a universal human desire to regress to an infantile state of dependency forces communities, particularly those attempting to survive in hostile environments, to design strategies to "toughen" its members. Although he exclusively discusses male initiation, Gilmore's ideas can be brought to bear on harsh female initiation as well; several scholars have noted the importance for many African women to demonstrate their ability to bear pain (see Obiora 1997 for a review of some of these). Carolyn Sargent was told by women in Benin that after the excruciating experience of clitoridectomy, "no pain will overwhelm a person" (Sargent 1989:175). In Chapter 6, Shell-Duncan, Obiero, and Muruli discuss how Rendille women in Kenya reject the idea of using anesthesia when being excised and instead emphasize the importance of being able to withstand the pain of being cut as preparation for enduring the pain of childbirth and as demonstrating maturity. Chapters 10, 11, and 12 in this volume point to similar concerns among women in Guinea-Bissau, Mali, and the Gambia, revolving around what one Kenyan woman described as "buying maturity with pain" (quoted in Davison 1996:60).

Often included, as well, in the list of long-term physical consequences of FGC is the way in which genital cutting may interfere with female sexual response (for a discussion of related issues of the control of female sexual behavior, the gendering of female bodies, and feminist discourses on pleasure and desire, see below). In a recent work, Toubia and Izett (1998) have reviewed studies on the effect of FGC on women's sexuality, documenting a broad range of findings: in some cases up to 90 percent of infibulated women reported pleasurable sex with frequent orgasm (Lightfoot-Klein 1989; see also Chapters 8 and 14), whereas in others as many as 50 percent of women claim to experience diminished sexual pleasure (El Dareer 1982). A reliable evaluation of the effect of FGC on sexual response is often difficult to obtain, since in many cases the procedure takes place at such a young age that the woman has no prior sexual experience with which to compare post-FGC sexual sensitivity (see also Obiora 1997). Nonetheless, Fuambai Ahmadu (1995; also Chapter 14) asserts that many women, herself included, who had sexual experiences prior to excision perceive "either no difference or increased sexual satisfaction" following the procedure. Toubia and Izett's (1998) review does demonstrate that FGC has the potential to interfere with sexual response but that it does not necessarily abolish the receptivity of sexual stimulation in women, since some of the sensitive tissues of the body and part of the clitoris are deeply embedded and not necessarily removed when the external genitalia are cut. Indeed, recent research involving dissections of female cadavers has revealed that the clitoris is at least twice as large as shown in any anatomy textbook (*The Guardian,* July 30, 1998). Moreover, British gynecological surgeon Harry Gordon reportedly has found during the performance of reconstructive surgery on "circumcised" Somali women that the extent of cutting during infibulation is actually quite variable. In 95 percent of the cases he has seen, beneath the infibulated labia majora, the clitoris has been left intact (Austveg et al. 1998:4245; see also Gruenbaum 1996:462).[8] Additionally, some studies suggest that other sex organs such as the labia minora or other erogenous zones become more sensitive in women having undergone clitoridectomies, thus allowing for greater sexual pleasure (Toubia and Izett 1998; see also Obiora 1997). In Chapter 14, Ahmadu also refers to the incidence of sexual dysfunction among Western, uncircumcised women and stresses the extent to which interference with sexual pleasure is often grounded in nonanatomical factors (see also Ogbu 1997:414).

Another question that has emerged from the discussion of health consequences of female genital cutting is whether the practice represents a "maladaptive" human behavior. The question that has been posed is: "Why would a society adopt and perpetuate a custom that is debilitating and potentially fatal?" The author of *Sick Societies* asserts that female "circumcision" is maladaptive and an example of the sort of problem that "populations might be said to bring on themselves or by maintaining traditional beliefs and practices that are harmful to people's health and well-being" (Edgerton 1992:15). According to Robert Edgerton, it should not be assumed that a persistent belief or practice is adaptive, a point similarly stressed in a popular medical anthropology textbook by Ann McElroy and Patricia Townsend (1989). Cited among customs with adverse outcomes, such as child abuse, female "circumcision" is presented as a cultural pattern that runs counter to "maximally adaptive responses, or wise, healthful choices" (McElroy and Townsend 1989:102). Gruenbaum (1996; Chapter 2 in this volume) offers a compelling critique of the medical ecology perspective and argues that "a trait should not be labeled maladaptive merely because it is risky or harmful to individual health" (1996:358).

An alternative perspective highlights behaviors that limit fertility as adaptive. Focusing on the fact that unchecked fertility allows for exponential population growth, female "circumcision" has been described as a mechanism for regulating population size in traditional societies. Rose Hayes (1975) argues that a "latent function" of infibulation is to keep aggregate fertility in check, maintaining a fine balance between population size and resource availability. Yet, as Deborah Balk notes (in Chapter 3 of this volume), this argument cannot be critically evaluated without separating the fertility-dampening effects of female "circumcision" from other factors that independently affect fertility. Systematic evaluations of the impact of female genital cutting on fertility, either directly or by influencing marital stability, are surprisingly absent from the literature, an issue that is addressed in detail by Balk.

Focusing on the individual, Gruenbaum suggests that an understanding of female genital cutting as adaptive or maladaptive might be better framed under political economic theory and prompts the question, "Who benefits?" (1996:460): "Some cultural patterns, in this view, are good for some people, but bad for others, harmful to the health of some but good for the power or wealth of others" (1996:460–461). From an evolutionary perspective, the adaptiveness of female "circumcision" can be evaluated, then, as it may relate to differing reproductive strategies of men and women in the environmental context of patriarchy, resource inequality, and the desire of men to control female fertility (see Chapters 2, 3, and 13 in this volume).

Trivialization of Culture

Several outspoken scholars have sharply criticized the tendency to describe the practice of FGC as desocialized and ahistorical. Reports from early travelers detail "curious customs" encountered in Africa or in contact with the slave trade as colonial physicians began publishing case reports highlighting the "medical atrocities of savage customs." Early medical accounts, in their numeracy and graphic detail, provided what has been described as a "voyeurist Western gaze . . . sanitized through a medical discourse" (Kirby 1987:37; see also Gosselin, in press). A striking example appears in a report by Carl Gösta

Widstrand of a 1762 expedition to Egypt during which members of the expedition "expressed a wish to see a circumcised woman" (1964: 80). This resulted in an eighteen-year-old village girl being brought out to display her genitalia while the expedition artist created a sketch. Subsequent sensationalized reports have presented decontextualized accounts of anonymous "mutilated" African women, what one author has termed "the exotic other female" (Engle 1992). These visual images, as Carla Obermeyer points out, elicit a contradictory response in which "the reader is both voyeur looking at sexual organs and clinician assessing damage" (Obermeyer 1999:90). Such reports have continued to appear throughout the twentieth century, often accompanied by photographs of the genitals of a faceless woman, serving to generalize about the plight of a homogenized African woman while overlooking the variations in the type of genital cutting performed or the conditions under which it occurs (Kratz 1994). Ahmadu asks trenchantly: "Can it possibly be a good thing for thousands of African immigrants who must soak in images of their nether regions literally spread open in 'education' pamphlets, women's magazines and so-called documentaries for the modern world to ponder?" (Ahmadu 1995:46). In Chapter 8 of this volume, Abusharaf concurs and cautions that "research on female 'circumcision' not only has to take into account the place of the practice in the culture in question but also has to be foregrounded in a multifaceted analysis of the lives of those women whose genitals have become the subject of study."

Much of the existing literature conveniently overlooks the cultural, political, and historical contexts of the various types of genital cutting performed by different actors in widely varying contexts. The tendency to present generalized lists of "reasons for the practice," Gosselin argues, contributes to the "trivialization of culture in the political literature" (Gosselin, in press). Although we do not wish to recreate here such a "laundry list" of rationales, we hope instead through this volume to highlight a wide range of local discourses, along with theoretical speculations surrounding practices of female genital cutting, agreeing with Stanlie James that "deceptively simple assumptions must be revisited and revised within the specifics of cultural context" (James 1998:1043). With Ahmadu, we caution that although each of the "explanations" for practicing FGC are discussed distinctly, they are in fact "interconnected and mutually reinforcing and, taken together, form overwhelming unconscious and conscious motivations" for its continuation.

Contributions to this volume fall along a wide continuum of approaches to the question of "meaning." At one extreme, Mackie argues in Chapter 13 that all female genital cutting ultimately stems from a concern with premarital female chastity, paternity assurance, and marriageability, although this association may no longer be explicit in all practicing societies (see also Chapter 3 by Balk in this volume, which discusses how, paradoxically, a practice that is in many instances a prerequisite for determining marriageability may, at the same time, undermine the stability of marriage). On the other extreme, Lori Leonard (see Chapter 9) found among the Sara—who have only recently adopted the practice, much in the manner of a "fad"—that their "narratives force us to ask not what it means, but, rather, whether it means anything at all." After repeated probing about the "meaning" of female "circumcision" among Sara today, Leonard was finally told by one impatient informant: "You are looking too hard—there is nothing!"

Between these two poles of a singular universal meta-theory and the dearth of any meaning at all beyond the desire to be fashionable lie a multiplicity of reported local understandings of female "circumcision." The Special Report found that, in a compilation of studies of attitudes to FGC, more than 54 percent of respondents stated that "tradition" was their primary reason for performing female "circumcision" (UN 1986:13), and Carr in her survey of infibulation concurs that the vast majority of women state that they favor the continuation of the practice because it is "custom" and "tradition." In Chapter 12 of this volume, Hernlund also found in the Gambia that respect for what was "found from the grandmothers" was the most strongly and commonly stated reason for performing FGC. Mackie discusses this sort of response, which "perplexes outsiders who suspect that the appeal to custom is merely obscurantist;" but goes on to argue that "the respondents are absolutely correct: FGC is a certain type of convention, involving reciprocal expectations about an interdependent choice, and that is exactly why it continues." Leonard's chapter, comparing two communities at different stages of adoption of FGC, demonstrates how quickly such significance can accrue.

A number of observers have commented on the often powerful nature of peer convention in perpetuating FGC, as girls and young women pressure each other to "join" in the practice (see, for example, Chapters 9, 12, and 14 in this volume). A particularly powerful account is provided by Lynn Thomas in Chapter 7, who describes the "Ngaitana" movement during which Kenyan girls defied various authorities and took it upon themselves to circumcise themselves and each other. Such conventions, Mackie argues further, often come to be seen as ethnic markers, but this is "a consequence, not a cause, of the practice." Hernlund, however, points out that conventions and markers often reinforce each other over time, as is demonstrated in Michelle Johnson's discussion of Guinea-Bissau in Chapter 11, where the practice of female "circumcision" has come to be perceived as intrinsically linked to the construction of Mandinga identity.

According to Mackie (1996; Chapter 13), the main force perpetuating the custom is the link between genital cutting and marriageability (for a critique of the marriageability perspective, see Obiora 1997:318). He argues that even if the originating conditions change, "as soon as women believed that men would not marry an unmutilated woman, and men believed that an unmutilated woman would not be a faithful partner in marriage, the convention was locked in place." Several contributors to this volume describe the association between FGC and marriageability. Yet many also emphasize that the significance of "circumcision" extends well beyond conferring marriageability to the legitimization of reproduction, as is the case in the Kono women's societies described by Ahmadu in Chapter 14.

Boddy has noted that in the Sudan not only does the procedure render a girl marriageable, but that undergoing it is "a necessary condition of becoming a woman, of being enabled to use her one great gift, fertility" (Boddy 1982:683). Boddy argues that infibulation is used to symbolically and physically enclose the womb, thus emphasizing the protection and sacredness of a woman's reproductive center. Moreover, Boddy articulates what many anthropologists have identified as the distinction between sexuality as procreation and sexuality as recreation. Infibulation, Boddy argues, is to many Sudanese women an "assertive, highly meaningful act that emphasizes female fertility by de-emphasizing female sexuality" (Boddy 1982:682).

A complete polarization of the sexes permeates Sudanese society, Boddy has argued, and circumcision reinforces this polarity by making women *less* like men—physically, sexually, and socially. Women are not so much preventing their own sexual pleasure, she argues, as "enhancing their femininity" (Boddy 1982:687). Boddy's analysis mirrors the work of anthropologists Nancy Lutkehaus and Marilyn Strathern, who have done extensive research on female initiations in New Guinea, although they do not write specifically about female "circumcision." Lutkehaus, with Strathern, argues that these rites are concerned with promoting the transition of boys and girls from an androgynous state of childhood to the gendered, and hence sexually differentiated, state of masculine or feminine adulthood (Lutkehaus and Roscoe 1995:196). Support for this theory has been drawn as well from widespread ethnographic reports of male and female "circumcision" (see, for example, Griaule 1965; Hansen 1972–1973; Meinardus 1967).[9] Similarly, Ahmadu maintains that Kono women of Sierra Leone "equate the female clitoris with the male penis, and hence, promiscuity, sexual aggressiveness, instability. . . . Removing the clitoris is ultimately what symbolizes the separation of women from men physically, psychologically and spiritually" (Ahmadu 1995:44). In Chapter 14 of this volume, Ahmadu extends this view and argues that excision is "a negation of the masculine in feminine creative potential."

The broad range of responses to the alteration of female genitalia reflects the widely differing views of meanings associated with women's bodies and women's sexuality. Whereas the procedure of genital cutting is seen by many as essential to the creation of femininity and full adult status, others view it as the obliteration of these very principles. For many Western feminists, the clitoris has become a powerful symbol of women's emancipation. In the wake of Shere Hite's influential *Hite Report* (Hite 1976) and the fight for the right to clitoral orgasms and sexual satisfaction, "female genital mutilation" became the symbol par excellence of patriarchal oppression for radical Western feminists (Gosselin 1996; see also Obiora 1997).

This approach has been sharply criticized by some African feminists, who argue that by letting sexuality become "assumed as an a priori issue around which 'all women' should organize . . . the specificity of women's experience is conveniently overlooked" (Abusharaf 1996:5–6). In Chapter 8 of this volume, Abusharaf discusses the way in which "some Western feminist representational discourses on female 'circumcision' as a signifier for sexual oppression have come under considerable critical reflection for their ethnocentrism and reductionism" and cautions that "by overemphasizing the effects of female 'circumcision' on sexual pleasure," much of the Western anticircumcision literature has distanced itself from the socioeconomic contexts of broader violations of women's rights.

Other anthropologists have also pointed to the way in which ideas about female sexual pleasure are culturally constructed and historically situated. In 1972, Henny Hansen wrote: "The most accepted view today is that sensitivity is concentrated in the clitoris. This contrasts with the older view, maintained by Freud and his pupils, that the erogenous zone is confined to the clitoris in the child and the young girl, while sensitivity in the adult woman is and should be vaginal" (Hansen 1972–1973:22). In Chapter 9 of this volume, Leonard offers an extensive analysis of such psychoanalytic theories regarding the effect of FGC on female sexuality. Interestingly, a similar view on the immaturity of clitoral and maturity of vaginal orgasms appears in Ahmadu's discussion of Kono women's thoughts on excision in Chapter 14.

Several scholars, including Gosselin (1996; and in press), Parker (1995), Obermeyer (1999), and Obiora (1997), as well as Ahmadu, Abusharaf, and Leonard in this volume, discuss the Western preoccupation with the clitoris as the primary site of female sexual pleasure, which has become incorporated into much of the anti-FGM literature. Dorkenoo (1994), for instance, refers back to the 1979 *Ms. Magazine* article in which Gloria Steinem and Robin Morgan accuse Sigmund Freud of performing "psychic clitoridectomies" on Western women with his theories. Inevitably, Western feminist discourses on sexuality are becoming incorporated into local anti-FGC campaigns throughout Africa, thus giving rise to new debates. Researchers often find, however, that perceptions vary widely, with supporters and opponents of the practice claiming alternately that FGC has no effect on sexuality; that it decreases or even annihilates a woman's ability to feel pleasure; or that it in fact causes more uncontrolled sexual behavior (see, for example, Chapter 11 in this volume). One anthropologist points as well to the contents of sexual education often accompanying "circumcision," arguing that "if any linkage exists between control of female sexuality and female 'circumcision' this linkage seems to be stronger within the transmission of knowledge about proper gendered behavior rather than through the removal of the clitoris" (Skramstad 1990:18).

Just as female genital cutting cannot, then, be linked in any simplistic, causal way to female sexual desire or pleasure, a similar ambivalence characterizes its perceived association with religious practice. Female "circumcision" is often seen to be somehow associated with Islam. This is perhaps not surprising, considering Islam's compulsory circumcision of males and the frequency with which female genital cutting is practiced among Muslim groups. It is important to note, however, that the Quran does not require female "circumcision," that not all Islamic groups practice FGC, and that many non-Islamic ones do. Contributions to this volume reflect the wide range of variation in the extent to which the practice of FGC corresponds with adherence to Islam. On one end of the continuum, the authors of Chapters 4, 6, 7, and 9 discuss the practice of FGC among non-Islamic groups. On the other extreme, in Chapter 11 Johnson points to the near complete correspondence between female "circumcision" and Islamic identity formation among Mandingas in Guinea-Bissau, where the practice has come to be seen as a prerequisite for the ritual purity necessary to pray as well as a marker of belonging to an Islamic community. In between these two extremes lie many specific contexts in which Islam is to various degrees invoked as associated with the continuance of the practice, and several chapters in this volume discuss local theological debates surrounding the practice. It has been suggested that "religion" is often offered, "almost reflexively," as a reason for performing FGC (see Gordon 1991:9). In response, Boddy argues that "the question of what is meant by 'religion' remains obscure" and points out that for many women "religion is nothing less than their entire way of life; religion and tradition are not merely intertwined, they are one and the same" (Boddy 1991:15; see also Coleman 1998). A great deal of effort by scholars and activists has been concentrated on demonstrating the lack of scriptural support for enforcing FGC (see, in particular, Abu-Sahlieh 1994), as is discussed in several of the contributions to this volume. It must, however, be emphasized that the "absence of clear textual dictates . . . does not automatically undermine the religious motivation" (Lewis 1995:22) of those who practice FGC, as is powerfully demonstrated in Johnson's discussion of Guinea-Bissau (see Chapter 11).

Strategies to Eliminate Female Genital Cutting: "Eradication" Efforts

Clearly, the perception of FGC in any one cultural context varies not only in its construction of "meaning" but also in its sense of relative importance. Even in cases where indigenous practitioners view it as a "problem," the practice often does not achieve the priority it receives in the international health community. In this volume, both Mandara (Chapter 5) and Gruenbaum (Chapter 2) point to local problems that are experienced as far more serious than FGC. Abusharaf, as well, reminds the reader that the "politics of priorities as articulated by Sudanese women are fundamentally distinct from those advocated in the West" (Abusharaf 1996:10).

It is not surprising, then, that identifying the most effective and appropriate strategies for eliminating female genital cutting is among the most bitterly contested issues surrounding this practice. As discussed by Thomas (1996, and in Chapter 7 of this volume), early colonial interventions alternately employed strategies based on the alleged adverse health effects of the practice and discourses framing the practice as uncivilized, barbaric, and unacceptable in the eyes of Christianity. Such campaigns have reappeared several times throughout the last century, each time with a slightly different focus. In the 1970s and early 1980s, when anticircumcision activists identified female genital cutting as "female genital mutilation," the practice again became targeted for "eradication," a term now almost as controversial as "FGM" (see also Obermeyer 1999). The custom of genital cutting came to be described as an "epidemic" and was singled out to be "treated as a public health problem and an impediment to development that can be prevented and eradicated much like any disease" (Hosken 1978:155).

Such statements became rallying cries at a series of conferences that launched the current international campaigns for the abolition of the practice but were not met without criticism. In the early 1980s, anthropologist Ellen Gruenbaum warned that the adoption of the medical view "implies not only that the practice is 'pathological,' but that its solution might lie in a sort of campaign-style attack on the problem. Social customs, however, are not 'pathologies'; and such a view is a poor starting point for change, since it is not one necessarily shared by the people whose customs are under attack" (Gruenbaum 1982:6). Other scholars have suggested that to confront FGC on medical grounds "has not proved productive" (Sargent 1991:24), and that a "disproportionate allocation of resources" have been earmarked for intervention studies (Obermeyer 1999:85).

Other activists have chosen a different direction in their anti-FGM activism, which came to a head in the 1970s when the practice increasingly became attacked as a violation of women's rights. However, through rhetoric such as Mary Daly's essay "African Genital Mutilation: The Unspeakable Atrocities," a combative tone was set that still lingers over the international debate. Reactions from African representatives, even those who had been advocating the abolition of the practice on health grounds, were often characterized by anger and indignation. The way that outraged "Western" women championed the issue has since been accused of revealing "latent racism," "intellectual neo-colonialism," and "anti-Arab and anti-Islamic fervor"

(Gilliam 1991:218), and efforts to "eradicate FGM" have been seen as an imperialistic intervention from meddling Westerners of privilege.

Although still offended by the often sensationalist manner in which the issue is discussed in the West, many African women have more recently invited assistance from the West in abolishing the custom of female genital cutting. Currently, "eradication" efforts are often supported by outside funding being channeled through indigenous women's organizations. A series of conferences and international meetings have been held to address strategies for eliminating FGM, starting with the 1979 Khartoum seminar on Traditional Practices Affecting the Health of Women and Children. After an initial reluctance to address the issue of FGC, the World Health Organization organized a meeting at which representatives from a number of African countries began identifying strategies for eliminating the practice. The seminar was seen by some as a major breakthrough for many campaigns, as "WHO gave its name and credibility to NGO's and campaigners working directly in the field" (Dorkenoo 1994:68). In the late 1980s, WHO issued an elaborate plan for action, and other major agencies have since joined the global campaign with their own platforms. To date, however, no consensus exits on the most appropriate approach to the elimination of female genital cutting.

The late-twentieth-century resurgence of international efforts to eliminate the practice of female "circumcision" forces scholars to confront a central question: Who, if anyone, has the moral authority to condemn this practice? As is discussed by Abusharaf (Chapter 8), the practice of FGC has generated heated debate on the conflict between cultural relativist and universalist paradigms.[10] In this light, female "circumcision" has emerged as a test case for cultural relativism as scholars struggle with how to approach the issue intellectually, emotionally, and morally. The doctrine of cultural relativism holds that there are no value judgments that are objectively falsifiable independent of specific cultures, and as such, moral judgments and social institutions in any one society are exempt from legitimate criticism by outsiders (Renteln 1988).

The work of scholars who stress the fundamental importance of offering perspectives on cultural factors that promote the practice of female genital cutting has brought the debate surrounding cultural relativism into sharp focus. Gruenbaum (1996) notes that analyses that *do* offer emic interpretations and cultural contextualizations are often criticized as bordering on advocacy for the practice. The authors of one work argue that anthropology's "pretensions to cultural relativity" have led to defensive attempts to counteract Western ethnocentrism, often causing the anthropologist to turn a "culturally blind eye" (Lutkehaus and Roscoe 1995:xiii), and another article accuses anthropologists of perpetuating a "cover-up" (Gordon 1991:13).

Janice Boddy, whose own work in the Sudan examines local views on infibulation, has replied that none of the scholars who study the practice in its cultural context is "so theoretically myopic or inhumane as to advocate its continuance" (Boddy 1991:16). Moreover, since researchers urging cultural sensitivity and understanding have often been equated with "cultural relativists," those who do in fact oppose female "circumcision" are accused of "intellectual dishonesty." Legal scholar Barrett Breitung contends that

> because they believe that female circumcision must eventually be eradicated, these advocates do not, in any meaningful sense, seek dialogue or consensus with supporters of female circumcision. Instead they attempt a discussion on the best way to eliminate the practice. This position, while reflecting the difficulty in addressing competing and differing cultural values, is intellectually dishonest. (Breitung 1996:661)

Confusion arises not only by equating Western scholarship with cultural relativism but by assuming uniform opposition to female "circumcision" among researchers. "No Western writer or cultural observer," Breitung writes, "is ambivalent toward or supportive in any way of the continuation or spread of female circumcision" (1996:685). The work of Sierra Leonean–American anthropologist Fuambai Ahmadu (Chapter 14) serves as a striking counterexample. As both a scholar working in the West and someone who describes herself as "neutral" on the subject of female "circumcision," her work challenges many of the assumptions of Western feminist scholarship, including formulations of "universal" human values (see also Obiora 1997:286).

In attempting to reconcile her own experiences surrounding excision with external discourses on women's bodies and sexuality, Ahmadu breaks what she describes as a "perturbing silence among African women intellectuals who have experienced initiation and 'circumcision.'" Ahmadu demonstrates that "insider" perspectives from Kono women of Sierra Leone stand in sharp contrast to prevailing human rights discourses; rather than characterizing female "circumcision" as a "peculiar manifestation of women's global subordination," they emphasize women's agency as well as the crucial dilemma faced by many African women in deciding the fate of their daughters—"to either be 'anticulture' or 'antiprogress'" (see Chapter 14).

Other scholars argue that cultural relativism, if read as moral relativism, "is no longer appropriate to the world in which we live" and that scholarly research must be "ethically grounded" (Scheper-Hughes 1995:410). Critics have targeted the profound dilemma of approaching, in praxis and writing, a procedure that potentially leads to severe and even life-threatening health consequences. Daniel Gordon, in a 1991 prize-winning essay, criticizes anthropology for its "inability to integrate a consideration of the medical complications of the practice into its description and denial of its own position of moral advocacy" (Gordon 1991:13). Gordon aligns himself with biological anthropologist Melvin Konnor in asserting that female genital cutting is one example of where anthropologists "ought to draw the line" of the limits of cultural relativism (Konnor 1990:5).

The universalist stance holds that certain individual rights are so funda-mental to humankind that they should be upheld as universal rights whose breach is subject to condemnation and, in certain instances, punishment through legislative force.[11] Through a series of UN conferences, "female gen-ital mutilation" has increasingly been conceptualized as a human rights viola-tion. In a keynote address at the UN Fourth World Conference on Women in Beijing in 1995, U.S. first lady Hillary Rodham Clinton stated unequivocally, "It is a violation of human rights when young girls are brutalized by the painful and degrading practice of female genital mutilation" (*San Francisco Examiner,* September 11, 1995).

The practice of female "circumcision" is not, however, universally recog-nized as a violation of basic human rights (see, for example, Brennan 1989). Hence, debate has centered on the challenge of balancing cultural values and autonomy against international standards of human rights. As outlined in an article by U.S. legal scholar Kay Boulware-Miller (1985), the human rights approach can be broken down into claims based on (1) the rights of the child, (2) the rights of women, (3) freedom from torture, and (4) the right to health and bodily integrity. As Boulware-Miller and others point out, however, each of these approaches carries with it potential problems.

The rights of the child. Numerous activists have urged that FGC be consid-ered a form of child abuse, a stance that evokes the UN Declaration of the Rights of the Child. This declaration, adopted in 1959, advocates that each child be given the opportunity "to develop physically, mentally, morally, spir-itually and socially in a healthy and normal manner and in conditions of free-dom and dignity" (Princ. 2) as well as be protected against "all forms of ne-glect, cruelty and exploitation" (Princ. 9). From this perspective, legal scholar Kellner argues that although labeling FGC as child abuse may "appear de-grading to the traditions of the African people . . . the physical and psycholog-ical well-being of the African children should be regarded as a higher con-cern" (Kellner 1993:131). As pointed out by, for example, Boulware-Miller (1985) and Barrett Breitung (1996), the rights-of-the-child approach is prob-lematic. For one, in cultural contexts in which most or all girls are "circum-cised," the child's right to develop "normally" includes being "circumcised." Second, labeling FGC as an act of child abuse implies that "parents who ap-prove of female circumcision are either incompetent or abusive" (Breitung 1996:9). Yet, as stressed by Mackie and Ahmadu (Chapters 13 and 14), par-ents choosing "circumcision" do so because they perceive this as acting in the best interests of their daughters.

The rights of women. At the UN Fourth World Conference on Women in Bei-jing, "female genital mutilation" was classified as a form of violence against women, equated with battering, rape, sexual abuse, and forced prostitution.

Eradication efforts focusing on FGM as a violation of women's rights often invoke the Convention on the Elimination of All Forms of Discrimination Against Women (CEDAW), enacted by the United Nations in 1981. CEDAW calls for an end to all gender discrimination and requires states to "modify the social and cultural patterns of conduct of men and women, with a view to achieving the elimination of prejudices and customary and all other practices which are based on the idea" of gender inequality or stereotyped roles (Art. 5a).[12] This line of argument, which often stresses the "private" nature of violations against women, has become the foundation for appeals for political asylum that may now be based on the claim that women escaping the perceived threat of forced genital cutting are escaping "persecution" (see, for example, Stern 1997; Bashir 1996). Another legal effort centers on seeking to secure gender as a possible category of oppression, much like membership in a political party (see Kassindja and Bashir 1998).

Although little consensus exists regarding the "true" background of FGC, it is an undeniable fact that in many cultures the practice is carried out by and remains firmly within the control of other women, as is borne out by several of the contributions to this volume. Fuambai Ahmadu, who has herself undergone excision in the context of initiation into a secret women's society in Sierra Leone, argues in what is destined to become a highly contested chapter that female initiation, including genital cutting, is an event that can be highly empowering to women and is in many contexts wholly unrelated to Western feminist ideas of patriarchal oppression (see also Hernlund in Chapter 12 for a similar assertion regarding initiation in the Gambia). Ahmadu argues against the standard anthropological view of "ritual officials as colluding with patriarchy in order to maintain the subordination of women in society" and asserts that "what *Bundu* teaches first and foremost is the subordination of young girls and women to female elders." And in Chapter 7, Lynn Thomas directs our attention to the importance of initiation events in bolstering the power of elder women over those from younger age groups (see also Lutkehaus and Roscoe 1995).

Nonetheless, a remarkable divergence in interpretation can be found in statements on the practice issued by various African women. Senegalese activist Awa Thiam, for example, writes in her 1986 book *Black Sisters, Speak Out:* "In Black Africa it would seem that males have forced women to become their own torturers, to butcher each other" (Thiam 1986:75). In contrast, "Haja," a Sierra Leonean businesswoman interviewed by Ahmadu, speaks for many others when she says about male domination: "It has nothing to do with us. Initiation is part of women's business. Circumcision is part of the process of initiation into our secret societies. We women continue to do it to ourselves. Men fear our medicine. . . . It is through our societies that we exercise leverage against men in our culture" (Ahmadu 1995:44).

An extensive literature from several disciplines has in recent years wrestled with "the potential tensions" (Ginsburg 1991:18) inherent in feminist analyses of FGC, but most of this discussion is unfortunately beyond the scope of this chapter. A number of contributions to this volume do, however, engage in discussions of how—if at all—Western feminists can or should position themselves regarding the practice of FGC. For instance, in Chapter 8 Abusharaf contrasts responses to FGC by Western and Sudanese feminisms, and in Chapter 10 Gosselin discusses the impact of international actions on a local campaign in Mali.

The history of much of Western feminist involvement has tragically been characterized by a "maternalistic" tendency to try to change the minds of women who practice FGC and—when this fails—to attribute to them "false consciousness" (Engle 1992:1525). Obiora asks, "What aspects of the anti-circumcision campaign are at odds with feminist epistemology and praxis?" (Obiora 1997:310), and criticizes the "inclination of some radical feminists to discount or marginalize the perspectives of African women" (Obiora 1997:316).[13] A statement issued in 1977 by African Women for Research and Development (AWORD) argued forcefully that although African women "must speak out in favour of the total eradication of these practices," they must "no longer equivocate or react only to Western interference" (in Davies 1983:219). Recent writings from both within and without Africa call for cooperation and coalition building and urge for prioritizing the role of African women in defining their own experiences of FGC (e.g., Lewis 1995).

Freedom from torture. Another approach to legitimizing opposition to FGC has considered defining the practice as a form of torture (e.g., Annas 1996). The 1984 UN Convention Against Torture and Other Cruel, Inhuman or Degrading Treatment or Punishment (CATCID) defines torture as "any act by which severe pain or suffering, whether physical or mental, is intentionally inflicted on a person for . . . purposes . . . including any reason based on discrimination of any kind." Specifically, the CATCID declaration requires that the torture be inflicted by "or with the acquiescence of a public official or other person acting in an official capacity" (Breitung 1996:682). Clearly, most FGC procedures take place in unofficial settings, although it has been argued that the failure of African governments to enforce existing laws against the procedure can be interpreted as satisfying this requirement (Breitung 1996:10). Invoking the term "torture," former U.S. Congresswoman Patricia Schroeder has supported legislation against the practice in the United States, arguing that if human rights abuse occurs due to racial or political reasons it is regarded as a human rights violation, but "if it happens to a woman, it's cultural" (*U.S. News and World Report,* February 7, 1994; see also Seddon 1993:285, and Gifford 1994). Likewise, in interviews following the release of her film *Warrior Marks,* novelist/activist Alice Walker has made such statements as: "There are a lot of people who think that to speak about this is to stick your nose into somebody else's affairs, somebody else's culture. But there is a distinction between torture and culture" (*Dateline,* February 10, 1994). As is shown in several of the contributions to this volume, however, many Africans view efforts to eliminate FGC as an attack on their culture. Again, we see evidence of what Breitung describes as "a great gulf . . . between what feminist commentators identify as the social purpose of female circumcision and what supporters of the practice claim that it means" (Breitung 1996:682).

The right to health and bodily integrity. A number of scholars and activists have come to the conclusion that the most reasonable angle from which to argue for the elimination of genital cutting is that of health. Boulware-Miller concludes that the right-to-health argument "integrates the issues of physical, mental and sexual health as well as child development" and may be seen as less exclusive and more politically acceptable than any other approach (Boulware-Miller 1985:177). This is the same conclusion that was reached in the Special Report issued by the UN Working Group on Traditional Practices in 1986. This document elects to not classify FGM as a human rights violation or manifestation of oppression of women and instead advocates for education focused on the potentially harmful effects of the practice.

In deciding how FGC could best be "remedied," the UN Sub-Commission for Prevention of Discrimination and Protection of Minorities did not, in the end, conclude that the practice of FGC constitutes a human rights violation. Instead, the sub-commission chose to frame the issue in terms of weighing the health consequences of the practice against its "cultural functions" (UN 1986). Arguing that FGC has become "obsolete" due to changing economic and social conditions, the report concluded that the health risks were deemed to be unwarranted.

Even simple educational campaigns designed to improve knowledge of the potential adverse health outcomes of genital cutting are not unproblematic, however. It has long been assumed that as people are made aware of the potential health risks they will abandon the practice. Carolyn Sargent, however, points out that health hazards are often recognized by women themselves and that basing a public health program on informing women about the risks of FGC would not alter their perceptions of its relevance (Sargent 1989, 1991; see also Obiora 1997:359). A well-known Sudanese women's health activist adds: "To argue against this practice on the grounds of physical damage and to attempt to eradicate it through health awareness and education are futile" (Toubia 1988:102). Female "circumcision" is not a medical problem, this author argues, but "essentially a social phenomenon reflecting the position of women." Toubia asserts that the cultural pressures on a girl to be "circumcised" in order to obtain the status of an adult—and thus marriageable—woman leads to a situation in which "loss of a woman's genitalia is not too high a price to pay" (Toubia 1988:102). Writing on the Rendille of Kenya in

Chapter 6 of this volume, Shell-Duncan, Obiero, and Muruli concur: "Awareness of the fact that female 'circumcision' is associated with adverse health consequences is widespread, yet the Rendille view the risks as worth taking in light of the implications for marriageability."

Nonetheless, a number of innovative educational campaigns have had some degree of success. In Chapter 13, Mackie stresses the importance of educational campaigns being nondirective and describes the process by which Senegalese women involved in the Tostan project themselves came to identify FGC as an issue needing to be addressed: "Villagers first look at what they and other villagers are doing now and understand why they are doing it. Next they receive new, relevant and often technical information. . . . Then they work as a group to discuss the information and to decide whether it is useful. . . . People are never told what to do."

Although many scholars do argue that the right-to-health approach is the most tenable human rights approach for opposing FGC, its practical application is faced by contradictions as well. One of the most contested areas of the debate over efforts to eliminate female genital cutting concerns its potential medicalization or "clinicalization" (Obiora 1997). A controversial approach has been to incorporate training on septic procedures for genital cutting as part of training programs for traditional birth attendants (van der Kwaak 1992). Traditional circumcisers are encouraged to perform the milder forms of genital cutting; given training on anatomy; and instructed to take precautionary steps such as using new clean razors on each woman, dispensing prophylactic antibiotics (powder on wound or oral), and using local anesthetic. In addition, in urban areas of some regions it is becoming increasingly common to have girls operated on in hospitals or clinics (Dorkenoo 1994; Caldwell, Orubuloye, and Caldwell 1997). In Djibouti, for example, a clinic run by Union National des Femmes de Djibouti reportedly conducted "mild" excisions under local anesthetic (UN 1991:19). Opponents argue that the incorporation of female genital cutting procedures in the biomedical healthcare system institutionalizes the practice and counteracts efforts to eliminate it (Gordon 1991; van der Kwaak 1992). Some argue that presently there is no evidence to suggest that a policy of promoting the less drastic form of genital cutting in hygienic surroundings will lead to its eventual eradication (Dorkenoo 1994:9).

Conversely, Shell-Duncan, Obiero, and Muruli argue in Chapter 6 that the medicalization of female genital cutting does not necessarily hinder efforts to eliminate the practice. This point is illustrated by the fact that in Nigeria, the practice of excision is gradually declining in urban areas where clinic-based procedures are available (Caldwell, Orubuloye, and Caldwell 1997). However, the option of obtaining medically assisted genital cutting procedures is becoming constrained by international policy. The official stance of the World Health Organization is that all forms of female "circumcision" should be abolished without intermediate stages and that the procedure should not be performed by health professionals under any circumstances. This position is held by many other organizations, including the International Federation of Gynecology and Obstetrics, the American College of Obstetricians and Gynecologists, the United Nations International Children's Emergency Fund (UNICEF), the American Medical Association (ACOG, 1995), and the Inter-African Committee (IAC). Shell-Duncan, Obiero, and Muruli criticize this staunch opposition to medicalization, arguing instead that "if improvement of women's health is truly targeted as a priority, intermediate solutions, including the improvement of medical conditions for female 'circumcision,' merit careful consideration" (for a similar view, see also Obiora 1997).

By juxtaposing divergent views, based respectively on idealistic and pragmatic perspectives on change, we are forced to confront a profoundly moral dilemma in regard to what Obiora calls "interim transitional strategies" (Obiora 1997:365). Should we assist in the improved health of women while lending legitimacy to a destructive practice? Or should we hasten the elimination of the practice while allowing girls and women to die from preventable conditions? In many African communities, particularly those only recently confronted with disapproval of female genital cutting, "circumcision" *will* for the time being be performed, the only question being under what conditions. The debate forces us to look more critically at some of our own assumptions and question why those who recoil in horror at the thought of African girls being genitally cut for the sake of marriageability spend no effort reflecting on the numerous, nonmedically indicated surgical procedures performed on Western women to make them more desirable (one anthropologist once remarked about breast implant surgery: "You don't hear anyone call that 'mammary mutilation.'"). However, as has been pointed out by Gunning (1997:457), for example, and others, medicalization of female genital cutting may, as has been the case with birth, lead to it coming under the control of male practitioners of biomedicine, thus resulting in loss of female influence.

If FGC can, in fact, be legitimately opposed on the basis of its health consequences, the question remains as to how women's health can best be protected. Some opponents advocate that legislation against female "circumcision" is a compelling solution. For example, Laila Bashir argues that criminalization will assist in deterring the practice by "fostering an environment . . . that is clearly intolerant to FGM" (Bashir 1996: 13), and Gunning concurs that "for those who are opposed to the surgeries already, the law could provide that extra needed support against social pressures to circumcise their daughters" (Gunning 1991–1992:228–229).[14] This view is receiving increasing support from Western nations, whose influence through economic means is perceived to threaten countries that do not outlaw or formally denounce all forms of genital cutting. The U.S. State Department now requires for its Human Rights Report that individual countries produce evidence of legislation or bans against FGC. There have been rumors, both on the ground in Africa and in U.S. media, of U.S. legislation making international aid conditional upon a nation's steps to criminalize and combat FGM, much as with conditions tied to drug trafficking, terrorism, or forced abortions.[15] No such binding legislation exists, but these perceptions may stem from the wording of a 1996 Treasury Department appropriations bill, which states that Section 579

> requires the United States, after September 1997, to oppose (abstain or vote NO) any loan or other utilization of funds, other than to address basic human needs, for the government of any country which the Secretary of the Treasury determines has a cultural custom, a known history of the practice of female genital mutilation, and has not taken steps to implement educational programs designed to prevent the practice.

Although we were told by State Department representatives that this bill has never resulted in denial of funds to any African country, Melissa Parker claims in a 1995 article that "one of the conditions of a recent loan by the International Monetary Fund to Burkina Faso was that the government should agree to further its activities to bring the practice to an end" (Parker 1995:506). Clearly it does evidence the U.S. government's opposition to FGC in an economic context and clarifies the rationale of countries who pass legislation to "please American sensitivities" (*The Economist*, February 13, 1999).

Formal legislation has proven, however, to be a poor instrument of cultural change. The few attempts to outlaw clitoridectomy or infibulation in Africa have been largely unenforceable. For example, the 1946 law criminalizing infibulation in the Sudan caused public uprisings, and following its enactment the prevalence has actually increased. Moreover, such efforts have triggered unexpected incidents of backlash, both in anticipation of and in response to legislation. When the British in 1945 made it known that infibulation would soon become illegal in the Sudan, "parents rushed to have their daughters infibulated, resulting in what one British observer reported as an unprecedented orgy of bloodletting" (Boddy 1991:16). Similarly, communities in varied locales that have been targeted by anticircumcision campaigns following film and media exposure have feared the enactment of legislation and have responded by performing excisions on all uncut females, including newborn infants (Eliah 1996; Chapters 11 and 12 in this volume). In Chapter 7, Thomas discusses the ban on clitoridectomy in the Meru District of Kenya in 1956, when adolescent girls defied the ban by excising each other.

Many advocates for women's health fear that legislation against genital cutting may result in increased risks for young girls and women as the practice goes underground. In a parallel to the abortion debate, it has been argued that victims of botched infibulations may simply be allowed to bleed to death rather than receive medical care when parents, circumcisers, and community members fear prosecution. In response to such a fear, in 1994 the Egyptian minister of health lifted a 1959 ban prohibiting health professionals from performing FGC. Since it is illegal for unqualified health professionals to perform surgical procedures, the regulation meant that no individuals were legally allowed to perform FCG (Toubia and Izett 1998). The 1994 reversal of this decree opened the opportunity for medicalization, with the intent of reducing harm and risk of death. However, deaths following medically supervised genital operations attracted widespread media attention and international scrutiny, resulting in a reinstatement of the original ban.

Despite the fact that legislation has been shown to be a poor tool for effecting change, under international pressure legislation continues to be drafted.[16] According to Toubia and Izett (1998), in 1994 Ghana became the first independent African nation to pass an explicit law prohibiting FGC. Similar laws have now been passed in Burkina Faso, Togo, the Central African Republic, Djibouti, and most recently in Senegal. The case of Senegal tragically illustrates the fact that legislation may, in some instances, actually undermine the success of programs aimed at ending FGC. Through a basic education program designed and implemented in 1998 by the Senegalese nongovernmental organization (NGO) Tostan, thirty-one villages publicly pledged to end the practice of female "circumcision" (see Chapter 13 for a more complete account). The success of this voluntary abandonment of FGC was reportedly stalled by opposition to a coercive law (*The Economist,* February 13, 1999), and top-down authority is being defied by communities who are continuing to "circumcise" girls, thus challenging whether the law will actually be enforced. Mackie's response, once again, emphasizes the limited utility of legislative action: "You simply can't outlaw cultural practices. . . . It is not possible to criminalize the entirety of a population, or the entirety of a discrete and insular minority of the population, without methods of mass terror. People have to decide to stop on their own" (*The Economist,* February 13, 1999).

An alternative view sees neither education, medicalization, nor legislation as central to attempts at eradication but argues instead that a decline in the incidence of female genital cutting will be the consequence of larger social change. This has been termed the "development and modernization approach." It is suggested that improvements in socioeconomic status and education, particularly for women, will have far-reaching social effects, including a decline in the demand for female "circumcision." Indeed, such changes have been shown to have an important effect on morbidity and mortality patterns (van der Kwaak 1992). Recognizing that "circumcision" is in many African societies a prerequisite for marriage and that marriage and children are vital aspects of women's roles and economic survival helps to contextualize this practice in a larger social setting. Hence, it is believed that effective change can occur only in the context of a women's movement directed at the social inequality of women, particularly economic dependency, educational disadvantages, and limited employment opportunities (Gruenbaum 1982). It has been argued, however, that changing social conditions will not automatically change strongly held beliefs and values on female "circumcision"; it is still important to convince men and women that female "circumcision" has an overall negative effect on their lives (van der Kwaak 1992).

The empirical evidence supporting the "development and modernization" approach is, however, unconvincing. The findings of John Caldwell, I. O. Orubuloye, and Pat Caldwell (1997), suggesting a decline in the practice of excision in urban areas of Nigeria, are a rare (and indirect) piece of supporting evidence for the "modernization" hypothesis in the African context. Additionally, John Kennedy (1970) notes that the reduction of infibulation to excision in Egyptian Nubia was accompanied by economic change and development. As Nubians lost their land after the construction of the Aswan High Dam, he argues, they took up wage labor; the loss of land inheritance deemphasized lineage continuity, and the complex of values that supported patrilineality and infibulation eroded. Based on discussions with gynecologists and clinic-based interviews, Assaad (1980:4) reports that at least 75 percent of Egyptian women have been excised and that "only the modernized and privileged few are spared." She maintains that "educated women see that their status may be derived from roles other than those of wife and mother . . . the more active socially and economically she is, the more she sees the health hazards of circumcision and looks upon it as an unnecessary mutilation" (Assaad 1980:6). What is not shown in these studies is a causal relationship between improved socioeconomic status and changes in the practice of female genital cutting. By contrast, Balk (1996b) finds in the Sudan a strong middle-class adherence to the practice of infibulation, with elite or poor women more likely to alter or abandon the practice. Obermeyer also cites a number of studies which "call into question the relevance of models that assume linear positive correlations among variables such as 'modernization,' education, and higher 'women's status,' and expect to find invariant negative associations between these variables and the prevalence of 'harmful practices'" (Obermeyer 1999:89).

Others scholars stress that in the context of development and modernization, the practice of female "circumcision" is actually spreading. Leonard's (1996) research among the Sara in Chad reveals that excision is a recently acquired practice, dating back only a single generation in some subgroups. Mackie (1996) reports that the practice of infibulation is spreading in the Sudan from the Arabized north to western and southern Sudan. He suggests that in urban areas, the less advantaged adopt the practice of infibulation to make their daughters more marriageable to the high status Arab traders that migrated from northern Sudan. Similarly, Pia Gallo and Franco Vivani (1992) report that infibulation, unknown a century ago among the Sab of Somalia, was adopted to emulate the nobility. Further, El Dareer finds that reinfibulation is associated with urban residence and higher levels of education in the Sudan, and Lightfoot-Klein (cited in Balk 1996b:14) concurs that the practice was initiated by wealthy Sudanese women within the past fifty years.

Mackie (1996 and Chapter 13 in this volume) similarly criticizes the "development and modernization" approach and proposes an alternative strategy modeled after successful efforts that eliminated footbinding in China. Footbinding, which was practiced on women in China for 1,000 years, ended in a single generation once successful eradication campaigns took hold. Mackie points out that footbinding and infibulation share a number of features in common, including near universality in communities where practiced and the aim of controlling sexual access to females and ensuring chastity and fidelity. Mackie argues that both "female genital mutilation" and footbinding are conventions maintained by interdependent expectations in the marriage market; once in place, conventions regarding access to reproduction are deeply entrenched since those who fail to comply also risk failing to reproduce. For footbinding, eradication efforts focused not only upon education about negative health consequences but also on forming associations of parents who pledged not to bind the feet of their daughters or let their sons marry women whose feet had been bound. Mackie suggests that the development of a similar "convention" approach for the elimination of female genital cutting may, as in China, decisively lead to change. Interestingly, whereas most suggestions for change include the caution to proceed slowly, Mackie's model and the Tostan project involve rapid change once a convention shift is in place. Although the Tostan initiative is arguably the most promising initiative for eliminating FGC, it does not necessarily indicate that rapid abandonment of FGC is imminent across Africa. As Shell-Duncan (in press:21) notes, "The time required to change beliefs and establish a consensus may take years in some societies. Parallel to the case of drug use, delivering the message of 'just say no'—in this case to female 'circumcision'—is much more simplistic in principle than application."

It is common for activists to argue that one of the reasons that FGC is so "entrenched" is that it has come to constitute an important source of income for those who perform the procedure (e.g., Dorkenoo 1994:50–51). Consequently, some eradication efforts have focused in part on schemes to compensate the cutters to replace lost income. There are several potential problems with this approach, however. In Chapter 13, Mackie offers a powerful critique of what he perceives as misguided functionalism. Although circumcisers immediately *do* cause the "circumcision" of girls, he argues, they do not cause parents to want FGC for their children and thus do not cause the continuation of the practice. Hernlund (Chapter 12) also reports on apparently unsuccessful schemes in the Gambia, where circumcisers allegedly received compensation for not circumcising but continued to do so in secrecy. As Mackie points out, however, in cases where circumcisers are extremely prestigious leaders of initiation societies, their genuine conversion is crucial (see Chapter 14 in this volume on the powerful position of secret society leaders in Sierra Leone). In the Tostan project in Senegal, the circumcisers publicly asked for forgiveness from their communities. In Mali, women from the blacksmith caste were publicly honored for their decision to cease cutting (see Chapter 10 in this volume). In the Gambia, the circumcisers participating in noncutting ritual were symbolically honored *as if* they had cut the girls (see Chapter 12).

A few communities have also experimented with alternative initiation rituals for girls, what Hernlund calls "ritual without cutting." In areas where FGC is associated with coming-of-age ceremonies, it is thought that a noncutting ritual event can contribute to elimination of the physical procedure. Most well-known is perhaps a project in Meru, Kenya, run by Maendeleo ya Wanawake Organization (MYWO) and the Program for Appropriate Technology in Health (PATH), in which a number of communities have organized events classified as "circumcision with words." In six years of operation, the project has prevented just over 1,000 genital cuttings (a formal evaluation of the project is forthcoming from the Population Council).[17] Likewise, the Ugandan group REACH received a UN award in 1998 after conducting similar replacement rituals in Sabiny communities. More recently, the Water for Life project in Somalia has carried out alternative rituals for girls, including symbolic infibulations (Gallo, personal communication). The success of such projects remains to be seen, however. A recent report from Uganda cautions that in the most recent "real" female initiation among the Sabiny, there was an increase in participation of 300 percent (*Newsweek,* int. ed., July 5, 1999:46).

In Chapter 12 of this volume, Hernlund describes the first such alternative ritual carried out in the Gambia. Although the success of these rituals remains to be seen, she argues that in the Gambian context these events have the potential to accomplish more than simply eliminate genital cutting and may assist in creating what one recent article terms "communities of resistance" (James 1998:1045). She cautions, however, that not everyone agrees that these rituals make sense, a view echoed by both Mackie and Johnson. In addition, Ahmadu warns that in the context of war-torn Sierra Leone, the idea of "new ritual" has taken on a far more sinister character. Nonetheless, in areas where FGC is closely tied to rites of passage, noncutting ritual may often be applicable, especially in political climates in which activists struggle to defend themselves against the argument that "to give up female 'circumcision' is to give up one's culture" (see Chapter 12).

In the preceding summary, we have for reasons of analytic clarity presented intervention strategies as if they were discrete and mutually exclusive, although in reality most campaigns combine a variety of strategies (see also Kratz 1994:346). "Integrated approaches," suggests one commentator, "combine domestic legal and nonlegal approaches, international standard-setting, and technical assistance and monitoring, with grassroots health and education campaigns" (Lewis 1995:45). Another scholar argues that it is the role of research "to show that these practices are unlikely to be challenged by a simple argument or to be changed by a single intervention" (Obermeyer 1999:97), and it is our hope that this collection of essays is a step in this direction.

In Lieu of Conclusions

The practices of female genital cutting appear to—more than almost any other issue—capture the popular imagination, trigger emotional responses, and reduce the complex to the nonnegotiable absolute. With this volume we hope to illustrate that it is impossible to offer simplistic solutions or pat answers, and we have attempted to problematize the intersection of global discourse and local practice. We have tried to raise questions, not only about an "exotic" and seemingly cruel "traditional" practice but about some of the assumptions that we as scholars hold about medicine, female bodies, and the right to speak with moral authority.

Regardless of one's stance on the appropriate level of the West's involvement with the practice of female genital cutting, encounters are becoming increasingly common in which a completely hands-off approach is untenable. On a legal and political level, the recent granting of political asylum to a Togolese woman on the basis of her fear of returning to Africa and being forced to undergo female genital cutting has established a legal precedent which—at least in theory—could apply to millions of women (but see Bashir 1996 for an argument against the fear of opening "the floodgates" of immigration). In the context of Western biomedicine, the recent influx of immigrants from communities that practice female "circumcision" has forced health practitioners, when confronted with the practice, to come face to face with issues of autonomy and multiculturalism (Schwartz 1994:431). Ethics committees are facing newly articulated "rights and wrongs" as they seek to adopt policies toward a procedure that has alternatively been described as a barbaric practice, an extreme act of misogyny, and an "affirmation of the value of women in traditional society" (Schwartz 1994:431).

Although many scholars correctly argue that the issue of determining the future of female genital cutting is best resolved by members of the communities in which the practice is found, the undeniable reality is that its eradication has already become, what Fuambai Ahmadu calls, "an irreversible 'international' political compulsion." Western governments have reclassified female "circumcision" as a "human rights violation," and the implied threat of withholding economic assistance to countries where the practice persists must be perceived as coercion for countries already reeling from structural adjustment programs. Morsy has offered a scathing critique of such global "rescue missions" and warns that "Western compassion can be nothing less than the kiss of death" (Morsy 1991b:22).

Clearly, the choice to continue or eliminate the practice of female genital cutting is no longer solely in the hands of those who currently engage in this practice. Consequently, any resolution of debated issues and the development of culturally sensitive approaches to eliminating female genital cutting require that we do not focus on this practice in isolation, but rather that we consider the lives and opinions of the people affected by it and the local and global domain of discourse and domination in which they are embedded.

Notes

1. Reporting on a lecture given by Mana Sultan Abduraham Issa at the University of Padova, Italy, on October 22, 1998.

2. For a discussion of the legal aspects of minors giving consent to genital cutting, see, for example, Coleman 1998 and Obiora 1997.

3. Although we find very compelling Obermeyer's point that the use of a full expression rather than an acronym "is a reminder that there are no easy equivalents and no simple way to understand" (Obermeyer 1999:84), we nonetheless use "FGC" for reasons of brevity. It is not our intention for this choice of terminology to "objectify the practice as if it were a rare or complicated syndrome" (Obermeyer 1999:84).

4. Due to space constraints, we are also unable to discuss here the well-documented history of female genital surgeries performed in Western biomedical settings.

5. DHS is a standardized survey that was administered to many nations worldwide in the 1980s and 1990s. It contains survey modules on topics such as fertility, family planning, and dietary intake. Modules on female "circumcision" were also included for a few African countries.

6. In Chapter 13, Mackie reports that Bamana women of southern Senegal performed "sealing," and it is plausible that this procedure is also practiced in Mali, although the literature refers more generally to "infibulation."

7. As this volume was going to press, an article was published, "Female Genital Surgeries: The Known, the Unknown, and the Unknowable" by Carla Makhlouf Obermeyer, which independently makes many similar assertions in regard to the alleged health effects of FGC and its impact on female sexual response as those made in this chapter. We refer readers to Obermeyer's excellent review for a more detailed analysis of the existing public health literature on "genital surgeries."

8. Austveg et al. (1998) report that traditional circumcisers often refrain from cutting the clitoris when performing infibulation in order to avoid hemorrhage from cutting the clitoral artery.

9. Accounts in the literature refer to ancient Egyptian beliefs about the bisexuality of the gods, which possibly merged with preexisting African ideas that identify the feminine "soul" of a man as located in the foreskin and the male "soul" of a woman in the clitoris. Although such a discussion is beyond the scope of this volume, interesting parallels can also be drawn to the well-documented Western discomfort with gender ambiguity that has resulted in routinely performing surgery on "hermaphroditic" infants.

10. For an alternative perspective, however, see Gunning (1991–1992). She argues that the relativist/universalist standoff is based on a false dichotomy and that

"culturally challenging" practices such as FGC are better approached through "multi-cultural dialogue and a shared search for areas of overlap, shared concerns and values" (1991–1992:191).

11. Gunning points out that responses to relativistic perspectives on human rights include not only universalist counterclaims but also what she calls the "positivist" view, which states that "as long as diverse nations sign and ratify human rights treaties they have willingly consented to be governed by the enumerated standards and cannot exempt themselves whenever it suits them" (Gunning 1991–1992:240).

12. Some countries, however, have entered reservations to this section. Malawi's reservation, for example, states that because of "their deep-rooted nature," certain "traditional customs and practices" are not to be included in the nation's adherence to CEDAW (Breitung 1996:683). Several articles point out that no other convention has been met with as many reservations as has CEDAW (see, for example, Funder 1993:421–422).

13. See Gunning (1997), however, for a response to Obiora, which cautions that the latter's view "begins to treat the views and experiences of Western feminists monolithically and as if they were diametrically opposed to those of African women" (Gunning 1997:448).

14. A number of legal scholars have recently written about anti-FGC legislation in the West (see, for example, Breitung 1996 and Coleman 1998). Of particular interest is the legal response to the practice in France, where both circumcisers and parents have actually stood trial for having girls circumcised, as was extensively covered in major news media February 17–20, 1999 (see also Obiora 1997).

15. For example, *The Economist* (February 13, 1999:45) reported that the U.S. State Department's Human Rights Report "lists those African governments that have banned female circumcision, and is used as a guide to allocating American aid."

16. But see Gunning, who argues for a separation of "the legal determination of right and wrong from the typical legal result of punishment" (1991–1992:244). She suggests that legislation be passed to establish norms but that the difficulty of enforcing human rights law is actually an asset in the context of FGC.

17. Presentation by Asha Mohamed of PATH, at USAID Symposium on Female Genital Cutting, June 3, 1999, Washington D.C., as reported in personal communication from Gerry Mackie.

2

Is Female "Circumcision" a Maladaptive Cultural Pattern?

Ellen Gruenbaum

The concept of cultural adaptation has been an extremely useful tool in anthropologists' efforts to explain many of the practices, technologies, and cultural beliefs that have become embedded in the cultural patterns of peoples of the world as groups of humans have adjusted to new environments or changed circumstances. In the concept of natural selection, physical traits were selected by the long process of differential reproductive success and survival over many generations, depending on appropriateness of a particular trait in helping individuals to live, find food, and mate in the context of the local environment. Adaptive success enabled individual members of a group to leave their genes behind in the next generation more often than those whose adaptive fit with the environment was less effective, which is the sort of understanding Charles Darwin and Alfred Russel Wallace developed from their observations of plants and animals in different environments in the nineteenth century.[1]

When, in the course of our own development as a species, humans acquired speech and therefore the ability to pass on knowledge in a very efficient way—through symbols, explanations, abstract thought, and acquired beliefs and values taught to others and to their young through language and example—it set in motion a dramatic process of change, and a far more effective type of adaptation became possible: cultural adaptation. This capacity to adapt using culture—instead of having to go though many generations of small physical changes resulting from the early deaths or failure to reproduce of those less well adapted to some new environment or changed condition—meant humans could think up solutions to problems and teach them to others fairly efficiently. If not well suited physically to a particular opportunity, say, a prey animal that could be eaten, humans did not need to evolve faster run-

41

ning or sharper claws but could work out tools like spears with stone points that could assist with the job of hunting. As additional behavioral complexities became useful, such as repetitive practice at throwing to improve accuracy, cultural supports such as imitative play and games probably formed part of the success of a particular practice in helping the individuals meet their food needs.

Similarly, even complex systems of cultural values can be said to serve a function in promoting survival of a population, which after the fact can be called adaptation. Cultural practices and values such as ethical prohibitions on killing other humans, customary sharing of food, marriage rules that encourage durable relationships and sexual exclusivity, or incest taboos—whether they are rooted in biological/psychological patterns or were developed as ways to control drives that might cause disruptive social effects—are examples of the sorts of cultural practices that can be identified as functioning to promote stability and survival of a group and its members. Such cultural practices can be called "adaptive" because they have positive results, promoting the survival of individuals, offspring, and the group. The proliferation of the population with a particular practice may lead to seeing this as group selection, although even if the behavior were clearly rooted in some genetically transmitted characteristic, it is not group selection in the strict sense, a concept that many population geneticists doubt can occur (Hartl 1980:349–350).

But for a cultural behavior, presumably not genetically transmitted, which is enforced by the group through a system of rewards and punishments, it becomes fairly clear why individuals choose to conform and how a new generation would acquire the behavior. Can the evolutionary success of such a behavior be judged by the differential rates of population growth of groups that do it and groups that do not? Those who reproduce prolifically and have the opportunity to enculturate more young in their system of values would be able to transmit the behavior to a growing population. This is the proximate explanation. But is there also a latent function, an ultimate explanation based on its effects on population survival? Looking back after several generations of population growth, could we say that a behavior was "adaptive"? Not necessarily, since the behavior may be unrelated to the reproductive success of the individuals in the population. However, if a practice promotes stability and social harmony (as the examples of mating rules and food sharing suggest), and this stability and harmony allows the members of a group to reproduce successfully and avoid excessive early mortality, it would not be entirely inappropriate to consider the contributing cultural practices as "adaptive" since they had positive results.

And what if a society hits upon a cultural practice or belief that has a positive effect on reproductive success of individuals but whose mechanism is not understood? Its preservation may, in retrospect, seem to have been preserved by its effect on the reproductive success of members of the group, since the population as a whole has grown. But they may simply preserve the practice or belief out of what could be called cultural inertia. The same thing could happen if they start a practice or belief that is not harmful, such as a taboo on sex during the menstrual period—it could be preserved and passed down to the next generations with the same confidence as they pass on knowledge of the proper way to plant yams. If, at some point, the environment changes in such a way that yam planting should be done differently, they will find out soon enough through the ineffective consequences of the old way. Similarly, if they hit upon a belief that sex should *only* be practiced during the menstrual period (thereby inadvertently avoiding women's fertile period around ovulation), they would soon observe a rapid decline in births except among the mavericks who violate the new taboo. The mavericks, teaching their own children these different values, might soon outnumber the conformists.

It seems to me, however, that most cultural anthropologists have somewhat less clarity about behaviors that have consequences for a group but that have different consequences for the individuals in the group. For example, it may well be that an island population of food growers who are not subject to a particularly high death rate will need to limit their births to balance their deaths, thereby avoiding overpopulation. But if a woman finds herself better off if she has more children to do the work and eventually support her in her old age, then the adjustment to a more sensible adaptation for the group as a whole may end up being in conflict with what is sensible for the individual (or pair of individuals) making the reproductive decision. For biological traits, the locus of selection is the individual, and what enhances the individual's fitness matters most. The effects of selection on many individuals may have a net effect on population growth. This should not, however, be confused with group selection in the strict sense. Does this mean that what is adaptive for a group may be less beneficial or even maladaptive to subgroups or individuals?

An additional complexity in considering what cultural practices are adaptive or maladaptive is that human cultural practices are sometimes highly distasteful from a different culture's perspective or from that of international standards on human rights. We are, of course, far from achieving an international consensus on human rights, even though the process has been accelerating in the last several decades. Nevertheless, one familiar example can serve to underscore the dilemma of attempting to balance cultural relativism and ethical standards: infanticide. In some of the cultures in which it has been found, infanticide can be understood as an adaptation to certain environmental, social, or economic conditions. In some conditions, an infant born too soon after its sibling may endanger the sibling's survival by the diversion of the supply of breast milk to the infant. This is particularly a problem where the older sibling might be weaned too soon without an adequate supply of weaning foods or uncontaminated water available, exposing the sibling to nutritional risks and potentially fatal contagious diseases. Rather than risk the survival of a child that has already established a social place and in whom the mother has invested a couple of years of her efforts, she might make the difficult choice to kill the newborn for the sake of the sibling. If the sex of the infant is female, and the sex of the sibling is male, and the survival of families in that culture is heavily dependent on having sons (either because sons have specific duties in the support of parents or, more generally, because polygyny rules and the longer reproductive years for males allow sons to produce more family members than daughters), the choice of the older sibling over the infant may be even more likely.

As difficult as the reality of this may be for those of us who don't have to make such choices, we can understand why it might have happened in some times and places. In fact, we might even say that the decision, in that context, is adaptive, since it helps the family to pursue security rather than risk the survival of a healthy two year old. They might console themselves with the thought that the mother can have another child when the timing is better. The genetic makeup of both children is such that the parents' genes have survived, but the likelihood of survival to adulthood and reproduction and hence future generations coming from them is positively enhanced if some, but not all, of the actual offspring are nurtured.

Clearly, by recognizing that this practice might have positive—though unpleasant—consequences, we do not necessarily condone it. More appropriately, we might want to say it is our responsibility as international observers to help to overcome the conditions, such as poverty or lack of access to clean water, that might lead to such hard choices.

But is the practice of infanticide in those conditions maladaptive or adaptive? Certainly, if it improves the survival chances of a healthy toddler, we could reasonably argue that it is an adaptive cultural practice because it seems to be a reasonable, understandable response to conditions and because it increases the reproductive success of that woman. Rather than risk losing both children, the mother has improved the chances for one. This may have a positive impact on group survival as well, since the availability of such a choice in such conditions may allow more members of the group to survive.

So, if disagreeableness is not enough to make a practice maladaptive, then under what circumstances might a cultural practice be considered so? In their popular medical anthropology text, Ann McElroy and Patricia K. Townsend use female "circumcision" as one example of what they term a "maladaptive cultural pattern" (1989:102–104). By doing so, they seem to be asserting that we should not assume that culturally institutionalized patterns have always developed for good reasons or that cultural patterns are necessarily going to promote health and well-being: "Humans do not invariably make maximally adaptive responses or wise, healthful choices."

I completely agree with the latter: our species has made many horrible choices at different times and places. But the assessment of whether female "circumcision" or any other cultural pattern is "adaptive" or "maladaptive" cannot be based solely on the judgment of its harmfulness to individuals. Rather, we need to consider whether there is an impact on reproductive success, which is a relative measure. It can only be determined by considering the effects of a practice on the two important factors, fertility and mortality. A practice that improves fertility relative to others without increasing mortality more than the relative fertility advantage could therefore still be considered "adaptive."

There can be little controversy over whether female "circumcision" is dangerous and potentially harmful to the health of the individual, yet that does not necessarily mean that it is *maladaptive*. If it were, then we might be justified in branding any resistance to change as irrational and even "backward." However, a better understanding of the role it plays in adaptation may help us to focus more appropriately—and less judgmentally—on more significant aspects, which I return to below.

McElroy and Townsend define adaptation as "the processes of adjustment and change that enable a population to maintain itself in a given environment" (1989:72). "Maladaptive" practices would presumably be ones that impede those processes and make population survival less likely. This is not an ideal definition of adaptation to work with, and indeed most evolutionary biology texts focus on individual reproductive success rather than group survival. Nevertheless, when considering the evolutionary implications of a cultural practice, it is not uncommon to want to consider group (population) survival, since practices can have contradictory effects on the individual and the group. Whether female "circumcision" in its many manifestations qualifies as a maladaptive practice—whether it affects individual survival or population survival—deserves consideration and an examination of some of the available data.

Nile valley populations have survived very well for centuries, if not millennia, with these practices. Leaving aside for the moment the degree to which the practices influence fertility, I would also question the assumption of a link between "individual physical health" and adaptation. If a condition is bad for individual health, is it maladaptive in relation to the population's survival? Unhealthy individuals often reproduce in large numbers, particularly if their conditions are not debilitating until after the reproductive years. Also, deaths among the young can serve as an adaptive process that selects against genetic or cultural traits that cause health problems, thus preventing them from being passed on. In short, one must agree with Hans Kummer's view, cited by McElroy and Townsend, that a trait preserved by a species need not be considered adaptive simply because it has been preserved: "All we can say with certainty is that it must be tolerable since it did not lead to extinction" (quoted in McElroy and Townsend 1989:119).

The same applies to cultural practices. A trait should not be labeled "maladaptive" merely because it is risky or harmful to individual health. Yet this is how McElroy and Townsend used the term "maladaptive": although female "circumcision" is performed for "both social and religious reasons," they label it "maladaptive for individual physical health and fertility" (1989:103–104). In my opinion, simply stating that female "circumcision" is not a "healthful choice" would be more accurate.

It is more important, in determining adaptiveness or lack thereof, to address the basic issues of survival and reproduction. If a practice inhibits the fertility of individuals, there is a stronger case for arguing that it is maladaptive, since reproduction is necessary to population survival over time. But that hardly can be asserted for "circumcision" as it is practiced in societies where it is valued. Indeed, if the rules of mating in a society require "circumcision," it would be justified to say that the fitness of uncircumcised women, who then have little or no opportunity to reproduce, is near zero and that of "circumcised" women is greater.

Although population survival may be irrelevant to biological adaptation via natural selection, since whatever the demographic outcome is could be considered "adaptive" (there being no teleological direction of evolution), I contend that it is nonetheless an important consideration in the debates over female "circumcision." In the late twentieth century, of course, we are aware that maximizing reproduction should not remain an unquestioned indicator of long-term "survival," since adaptive success clearly requires maintaining a balance between population and resource use. But if female "circumcision" inhibits fertility in any way (as Deborah Balk's analysis of Sudanese data in Chapter 3 suggests that infibulation does), an argument could be made that it is maladaptive to individual reproductive success and evolutionary survival. If statistical differences in reproductive success can be measured between populations with and without certain forms of the practice, the term "maladaptive" might not be entirely appropriate, and yet the difference would be important to policy debates.

In order to persuade people from pro-natalist cultural environments to end female "circumcision," some critics (e.g., Hosken) would like to be able to assert that female "circumcision" inhibits fertility. Certainly pharaonic "circumcision" (infibulation) is associated with lowered fertility for individuals as a result of scar tissue inhibiting sexual activity; of chronic infections resulting in higher rates of miscarriage, stillbirth, and infertility; or of obstructed labor and consequent damage to reproductive organs.[2] In Chapter 3, Balk demonstrates that low fertility and greater likelihood of marital disruption are important consequences of infibulation.

However, I know of no strong evidence that group fertility is seriously impaired, from either a population or even an extended family perspective, and my own ethnographic research supports this conclusion. I found that achieving high fertility did not, in fact, seem to be a problem in rural Sudan where pharaonic "circumcision" is practiced, despite the prevalence of many health risks and the inadequacy of hygienic conditions. Indeed, Balk's analysis of survey data supports this; she finds that on average people do achieve high fertility. The data cited (from a stratified random sample of 5,856 northern Sudanese women) include the finding that 78.1 percent of the women with six or more children are infibulated, which is only one-half of 1 percent less than the percentage of those with no children and a higher percentage than the sample as a whole.

In 1989, in an effort to seek some understanding of the ways in which different forms of "circumcision" might influence reproduction, I collected twenty-nine reproductive histories from married Sudanese women in a village in the southern part of the Rahad Irrigated Scheme, east of the Blue Nile.[3] This work was part of a long-term project with two ethnic groups, the Kenana and the Zabarma, with whom Jay O'Brien, Salah-el-din El-Shazali, and I had done research in the mid-1970s.

The groups have different traditional female "circumcision" practices.[4] The Kenana perform the most severe pharaonic "circumcision," characterized by total excision of the clitoris, prepuce, labia minora, and labia majora and infibulation, which closes the vaginal opening except for a tiny opening for urination and menstrual flow. The Zabarma, however, practice clitoridectomy (or partial clitoridectomy) only, which they call "sunna circumcision." The term "sunna" suggests that the practice is acceptable or even recommended or required for Muslims, although most Islamic theologians consider it to be either optional or discouraged by Islam.

A comparison of my network samples from the two groups offers insight into the effect of pharaonic "circumcision" on fertility. If we hypothesize that reduced fertility of "circumcised" women is due either to failure to become pregnant or to pregnancy and childbirth difficulties leading to stillbirth or perinatal death, the number of live births among pharaonically circumcised women would be lower than among sunna circumcised women. But as is clear from Table 2.1, the birthrate (an average of 6.8 births per woman for the Zabarma sample and 7.15 for the Kenana sample) is approximately the same for both groups, even though the samples include some young women who have not yet completed their reproduction. For women with completed reproduction, the averages are 8.0 for Zabarma women and 9.2 for Kenana women. Thus, birth rates are actually somewhat higher for the pharaonically circumcised sample. Only one of the twenty-nine women—a pharaonically circumcised Kenana—was apparently infertile: she had already been divorced twice, although she was still in her twenties.

My data do not include adequate information on maternal mortality, but they suggest nevertheless that female "circumcision" per se does not seriously imperil fertility; indeed, their fertility is quite high.[5] Although a poorly done surgery or related complications may contribute to infertility for some individuals, particularly where adequate health care is unavailable, certainly the community as a whole is in no danger of dying out due to the presumed

Table 2.1   Comparison of Zabarma and Kenana Fertility (live births
             only)

	Zabarma (sunna)		Kenana (pharaonic)	
	Total per Woman	Average	Total per Woman	Average
Births to all women in sample	68 (n = 10)	6.8	136 (n = 19)	7.15
Births to women with completed childbearing only	64 (n = 8)	8.0	92 (n = 10)	9.2
Apparent sterility	0		1	

maladaptiveness of the practice. And in rural central Sudan, where divorce is easy and polygyny not uncommon, patrilineal kin groups do not seem to have experienced any difficulty in generating offspring due to female "circumcision." The lack of dramatic negative effect on group fertility allows these sociocultural and kin groups to perpetuate the beliefs and practices. Nevertheless, the risk to fertility for the individual, substantiated by studies such as Balk's, may be an important argument for reformers to use.

Although female "circumcision" and its complications certainly affect death rates, high fertility compensates, making female "circumcision" a relatively minor factor in net population growth. In the reproductive histories of Sudanese women that we collected, for example, none of the forty-nine deaths of offspring that women reported was due to complications of "circumcision," and only one death of a girl of a possible age for "circumcision" to be a factor (twelve) was mentioned, although the mother did not report the cause of her death. The vast majority of deaths of children of both sexes were attributed to fever, diarrhea, or malaria (cf. Mairo Usman Mandara's discussion of physicians' rankings of relative importance of health issues in Chapter 5). In my estimation, improvements in the water supply and storage, sanitation, mosquito control, and nutrition, as well as improved basic health services, are needed to reduce child and infant mortality.

Clearly then, even if female "circumcision" contributes in some small way to lowered fertility or premature deaths, it is not as significant as malaria and diarrheal diseases. Since so many pharaonically circumcised women are fertile, it is unlikely that at an evolutionary level this type of "circumcision" is a problem for fertility or that it functions as a selective factor in adaptation. In these senses, it is thus inappropriate to argue that female "circumcision" is "maladaptive."

Even so, we are left with an interesting problem. Why do societies that practice female "circumcision" preserve it, and in fact, give it a prominent symbolic role? Does it serve a positive function? Or does it fall into Kummer's "tolerable" category?

Those who have argued that there is a symbolic value for female "circumcision" in maintaining gender relations and kin group cohesion (e.g., Boddy 1982, 1989; Hayes 1975)—a position that suggests a positive function for the practice—leave themselves open to occasional accusations of complicity via excess "cultural relativism" (cf. Gordon 1991 and Hosken 1982). One might even argue that precisely because practices like "circumcision" are important symbolically, they should be preserved or interfered with only cautiously, despite their drawbacks. There is some merit in this argument, particularly because practices of "circumcision" are entwined with gender identity (Boddy 1982, 1989) and ethnic identity (Gruenbaum 1988), both of which are very closely guarded and not easily changed.

Along these lines, if it helps people to make sense of a harmful practice whose origins are unknown, one can speculate that there were formerly some practical reasons for the infibulation (e.g., perhaps the scar barrier made rape less likely in areas where girls might be exposed to strangers on caravan routes). But as conditions changed, it may be that the cultural practice was preserved in the "tolerable" category.

It is important to remember that, as Soheir Morsy (drawing on the work of historian Christine Delphy) pointed out for *zar* spirit possession, to know the origin of a social practice cannot explain its present existence (Morsy 1991b:193). Thus the persistence of a practice that has negative consequences still must be explained in terms of present circumstances that encourage or discourage its continuation. No meaningful effort to change cultural practices can neglect this inquiry.

Forces for Continuity and Change

So what are these forces, both for change and for preservation? In its various forms and contexts, female "circumcision" has served meaningful purposes, and practitioners' attachment to it is rooted in those meanings, not just in a purported reluctance inherent in our species to resist change.

Elsewhere, I argue that the forces for preservation can be analyzed in part by understanding the differences in interests of men and women, old and young, and people of differing social statuses in a society. In the case of the rural areas of Sudan where I did research in the 1970s, 1989, and 1992, I found the interest in preservation of or change in the practices to vary starkly depending on gender, age, education, status, ethnicity, and religious background (see Gruenbaum 1988, 1991, 1996). The practice of pharaonic "circumcision," for example, in some cases reinforces social class and ethnic group superiority by functioning as an ideological marker of superior morality and propriety for the dominant ethnic groups of specific areas, and by serving as justification for the socioeconomic subordination of West African and southern Sudanese groups that do not practice pharaonic "circumcision."

In terms of physical harm, clearly women and girls bear the effects, whereas men's bodies are not similarly damaged. In Muslim areas, of course, males are also circumcised in boyhood or, increasingly, infancy, but that involves only foreskin removal—painful and medically unnecessary but far less risky or damaging than most forms of female genital cutting. There is another aspect to consider, though, in the effects on men's bodies of female "circumcision," and that is in terms of sexual pleasure. Although not a common topic of conversation, in some of my candid research interviews Sudanese women indicated that men gained greater sexual stimulation from a tightly infibulated woman, a point that was particularly convincing when discussed by a trio of co-wives, in a polygynous marriage, who had different forms of "circumcision." Indeed, many of the women whom I have interviewed, including ardent reformers, are convinced that men's sexual preference for infibulation—combined with families' desires to ensure their daughters' virginity and marriageability—is a major barrier to wholesale reform. Although there are certainly men in Sudan and elsewhere who find more pleasure in sex with an uninfibulated woman (and despite the inference from Balk in Chapter 3 that the higher rate of divorce of infibulated women may be due to sexual difficulties), the fear of male preference for infibulation is indeed a major factor to address in reform efforts. It has been heartening, therefore, to see more and more men of several countries becoming involved in efforts at change.

Thus, despite a picture of females being harmed and many men benefiting in some way, I categorically reject the simplistic analysis that female "circumcision" is a conspiracy of men to oppress women. That is no more sensible than to say that the fact that female midwives carry it out makes it the fault of women. What does make sense is to understand that rural Sudanese women live their lives in a social context in which they have lesser autonomy and stature than the men in their families, but in which social stratification of other sorts—economic, ethnic, family, and religious—has a profound bearing on how they will analyze and act on their subordination as women. Indeed, many Sudanese women, and no doubt many other African women as well, would argue eloquently that they have honored places and arenas of autonomy in their families and communities and should not be pitied by Western women who think themselves liberated.

Western disgust at female "circumcision" and the often oversimplified analyses strike many African women scholars as arrogant. They can point to Western aesthetically motivated medical disasters such as silicone breast implants and useless but risky cosmetic surgeries. The ethnocentric views of outsiders fail to recognize the dynamic nature of cultural patterns, imagining "the other" perhaps as frozen in time, bound by "traditional" ways of doing things (e.g., Walker 1992, Walker and Parmar 1993), and as "prisoners of ritual" (Lightfoot-Klein 1989) who are not rational makers of their own history. But as Robert Edgerton makes clear in his discussion of customs such as suttee in India as well as female "circumcision" in Africa, insiders to such cultures often have widely differing opinions and disagreements about them (1992:139). Culture is always dynamic, and that is even more the case when the issue at hand is the subject of international controversy, health education, and political discord.

In the areas of Sudan where I did research (especially the two main rural villages where I worked, one in Gezira and one in the Rahad irrigation project area), there are widely different opinions about female "circumcision." Change is by no means general but is happening in different ways and at different paces. The forces for change include health education, the spread of schools, and the efforts of local people who advocate reform. Some advocate reform from new understandings of religious teachings—that Islam does *not* mandate female "circumcision" as they had previously assumed—and others combine that insight with an appreciation of the health issues and growing national and international opposition. But there are strong countervailing forces in the form of ideologies of superiority—ethnic, economic, and moral—associated with pharaonic "circumcision."

Debates and discussions about the proper course of action, then, are not confined to the large cities like Khartoum and Wad Medani but are also taking place in the electrified villages of Gezira where people can watch national television and even in remote areas and among ethnic groups outside the mainstream of Sudanese national culture—though somewhat less vocally there. Although the ideas gaining ground in the rural areas more often favor reform (to the modified sunna "circumcision") rather than total elimination of female "circumcision," there is great cause for hope.

Unlike the spontaneity of genetic variations (i.e., mutations and chance combinations), which serve as the raw material for adaptation through natural selection, cultural variations are the product of thinking human beings who actively search out their best interests and who argue and decide, alone or in groups, whether to preserve one way of doing things or to invent others. Thus biological adaptive constraints—differential death and birth rates—are only a small part of the process of cultural adaptation, and it is necessary to ask political and economic questions as well as ones about biological adaptiveness (cf. Singer 1993).

The efforts to change female "circumcision" are not simply adaptive improvements on an otherwise maladaptive cultural pattern. Rather, both change efforts and resistance to such efforts involve contradictory political-economic implications. Forces for preservation of "Sudanese traditions" may be motivated by nationalist or partisan opposition to political repression and yet at the same time contribute to suppression of the female population (via the harmfulness of female "circumcision"). The Islamist movement may oppose pharaonic "circumcision" for religious reasons and yet impose more restrictions on women in the workplace, in dress, and in the curtailment of freedoms labeled as "Western" or un-Islamic—with the result that such cultural practices are suppressed without improving women's lives. In Sudan, the Ministry of Health supports abolition of all forms of these surgeries through education and by recommending against it, positions that are perceived by many rural people as somewhat elitist; that is, they see them as views of educated, middle-class, urban people. Many educated Sudanese, especially feminists, support the idea of gradual elimination of female "circumcision"—led by energetic efforts—while maintaining respect or patience for the sentiments of those not espousing their view (Toubia 1993). But they also recognize that the "circumcision" issue is only one of dozens of obstacles to balanced lives for women.

The international dimension of political-economic issues should not be overlooked. When outsiders take strong positions on practices such as pharaonic "circumcision," they can appear to be ethnocentric or arrogant. Their posturing can seem to deliberately ignore the salient factors affecting Third World poverty and ill health (such as centuries of economic exploitation and political interference) and to place blame instead on the people themselves or their cultural maladaptation. To repeat Janice Boddy's rejoinder to Gordon (1991), if we have not analyzed how change might occur, then "of what practical consequence [is it to] draw the line" at female "circumcision" (1991:16)? Instead, we must analyze the conditions and contribute to their amelioration.

Outsiders must recognize that our knowledge of the existence of this practice does not turn the tide: it is the women who practice "circumcision" who will be the ones to change it (Gruenbaum 1982). Nahid Toubia has commented that

> over the last decade the . . . West has acted as though they have suddenly discovered a dangerous epidemic which they then sensationalized in international women's forums creating a backlash of over-sensitivity in the concerned communities. They have portrayed it as irrefutable evidence of the barbarism and vulgarity of underdeveloped countries . . . [and] the primitiveness of Arabs, Muslims, and Africans all in one blow. (1988:101)

Thus, for outsiders to target female "circumcision" as the social problem in need of the most urgent attention seems outrageous to many African women—among them anthropologist Soheir Morsy (1991a)—since there are so many worse problems that wealthy countries have caused, exacerbated, or at any rate failed to help solve (for a similar perspective from Nigerian medical doctors, see Chapter 5).

In Sudan, for example, at least a quarter of a million people died of starvation caused by drought and war in 1988–1989. In 1991, millions of people were at risk of death from starvation because of an unhappy combination of failed rains, protracted civil war and population displacement, repressive government, and international isolation following the Sudanese government's refusal to support the coalition against Saddam Hussein during the Gulf War. Although the United States and other countries offered some assistance, it was too little and too late, relating to the "donor fatigue" phenomenon. Thousands of little Sudanese girls died—whether "circumcised" or not—along with their brothers and elders. Such international injustices and human tragedies are, perhaps, what really constitutes maladaptation.

I must conclude that maladaptiveness is not the problem with female "circumcision." Invoking evolutionary processes—with their teleological echoes of "progress"—may be a colorful rhetorical device for arguing against female "circumcision," but it falls short in the light of data. To say that cultural practices are adaptive or maladaptive is to suggest they have a role in survival of a species or population, something very difficult to address for a contemporary situation in which the future is not known and on a planet where population growth itself may turn out to become a sign not of evolutionary success for this species, but a medium in which future disasters fester.

If we wish to address the broad question of what is good for a single society, we would have to examine differences in social interests by gender, ethnicity, age, and social class. In the case of Sudan, arguments for the abandonment of controversial cultural practices such as female "circumcision" can serve a variety of political ends—from hiding international injustices to undercutting the authenticity of traditional Sudanese culture under the banner of the Islamist movement, advocating women's liberation, or supporting stricter Islamic interpretations of limitations on women's roles.

If such widely divergent interests can be served both by a cultural practice and by opposition to it, it is important that analysts increase the sophistication with which questions are approached, including not only health impacts but the political-economic context in which the cultural practices are pursued. The cultural debates underway in Sudan are an indication of the leadership rural women provide in the struggle to change female "circumcision." In their use of their intellectual and moral facilities, they are participating in cultural change.

Notes

I am grateful to the Development Studies and Research Centre of the University of Khartoum for research affiliation in 1989 and 1992 and the Department of Rural Development at the University of Gezira for affiliation in 1989. The quantitative data and several of the ideas for this chapter first appeared in my article in *Medical Anthropology Quarterly* (Gruenbaum 1996). Funding for research and writing was provided by California State University at San Bernardino (travel grant and sabbatical), a Grant-in-Aid from the American Council of Learned Societies, and a summer fellowship from the National Endowment for the Humanities. Helpful comments on a previous version of this paper by anonymous reviewers and editors of *Medical Anthropology Quarterly,* as well as the suggestions of the editors of this volume and Roger LaJeunesse, are gratefully acknowledged. The final responsibility, of course, is my own. I am especially grateful to my Sudanese academic colleagues, Mohamed El Awad Galal-el-din and Ibrahim Hassen Abdal Galil; to three research assistants in different projects, Awatif Al-Imam, Ekhlas Musa, and Saida Mohamed El Amin Ahmed; and to the people of the communities where I did my research for their assistance, insight, hospitality, and friendship. Correspondence may be addressed to the author at the College of Social Sciences, California State University, 5340 North Campus Drive, Fresno, CA 93740-8019.

1. See part 2 of Quammen (1996) for a lively account of the development of Wallace's and Darwin's contributions to evolutionary theory.

2. Pharaonic "circumcision" is the most severe form of the surgeries and is still practiced widely in Sudan and Somalia. It consists of removal of the clitoris, prepuce, inner labia, and part of the outer labia, followed by the closure of the tissues over the vaginal opening. The resulting scar tissue occludes the urethral and vaginal openings, with only a single tiny opening preserved for the passage of urine and menses. First intercourse often requires tearing or cutting, and childbirth requires cutting, followed by re-infibulation (restitching) of the opening. For more information, see Rushwan et al. 1983 and El Dareer 1982.

3. The interviews were conducted in Arabic using an outline of topics, including personal background, a reproductive history, and questions on labor tasks of the women and children. I was assisted by a Sudanese woman schoolteacher who accompanied me on the majority of interviews and explained in standard Sudanese Arabic unfamiliar words from the local speech. Her assistance in facilitating the interviews through her friendliness, personal knowledge of families and relationships, and stature in the community was very valuable. She also used the opportunity to encourage mothers to send their children to school.

4. For an overview of and survey data on female "circumcision" practices in Sudan, see El Dareer (1982) and Rushwan et al. (1983).

5. From my discussions, it seemed that mortality from childbirth was not a major problem in this region at the present time when compared with other causes of mortality. These families moved to the development project village, which has a clinic staffed by a medical assistant, in 1978. Births are attended and "circumcisions" performed by the village midwife, who has not received full formal training but sterilizes her instruments, uses local anesthesia for incisions and suture, and participates in Ministry of Health seminars from time to time. It is quite possible that maternal mortality was a more serious problem in the recent past.

3

To Marry and Bear Children? The Demographic Consequences of Infibulation in Sudan

Deborah Balk

In Sudan, as elsewhere in the Horn of Africa, female "circumcision" is a critical part of gender identification (e.g., van der Kwaak 1992; Talle 1993) and is thought to ensure a daughter's place in the marriage market and ultimately as a fertile wife (e.g., Boddy 1982; Cloudsley 1983; Gordon 1991). Other factors—such as ethnic and socioeconomic class differences—may also play an important role in the perpetuation of these practices, but the associations with gender identification, marriage, and reproduction are paramount (e.g., Gruenbaum 1988; Balk 1996b). So strong are the associations with gender that studies identify women—mothers, grandmothers, midwives—rather than families or institutions as key actors in the maintenance of these practices (e.g., Hayes 1975; Gruenbaum 1982). For some women, however, the consequences of their "circumcisions" may be so great as to jeopardize the very institutions they seek to maintain.

This chapter considers how female "circumcision," although considered central to the institutions of marriage and reproduction in Sudan, concomitantly may be the central cause for dissolving unions, in large part by dampening fertility. I focus on Sudan because infibulation, the most extensive form of "circumcision," is commonplace there. It can be argued that the extensiveness of infibulation makes for more frequent and numerous consequences, in turn making an understanding of its causes more salient. I give an empirical example based on data from the Sudan Demographic and Health Survey (DHS).

Numerous clinical studies have suggested that there are serious demographic and health consequences of various forms of the practice, ranging from minor infection to infertility and death (e.g., Cook 1979; El Dareer 1982; Aziz 1980; Verzin 1975; Shandall 1967; Inhorn and Buss 1993). Unfortunately, there is a notable lack of attention given to this subject in the African social demographic literature. Nevertheless, research on fertility suggests that the levels of infertility (i.e., childlessness) and subfecundity (i.e., when the capacity to produce live births is lower than normal) are high in the regions where these practices exist (e.g., Frank 1983; Mammo and Morgan 1986; Bongaarts, Frank, and Lesthaeghe 1984), despite the overwhelming cultural "preference" for high fertility (e.g., Caldwell and Caldwell 1987). High proportions of childlessness are commonly attributed to the widespread incidence of sexually transmitted diseases (STDs), but few sociodemographic studies have considered the effects that ritual female genital practices may have on infertility (or subfecundity) directly or indirectly through their effect on STDs (e.g., Mammo and Morgan 1986). Even fewer have considered the effects of infibulation, either directly or indirectly through infertility, on marriage. This chapter seeks to narrow that gap.

Although infibulation is by far the most commonly practiced form of "circumcision" in Sudan, some additional description of the practice is useful. According to the DHS data, in Sudan, 13 percent of women have had a sunna "circumcision," 73 percent have had a pharaonic (also called, Sudanese) "circumcision," and 2 percent have had *matwasat*—literally meaning intermediate—"circumcisions" (DHS 1991). Girls are usually (initially) "circumcised" somewhere between the ages of four and eleven (e.g., El Dareer 1982; Hicks 1993), although the range spans from shortly after birth until puberty, at least in northeastern Africa. According to two prior surveys in Sudan, the mean age of "circumcision" is about 6.5 years, or between six and eight years (Ministry of Planning 1979; El Dareer 1982; respectively). The simpler forms of "circumcision," such as the sunna type, typically occur only once in a woman's lifetime, but women who are once infibulated need to be de-infibulated for childbirth and often for sexual intercourse before that; and many are then restitched after giving birth. Some women who are excised may also need to be de-infibulated, either at marriage or childbirth because their remaining labia have fused together, producing a closure similar to an infibulation (e.g., Agugua and Egwuatu 1982; Hosken 1982; Widstrand 1964). Re-infibulation also occurs among some women whose husbands are absent from the household for a time and among divorced and widowed women who want to remarry (e.g., El Dareer 1982; Boddy 1982; Hayes 1975; Cloudlsey 1983).

Evidence from the Literature

Elsewhere I have synthesized the mostly anthropological literature describing how the institutions of marriage and fertility cause, or perpetuate, the practice of "circumcision" (Balk 1996b). Here I focus on the literature that illuminates the demographic consequences, that is, on fertility and marriage. Mortality and morbidity are not the subject of this chapter, but a quick overview is relevant: "Although the incidence of mortality and the extent of morbidity is sketchy at best, the complications of female genital operations have been described, if not quantified, with some consistency" (Gordon 1991:6; also see El Dareer 1982; El Saadawi 1980; and Hosken 1982). Among the many health consequences of the practice (see Chapter 1), urinary tract infections, reproductive tract infections (RTI), and pelvic inflammatory disease (PID) are of particular importance because they are among the leading causes of infertility. Thus, the presence of these infections in "circumcising" populations is also reviewed below. Before so doing, it is worth commenting on how the severity and frequency of "circumcision" may affect any of these outcomes.

Logic would suggest that the more severe the procedure, the more severe the implications for the immediate and distant future. For example, in a comparison of urinary complications in women who are sunna circumcised and excised, N. Agugua and V. E. Egwuatu (1982) find that severe early or delayed complications are relatively rare in women who are only sunna circumcised; Ulla Larsen (1989) finds that those who had pharaonic circumcision had a higher incidence of sterility (in the five years preceding a 1978–1979 survey) than women who were not "circumcised" or who had any other form of "circumcision." More generally, Verzin (1975:164) notes that "the complications are both immediate and remote and their frequency and seriousness are in direct relation to the severity of the tissue mutilation performed." Each de-infibulation and re-infibulation increases the risk of complications (e.g., Laycock 1950; El Dareer 1982; Mustafa 1966). Recall that many infibulated brides need to be de-infibulated at the time of marriage to permit penetration, and all infibulated women need to be deinfibulated at the time of childbirth (El Dareer 1982; Laycock 1950; De Silva 1989; Lightfoot-Klein 1989; Melly 1935). El Dareer estimates that about 50 percent of Sudanese women are re-infibulated, one or more times, at some point postpartum (1982:56).

Fertility

Anecdotal and case study evidence leads us to believe that "circumcised" women, especially those who are infibulated, should have a harder time getting pregnant, staying pregnant, and bearing healthy babies. These effects have been difficult to demonstrate, owing in large part to the lack of studies designed explicitly to examine them (and accompanying appropriate data) and the resistance or inability of women to identify problems of fertility with their "circumcision" status and history (e.g., Inhorn and Buss 1993; El Dareer 1982). Another problem is that all but one of the clinical studies I found rely on self-selection of patients, that is, hospital or clinic patients seeking treatment of one form or another (although often not for infertility) or prenatal care; one study relied exclusively on infertile couples (Meuwissen 1966). I reviewed those studies that consider, however vaguely, whether the following occur at higher rates in "circumcising" groups and especially in infibulating groups: (1) pregnancy loss and stillbirths; (2) secondary sterility (i.e., infertility after a known pregnancy); (3) primary sterility (i.e., unable to conceive despite exposure over a prolonged period); and (4) infections (e.g., PIDs and RTIs) that cause infertility.

Infibulation also inhibits coitus. Although this would generally affect only the first few weeks or months of a marriage, it would increase the interval between marriage and first birth among infibulated women but probably have a small effect, if any, on overall fertility. These effects would be greater if coital difficulties lead to the use of unsterile interventions (e.g., use of unhygienic blades or insertion of unhygienic objects to cut or widen the vaginal opening), which increase the risk of infection (Shandall 1967; El Dareer 1982). There are no studies reporting coital differences to review.

The issue of pregnancy loss has not been addressed empirically, even in the clinical literature. Mark Belsey (1979) proposes more generally, however, that cutting of female genitalia may produce infection or injury that interferes with conception or increase the risk of pregnancy wastage. Stillbirths may result from a number of causes, but the evidence in medical literature clearly suggests that infibulation increases the probability of pregnancy ending in a stillbirth, largely due to the fact that labor is obstructed by an extreme narrowing of the vagina and accumulated fibrous and scarred vulvar tissue that favors a prolonged and painful labor and fails to dilate during contractions (e.g., Gordon 1991). Laycock (1950:448–449), who provides case study evidence from Somalia, speculates as follows: "It is hardly surprising that the mutilation of the vulva produced by infibulation, and more particularly by subsequent septic infection, should produce a condition of the soft tissues incompatible with parturition." In a controlled study of Sudanese expatriate women in Saudi Arabia, S. De Silva (1989) finds that "circumcised" women are three times more likely than uncircumcised women to experience prolonged (stage II) labor, but they appear not to be more likely to have a pregnancy end in a stillbirth or early neonatal death (also see Daw 1970); both groups received pre- and neonatal care. Of statistical significance, however, is that the infants born to "circumcised" women are much more likely to experience severe asphyxia (De Silva 1989:237–238), which may lead to brain damage, other morbidities, and death. In another study of twelve Somali refugee women in the United States, eleven of whom were "circumcised," Arbesman et al. (1993:38) found that out of forty-eight pregnancies, four resulted in stillbirths. This rate is much higher than that found in noninfibulating populations.

The issue of primary and secondary sterility has been addressed by a few studies, mostly through consideration of infertility-causing infections. In an oft-cited paper, Asim Zaki Mustafa (1966:304) claims that "20 to 25 percent of the cases of infertility in the Sudan are due to infibulation, which may cause chronic pelvic infection or may prevent sexual intercourse," but he offers neither data nor citations to support this. Others do provide evidence. Eugenio Lenzi (1970), for example, discusses four Somali case studies describing chronic inflammation of the fallopian tubes secondary to an ascendant infection contracted at the time of infibulation. In a clinical study of PID, Hamid Rushwan (1980) finds far lower rates of gonorrhea and septic abortion than expected and, therefore, suggests that female "circumcision" is likely the leading cause of PID in Sudan. Although he made no direct assessment of the effects of "circumcision," in the 147 patients in which organisms were isolated and tested for gonorrhea, all but one were "circumcised," with the pharaonic type being overwhelmingly prevalent. In a study of 398 women in infertile marriages in central Ghana, J. Meuwissen (1966) finds that there are vaginal changes (i.e., mostly, the hardening and narrowing of the vaginal passage) resulting from "ritual circumcisions and native treatments in 41 women (10 percent)." Although this suggests that "circumcision" (probably excision, which is prevalent in that area) contributes to infertility, it is impossible to conclude anything about the extent to which it contributes. De Silva (1989) also finds a much higher incidence of urinary and genital tract infections among "circumcised" Sudanese women (in his Saudi Arabian hospital study). In a study of more than 4,000 obstetric and gynecological patients attending the outpatient clinic at the Khartoum General Hospital between 1962 and 1966, A. Shandall (1967) finds, among 436 cases of nontuberculous chronic pelvic infection, that the incidence among those who are pharaonically circumcised is more than three times as great than the incidence among those who are sunna circumcised.[1] Such findings are strongly confirmed by Marcia Inhorn and Kimberly Buss (1993:232) in a case-control study of tubal-factor infertility (TFI) (i.e., infertility resulting from postinflammatory damage to the fallopian tubes such as PID causes) among 190 Egyptian women. They show that women with TFI are more likely to have had an excision (rather than a clitoridectomy) than are their fertile controls, and they are more likely to have had their "circumcision" performed by a traditional provider than are the fertile women in the control group. The joint risk of these factors is highly significant. Controlling for other factors, they show that "women who had had either an excision or a clitoridectomy by a traditional provider are at 2.0 times greater risk of TFI than are women who had had neither, and women who had had both excision and a traditional practitioner are at a four times greater risk of TFI than are women who had had neither."

At the population level, in a cross-national analysis, Larsen (1994) finds that primary sterility (measured by the proportion childless among women who married before reaching age twenty) is relatively high (5 percent) as measured in 1978–1979 and relatively low (2 percent) as measured in

1989–1990. (She does not consider the decline in the prevalence of pharaonic "circumcision" in the interval; rather she sees this decline as part of a trend in Africa in the declining prevalence of sterility.) She also finds that sterility is quite high in the upper age groups (in both periods) relative to other African countries. In another study looking at the determinants of sterility in Sudan, Larsen (1989) finds that those who were pharaonically circumcised have a higher incidence—that is, rate of new occurrences in a given time period—of sterility in the five years preceding the 1978–1979 World Fertility Survey than all other women, other things being equal, but that they did not have a higher prevalence—that is, the number of total cases in population in a given time period—of sterility overall. She adds that although there may be real downward pressures on fertility from "circumcision," these are difficult to identify in a population with so little variation in the practice. Larsen's lack of a significant finding may be in part due to her classification of "circumcision" types. Because of the small number of cases, she puts all "circumcised" women who were not pharaonically circumcised in one category, thus erroneously grouping women with *matwasat* circumcisions, which are most like pharaonic circumcisions, with women who have had sunna circumcisions, from whom they vastly differ.

Marriage

"Circumcision" may affect marriage in three ways. First, it affects one's ability to marry. Second, difficulties arising from one's initial "circumcision" or re-infibulation may affect the quality and stability of the marital union. Third, by increasing the chances of infertility, "circumcision" greatly enhances the likelihood of dissolution. Each of these is reviewed in turn.

Most of the literature identifies female "circumcision"—especially infibulation—as a prerequisite for marriage in Sudan and the neighboring areas (see, for example, my review in Balk 1996b). A few analyses provide empirical evidence of the real or perceived difficulty in finding husbands for uncircumcised women who belong to "circumcising" social groups (e.g., Sequira 1931; Lowenstein 1978; Gruenbaum 1991; Dirie and Lindmark 1991; Huddleston 1949). Yet the question of whether "circumcised" and uncircumcised women marry in two different marriage "markets," to my knowledge, has not been addressed.

There are many ways in which these practices may affect the quality of marriage. For example, coital difficulty, an unsatisfying sex life, the chronic retention of urine and menstrual fluids, or the development of fistulae that may produce foul odors may challenge the stability of the union (e.g., Toubia 1985; El Dareer 1982). Shandall (1967:195–196), for example, reports that of 300 polygynous Sudanese men, married to both pharaonically circumcised and sunna circumcised or uncircumcised women, sixty (i.e., 20 percent) stated that they married their second, nonpharaonically circumcised wife because they could not keep up with the ordeal of perforating the progressively toughened "circumcision" scars of their wives every time they have a baby.

Most important, if marital unions are established in large part to produce children (for the lineage), as I believe they are in northeastern Africa, then it stands to reason that if unions do not produce children, they may dissolve. Indeed, when women are unable to produce children, the likelihood that they will be divorced or that the husband will take another wife has been shown to increase (e.g., Larsen 1995; Sami 1986; van der Kwaak 1992; Meuwissen 1966; Ammar 1954). Mohamed Al Awad Gala El Din (1977:625–626) makes the related point that when a Sudanese woman bears no children (or none that survive), a husband may ask for a refund of half of the marriage cattle (i.e., bride wealth paid from the groom's family to the bride's) to help him find another wife more likely to bear children. Lewis's (1994:63) research in Somalia

> suggest[s] that one of the commonest and most important contributory factors in the break-down of a marriage is infertility. In most cases the marriage histories of barren women reveal a series of short unions. Men, certainly, readily divorce a woman who after a few years of marriage has borne no children, unless other attributes compensate for her sterility.

Among northern Somali pastoralists, Lewis finds that between 24 and 32 percent of marriages end in divorce (Lewis 1994). In a study of sterility in East Africa, Henin (1981:696) finds "evidence that women in polygynous unions as well as women with a high frequency of remarriage have a higher incidence of childlessness than those in monogamous unions who are married only once." Although being in a polygynous union may or may not reduce the relative welfare of women, divorce due to infertility carries especially harsh consequences for women and their natal families (e.g., see Inhorn and Buss 1993 for evidence in Egypt). In sum, although much is known about marriage and marital dissolution in "circumcising" populations, it remains an empirical question as to how "circumcision" contributes directly and indirectly to the ability of women to get married and remain in stable, quality unions.

An Empirical Example from Sudan

Data from the Sudan DHS are used to determine the effects of infibulation in northern and central Sudan. The DHS covers these provinces: Northern (including Nile), Darfur, Kordofan, Eastern (including Kassala), Central (including Blue Nile), and Khartoum and excludes the southern regions (i.e., Equatoria, Bahr el Ghazal, and Upper Nile provinces).[2] For simplicity's sake, in the empirical analysis below I use the words Sudan and Sudanese to refer to those in the surveyed regions only. I do not intend to refer to the populations of southern Sudan. The DHS is broad-based and intended for cross-national comparison as well as many types of social and demographic analyses on Sudan. Some data were collected on "circumcision," but in-depth analysis of the practices themselves was not the intended use of these data. Nevertheless, the data set contains sufficient information on these practices, marital dissolution, and fertility to test some of the above ideas. Thus, I ask, what are the effects of infibulation, in particular, on divorce and fertility?

The DHS interviewed more than 5,000 ever-married women of reproductive age in Sudan, except in the southern regions, in 1989 and 1990. The survey was designed to obtain 5,000 completed interviews from ever-married women fifteen to forty-nine years of age who slept in the selected household the night before the interview. With the exception of the southern regions, it is a nationally representative sample (i.e., it was a multistage, stratified, self-weighting probability sample) of the settled population but excluded the nomadic population in urban and rural areas. The nomadic population was estimated, by the Sudanese census, to be about 10 percent of the total population in 1983 (DHS 1991:2–5). All interviews were conducted in Arabic by trained female interviewers who were unknown to the respondents.

The survey faces some important limitations. Concerning the practice itself, rather than asking respondents to describe their "circumcision," they were asked what form of "circumcision" (or *tahur,* literally translated as "cleanliness" or "purity") they had had and were supplied with three choices: sunna, intermediate (*matwasat*), and pharaonic. No data on de- and re-infibulation were collected, nor was any direct information collected on consequences the respondents believed arose from their *tahur*s. Data on ethnic affiliation were not collected, although adherence to the practice (as well as general rules about marriage, childbearing, and the role of women) seems to vary strongly by ethnicity (e.g., Hicks 1993; El Dareer 1982). Because the survey is restricted to ever-married women, it is not possible to consider directly whether marriage itself is a consequence of the practice (let alone the more complex questions about marriage markets). Although each woman was asked how many times she had been married, full marital histories were not taken. Among women married more than once, I know neither how prior marriage(s) ended nor the number of births that occurred in each marriage nor the duration of each union. This information would, of course, be important if divorce due to infertility or subfecundity is a consequence of the practice. Although Sudan is a polygynous society, for reasons related to the sampling criteria, the DHS does not collect data on all the wives of any particular husband (i.e., only those in the sampled household, and even then their relationship is not identified as co-wives), nor does it ask of divorced and widowed women whether their union(s) had been polygynous. This prohibits comparisons of the "circumcision" status among co-wives and of the likelihood of divorce by marriage type. Finally, live birth histories were taken rather than full pregnancy histories, which prohibits an assessment of fetal loss and stillbirths.

Table 3.1 shows selected socioeconomic and demographic descriptors of the survey respondents according to their "circumcision" status. As expected, adherence to the practice declined over time: the decline in any form is slight, but a tendency away from infibulation and toward sunna "circumcision" in more recent times clearly exists. The small Christian minority is less likely to be "circumcised" at all, but when they are, they are more likely to have had the sunna type. Urban residents are less likely to be "circumcised" or infibulated. Women born in Darfur or any of the southern Sudanese regions are much less likely to be "circumcised" than women from any of the other Sudanese regions, Egypt, Ethiopia, or Somalia. A sizable proportion of the women from Egypt, Ethiopia, and Somalia, however, have the sunna type rather than infibulation. There are also important differences by education and socioeconomic status, which are discussed in the multivariate analysis below.

Effects on Marital Dissolution

Theory suggests that "circumcision" and, in particular, infibulation may dissolve marriages because of its effects on marital quality or output (i.e., children). Because the consequences of sunna circumcision are likely to be relatively mild and the sample size was small, here I consider only the effects of infibulation. In considering the consequences, I control for external or exogenous factors that affect the likelihood of infibulation (discussed above); I call this the "exogenous model." I also consider, when predicting the likelihood of divorce, the effects of having borne children; because divorce itself may halt or reduce childbearing, this variable is clearly endogenous and thus labeled the "endogenous model." However, because low fertility (discussed in the next section) may be the primary direct cause for divorce, it is important to account for it despite its potential endogeneity (i.e., lacking appropriate "instrumental" variables). In these analyses, I am concerned with explanatory factors rather than the levels at which infertility and divorce occur in the population. It has been argued that surveys of this sort tend to underreport childless women; given the high value placed on childbearing, such women may avoid being interviewed or answer "don't know" to questions about fertility, thus nullifying analysis of those cases (Larsen 1989). These arguments can be extended to divorced women, if divorce arises from childless marriages.

The data allow us to consider whether currently divorced women are more likely to have been infibulated. For reasons of data limitations discussed above, I restrict the outcome to current divorces only and the sample to re-

Table 3.1 Percentage of Women According to Their "Circumcision" Status, by Selected Socioeconomic and Demographic Characteristics

Demographic and Socioeconomic Characteristics	"Circumcision" Status			Number of Observations
	Never "Circumcised"	*Sunna* "Circumcised"	Infibulated	
Age				
15–24	11.2	17.6	71.2	1,317
25–34	10.9	13.6	75.5	2,324
35–44	10.9	11.2	77.9	1,675
45–49	9.1	8.5	82.4	540
Number of Unions				
One	10.3	13.3	76.4	5,259
Two or more	15.2	14.2	70.6	586
Number of Children Ever Born				
0	7.5	13.9	78.6	583
1	10.2	15.2	74.6	785
2	14.5	14.5	71.0	676
3	11.9	14.7	73.4	653
4	9.9	15.5	74.5	593
5	8.9	14.4	76.7	550
6 plus	11.1	10.8	78.1	2,016
Level of Education				
No formal	17.1	14.4	68.5	3,423
Primary	1.8	10.6	87.6	1,541
Secondary	1.8	13.4	84.8	821
Highest	7.0	21.1	71.8	71
Religion				
Muslim	10.0	13.1	76.9	5,741
Christian	52.7	25.9	21.4	112
Location of Current Residence				
Urban	13.1	13.4	73.6	2,180
Rural	7.0	13.3	79.7	3,676
Region of Childhood Residence				
Egypt, Ethiopia, Somalia	8.0	40.0	52.0	75
Southern regions[a]	59.3	12.8	27.9	86
Darfur region or Chad	33.8	18.3	47.9	1,115
Other regions[b]	4.3	11.7	84.0	4,580
Socioeconomic status[c]				
Lowest quartile	22.8	15.9	61.3	1,560
Second quartile	9.4	15.1	75.5	1,496
Third quartile	7.0	12.9	80.1	1,465
Highest quartile	2.4	8.8	88.8	1,327
Total	10.8	13.4	75.9	5,856

Notes: a. These include Equatoria, Bahr el Ghazal, and Upper Nile regions. b. These include Khartoum, Northern, Eastern, Central, and Kordofan regions. c. See Table 3.2 for an explanation of this variable.

spondents who have been in only a single union, whose marriages began at least five years prior to the survey, and who were at least twenty-five years old. Among the 3,596 women meeting these criteria, 160 women (4.4 percent) are currently divorced.

Table 3.2 shows that infibulated women are about 2.3 times more likely to be divorced currently than other women, whether the model is endogenously or exogenously specified. This effect is strong. The only other socioeconomic or demographic characteristic affecting the likelihood of divorce in the exogenous model is whether the respondent's childhood residence was in Egypt, Ethiopia, or Somalia. Although the number of cases is small, these women are also somewhat more likely to be divorced. Whether this may be because divorce is more acceptable to these women (e.g., Lewis 1994), for example, is beyond the scope of this chapter. In the endogenous model, as expected, I find that the number of children born considerably lowers the odds of being divorced: each additional child lowers the odds about 1.8 times. Additionally, when controlling for children ever born, it appears that age increases the odds of divorce, although at a diminishing rate, and schooling somewhat lowers the odds. In this model the effect of being from Egypt, Ethiopia, or Somalia has diminished (either because it is correlated with the number of children ever born or because the estimate is based on a small sample size).

Given that the effects of infibulation on divorce remain strong even when the number of children ever born has been taken into account suggests that infibulation may cause divorce, not only through its effects on fertility but also by reducing other aspects of marital quality. Future studies should be designed to test some of these other aspects, as well as to account for the probable endogeneity discussed above.

Effects on Fertility

The primary direct consequence of infibulation may be low fertility or sterility. For the purpose of this exercise, I define low fertility as having borne two or fewer children, thereby including permanently sterile women. As in the analysis of divorce, I include an exogenous and an endogenous model. The exogenous model is identical to that predicting divorce, and the endogenous model of low fertility also takes into account whether the respondent is currently divorced. The fertility model is endogenous because divorce may result as a consequence of low fertility arising from infibulation. However, because divorce may also result from other factors and in and of itself curtails fertility in a population in which childbearing occurs within marriage, it is an important variable to consider despite its probable endogeneity. The sample is restricted to women who have been in only a single union, whose marriages began at least ten years prior to the survey, who were at least thirty years of age, and who had never used contraception. Widows are excluded from the analy-

Table 3.2   Odds Ratios of Selected Variables on the Likelihood of Being Currently Divorced or of Having Low Fertility (i.e., two or fewer children ever born), Sudan

Background Variables	Currently Divorced[a]		Low Fertility[b]	
	Exogenous Model	Endogenous Model	Exogenous Model	Endogenous Model
Age	1.154	1.667**	0.618*	0.548*
Age^2	0.998	0.993**	1.006+	1.008*
Christian	1.311	0.962	(2.379)	(4.424+)
Urban resident	1.316	1.064	0.936	0.693
Years of education	1.003	0.946+	1.102*	1.116*
Socioeconomic status[c]	0.905	0.693	2.856*	3.226*
Region of childhood residence[d]				
Darfur region or Chad	1.008	0.842	1.334	1.276
Southern Sudan regions	0.007	0.022	(0.007)	(0.002)
Egypt, Ethiopia, Somalia	(3.119*)	(1.960)	(5.123**)	(2.679)
Infibulated	2.346**	2.293**	2.064**	1.490
Children ever born	—	0.542***	—	—
Currently divorced	—	—	—	14.732***
Overall % predicted correctly	95.55	95.58	91.88	92.24
Chi-square	30.770**	306.240***	56.301***	162.188**
Number of observations	3,596	3,596	1,675	1,675

Notes: a. Regression includes respondents who have been in a single union, whose marriages began at least five years prior to the survey, and who were at least twenty-five years of age.

b. Regression includes respondents who have been in a single union, whose marriages began at least ten years prior to the survey, who were at least thirty years of age, and who never used contraception. Widows are excluded.

c. This variable is a composite index ranging from a low of 0 to a high of 1. The index is composed half of structural goods and half of consumer durables. To represent structural goods, each of the following is classified, as 0 for relatively poor and 1 for relatively wealthy: type of wall construction, type of floor construction, toilet type, water source, and electricity. To represent durable goods, each of the following items is assigned a 0 if no one in the household owns one and a 1 if anyone in the household owns one: radio, television, bicycle, refrigerator. These two parts are added together and divided by 2 to produce a standardized bundle ranging from 0 to 1.

d. Omitted category includes all other regions of Sudan, except Darfur and the southern regions.

Significance levels are denoted as follows: +p < 0.10, *p < 0.05, **p < 0.01, ***p < 0.001.

( ) denotes that there are fewer than fifty cases in the given category.

sis. Of the 1,675 women meeting these criteria, 135 women (8.1 percent) had low fertility; the mean and median number of children born were 6.9 and 7, respectively.

The exogenous model indicates that infibulated women are twice as likely to have low fertility than other women, other things being equal (see

Table 3.2). As might be expected, age lowers the likelihood of low fertility; this effect is weak, however, probably because the sample is restricted to women ages thirty and older. Higher education and socioeconomic status—which themselves increase the odds of being infibulated (see Balk 1996b)—raise the likelihood of having low fertility, presumably because education and wealth create preferences for small families; since infibulation is directly accounted for here, reasons other than their associations with it likely explain their effects on fertility.

The only regional or ethnic difference found is that women from Egypt, Ethiopia, and Somalia are also much more likely to have low fertility. This is consistent with the finding that they were also more likely to be divorced, and when the variable for being divorced is introduced, the effects dissipate.

In the endogenous model, where current marital status is controlled for, the effects of infibulation are no longer significant ($p = 0.167$). Women who were currently divorced (n = 96) are vastly more likely (i.e., nearly fifteen times more likely) to have low fertility than women who are still married. Because the introduction of this variable washes out the effects of infibulation from the exogenous model and because the effects of infibulation are found on current divorce status both in the presence and absence of the number of children ever born, current divorce status may act as a partial but effective proxy for infibulation. (It cannot act as a complete proxy because much more of the population is infibulated than is currently divorced.) So close is the relationship between divorce and infibulation that of the ninety-six currently divorced women, only five women were not infibulated; whereas among the currently married women, 27 percent were not infibulated. If I consider the joint probability that the above respondents have low fertility and are currently divorced, I find a very strong relationship to infibulation: 73 percent of the 1,497 women who have more than two children and are in intact marriages are infibulated; this compares to 81 percent of women with low fertility who are not divorced (n = 89), 94 percent of women who have two or more children and are divorced (n = 49), and 96 percent of women who have low fertility and are divorced (n = 47). Among women in intact unions, women whose fertility is less than two are 40 percent more likely to be in polygynous marriages than women whose fertility is greater than two (not shown), thus demonstrating the importance for future studies to examine polygyny concomitantly with divorce.

Using multinomial logistic regression, I estimate the joint likelihood of being divorced and having low fertility (Table 3.3): that is, being divorced, having low fertility, or both. As might be expected from Table 3.3, infibulation is likely to considerably raise the relative risks of being divorced regardless of one's fertility. Among women with more than two children, it raises the likelihood 6.6 times, and among women with fewer than two children, it raises the likelihood 7.5 times. It does not statistically increase the odds of low fertility among women in intact marriages ($p = 0.138$).

Table 3.3   Multinomial Logistic Regression Results:
Relative Risk Ratios of Selected Variables on the
Likelihood of Being Currently Divorced and/or Having Low
Fertility (i.e., two or fewer children ever born) as Compared to
Being in an Intact Marriage and Having Borne More Than Two
Children

Background Variables	Marriage Intact, Fertility 2 (n = 89)	Divorced, Fertility > 2 (n = 49)	Divorced, Fertility 2 (n = 47)
Age	0.507*	1.369	0.966
Age^2	1.008*	0.995	1.000
Christian	2.603	[a]	0.757
Urban resident	0.850	3.282***	1.303
Years of education	1.094+	0.916	1.099
Socioeconomic status[b]	2.786+	0.524	2.704
Region of childhood residence[c]			
Darfur region or Chad	1.420	1.535	1.006
Egypt, Ethiopia, Somalia	5.258*	15.200**	12.323**
Infibulated	1.561	6.619**	7.535**
Equation-specific Chi-square[d]	33.99***	31.78***	34.07***
Number of observations	89	49	47

Notes: Regression includes respondents who have been in a single union, whose marriages began at least ten years prior to the survey, who were at least thirty years of age, and who never used contraception. Widows are excluded.

a. No coefficient is estimated because all women with this outcome belong to the reference group (i.e., Muslims).

b. See Table 3.2 for explanation of this variable.

c. Omitted category includes all other regions of Sudan, except Darfur and the southern regions; no coefficient is estimated for women of southern Sudanese origin because they all fall into the reference outcome group (i.e., they are in intact marriages with greater than two children).

d. The overall model chi-square statistic is 104.28*** with a total of 1,675 observations.

Significance levels are denoted as follows: +$p < 0.10$, *$p < 0.05$, **$p < 0.01$, ***$p < 0.001$.

In a subset of equations applying only to women in intact unions, I control for whether the respondent is in a polygynous marriage (not shown). With this control, I find that infibulated women are 1.79 times more likely to have low fertility even in intact unions ($p = 0.054$). Further, women in polygynous marriages are 1.81 times more likely to have low fertility, as might be expected.

The covariates associated with low fertility among women still in their first union suggest that very different types of constraints or preferences are driving their low fertility. Relative youth increases the odds of being in one's first marriage, despite low fertility. Similarly, wealthier and better-educated women are more likely to have lower fertility but remain in intact unions, as argued above, presumably because they desire smaller families. Women from

Egypt, Ethiopia, or Somalia were more likely to be divorced *or* to have low fertility than women from other regions; the strength of this variable increases when predicting divorce as an outcome, further suggesting that divorce is more common among these women. The consistency and strength of this variable, about which I can only speculate, clearly indicates that ethnicity needs to be considered more closely. Finally, divorced women with high fertility are more likely to live in urban areas. This may result from a spurious relationship whereby these women—for reasons due to their divorced status or higher fertility (e.g., they have many children for which they are the sole provider)—move to urban areas where they are more likely to find work. The data confirm that these women are more likely than other women to be working presently (not shown), but they cannot discern residential histories in relationship to the marital history. Thus, I do not know whether there was fertility- or divorce-specific migration.

The results of the exogenous model alone are suggestive. The results of the endogenous model, as well as those from the multinomial logistic regression, show that although infibulation may affect fertility, it is inextricably linked to divorce, the effects on which cannot be separated here. Clearly, future research must be based on purposive collection of data to rigorously test, using appropriate methods, the complex relationships among fertility, marital dissolution (both through divorce and polygynous remarriage), and infibulation. Such data collection will have to pay much greater attention to marital and fertility histories than did the present data set.

Conclusion

In patriarchal northeastern Africa, "circumcision," and most notably infibulation, is a highly valued institution that co-exists with the institutions of marriage and reproduction. These institutions together mold female identities and livelihoods. So closely associated are these institutions that women insist on "circumcising" their daughters because not to do so would likely reduce or obliterate their daughters' ability to marry and become mothers. Infibulation and other forms of "circumcision" are thus closely associated with gender identification. Infibulation much more than other forms of "circumcision" emphasizes the virginal and reproductive roles of women. By securing the vaginal opening with sutures, infibulation highlights the importance of females being virgins at the time of marriage; and by the husband's right to open those sutures, he (and his lineage) demonstrate the propriety of his wife's reproductiveness (e.g., Boddy 1982). Infibulation thereby maintains a system of patriarchal control and honor.

Although important to the maintenance of social structure, infibulation comes at a high cost, at least for some participants. Although the literature has not documented the population-wide levels of adverse consequences resulting from these practices, small-scale and anecdotal studies have nevertheless found associations between these consequences and practices. (Additional evidence is found in a few systematic studies whose purposes were not explicitly to consider this relationship.) Through any number of medical sequelae, infibulation raises the chance of infertility and subfertility and in doing so also increases the likelihood of divorce or polygyny. Through other mechanisms (e.g., coital difficulty), infibulation may also directly reduce the quality of marriage and thereby cause marital disruption. I was able to estimate these consequences, using data from the Sudan Demographic and Health Survey. Although my analysis was limited by the data—notably by the absence of data on ethnicity, the lack of thorough marital and pregnancy histories, and omissions in the "circumcision" practices (individual histories, other household members)—it is nonetheless a more systematic assessment of these consequences of practices than any previous study.

I find that infibulated women are more than twice as likely to be divorced currently than women who are not infibulated, other things being equal. This effect is strong and remains intact even when the number of children ever born—an endogenous variable that itself reduces the likelihood of divorce considerably—is introduced into the model. This suggests infibulation can cause divorce through its effect on fertility and by reducing marital quality in other ways.

After controlling for other factors, I find that infibulated women are also about twice as likely to have low fertility—that is, two or fewer children—than women who are not infibulated. However, this effect dissipates when the respondent's current marital status, clearly an endogenous variable, is introduced: divorced women are nearly fifteen times more likely to have low fertility than still-married women. Whether the effect diminishes because the relationship between divorce and infibulation is itself so strong as to account for the effects of infibulation on fertility or because of other unmeasured or potentially spurious factors unfortunately could not be determined with these data.

Thus, my findings present an inherent paradox. Infibulation inhibits a woman's lifetime marriage potential and decreases her fertility despite what northeastern African societies have identified as its function (latent or otherwise) to facilitate these outcomes. Does this mean that infibulation is maladaptive, as Gruenbaum asks in Chapter 2 of this volume? This chapter has not considered that question head-on but tends to support Gruenbaum's finding that it is not: most Sudanese women achieve high fertility and remain in intact marriages despite the risks associated with "circumcision," thus allowing for the institutions of marriage and fertility to remain (more or less) intact. However, a practice need not be maladaptive to be harmful to many women and their families. This conclusion leads to my last question.

Are the risks posed by the consequences—marital disruption and child-lessness—less than those posed by not adhering to the practice—that is, rendering one's daughters "unmarriageable"? This question assumes, perhaps mistakenly, that such risks can be weighed equally. Perhaps the risks that all women face (e.g., initial marriageability) outweigh those that only some women ultimately face (e.g., marital disruption); this is to say that infibulation is such an important part of the social structure that the costs borne by particular individuals are expected to be overlooked. Alternatively, it may be that the risks appear—seemingly anew—to each generation adhering to these practices. Women who suffer the greatest ill-effects of "circumcision" are the least likely to continue the practice because they have the fewest children to "circumcise" and because they are most likely to be divorced, thus having less access to whatever children and associated resources they may have had. Gerry Mackie (1996:1,009, see also Chapter 13 in this volume) strongly makes this point: "once in place, conventions regulating access to reproduction are deeply entrenched, in part because dissenters fail to have descendants."

Future research should estimate the level of effects—on individuals as well as on families—of these practices in the population at large, bearing in mind its many variants. Empirical analysis of the determinants of marriage and marital stability is just as important as additional research on fertility; and both of these will require better data than those used in the present analysis. The shortcomings from this analysis would suggest that future studies could easily find stronger adverse effects than I have found here. Thus, the most salient questions for future research are why, how, and by whom are these practices embraced in the face of adversity?

Notes

I wish to thank Frank Zimmerman, Lindy Williams, Zeinab Khadr, Gerry Mackie, Karen Ericksen, Meg Greene, Jim Orrcut, Lynn Morgan, and the editors of this volume for comments from which I benefited at various stages in my study of this subject.

1. Shandall (1967) also finds that women with no form of "circumcision," whose incidence of infection was lower than pharaonically circumcised women, were about 1.5 times more likely to have chronic pelvic infection than women with sunna circumcisions. He attributes this to the fact that the uncircumcised women included a larger share of women from southern Sudanese and western Sudanese low-income groups.

2. Localities noted in parentheses are for comparability with other studies.

4

Female "Circumcision" Among the Yoruba of Southwestern Nigeria: The Beginning of Change

I. O. Orubuloye, Pat Caldwell & John C. Caldwell

Many of the ethnic groups of West Africa have traditionally practiced, and still practice, both male and female circumcision. This is the situation among the 20 million Yoruba people of southwestern Nigeria, with the exception, in the case of female "circumcision," of two ethnic subgroups. The authors' recent interest in "circumcision" among the Yoruba is the result of the confluence of two activities, social demographic research over three decades in southwestern Nigeria and recent investigations of interrelations between male circumcision status and HIV/AIDS in sub-Saharan Africa (Caldwell and Caldwell, 1993, 1996).

In 1994–1995 we carried out a sociodemographic survey, supplemented by in-depth interviews, in Ondo, Oyo, and Lagos States. In that research, the Southwest Nigerian Study, there were 1,749 male and 1,976 female respondents. We reported separately on the three major avenues of the inquiry, one of which focused on "circumcision" (Caldwell, Orubuloye, and Caldwell, 1997). The findings of this strand will be briefly summarized here. It was these findings that demonstrated that important change in the practice of female "circumcision" was under way and that further research, employing an intensive anthropological demographic approach, was needed to establish the cause of this change. This further research, the Yoruba Female Circumcision Study, was in the field from October 1997 until January 1998 and is reported on in this chapter.

The 1994–1995 research confirmed that the Yoruba continued to practice both male and female "circumcision," almost entirely during infancy and mostly in the first week of life. The important finding was that it was no longer universal. Of the sons and daughters of the respondents, 1 percent of the boys and 4 percent of the girls beyond infancy had not been circumcised. This was apparently capricious among the boys because no socioeconomic correlates could be established, and it is probably a measure of neglect or destitution and perhaps orphanhood. The situation was very different among the girls. Although only 2 percent of rural girls were uncircumcised, 6 percent of urban ones were. Nearly all uncircumcised girls in urban areas had relatively young parents with at least some secondary education. Where the mother lived in a town, was under thirty-five years of age, and had at least some secondary education, one-eighth of the daughters had been left uncircumcised. Because education levels are higher among Christians than Muslims and because most educated parents work in nontraditional occupations, most uncircumcised girls in town are found in middle-class, Christian families. It might be noted that Islam mandates male but not female circumcision. Although Christianity makes male circumcision optional, Christianized traditionally circumcising ethnic groups are sufficiently familiar with Old Testament Jewish male circumcision to feel that Christianity favors the practice. The finding of near-universal but no longer universal circumcision is compatible with the situation reported in nearby (but not Yoruba) Bendel State (Myers et al. 1985:583–584) but is not compatible with a study of two clinics in Ibadan city, where much lower levels of circumcision were found (Onadeko and Adekunle 1985:180–181). The explanation for lower levels in the latter study may be that Ibadan has a disproportionate level of upper-middle-class clientele as well as a significant immigration of the two noncircumcising ethnic subgroups, Ijebu and Egba.

The study also showed why change may be taking place. Everyone agrees that circumcision has been traditionally expected, but the traditional way of life has in this century been overwhelmed by economic growth, the coming into being of the nation-state, and wholesale religious change. Traditional religion has underpinned circumcision and especially circumcision rites, and yet only 4 percent of the Southwest Nigerian Study respondents reported themselves to be adherents of traditional religion. It is also important that the Yoruba have had only one specific explanation for the need for female "circumcision" and that is to preserve the lives of the next generation, for the tip of the clitoris touching a baby's head during birth is thought to result in the baby's death. This view should not be taken lightly: the Yoruba have been willing to undergo the world's longest postpartum sexual abstinence in order to preserve the lives of their infants (Caldwell and Caldwell 1977; Orubuloye 1981; Page and Lesthaeghe 1981). However, it is vulnerable to changes in beliefs about the causes of death. There is no emphasis on the ugliness of the pubes of uncircumcised women, perhaps because universal infant circumcision has not allowed comparisons. It has been assumed that uncircumcised young women would find it difficult or impossible to marry because of their unnatural or wicked condition, but the lack of emphasis on their repulsiveness would be likely to make change easier. One respondent in twenty, both in rural and urban areas, claimed that the new religions, Christianity and Islam, expected circumcision, but this is little more than the expectation that religion will sanction accepted morality. Similarly, no rural women, but 2 percent of those living in urban areas with more access through the media to global debates and ideologies, said that men had continued female "circumcision" to curb nonmarital female sexual activity.

Much change in associated behavior has already taken place, and this must modify attitudes toward the operation. Real tradition expected not only circumcision but its performance by a traditional specialist at a specific ceremony. These ceremonies were universal a century ago, although perhaps because they occurred in infancy and not adolescence, they had none of the flamboyance or protractedness of many other African circumcision rites. By 1994–1995, only 28 percent of rural circumcisions and 13 percent of urban circumcisions, both female and male, were performed by specialists because the operations were increasingly performed by nurses and doctors in health facilities, invariably with no ceremonial overtones.

The Southwest Nigerian Study raised as many questions as it answered. Exactly what form did Yoruba female "circumcision" take? An adequate answer to this question in any future study would need the involvement of health personnel. Had the first uncircumcised women faced problems finding sexual partners and in making a suitable marriage? How could parents allow their daughters to face such problems? How had the trend against "circumcision" begun, and was it likely to herald a steep decline in the practice? How did parents make the decision not to "circumcise" and what motivated them? In contrast, why did most urban, educated, middle-class parents continue to have their daughters "circumcised"? Did they now have doubts, and what was the source of these doubts? These matters could be adequately investigated only by an intensive study of each family and needed a more anthropological approach. Finally, had many of the respondents in the Southwest Nigerian Study employed the wrong terms in describing the circumcisers, or was it true that there had been a massive movement of the operations into the modern health sector? The 1997–1998 Yoruba Female "Circumcision" Study was planned to answer these questions.

The 1997–1998 Yoruba Female "Circumcision" Study

The need for a more intensive study could be more easily met by making the research more geographically focused. We decided to confine the work to

Ondo State's northernmost part, Ekiti Division, which by the time of the fieldwork had been separated to form Ekiti State. One of the global network of Demographic and Health Surveys (DHS 1989) had been held in Ondo State in 1986. It showed that more than 40 percent of the population was urban, with that level increasing by about 1 percent per year. The religious breakdown was 85 percent Christian, 13 percent Muslim, and 1 percent adherents of traditional religion, a marked contrast to the situation in the early decades of the century, when the great majority adhered to the traditional religion. Ondo is a Yoruba state, with 85 percent of the population describing themselves as such. Almost two-thirds of adult females of reproductive age had experienced some schooling, and 40 percent had at least some secondary schooling. Among women under twenty-five years of age (under thirty-six years in 1997), more than 70 percent had some secondary schooling, with the level exceeding 80 percent in urban areas. The levels of urbanization and education suggest extraordinarily rapid social change, and these measures are higher still for Ekiti. There are also signs of resistance to change, particularly the fact that almost half the wives were in polygynous unions. Nevertheless, the typical younger woman now marries after she turns twenty years of age. Furthermore, the majority are practicing contraception, and the transition to smaller families—and all that means in terms of how children are seen and treated—is underway (Caldwell et al. 1992). Nevertheless, it should not be forgotten that these changes are taking place in a society where mortality rates are still high and most of the population is poor. In 1986, 11 percent of births resulted in deaths by five years of age, and the rate was 10 percent even in the towns (DHS 1989:55), levels which have probably not improved since. The national per capita annual income is under U.S.$300 (World Bank 1996:188), and Ekiti's income level is not likely to be above U.S.$400.

Two sites were chosen for the study, one urban and one rural. The urban location was Ado-Ekiti, the capital of the new Ekiti State. Its population was recorded as 150,000 by the 1991 Nigerian census (NPC 1994:19) but is now rising as public service positions for the new state are filled. The rural location was Efon-Alaaye, in Ekiti West Local Government Area (LGA). The whole LGA (the smallest unit for which figures have yet been released) recorded a population of 219,000 in the 1991 census (NPC 1994:19), but Efon-Alaaye constituted only a small fraction of the total population. It is located 30 miles west of Ado-Ekiti and straggles for some miles along a prominent, wooded ridge. It is a typical Yoruba rural township where most households have some connection with farming even though some of their farms are miles away. This concentration of population—large enough to be called a town in most societies—along a mountain ridge on Ekiti's western border was brought about for defensive reasons during the war-torn nineteenth century when the slave armies of the city of Ibadan ravaged nearby areas. In spite of its considerable population, Efon-Alaaye will be shown to contrast

markedly with Ado-Ekiti in its socioeconomic characteristics and to be typically rural. It is, of course, likely that some of the smaller, more isolated rural
populations would have evidenced an even greater preponderance of female
"circumcision."

Apart from work carried out by principal investigators, all urban interviews and subsequent open-ended discussions were carried out by qualified
nurses. Nearly all had performed female "circumcisions," and one had specialized in the practice. In addition to survey and anthropological demography training at Ekiti State University's Population and Health Research Centre, further training on the identification of female "circumcision" by type
was provided by the University's Medical Service. In contrast, only two of
these nurses were available for the rural interviews, and the other interviewers
had social science training. Even the nurses could not tap into a network of
nurses whom they knew and from whom they could seek information to the
extent that had been possible in Ado-Ekiti. This had little impact on the quality of most of the data but almost certainly made that on the extent of "circumcision" in the rural area less trustworthy.

The respondents in the survey were Yoruba women under fifty years of
age with at least one daughter older than twelve months. The restriction to
Yoruba, who constitute almost 90 percent of the population of Ekiti State, was
meant to eliminate the complexities of considering immigrant groups with
different cultures, although it did not eliminate Yoruba noncircumcising ethnic subgroups such as the Ijebu. Efon-Alaaye was mapped, and every house
was visited, yielding a total of 298 interviews. The Population and Health Research Centre had mapped Ado-Ekiti in 1991, recording every house. An updated version of this map was employed, and the city was divided into six
strata, each fairly homogeneous socioeconomically. A random selection of
one household in twenty was made in each stratum, yielding 738 interviews.
The sampling fraction had been deliberately chosen to provide more urban
than rural interviews so as to maximize the number of interviews in households with uncircumcised females and provide a satisfactory number for in-
depth investigation.

The preliminary work and testing of prototype questionnaires revealed a
situation of basic significance for the study. First, a relatively old and respected nongovernmental organization, the Nigerian Council of Women, had
been campaigning against female "circumcision" and had been widely heard
of or read about in Ekiti State. Second, the Federal Ministry of Health had instructed all government health facilities, such as hospitals and clinics, to present the case against female "circumcision" to all pregnant women having
prenatal checkups at these facilities and to all new mothers being released after hospital births. A considerable proportion of all women had heard this
message, and they took it to be government policy. The impulse for activity
by both governmental and nongovernmental organizations had undoubtedly

come from international organizations, particularly such high-profile events as the World Health Organization (WHO) conference on female "circumcision" held in Khartoum in 1979, a WHO Position Statement in 1982, and the *Programme of Action* of the International Conference on Population and Development held in Cairo in 1994.

It should also be noted at this stage that the study supported the finding of the 1994–1995 survey (Caldwell et al. 1997:1186) that the decline in female "circumcision" had begun, showed that there was a marked urban-rural differential in change, and provided enough uncircumcised females for satisfactory further study. The 1994–1995 survey reported that 6 percent of daughters in urban areas and 2 percent in rural areas of traditionally circumcising societies of southwest Nigeria were no longer being "circumcised." The 1997–1998 study being reported here found that in Ekiti State, unusually highly Christianized and with some of Nigeria's highest educational levels, 13 percent of daughters in the state capital, Ado-Ekiti, were uncircumcised, as were 3 percent of daughters in a large rural village, Efon-Alaaye. In all studies and localities, usually through mishap and chance, 1 percent or fewer sons were uncircumcised, and there appeared to be no pattern of change and no ideologies aiming at change in that case.

The characteristics of the 1997–1998 respondents are shown in Table 4.1. Henceforth, Efon-Alaaye will be shown in tables merely as "rural" and presented on the left-hand side as the least changed population, and Ado-Ekiti will be described as "urban." Table 4.1 evidences great change, especially in urban areas. In the course of the present century, traditional religion (as nominated adherence and not as contributor to culture) has almost disappeared. Muslims are usually traders and are more likely to be found in the larger towns. Education levels are high but not suspiciously so, for by age and residence they are in keeping with the findings of the 1986 Ondo State Demographic and Health Survey (DHS 1989:7). These levels are driving the demand for nontraditional jobs, more easily met in Ado-Ekiti with its state public service jobs. In recent years, male age at first marriage has remained at about twenty-nine years, but female marriage age has been rising so that the age gap between spouses is down to about ten years in the villages and six years in the towns. This may make discussion easier between husbands and wives on matters like their daughters' "circumcision."

The Prevalence of Female "Circumcision"

Even in urban areas, the decline of female "circumcision" is a recent occurrence, although among both the respondents and their mothers, there have long been up to 5 percent of Ekiti wives uncircumcised. This is partly because some Ijebu, a Yoruba group who do not practice female "circumcision" and

Table 4.1   Characteristics of Female Respondents Under Fifty Years Old with at Least One Daughter over Twelve Months, Ekiti State, Rural and Urban, 1997–1998

Characteristic	Rural (n = 298)	Urban (n = 738)
Median age of respondents (wives[a])	35 years	35 years
Median age of husbands[a]	45 years	41 years
Median age of respondents at first marriage[b]	20 years	24 years
Median age of husbands at first marriage[b]	29 years	29 years
Education of respondents		
no schooling	24%	12%
primary schooling only	27%	18%
at least some secondary schooling	49%	70%
Education of husbands		
no schooling	21%	13%
primary schooling only	26%	12%
at least some secondary schooling	53%	75%
Respondents' occupations[c]		
traditional sector	76%	50%
modern sector	22%	47%
other	2%	3%
Husbands' occupations[c]		
traditional sector	62%	41%
modern sector	25%	51%
other	13%	8%
Respondents' religion		
Christian	92%	84%
Muslim	6%	14%
Traditional	1%	1%
Husbands' religion		
Christian	94%	83%
Muslim	7%	14%
Traditional	1%	2%

Notes: a. In marriage or stable unions; husbands are the children's fathers.
   b. Marriage or first stable union.
   c. The traditional sector includes farming, marketing, and artisanship. The modern sector includes all "white collar" (clerical) occupations, and also professional, managerial, and shopkeeping work.

live only 100 miles away on the way from Lagos to Ekiti, had been brought to Ekiti as wives. It was no longer possible to ascertain whether this was just happenstance or whether their husbands had sought them out because of their "circumcision" status and the belief that this led to more mutually enjoyable sex. Therefore, when we come to consider change, the focus will be increasingly on the respondents' daughters. However, we will first examine the respondents and their situation. Defining the extent of "circumcision" was a major aim of the present project and determined the interviewers chosen.

Among those respondents who had been "circumcised" (94 percent of the total), a conclusion was reached about the degree of mutilation for about 91 percent of rural respondents, on whom the interviewers had sometimes performed the operation, and 64 percent of the urban ones. About 15 percent had little more than the prepuce removed, 50 percent had a nick in the clitoris aimed at its end, and 35 percent had more of the clitoris removed. These categories grade into each other both in physical fact and in diagnosis. The tip of the clitoris is regarded as endangering the survival of babies who are being born, and where more of the organ had been removed, this was not necessarily the aim of the circumciser. Rather, the cause was more often the speed at which the traditional circumciser was expected to operate and the tiny size of the clitoris when the Yoruba operation was usually carried out during the first days of life.

Even when the respondents were "circumcised," change had already begun with regard to the totality of the "circumcision" experience. Such erosion of tradition could in time weaken the belief in the necessity for the operation itself. The changes were made possible because the central player, the infant girl being "circumcised," was hardly a conscious participant, and in any case Yoruba rituals surrounding birth are far less ceremonial than those concerning the old, especially their death. Not surprisingly, full details of their infant "circumcisions" could be obtained for only about six-sevenths of the respondents. Around 11 percent had a full traditional ceremony in which chickens, goats, or the large forest snails were sacrificed. Only 37 percent were operated on by traditional circumcisers, although traditional doctors and traditional birth attendants, both of whom may have been used as substitutes in the case of female infants for a long time past, accounted for another 37 percent, leaving 24 percent to nurses and doctors in the modern sector, and 2 percent to parents. These changes have accelerated: as we will see when we turn to the present generation of children, only 5 percent of "circumcised" girls used the services of traditional circumcisers, whereas for 50 percent, nurses or doctors in the modern sector were employed.

Reasons for Female "Circumcision"

We attempted to investigate both changing attitudes toward female "circumcision" over time and contrasts between general societal attitudes and the specific situation of individual parents (see Table 4.2). The question of why the Yoruba "circumcise" women was asked when discussing the respondents' own "circumcisions." Two other questions were posed when discussing their attitudes toward their daughters' operations. The category "tradition, culture, social conformity" may not seem homogeneous, but it became increasingly clear in discussions that many who believe that they should conform to culture mean little more than that they should not expect their daughters to bear the brunt of breaking with the social consensus.

Table 4.2   The Reasons for Female "Circumcision"

	Rural (n = 298) %	Urban (n = 738) %
Why do the Yoruba "circumcise" females?		
tradition, culture, social conformity	62	60
prevents death at birth	27	11
reduces sexuality and promiscuity	5	16
other responses	1	1
don't know, no response	5	12
What are the present-day advantages of "circumcising" daughters?		
tradition, culture, social conformity	21	25
prevents death at birth	33	10
reduces sexuality and promiscuity	24	25
no advantages	2	17
don't know, no response	20	23
Why do you and your husband want your daughters to be "circumcised"?		
tradition, culture, social conformity	90	65
prevents death at birth	2	4
reduces sexuality and promiscuity	2	6
grandparents expect it	4	2
don't want "circumcision"	2	23

Table 4.2 shows that most people believe that many Yoruba are still motivated to "circumcise" their daughters by the fear that their grandchildren's survival might be jeopardized and that the newer concept of controlling females' sexuality is widely known, at least in large urban areas. What is important, however, is that few of the respondents said that their own families are now motivated by these considerations. Overwhelmingly, the motivation is now social conformity, the fear that, if they innovate, their daughters and consequently they themselves will suffer. Their fears center on whether an uncircumcised girl would be marriageable. The study did not include male respondents, but the fact that such fears are not baseless is shown by the female respondents' attitudes to uncircumcised males, set out in Table 4.3.

Only 1 percent of both urban and rural women are certain they would marry an uncircumcised man. Even that small number probably largely comprises those who did do so (Caldwell et al. 1997:1186). Admittedly, male circumcision has not been under assault and shows no sign of declining, but the women's reaction to uncircumcised men reflects what the situation of uncircumcised women must have been until very recently. Indeed, most parents of daughters believe this still to be the position and fear to be the first innovators.

Table 4.3   Respondents' Attitudes Toward Uncircumcised Males

	Rural (n = 298) %	Urban (n = 738) %
Would you have sex with an uncircumcised man?		
yes	5	4
no	94	89
not certain	1	7
Would you have married an uncircumcised man?		
yes	1	1
no	98	91
not certain	1	8

Effects of Female "Circumcision"

All but 6 percent of the respondents had been "circumcised," and they partic-ipated in long discussions about what they believed the effect upon them had been. They were, of course, aware—and the interviewers were more so—that they had no completely satisfactory way of comparing themselves with the uncircumcised. These discussions are summarized in Table 4.4. As yet, there is no pronounced female hostility to female "circumcision." Very few believe that the operation has reduced their capacity for sexual enjoyment, although that concept is beginning to get a foothold in more sophisticated and better read Ado-Ekiti.

There is not the same urban-rural differential with regard to their hus-bands' enjoyment, perhaps because this is a matter that the Nigerian Council of Women and the women's movement literature more broadly rarely address. Few rural women believe they have been physically distorted or genitally mu-tilated, although that view is now growing in the urban population. Few town women any longer believe that there is any impact on child survival, a change that has probably been reinforced by the drop in infant mortality over the last half-century. There has certainly been attitudinal change, especially among the urban population, and key questions are the nature and origins of the in-formational flows that have catalyzed the change.

Awareness of the International Movement Against Female "Circumcision"

Half of all rural women and a slightly higher proportion of urban women had heard or read the case against female "circumcision," which is not surprising

Table 4.4   Reactions of "Circumcised" Women to Their Condition

	Rural (n = 290) %	Urban (n = 676) %
Whether they believe their "circumcision" has reduced their enjoyment of sexual activity		
Increased enjoyment	53	16
No effect either way	40	63
Reduced enjoyment	4	16
Cannot evaluate	3	5
Whether they believe their "circumcision" has reduced their husbands' enjoyment of sexual relations with them		
It increases his enjoyment	55	18
No effect either way	36	71
It reduces his enjoyment	7	8
Cannot evaluate	2	3
The aesthetic effect of their "circumcision" on their genitalia		
More beautiful	76	24
Neutral or little effect	21	73
Uglier	2	2
Cannot evaluate	1	1
The effect of their "circumcision" on the chances of children surviving birth		
More danger to infant	8	3
No effect either way	13	80
Less danger to infant	77	16
Cannot evaluate	2	1

because all government prenatal clinics and government obstetrical services are supposed to advocate against female "circumcision." The Nigerian Federal Department of Women's Affairs had, in 1994 when its minister was a woman, issued a decree banning female "circumcision." A substantial proportion of women attend the prenatal clinics, but few can afford to give birth in hospitals. Many have also read about or heard the views of the Nigerian Council of Women, especially on regular radio sessions. One might expect the most vibrant institution in most women's lives, the Christian church, to play a role, but only 7 percent of rural women and 9 percent of urban women had ever heard their religious leaders broach the subject. This is in keeping with earlier research findings on the lack of importance of religious leaders in combating HIV/AIDS (Orubuloye, Caldwell, and Caldwell 1993). Table 4.5 summarizes the chief message respondents remember.

The main thrust of the message against female "circumcision" is that it may endanger the child's life and that this risk is unnecessary because there is neither a need nor a reason for the operation. The message about not impair-

Table 4.5   The Main Message Remembered Against Female
             "Circumcision"

	Rural (n = 298) %	Urban (n = 738) %
Unhealthy and dangerous	24	22
Unnecessary, crude, primitive	15	3
Reduces sexual enjoyment	1	4
Endangers childbirth	1	4
Not a good practice	8	4
Females should not be "circumcised"	2	12
Mutilations, alters genitalia	0	(.03)
Not Christian, not in the Bible	0	1
Have not heard messages	49	50

ing sexual enjoyment has little effect, not because the Yoruba feel sexual enjoyment to be unimportant, but because few women believe that their own "circumcision" has had any significant effect on their sexual pleasure.

Attitudes Among Uncircumcised Respondents

Five rural women (2 percent of respondents) and fifty-six urban women (8 percent of respondents) had not been "circumcised." The higher urban level was not entirely explained by social change since eleven, or almost one-fifth of them, were immigrant wives from noncircumcising Yoruba groups, mainly Ijebu. Even these women are included in the analysis below because nearly all their fathers were Ekiti Yoruba, and they so regarded themselves. Because of the very small number of uncircumcised rural women, the analysis in Table 4.6 includes all uncircumcised women combined. The responses suggest that among Ekiti Yoruba, who have traditionally "circumcised" women, the failure to "circumcise" daughters is largely deliberate and is mainly a reaction to messages received directly or indirectly from the campaigns against "circumcision."

Uncircumcised young women do feel different, but there are now sufficient messages in the community against "circumcision" for three-quarters of them to be satisfied with their parents' decision. Nevertheless, they are still stigmatized and encounter some difficulties in marrying. In compensation, most believe they enjoy sexual activity more than "circumcised" women, a belief that may be factual but that may also be largely derived from the messages of the campaign against "circumcision."

Table 4.6   Attitudes Among Uncircumcised Respondents (n = 52)

	Distribution (n = 61) %
Why weren't you "circumcised"?	
Parents influenced by the campaign or by the argument that the operation was dangerous to the child	20
Parents' decision (don't know influence)	40
Sub-ethnic group did not practice	25
Don't know	15
Do you now wish you had been "circumcised"?	
Yes	23
No	75
Not sure	2
For those who now wish they had been "circumcised" (n = 14): Why would you like to be "circumcised"?	
To avoid stigmatization and ridicule	67
So as not to feel different	25
No response	8
For those who are pleased that they are not "circumcised" (n = 40)[a]: Why are you pleased?	
Believes sex life better	64
Believes births easier	24
Glad life not endangered in infancy	3
No response	9
Did being uncircumcised cause problems in finding a husband?	
Yes	13
No	67
Not certain, no response	20
For those who had problems in finding a husband (n = 14)[b]: Why didn't men want to marry you?	
Social stigma, believed was physically different	79
Believed I might be promiscuous	21

Notes: a. Excludes six respondents who neither wish they had been "circumcised" nor are pleased that they were not.

b. Includes six women who were not certain about whether they had problems in getting married but still answered this question.

The Younger Generation—
"Circumcision" of Girls Today

The proportion of females not "circumcised" has climbed between the respondents' generation and that of their daughters, today's girls. In Ado-Ekiti the proportion of uncircumcised females has almost doubled between the generations to 13 percent, close to being a mass phenomenon, and the proportion in rural Efon-Alaaye has more than doubled to 4 percent. All sons continue to be circumcised. Table 4.7 continues to amalgamate rural and urban responses, partly because rural noncircumcision levels are still low but largely so as to make comparison with Table 4.6 easier. It should be noted that the figures quoted earlier for the "circumcision" of the youngest female generation, 13 percent uncircumcised in Ado-Ekiti and 3 percent in Efon-Alaaye, were a count of the daughters and not of mothers with uncircumcised daughters. The point is that an increasing number of women have been converted by the campaign against "circumcision," and many now have "circumcised" older daughters and uncircumcised younger ones. There is a parallel here with the situation in the United States and other English-speaking countries in the 1950s and 1960s as the movement toward not circumcising sons gathered strength, which resulted in older sons being circumcised and younger ones not being circumcised.

Clearly, the changes are not spontaneous. They have been influenced both by the organized campaign and by other debate and discussion originating either from the campaign or from information journalists have picked up from sources outside the country. The message carrying the most influence is that there is no real reason for the operation and that it is unnecessary, hazardous, and painful. The strongest external influence comes from the local doctors and nurses at prenatal clinics or in obstetric wards.

Within the family, the influences are uneven. It is mainly the wife who hears the doctors and nurses, and she is also the one who most identifies with the daughters. But only 8 percent of those not circumcising refused to countenance their husbands' opposition or indecision. In the great majority of cases, the husband concurred that the operation should not be done, and this is the way the survey results are reported. Yet it is quite clear from the in-depth investigations that it was usually the wife who felt strongly on the matter and the husband who left such children's matters—especially as they concerned daughters—to their wives. Not infrequently the wife had the strong support of her mother.

It should be noted that the respondents have few worries about their uncircumcised daughters' chances of marriage. They—at least those who live in the town—feel that society is changing and will change much more. They do not worry about increased promiscuity, but neither do they think the maintenance of the libido an important matter. The problem here is that they are talking about their daughters, many of whom are young. Table 4.6 clearly showed that they thought that the maintenance of their own libido was important.

When we explored further the social pressures on uncircumcised girls and their mothers, we found they were less than we had anticipated (see Table 4.8). The spouses' relatives generally either support the decision or are not informed or asked. Only one in five or six of the respondents reported that opposition had been expressed.

Table 4.7   The Situation of the Respondents' Uncircumcised Daughters
            (n = 115)

	Distribution (n = 115) %
Why weren't your daughters "circumcised"?	
Responded to the campaign against "circumcision"	30
Believe the operation is dangerous	30
Believe the operation might make childbearing more difficult	19
Believe the operation decreases sexual pleasure	10
No biblical warrant	10
No response	1
What do you now think is the best outcome of their not being "circumcised"?	
They have not been physically mutilated	29
Their lives were not endangered by the operation	29
They did not have the pain of the operation	6
They will have an easier childbirth	28
They will not have diminished sexual pleasure	1
We have obeyed God or the Bible	4
No response	3
Who made the decision not to "circumcise"?	
Mother (respondent)	11
Father	13
Both parents	52
Spouses' parents	11
Doctor or nurse	7
Others	4
No response	2
Who influenced your decision?	
Spouse	32
Parents	12
Doctor or nurse	39
Minister/priest	2
Others	11
No response	4
What problems are your daughters likely to face because they are uncircumcised?	
None	85
Social stigmatization	6
Difficulty in marrying	2
Suspicion of promiscuity	5
No response	2

In fact, the chief reaction to changing attitudes about female "circumcision" is silence. Parents quite often let the time for "circumcision" pass without discussing it with each other. They find it difficult and are usually reluctant to raise the matter with their own parents. Mothers do not wish to discuss with their daughters whether or not they have had them "circumcised." Fa-

Table 4.8   Pressures on the Mothers of Uncircumcised Girls

	Distribution (n = 52) %
Attitude of the mothers' relatives	
In favor of the decision not to "circumcise"	45
Against the decision	16
Relatives don't know about the decision	23
Respondent doesn't know or care about her relatives' attitudes on these matters	13
No response	3
Attitudes of her husbands' relatives	
In favor of the decision not to "circumcise"	50
Against the decision	20
Relatives don't know about the decision	19
Respondent doesn't know or care about her in-laws' attitudes on this matter	10
No response	1

thers hardly ever discuss such matters with their daughters. Parental reluctance is greatest when the girls have been left uncircumcised. Thus, many uncircumcised girls become quite old before they realize their condition. This silence may break as an ever-larger proportion are left uncircumcised, which may hasten further change.

The Changing Nature of "Circumcision"

Profound changes in the nature and even the fact of "circumcision" were likely once the operation began to move from its age-old moorings, the traditional circumciser and accompanying community ceremonies. Just how much movement has taken place is shown in Table 4.9. "Circumcision" is being rapidly taken over by modern health providers, especially in urban areas. In the modern sector it is monopolized by trained nurses, perhaps because doctors are conscious of their training and the attitudes of the government health departments. Infection is rare and in all cases was treated with antibiotics, mostly at government or private hospitals. Because of the involvement of the modern health sector and the fact that most "circumcisions" are limited clitoridectomies, there may be a very low level of circumcision-related mortality for both girls and boys.

As to the extent of the "circumcision," the medical expertise available to the research program was greater in the urban than the rural area, and it is

Table 4.9   Aspects of the Respondents' Daughters' "Circumcisions" (respondents with "circumcised" daughters only)

	Rural (n = 280) %	Urban (n = 629) %
Circumciser		
traditional circumciser	5	3
traditional doctor	5	5
traditional birth attendant	39	6
nurse	49	81
doctor	1	3
parents	1	2
Median age at "circumcision"	one week	one week
Whether daughter reacted as if hurt		
yes	46	61
no	48	27
don't know, no response	6	12
Whether there was a subsequent infection		
yes	0.4	1.9
no	99.2	98.1
no response	0.4	0.0
Daughters dying as a result of "circumcision"		
none	100	100
Whether respondent has heard of any girl who has died as a result of infection from "circumcision"		
yes	0.4	1.0
no	99.6	99.0
Whether the respondent has heard of any boy who has died as a result of infection from "circumcision"		
yes	1.4	1.5
no	93.2	97.5
no response	5.4	1.0
Extent of daughters' "circumcision"		
prepuce/hood only	4	21
clitoris nicked	83	28
end of clitoris cut off	11	32
clitoris removed	1	3
uncertain	1	16
Whether daughters know they have been "circumcised"		
yes	33	32
no	56	65
not certain	11	3
For those daughters who know they have been "circumcised": whether happy about it		
yes	60	25
no	5	8
no reactions expressed	35	67

likely that the tip of the clitoris is cut off in about one-third of cases, with this more likely when the operation is performed outside the modern health sector. The removal of more of the clitoris is rarer. It is perhaps significant that a small number of older girls are now resentful of the fact that they were "circumcised," mostly because they too have heard the message against "circumcision."

Because the identification of the extent of the clitoridectomy in the urban population was generally performed by health professionals, information on the extent of the procedure is more trustworthy for the urban than the rural population. Even the higher level of "uncertain" responses is a measure of the nurses' determination to report the situation only if they were certain. This explains the apparent anomaly that, in a period of change, the reported extent of clitoridectomy was greater for the urban than the rural population. Taking the urban information to be more trustworthy, the situation seems to be that doing more than cutting off the top of the clitoris is now rare. Perhaps it always was because the main aim of the Yoruba was always to protect the baby's head from being touched by the tip of the clitoris during birth. What is perhaps more striking is that, for those urban daughters among whom the extent of "circumcision" was certain, almost three-fifths were "circumcised" to a lesser extent than the removal of the tip of the clitoris.

The most important engine of change is provided by the medicalization of the operation and was explained to the researchers by nurses. Nurses are less influenced by their training to be against female "circumcision" than are doctors, and many rely on it for an important part of their income. Nevertheless, their training and the continuing campaign against the operation make them cautious and reluctant to have any fuss about a messy operation or an infection. The result is that they usually nick the clitoris just enough to cause visible bleeding, leaving parents unaware of just how little has been removed.

The Conditions of Change

The Yoruba people have no great emotional investment in retaining female "circumcision." It is not a pillar of Yoruba culture or their new religions, and it does not distinguish them from neighboring groups. When they answer that it is their tradition, most mean that they do not want their daughters to be the innovators, to be regarded as "unnatural" and perhaps to be unmarriageable. Uncircumcised boys would still suffer all these fates.

Female "circumcision" is different from male circumcision only in that there are new forces that regard it as an unnatural condition. The anticircumcision message is being heard. Many mothers who continue to "circumcise" their daughters say that they would desist if only that message were much stronger, thus guaranteeing that uncircumcised girls were in the majority.

Table 4.10   Female "Circumcision" down the Generations

	"Circumcised" Respondents (n = 966) (%)	Uncircumcised Respondents (n = 61) (%)
Proportion of respondents with uncircumcised mothers	3	25
Proportion of respondents with uncircumcised daughters	8	58

They feel that is it unfair of the government to promote the change without doing it very loudly and clearly so that every health worker as well as every official expresses shock at any female "circumcision" as being against the Yoruba way of life and all civilized values. Change will probably become certain when the case against female "circumcision" is taught in the schools.

In the present circumstances of a somewhat weaker message—almost certainly heard to some degree by nearly all and not merely the 50 percent of respondents who admit to it—there are three additional pressures that influence women to give up female "circumcision": the fact that the mother is not "circumcised," the spread of education, and urbanization.

There have long been some uncircumcised wives, women from the Yoruba noncircumcising Ijebu, a group only 100 miles from Ado-Ekiti and on the road from Lagos. The in-depth studies showed much more clearly than the survey that mothers are ultimately the main decisionmakers about female "circumcision," and the men are beginning to feel that it is women's business. An uncircumcised mother is likely to feel even more isolated if her daughters are "circumcised." Furthermore, her husband, or at least the daughters' father, is a man who tolerated or even preferred an uncircumcised wife. Real life is more complex than this, however, for once resident in areas in Ekiti where "circumcision" is common, even couples including an uncircumcised wife often try to conform. Table 4.10 shows that uncircumcised women are, nevertheless, eight times as likely to have had uncircumcised mothers as are "circumcised" respondents, and they are seven times as likely to have uncircumcised daughters as are "circumcised" women. Among the grandmothers' generation, 3 percent were uncircumcised, compared with 6 percent of the mothers and 16 percent of the daughters.

In spite of the fact that uncircumcised mothers are far more likely than "circumcised" mothers to have uncircumcised daughters, intergenerational conformity is not the major explanation for the larger numbers of uncircumcised girls in the present generation. The major source of recruits to the uncircumcised group is, in fact, because of intergenerational change by "circumcised" mothers, who outnumber uncircumcised ones by sixteen to one. Thus, two-thirds of the uncircumcised girls had "circumcised" mothers.

Another reason for change is education. The majority of respondents had at least some secondary education, and their husbands were somewhat more educated still. Educated people expect change and confrontation with tradition. They understand more of the messages read or heard on the radio or at meetings or hospitals. They are more likely to attend meetings. Thus, the relationship between education and the increasing likelihood of giving up female "circumcision" looks simple. In fact, it is far more complex.

We compared those with at least some secondary schooling with the less educated. The more and less educated interpret female "circumcision" in an almost identical way. In both groups, more respondents believed that "circumcision" enhanced rather than diminished sexual enjoyment. Only 2 percent of either group held that "circumcision" rendered the genitalia uglier, perhaps because Yoruba "circumcision" is somewhat limited. Only one-third of each group any longer believes that "circumcision" prevents deaths during the birth process. A majority of each group employs the modern health sector for "circumcisions."

The contrast lies in the fact that almost twice the proportion of the more educated compared with the less educated claim to have heard or read the message against "circumcision." Furthermore, 16 percent of the more educated, in contrast to only 8 percent of the less educated, have not "circumcised" any of their daughters. What has happened is that among the minority who think there are few advantages in "circumcision" or that it matters little either way, the more educated are both more likely to be swayed by "expert" opinion and are more decisive, or less influenced by others, when they are swayed.

The strongest factor in changing attitudes is the urban-rural differential, and most of the differential is not the product of educational differences. The explanation seems to be that townspeople can go their own way with less interference than in rural areas. Parents do not worry so much about their daughters being regarded as different and believe there is less chance that potential husbands will turn them down. In the town, 13 percent of respondents believe that the uncircumcised have greater sexual enjoyment, compared with only 4 percent in the village. Although only 2 percent of each group believe that "circumcision" renders the genitalia uglier, only 24 percent of townswomen, compared with 76 percent of villagers, believe that the operation enhances beauty. Only 16 percent in the town, compared with 77 percent in the village, believe that "circumcision" protects infants at birth.

Townswomen are more sophisticated, but they are also much more likely—six times as likely—to hear the new messages. In town, government health providers are more likely to spell out the message, and women's groups are more likely to discuss it. The result is that more than two and a half times the proportion of daughters remain uncircumcised. Those who are "cir-

Table 4.11   Proportion of Uncircumcised Daughters by Mother's Religion and Education

	Christian		Muslim		All Religions[a]	
Education	Number	%	Number	%	Number	%
Up to primary school	292	7	62	11	360	8
Secondary or more schooling	580	14	60	28	656	16
All schooling	872	12	122	20	1,016	13

Note: a. Includes traditional and no religion.

cumcised" are much more likely to have the procedure performed by modern health workers.

Another factor is also at work—religion. The situation is very different from that found in Somalia, Eritrea, or Sudan, where extreme forms of "circumcision" are regarded as extensions of purdah. Muslim Yoruba women do not practice purdah, and with rising educational levels, in Ekiti they are increasingly taking the view that the failure of Islam to mandate female "circumcision" is really a prohibition. As Table 4.11 shows, Muslims are now almost twice as likely as Christians not to "circumcise" their daughters, and 28 percent of the daughters of Muslim mothers with some secondary schooling are not "circumcised."

The Future

The Yoruba are ever less likely to believe there is a strong case for female "circumcision." The major reason that the practice persists is the fear that their daughters will be penalized in the marriage market, as well as in other ways, if the operation is not done. In these circumstances, both nongovernmental and governmental programs have had some success, since female "circumcision" became an international issue, in reducing its incidence. The arguments that it is mutilating and dangerous and that it reduces the libido are not very effective because few women believe any of these propositions. The operation is limited in scope. Either it is carried out by modern health personnel, or they are available to stem infection. Almost half the minority of mothers who believe the operation would reduce their daughters' libido see little harm in that.

The anticircumcision movement is slowly winning, especially in the towns, because it argues that the operation is uncivilized, not done by enlightened people, and not sanctioned by either the Bible or Quran. At the present rate of acceptance of the message not to "circumcise," full change would take several generations. It is probable, however, that change will begin to snowball, especially if health officers become more certain of their message and if other officials and teachers join the struggle.

Note

The authors wish to acknowledge the assistance of Dupe Orubuloye, Folakemi Oguntimehin, and Pat Goodall.

5

Female Genital Cutting in Nigeria: Views of Nigerian Doctors on the Medicalization Debate

Mairo Usman Mandara

Female genital cutting is one of the most discussed issues among international agencies, international and local nongovernmental organizations (NGOs), and to a lesser extent, government health agencies in Nigeria. Most of the discussion centers on debate forwarded by feminist activists in NGOs. These activists believe genital cutting is harmful both medically and psychologically, and therefore they advocate the total eradication of all forms of the practice not only through education but also by legislative intervention. The call for intervention to stop female genital cutting is based on the belief that female genital cutting is not only undesirable and disfiguring (thus the term "mutilation") but poses serious health consequences for the women concerned.

Much has been written on the medical consequences of female "circumcision," and a long list of health consequences is repeated time and time again. This was particularly made popular by the famous *Hosken Report* of 1982 but has continued in many forms, including the statement of the director-general of the World Health Organization (WHO), who in 1994 denounced all forms of female genital cutting on health grounds. The health consequences that are reported in the literature repeatedly are so extensive and severe that if they do occur, then these procedures are truly mutilation of the female external genitalia.

The long-term sequelae, usually described in association with infibulation, include problems such as the development of keloid scars, vulval cysts, vaginal stenosis, pelvic inflammatory diseases, and subsequent infertility (see Chapter 1 for a fuller discussion of adverse consequences of different forms of genital cutting). The milder forms of female "circumcision," clitoridectomy and excision, have been found to be associated with immediate complications of surgery: excessive bleeding, pain, and infection, among others (see Chapter 6 of this volume). Interestingly, these early complications of surgery are preventable. Yet a central question remains: should medical practitioners intervene to prevent the medical complications that may arise from female "circumcision"?

The views of anticircumcision advocates have been heard: medicalization, it is argued, will institutionalize female "circumcision" in the medical profession and, by seemingly condoning the practice, undermine eradication efforts. By contrast, the view of people practicing female "circumcision" is not heard but seen: despite formal or informal prohibition, female genital cutting is becoming increasingly medicalized (for a discussion of the trend in medicalization in Nigeria, see Chapter 4 of this volume). Although formal statements have been issued by medical organizations and associations, including the World Health Organization and the International Federation of Obstetricians and Gynecologists, the view that has not been heard widely is that of African medical practitioners themselves. To remedy this situation, in this chapter I (1) assess the attitudes and practices of women who present themselves for obstetrical and gynecological care at Ahmadu Bello University Teaching Hospital in Zaria, Nigeria; (2) assess the views of Nigerian doctors on the magnitude of female "circumcision" as a health problem when compared with other known medical conditions in the country, and identify the sources and perceived adequacy of information on female "circumcision" provided to Nigerian doctors; and (3) seek to understand the views of Nigerian doctors as to whether female "circumcision" should be medicalized.

Nigeria: The People and the Place

The West African nation of Nigeria is the most highly populated country in Africa, with an estimated population of more than 100 million people and a population growth rate of 3.2 percent annually. When it gained political independence in 1960, the country was subdivided into only three regions. Now, however, this burgeoning nation is demarcated into thirty-six states, which are inhabited by more than 250 different ethnic groups. The northern part of the country is inhabited mainly by the Hausa-, Fulani-, and Kanuri-speaking peoples, most of whom are Muslims. The majority of people in the southwestern region of the country, both Christian and Muslim, speak Yoruba. These groups have strong cultural affiliations with each other despite their religious differences. The southeast is dominated by the Igbo, who are mainly Christian. Nigeria is, therefore, a heterogeneous collection of peoples with different religious beliefs and customs, making it difficult to generalize about cultural practices in the country.

Prior to independence, agriculture was the mainstay of Nigeria's economy. Crops such as maize, cassava, millet, rice, and yams were produced at subsistence level, and agricultural products such as cocoa, palm kernel, palm oil, ground nut, and cotton were produced for export (IAC 1997). In the early 1970s, there was a major shift from agriculture to petroleum exports. As Nigeria became a major world producer of petroleum, the rise in revenue allowed the nation to initiate development programs directed at improving socioeconomic conditions. Evidence of these efforts can be seen in changes in the nation's epidemiological and demographic profile: the under-five mortality rate has dropped from 192 per 1,000 live births in 1990 to 147 in 1995; in the 1990s, life expectancy has risen from forty to fifty-two years; 49.9 percent of Nigerians now have access to safe water and 53 percent to sanitary toilets (IAC 1997). However, the process of development and modernization has not equally affected all sectors of the population or addressed all segments of social life. Indeed, Nigerian society is best understood as a society in transition, with a complex melding of old and new practices.

Despite improvements in health and socioeconomic conditions, women's status in Nigeria remains low. Nigeria is essentially a patriarchal society in which authority is held by the extended family. Patriarchal control over women is held to be responsible for women's low autonomy in decisionmaking and unequal access to family-based resources. Consequences include underutilization of health services by women with absentee husbands, which contributes to high levels of infant and maternal mortality (IAC 1997). In many traditional communities, women cannot own land and are denied rights of inheritance when they become widowed (Aderibige 1996). Polygyny, which is endorsed by Islam and the Nigerian Native Laws and Customs, is widely practiced. Criticized not only as a by-product of patriarchy, polygyny is thought to constitute a health hazard for women, increasing their risk of contracting sexually transmitted diseases such as HIV (IAC 1997). Extramarital affairs and the keeping of mistresses are also common and is silently accepted as "normal" even by the women. Marriages are still often arranged, and early, or "child," marriages are commonplace. This tradition is listed among factors responsible for high rates of pregnancy among young adolescents, which carry an elevated risk of complications, including obstructed labor (IAC 1997). Also listed among "harmful traditional practices" in Nigeria is female "circumcision," referred to by many activists as "female genital mutilation" (FGM).

Female Genital Cutting in Nigeria:
Forms and Frequency of the Practice

Awareness of the adverse health consequences of female genital cutting (FGC) increased following two international meetings sponsored by the

World Health Organization, the first held in 1977 in Cairo and the second in 1979 in Khartoum. Following these landmark meetings, the WHO and other United Nations agencies, such as UN Children's Fund (UNICEF) and UN Population Fund (UNFPA), began to sponsor educational programs aimed at eradicating the practice. Further impetus was given when a seminar, entitled "On the Traditional Practices Affecting the Health of Women and Children," was held in Dakar in 1984. At this seminar participants from twenty African countries, including Nigeria, resolved to "regard FGM as a health hazard and as an unnecessary human suffering" (IAC 1997:7). Afterward, the Inter-African Committee (IAC) was formed, with one of its twenty-six chapters established in Nigeria. Since that time, studies sponsored by the IAC and other agencies have yielded an increasing, although still fragmentary, body of information on the practice of female genital cutting in Nigeria.

Aside from the most commonly described forms of female genital cutting, clitoridectomy, excision, and infibulation (see Chapter 1 for definitions), two other forms of genital cutting are found in Nigeria. The first is a practice referred to by the Hausa as *gishiri* cut or *yankan gishiri* (literally, salt cut), which is a surgical cut on the anterior or posterior vaginal wall made with a razorblade or penknife. Unlike female "circumcision," *gishiri* is performed commonly as a "cure" for a variety of ailments, including obstructed labor, amenorrhea, infertility, pruritus vulvae, and others. The Kare-kare of the north have a similar practice called *zur-zur* cut, which is an incision made during obstructed labor on the anterior or posterior lip of the undilated cervix in the hope of achieving vaginal delivery in the case of prolonged or obstructed labor. This practice is usually associated with severe hemorrhage, which may lead to shock or even death. Adverse consequences of this procedure for women who survive include cervical incompetence in subsequent pregnancies and a high risk of vesico-vaginal and recto-vaginal fistulae.[1]

A second form of genital cutting not included in traditional classifications is hymenectomy. Hymenectomy, referred to as *chire angurya, chire haki,* or *chire belun gaba* (excision of abnormal growth) by the Hausa, involves excision of the hymen when it is considered too thick. This form of cutting is usually performed by a *wanzami* (traditional herbalist-barber) on infant girls soon after birth. Although most women do not know why it is done, some report that it assists a woman in consummating marriage (i.e., thickened hymen makes penetration difficult).

The prevalence of different forms of genital cutting in Nigeria varies widely across geographic regions and ethnic groups, and enormous variation exists within ethnic groups. For example, excision among the Yoruba women in southwestern Nigeria ranges from a prevalence of 60–70 percent in Oyo State (Onadeko and Adekunle 1985) to more than 95 percent in Ondo State (IAC 1995). By contrast, excision is seen in only 35–45 percent of Yoruba women in Ogun State and is virtually nonexistent among Yoruba women of Ijebu (Adeneye 1995).

The Inter-African Committee of Nigeria has recently reviewed the existing literature in an attempt to describe the prevalence of female genital cutting across the states of Nigeria (Table 5.1). The reliability of some of these figures is, however, uncertain and will be reevaluated once the results of a recently conducted National Baseline Survey are released.

No generalizations can be made about the practice of female genital cutting in Nigeria except that it occurs to different degrees among different localized groups. The practice transcends any distinct beliefs, culture, or ethnic affiliation. Despite improvement in the education, health, and economic status of communities where it is practiced, the custom of genital cutting persists.

Female Genital Cutting in Zaria:
A Clinical Appraisal

In the first segment of this study, I evaluated the practices and attitudes of women seeking clinical treatment so that similarities or differences in views of practitioners and patients might be identified. A clinical study was conducted among patients patronizing the Obstetric and Gynecology Unit at Ahmadu Bello University (ABU) Teaching Hospital in Zaria, Nigeria, in 1995. The Ahmadu Bello University Teaching Hospital serves an estimated population of more than 50,000 people in Zaria, and receives referrals from about eight surrounding states for specialized cases. Zaria is populated by people from different parts of Nigeria, mainly because of the presence of one of Nigeria's biggest universities, Ahmadu Bello University. A sample of 500 women who presented themselves to the Obstetric and Gynecology Unit were recruited to participate in this phase of the study. Participants were interviewed using a standardized questionnaire and were given a full examination of the external genitalia. The aim of the interview was to elicit background information in order to construct a sociodemographic profile of the clientele and to collect information on each woman's experience with female genital cutting, complications resulting from the procedure, and attitudes regarding the continuation of the custom. Physical examination of the lower genital tract was done by simple inspection of the vulva and perineum and parting of the labia to inspect the vaginal introitus. Those women who were found to have any form of genital cutting were then subjected to more detailed digital and speculum examination. Information on hymenectomy was, however, based on informant knowledge. This information was then used to classify the form of genital cutting for each subject according to the classification described earlier.

Table 5.1   Prevalence of Female Genital Cutting in the States of
            Nigeria

State	Type of Genital Cutting	Prevalence (%)
Adamawa	*gishiri* cuts	60–70
Akwa Ibom	excision	65–75
Anambra	excition	40–60
Bauchi	*gishiri* cuts	50–60
Benue	excision	90–100
Borno	excision, infibulation, *gishiri* cuts	10–90
Delta	excision	80–90
Edo	excision	30–40
Imo	excision	40–50
Jigawa	*gishiri* cuts	60–70
Kaduna	*gishiri* cuts	50–70
Kebbi	*gishiri* cuts	90–100
Kogi	*gishiri* cuts	0–1
Kwara	clitoridectomy and excision	60–70
Lagos	clitoridectomy	20–30
Ogun	clitoridectomy and excision	80–90
Ondo	excision	90–98
Osun	clitoridectomy	80–90
Oyo	clitoridectomy	60–70
Plateau	clitoridectomy and *gishiri* cuts	30–90
Rivers	clitoridectomy and excision	60–70

Source: Adapted from IAC 1997.

For convenience, I describe my findings by ethnic group. Among the Hausa women (n = 226), most of whom read up to secondary school level and are all Muslims, genital cutting is still widely practiced (Table 5.2). The type of genital cutting found in this group is mainly clitoridectomy (51 percent). Hymenectomy was determined to have been performed on 28 percent of Hausa girls, in most cases on the seventh day postnatal. No medications were reported to have been applied on the area, and no cases of complications were recalled. An additional 8 percent of women had *gishiri* cuts. When questioned about their attitude toward sex, Hausa women reported that it was not affected by genital cutting. Additionally, when questioned about their attitude about

Table 5.2   Prevalence of Genital Cutting Among Patients at Ahmadu
Bello University Teaching Hospital Obstetrics and
Gynecology Unit

	Hausa (%)	Ibo (%)	Yoruba (%)
Religion			
Muslim	100	0	53
Christian	0	100	47
Education			
primary	28	28	51
secondary	40	68	38
none	32	4	11
Prevalence of FGC	41	76	75
Type of FGC			
clitoridectomy	51	—	5
excision	13	88	83
infibulation	0	13	7
gishiri cuts	8	—	2
hymenectomy	28	—	—

Note: n = 226 Hausa; 53 Ibo; 55 Yoruba.

the continuation of the practice of genital cutting, most women said they were indifferent and did not intend to have their daughters cut.

Yoruba women (n = 55) were a mixture of both Christians and Muslims. Most of the women I examined have had some form of genital cutting (75 percent). The form most commonly practiced among this group is excision, performed mainly by traditional midwives or healers for reasons thought to include safeguarding virginity, attenuating sexual desire, and fulfilling a religious rite. The procedure is usually done on the eighth day after birth, and is variously called *idi dida* or *ila*.

Among the Ibo women interviewed at ABU Teaching Hospital (n = 53), most have attended at least secondary school and were either self-employed or working for companies. All were Christian. Although some were aware that part of their genitalia were excised, others did not know that they had been cut. The majority of Ibo women (76 percent) had some form of genital cutting, most commonly excision (88 percent), but several cases of infibulation were also observed (13 percent). Most women reported that the "circumcision" procedure was performed by "an old woman" at puberty; a minority had the procedure done by professional nurses and midwives in private clinics. The reasons given for the custom varied. Although most of the women said it was done to safeguard virginity and prevent promiscuity later in life, others said it was to initiate a girl into womanhood.

Table 5.3   Attitudes of Patients Toward Female Genital Cutting (n = 500)

| | Number | How do you feel about the continuation of FGC? | | | Do you intend to circumcise your daughters? |
		Approve (%)	Indifferent (%)	Disapprove (%)	Yes (%)
Education Level					
None	115	26	25	49	26
Primary	110	20	31	49	20
Secondary	163	22	33	47	20
Tertiary	69	13	28	60	13

Among "circumcised" women, 11.6 percent (n = 23) reported complications. Specifically, seven women had difficulty with urination, nine women had excessive bleeding, and four reported collapse. Noteworthy as well is the fact that 30.3 percent of women who had *gishiri* cuts sustained vesico-vaginal fistulae. Most women said that the practice had no effect on their sex life. The attitude of women toward the continuation of genital cutting (Table 5.3) varied somewhat by education. Overall, many women either disapproved of (50 percent) or were indifferent to (29 percent) the practice. A significantly higher proportion of women with higher education opposed the practice (60 percent), as compared to women at other educational levels. A substantial number of women (21 percent) said they intended to have their daughters "circumcised," particularly women with no education (26 percent), as compared to women with tertiary education (13 percent).

Views of Nigerian Medical Doctors

If as many as 21 percent of women seeking obstetrical and gynecological care believe the practice of female genital cutting should continue, then what do medical practitioners think? Are these 21 percent entitled to female "circumcision" by trained experts? Should they enjoy orthodox medical facilities to decrease the complications associated with these practices, or should they be left to the mercy of untrained personnel to perform the procedures in unclean environments with all the hazards of infections, hemorrhages, and excessive pain? To assess opinions in the medical community, 250 Nigerian doctors were interviewed in 1997 using standardized questionnaires. One hundred and forty-five were obstetrician/gynecologists, eight were community physi-

Table 5.4   Complications Related to Female Genital Cutting Encountered by
Twenty-six Doctors

Complication	Number	%
Hemorrhage following "circumcision"	4	15
Hemorrhage following *zur-zur* cut	7	27
Hemorrhage following *gishiri* cut	12	46
Vesico-vaginal fistulae	3	17

cians and general practitioners, and the remaining twenty-five were of other specialties. The respondents filled out questionnaires individually while remaining anonymous. One-on-one discussions were also conducted with seventy doctors who feel strongly about their views on the medicalization of female genital cutting.

Although almost all the doctors interviewed obtained information on female genital cutting through the media, activities of nongovernmental organizations (NGOs), and professional journals, 10 percent (n = 26) have had personal experiences and encounters with women who have had some form of genital cutting. These twenty-six doctors had seen and treated various complications related to different forms of genital cutting (Table 5.4).

Of the 250 medical practitioners interviewed, 40 percent believe the available information on the practice of female genital cutting is adequate within Nigeria, and 95 percent believe there is adequate information on the subject internationally. The majority (213) of medical practitioners interviewed consider female genital cutting to be a health problem. Notably, of these 213, 75 percent consider it to be a minor health problem when compared and prioritized with other known medical problems in the country (Table 5.5). Maternal mortality, diarrheal diseases, and malnutrition are some of the most serious leading causes of morbidity in the country. Hypertension, although present, is not a serious and life-threatening condition in Nigeria. Alzheimer's disease, although recognized as a medical condition and identified as a serious problem elsewhere in the world, is practically nonexistent in Nigeria. A medical practitioner could easily go through his or her entire medical career without encountering a single case of Alzheimer's disease.

When asked how they would prioritize FGC as a health concern of the Nigerian people when confronted with limited resources, several respondents said that they had not thought about it and were reluctant to make definite comments. Forty-two percent said there were other more pressing and serious health issues in the country, such as maternal mortality, prenatal mortality, communicable diseases, and malnutrition; they indicated that they would not consider FGC to be a priority. Thirty-nine percent of the respondents said that

Table 5.5   Relative Ranking of the Importance of FGC as a Health Problem in Nigeria

	Number Agreeing	%
Responses to the statement: FGC is as important as		
Maternal mortality	—	—
Diarrheal diseases	—	—
Malnutrition	—	—
Hypertension	53	25
Alzheimer's disease	160	75

they would encourage NGOs to deal with the problem while they deal with more urgent and serious health issues. One doctor responded:

> All these campaigns are being engineered by international NGOs for whatever reason, since they have money to indulge in these campaigns for whatever reason. I will encourage local NGOs to use the money and help them do the campaign. After all it is good that our people should stop these harmful practices. I will, however, not use the limited resources of the Nigerian people in something as trivial—Oh! Sorry—not so serious while hundreds and thousands of men, women and children are dying of malnutrition, communicable disease, malaria, etc. Even if they are all healthy, I will use Nigerian money to invest in education. We have more pressing issues than to sink our money—limited money—in such ventures.

All the 250 medical practitioners interviewed advocate the eradication of female genital cutting in all its forms. To do so, they suggest making use of local NGOs, involving community leaders, and planning individual activities. Surprisingly, less than 10 percent believe the government can exert any influence in eliminating the practice.

In response to the question of whether female genital cutting should be medicalized as an interim measure before total eradication, if that is not immediately possible, 20 percent of the 250 practitioners support the idea. Supporters explain that if the practice of "circumcision" cannot be eradicated completely, then it is in the interest of the girl or the woman to have the procedure performed safely. It should be carried out by adequately trained gynecologists, urologists, or general practitioners in good health centers not only to minimize the pain and trauma of the procedure but also to prevent complications. They argue that if these preventive measures are not taken, women will have the procedure performed by untrained personnel, and any complications that arise would, in all likelihood, be treated by the same doctor that had earlier refused to perform the "circumcision." Women who do not seek professional medical treatment for resulting complications may die. All the doctors advocating this view suggested limiting "circumcision" to only the mildest form, clitoridectomy, and they maintain that the service should then be paid for completely without any subsidy from the state.

By contrast, most of the doctors interviewed (80 percent) are of the opinion that there is no medical indication for female "circumcision," and thus performing the procedure could be equated to malpractice. They argue that there are no medical benefits from female "circumcision" and distinguish it from the case of male circumcision, which is believed to reduce the incidence of carcinoma of the cervix in sexual partners of circumcised males. The sentiment of the majority of Nigerian medical doctors was that medicalizing female "circumcision" will only encourage the practice and make eradication difficult.

Conclusion

Among people practicing female "circumcision" in Nigeria and elsewhere in Africa, a strong adherence to the practice is commonly observed. Anticircumcision efforts have been under way in Nigeria for nearly two decades, emphasizing the health consequences of the practice. Nonetheless, a large segment of the population not only condones the practice of genital cutting but advocates it for their daughters. In my survey of attitudes of women utilizing the obstetrical and gynecology services at Ahmadu Bello University Teaching Hospital, 75 percent had experienced some form of genital cutting and, disturbingly, more than 20 percent approved of continuing the practice by having their own daughters "circumcised."

Despite the continued demand for female "circumcision," the practice is changing in that it is becoming increasingly medicalized. Once primarily the responsibility of traditional circumcisers, it is now being performed increasingly by professional nurses (see Chapter 4 in this volume). For this reason we must critically examine the role and responsibility of the medical community and understand the attitudes of medical practitioners.

Nigerian doctors surveyed in this study unanimously support the total eradication of all forms of female genital cutting. The question that remains is whether and how they should treat women who elect (or whose families elect) "circumcision." Should doctors or nurses give them medical assistance during a period of transition while gradually trying to change their attitudes? Or should their innocent daughters be allowed to suffer and pay the price of the decision taken by their mothers? Are women entitled to a period of transition from the practice as it is known to an interim period of relative safety before complete eradication is achieved? Among Nigerian doctors in this study, only 20 percent believe that medical assistance to improve the safety of "circumcision" should be offered in a transition period prior to total eradication. Although those supporting medicalization believe it is ethical to minimize pain and arrest complications before they arise, the majority of medical doctors oppose this stance. Rather, they support the position of the World Health Organization:

> Given WHO's commitment to advance the health, and protect the lives of women and children, including their reproductive and psychological health, the Organization continues to advise unequivocally that FGM must not be institutionalized, nor should any form of FGM be performed by any health professional in any setting, including hospitals or other health establishments. (WHO 1996)

Those who accept this statement regard medicalization as unethical and often equate it to medical malpractice.

What is most interesting in this research is that less than 5 percent of the doctors were ready to use part of the country's health budget to achieve eradication, despite their belief that female genital cutting should be eradicated. Overall, the health consequences of female genital cutting were viewed as a low priority when compared to other serious health problems in the country. Maternal mortality, diarrheal disease, and malnutrition were recognized as pressing health concerns, whereas health complications from "circumcision" were regarded by most to be of equal importance to Alzheimer's disease, a condition rarely found in Nigeria.

Although complications associated with female "circumcision" are seen as a low healthcare priority, confronting the question of whether and how to provide medical care is becoming unavoidable. Indeed, the practice of female genital cutting is one area that tests a medical practitioner's ability not only to diagnose and treat medical conditions but to appreciate the complex social issues involved. The challenge is formidable in light of the enormous cultural diversity found in Nigeria. There, female genital cutting is performed for numerous and varied reasons throughout the country. Whereas among the Shuwa of the extreme northeast and the Ibos of the southeast it serves to attenuate sexual desires, in the Delta region female "circumcision" is seen more as an initiation rite into womanhood. Among the Yoruba of Atakumasa, the clitoris is excised because it is believed that if the clitoris touches the head of a baby during childbirth, the infant will die. *Gishiri* cuts and *zur-zur* cuts, however, are performed in an attempt to assist women with prolonged labor, in the belief that the cut will dilate the birth canal and aid vaginal delivery. Consequently, generalizing about the social meaning and importance of genital cutting practices throughout Nigeria is difficult, if not impossible.

How, then, shall we target and treat these varied customs? Clearly, uniform solutions are not tenable because effecting change requires understanding the attitudes and beliefs associated with the practices. I believe that successful change requires not only understanding but also appreciation of the reasons for sustaining the practice. Only by offering alternative ways of achieving the same objective can we hope to completely and permanently eradicate female genital cutting.

Meanwhile, in the debate on medicalization there are no easy solutions because each stance involves tradeoffs regarding women's health. Additional complexity is added by the fact that in Nigeria there is currently no legislation regarding the practice of female genital cutting or the provision of medical support. As professionals trained to assist and promote health, in this arena we are asked by international health organizations to remain hands-off. Yet we must at least consider the fate of those being denied medical care. Although most Nigerian doctors oppose the medicalization of female genital cutting, questions do remain, and we can only hope that actions supported by the medical profession best serve to promote the health and welfare of Nigerian women.

Note

1. Vesico-vaginal fistula is an abnormal condition in which there is a connection between the bladder and vagina, leading to uncontrolled leakage of urine via the vagina. Recto-vaginal fistula is an abnormal connection between the rectum and vagina, resulting in leakage of feces through the vagina. These are very distressing situations, and the affected woman is usually deserted and possibly divorced by her husband. She is usually ostracized by society and left to fend for herself.

6

Women Without Choices: The Debate over Medicalization of Female Genital Cutting and Its Impact on a Northern Kenyan Community

Bettina Shell-Duncan,
Walter Obungu Obiero
& Leunita Auko Muruli

No action will entrench FGM more than legitimating it through the medical profession. If doctors and hospitals start to perform it, rather than condemn it, we will have no hope of ever eradicating the practice. All the respect and authority given to doctors will be transferred to the practice and we [activists] lose our credibility.

—Aziza Kamil

Some of the most contentious debates surrounding the practice of female "circumcision" emanate from the health risks associated with genital cutting procedures. The medical consequences of female genital cutting (FGC) are central in two prominent—yet contradictory—arguments. On the one hand, by emphasizing that female genital cutting exposes women to unnecessary and often severe health risks, a medical argument forms the foundation of most anticircumcision campaigns. On the other hand, any efforts to minimize the health risks through medical interventions are strongly opposed by anticircumcision advocates, based on the belief that medicalization counteracts efforts to eliminate the practice.

In the anticircumcision literature, fragments of information about different types of genital cutting performed under widely varying conditions are melded and repeated as the "medical sequelae."[1] As variations in the practice (degree of cutting, training of the circumciser, sanitary conditions, degree of medical support) are obliterated, what remains is a seemingly objective, scientific discussion of the medical "facts" of a single practice—"female genital mutilation" (FGM). This discussion is often divided into three categories: short-term, long-term, and obstetrical consequences (see Chapter 1 for a detailed discussion). A recitation of detailed descriptions of adverse health outcomes takes center stage in most educational campaigns, based on the hope that as awareness of the dangers of female "circumcision" increases, support for the practice will diminish. One serious problem with these accounts of the medical "facts" is that they largely fail to distinguish differences in the types and frequency of complications associated with different types of genital cutting. Often details from select case reports of infibulations with extreme complications are presented in reports generalizing about the health risks of *all* forms of genital cutting. Graphic descriptions of physical trauma, torturous pain, and psychological damage are often accompanied by photographs of faceless women displaying scarred genitalia. Although these sensationalized images are intended to motivate change in communities practicing FGC and to ignite public outrage and fuel political action worldwide, they also base many campaigns (those in communities practicing clitoridectomy or excision) in misinformation. Yet it has long been recognized privately but not declared publicly that the dissemination of distorted, exaggerated, or incorrect information to target communities undermines the credibility of anticircumcision campaigns (see also Chapters 10, 11, and 14 in this volume). For example, in 1939 Paul Chiono was asked by the Catholic Mission in Nyeri, Kenya, to investigate whether clitoridectomy did, in fact, cause scarification that obstructs labor, as claimed by opponents to the practice. He concluded "after many careful observations . . . [that] clitoridectomy does not deprive the local muscular tissue of the necessary elasticity as to hamper childbirth. Therefore campaigning against the custom based on this argument leaves people indifferent and suspicious because [it is] not justified by every day experience."[2]

Paradoxically, those who emphasize female "circumcision" as a public health issue at the same time oppose any medical intervention designed to minimize health risks and pain for women being cut. Medical interventions have been attempted in various forms. In some regions, local health workers promote precautionary steps, such as the use of clean sterile razors on each woman, and dispense prophylactic antibiotics and antitetanus injections. Other regions have incorporated training on genital cutting as part of traditional birth attendant programs (van der Kwaak 1992). Traditional circumcisers are encouraged to perform the milder forms of genital cutting and receive training in anatomy and septic procedures. In addition, in some areas, genital operations are performed in clinics or hospitals by trained nurses and physicians (see, for example, Chapter 4 in this volume for a discussion of this trend in Nigeria). The impact of these programs on the health of women in rural communities has received surprisingly little attention. Without consideration of health improvements resulting from these training programs, this approach has been strongly criticized. Opponents argue that incorporation of female genital cutting procedures in the biomedical healthcare system institutionalizes the custom and counteracts efforts to eliminate the practice of female "circumcision" (Gordon 1991; Toubia 1993). The position of the World Health Organization (WHO) is that all forms of female "circumcision" should be abolished without intermediate stages (WHO 1982). The purely medical arguments for abolition of even the mildest forms of female "circumcision" lose weight when health risks of female "circumcision" are minimized.

A less controversial approach has been to promote change in values and attitudes toward female "circumcision" as part of a larger process of social change. This approach, termed "development and modernization" (van der Kwaak 1992), suggests that improvements in socioeconomic status and education, particularly for women, will have far-reaching social effects, including a decline in the demand for female "circumcision."[3] By analogy, such changes have been shown to have an important effect on morbidity and mortality patterns (van der Kwaak 1992). Recognizing that in many African societies "circumcision" is a prerequisite for marriage and that marriage and children are vital aspects of women's roles and economic survival helps contextualize this practice in a larger social setting. Hence, it is believed that effective change can occur only in the context of a women's movement directed at the social inequality of women, particularly economic dependency, educational disadvantages, and limited employment opportunities (Gruenbaum 1982). It has been argued, however, that changing social conditions will not automatically change strongly held beliefs and values on female "circumcision"; it is still important to convince men and women that female "circumcision" has an overall negative effect on their lives (van der Kwaak 1992). It is also recognized that changing traditions and values is possible but will not occur quickly.[4] Lessons can be learned from family planning initiatives in Kenya and other parts of sub-Saharan Africa, demonstrating that change in deep-seated values, such as high fertility and large family size, can occur. However, the process of change is slow. Family planning programs were under way in Kenya for more than twenty years before taking hold (Brass and Jolly 1993). There is no reason to assume that attitudes toward female "circumcision" would change more quickly. Therefore, we believe that short-term "intermediate" solutions, including medical support for female "circumcision," need to be at least considered and evaluated.

Female "Circumcision" Among the Rendille of Northern Kenya

In this chapter, we examine the context and consequences of female "circumcision" among a non-Islamic African group in northern Kenya, the Rendille.

This group inhabits the Kaisut Desert of northern Kenya, a hot, arid semi-desert that receives, on average, less than 300 mm of rain each year. The desert terrain is dotted with isolated mountains that support forest growth. The majority of space is lowland acacia scrub desert that has been character-ized as one of the harshest and least productive regions of East Africa (Bea-man 1981). Traditionally, the Rendille subsist in this inhospitable environ-ment as nomadic herders of mainly camels and to a lesser degree cattle and small stock (goats and sheep). The nomadic community is entirely dependent upon their animals for subsistence, consuming direct animal products of milk, blood, and meat or exchanging animals for farm goods such as sugar, tea, and cornmeal. Moving with their animals, the Rendille live in patrilineal, patrilo-cal clan-based settlements (*gob*). The settlement pattern of the Rendille began to change when a series of droughts in the 1970s and 1980s diminished large portions of Rendille livestock (Fratkin 1991). The Rendille were forced to settle alongside mechanized waterholes which were also sites of famine relief food distribution (Fratkin 1991). Today more than one-half of the estimated 22,000 Rendille people are settled in towns formed around these permanent waterholes (Fratkin 1991). The lifestyles in newly formed towns vary consid-erably, representing a broad range of development in terms of infrastructure, market integration, and educational and economic opportunities.

This setting provides a unique opportunity to examine the manner in which the practice of female "circumcision" and surrounding attitudes change as a society experiences the transformations brought about by settlement and development. The people here share a common language and common cultural beliefs and practices yet participate in widely varying social and production systems (Nathan, Fratkin, and Roth 1996). Hence, it is possible to examine whether and how the practice and perceived value of female "circumcision" has altered in segments of this society that have experienced dramatic change. Noteworthy, however, is the fact that even in the most "urbanized" location, Marsabit Town, which is the capital of Marsabit District, the level of develop-ment lags far behind that of central Kenya. Because of the rugged terrain, lack of any paved roads, and threat of banditry, this northern region is quite isolated from the rest of Kenya. Additionally, because this region is sparsely populated as well as remote, it is commonly overlooked in national surveys and given low priority in national development efforts.

Another interesting feature of this study setting is that it allows us to pre-liminarily evaluate the effect of medical support on the health consequences of female "circumcision." In the settled sector of the Rendille, community health workers have in recent years been promoting the use of sterile razors, antibiotics, and antitetanus injections. A comparison of the long- and short-term health consequences following medically assisted versus unassisted op-erations will provide insight into the degree to which minimal medicalization can alter the health risks of female genital cutting.

The Rendille Maternal and Child Demographic and Health Study

Data on female "circumcision" were gathered as part of a larger demographic and health survey of women ages fifteen and over in five distinct Rendille communities. A questionnaire was constructed to obtain information on socioeconomic characteristics, reproductive history, obstetrical outcomes, and female "circumcision." This questionnaire was pretested once in 1994 and again in 1995. Interviewers were trained by Walter Obiero, and data collection was completed in 1996. We first interviewed women in the traditional nomadic pastoralist sector of the population and obtained information that could serve as a baseline for comparison with various settled communities. We then randomly sampled women in four different settled communities:

1. The district capital, Marsabit Town, which is located atop an isolated mountain in the Kaisut Desert. Many women here are involved in wage labor or small businesses, such as working at the post office or in local markets.
2. The town of Songa, which is also atop Mt. Marsabit. It is inhabited by approximately 2,000 people who practice irrigation agriculture in a mission-sponsored project in Marsabit National Forest. Women here grow and sell vegetables at the Marsabit market. We expected to see the greatest amount of difference in beliefs, values, and practices of female "circumcision" in these two communities in comparison to the nomadic community because their lifestyles and subsistence strategies differ the most.
3. The third community we surveyed is Karare, a town on the slopes of Mt. Marsabit where people subsist by either sedentary cattle keeping and milk marketing or by dryland horticulture.
4. Finally, we visited a lowland desert town called Korr, which emerged when the Catholic mission dug permanent mechanized waterholes and began distributing famine relief food in the 1970s. Some people here are involved in market trade, but as is the case with Karare, many people still rely on animal production for subsistence and seemingly have a greater degree of connection with the nomadic sector of the population. We therefore expected changes in the practice of female "circumcision" to be intermediate in these locations.

Characteristics of survey respondents are shown in Table 6.1. A total of 920 Rendille women ages fifteen to seventy-six years were surveyed across the five communities in Marsabit District. Respondents from each community shared similar socioeconomic characteristics. Overall, 16.1 percent of women

Table 6.1   Socioeconomic Characteristics of Female Respondents,
             Ages Fifteen to Seventy-six, in Five Rendille Communities,
             1996

	Nomad	Korr	Karare	Songa	Marsabit	Total
Number sampled	95	246	223	219	137	920
Percent ever married	92.5	93.5	89.6	88.8	94.9	91.6
Percent ever given birth	93.7	95.1	92.8	97.2	98.5	95.4
Percent poor	12.6	16.7	19.8	13.3	16.1	16.1
Percent ever attended school	11.6	17.5	17.6	13.2	8.8	14.6
Religion						
Catholic	15.9	51.4	39.6	41.6	50.0	42.4
Protestant	3.2	3.7	18.0	14.4	2.2	9.4
Mulsim	0.0	1.2	1.8	0.9	1.5	1.1
Traditional	80.8	42.5	58.1	45.0	46.3	48.6

were from poor families.[5] The majority of respondents have never attended school and are illiterate. Of those who attended school, less than 1 percent continued their education beyond primary school. The majority of women practice the traditional Rendille religion, although in the towns of Korr, Karare, and Marsabit where Catholic missions are present, a large number of Catholics are found. The majority of respondents are ever-married women (91.6 percent) and have given birth to at least one child (95.4 percent).

As a followup to the survey we returned to Marsabit District in 1997 to conduct in-depth interviews and focus group discussion on the cultural context of female "circumcision." Focus group discussions were stratified according to marital status and gender as follows: unmarried teenage boys and girls, men and women married for less than ten years, men and women married for more than ten years. Each group was split by gender to facilitate open discussions. Interviews were also conducted among traditional circumcisers (usually in the course of observing the "circumcision" ritual) and local health-care personnel. This qualitative information allowed us to develop an understanding of gender and intergenerational differences in perspective and factors promoting change.

Cultural Context of Female "Circumcision" Among the Rendille

In the Rendille language, the term *khandi* is used to refer to the circumcision of both men and women. Today excision is the form widely practiced among Rendille women. In contrast to other regions of Kenya, discussions about this practice are not shrouded in secrecy. In 1994 before conducting the first pretest of the survey questionnaire, I (BSD) inquired about the sensitivity of raising questions on female "circumcision." My assistant assured me that women would speak openly on the topic, and shortly afterward I was invited to attend a wedding celebration the following morning. It was there that I discovered that excision is performed as part of the wedding ceremony. Being unprepared for what I was to witness, I watched with amazement the bravery of the newly cut bride and the joyous celebration that ensued. Although I was asked to not take photographs, the circumciser, the bride, and attending women all spoke freely with me about the importance of this custom for Rendille women. And as so often happens to anthropologists, many questions were asked of me regarding the customs in my country. Women politely tried to conceal their disgust when they learned that I, a married woman and mother, was not excised. One woman replied: "In your place this might be fine, but for Rendille women, circumcision is the only thing that separates us from animals."

Among the Rendille, excision is traditionally performed during the marriage ceremony. Marriages are typically arranged by a woman's family without her involvement. Marriage negotiations are conducted between the elders of the bride's and groom's clans, and once completed, the girl's mother is informed about the decision and begins preparations for the celebration. Marriage is one of the most important rites of passage for Rendille men and women, and the celebration extends over several days. All preparations are kept secret from the bride-to-be if the family suspects that she may object to the chosen husband and run away, disgracing the family.

Two days before the wedding, the groom and his family form a ritual procession (*guro*) from their home to the bride's home, and outside the hut women sing the praises of the groom and the fortuitous union of the two families (Beaman 1981). A ram is slaughtered and presented to the bride's mother for a feast among married women, and the skin of the ram is prepared for the bride to sit upon while being cut. The procession arrives again on the eve of the wedding, and girls bring red ochre to smear on the bride's beaded necklaces.

On the wedding day, before dawn the circumciser (*kamaratan*), who was selected by the bride's mother, is brought to the hut, and at first light the young bride is circumcised. The groom's family brings animals to pay the *kamaratan* for her service, and one sheep is given as a gift to the bride's mother and tied to the outside of the hut. It is said that the sheep, as it bleats in the midday heat, forewarns the bride of the burden and responsibilities accompanying marriage.

Among the Rendille, excision is not performed by a traditional birth attendant (*tagan*), but rather by a woman who is a specialized circumciser (*kamaratan*). A *kamaratan* is usually an elderly woman with a reputation for being careful and observant who acquires her skills by watching many ritual "circumcisions." A skillful circumciser is considered to be one who cuts quickly and accurately. In the past the cutting was done with a knife, although now razor blades are more commonly used. Excision typically takes place inside a traditional hut in the early morning hours, lighted by a low fire. Males and uncircumcised girls are required to leave the hut, the latter for fear of elevating their anxiety over their future fate. And often the mother of the bride waits outside as well, to avoid the torment of watching her daughter suffer. While being cut, the girl is held still by two women, one holding her legs and the other holding her torso. The *kamaratan* kneels between the girl's legs and quickly removes the clitoris and labia minora, and the cut tissue is buried beneath a hearthstone in the center of the hut. The fresh wound is rinsed with milky water steeped with herbs (*ikiroriti*) and examined for mistakes. The bride is then advised to sit quietly with her legs together, and periodically women tending her check to see if her blood has clotted. If the bleeding continues, several remedies may be tried. In some cases the girl is told to drink plain milk or milk mixed with blood until the bleeding stops. Alternatively, she is given water boiled with small bitter seeds known locally as *khankho*, which are said to make the blood clot. For the next several days the bride will be nursed, resting and rinsing the wound with water boiled with herbs several times a day. Additionally, it is believed that a good diet, one of milk, blood, and meat, will help the bride replace lost blood and regain strength.

Once the operation is complete, the bride's mother and mother-in-law are allowed to enter the hut to see that the bride has fared well. When the news is announced, a collective sense of anxiety vanishes, and a festive celebration begins. The *guro* procession is repeated, with relatives singing praises of the bride and groom in echoing choruses. This time, the procession also delivers the initial payment of bride wealth.[6] Amid songs of praise, visitors come to congratulate and bless the new couple, bringing gifts of sugar, tea, and small livestock, and the families feast on a sacrificed sheep.

Later in the day the families select a site for building a new hut for the couple. The Rendille term for marriage, *min discho*, literally means "house building," and no unmarried man can have his own house (Beaman 1981). Women in the bride's family will have walked long distances to gather new green branches for building a new hut and rebuilding the bride's mother's hut. Dried sticks from the mother's hut are removed and divided, half remaining and half being used to build a new hut for the bride and groom, symbolizing that this house will join the two families. That evening, in a ceremonial procession, the bride and her new husband walk to their new hut. The bride carries her possessions on her back in a manner that she will carry an infant, symbolizing the anticipation of children. As Beaman (1981:336) notes, "Children are the most important reason a man marries, and are the central focus of a woman's life, assuring her place in her husband's clan, her allotment of milch camels, and her social acceptance throughout society." The groom makes a fire anew from sticks, rather than from burning embers, to symbolically mark the beginning of their new life together. The marriage is consummated after the bride's wounds have been allowed to heal, usually one week.

"Circumcision" symbolically marks that the bride is no longer a girl (*inam*), but now a woman (*aronto*). To mark the transformation, the bride discards her father's name and takes her husband's name and leaves her clothes and ornaments of a girl behind. She is given new skins, a large woven necklace (*bukhurcha*) made of sisal or giraffe hair, and a strand of red and white marriage beads (*irtitior*) that she will wear until she bears her first child. Women stress the importance of "circumcision" as a central part of their rite of passage into womanhood, marking that they are now mature and worthy of respect. The bravery and self-control displayed by enduring the pain of the operation is seen as central to the transformation from childhood to womanhood. By withstanding the pain of being cut, a woman demonstrates her maturity and readiness to endure the pain of childbirth and hardships of married life. One issue raised in focus group discussions was the acceptability of using anesthesia on women when excised. This suggestion stemmed from the fact that when the most recent age-set of warriors was initiated, circumcision was performed by a nurse who used a local anesthesia. When asked if this same practice would be acceptable for girls, women, particularly recently married women, strongly objected, viewing the proposed change as a trespass on women's affairs. Enduring the pain, they explained, is a constitutive experience in preparing a woman for her role as wife and mother, her central role in Rendille society.

Concomitant with "circumcision" is improved social status. A woman, once circumcised, is recognized as the female head of her new household. She is allocated livestock, and most important, she is now allowed to bear children. Prior to marriage, it is acceptable for Rendille girls to be sexually active. Adolescents often spend weeks or months tending animals in the bush, where they are free to have sexual partners. It is taboo, however, for unmarried girls to become pregnant. Young warriors are counseled by elders on how to avoid impregnating their girlfriends by practicing withdrawal. If an unmarried girl becomes pregnant, both she and her boyfriend are disgraced, and the girl is faced with the danger of forced abortion. One young married man explained, " Children of girls are outcasts or can be killed. You must have a circumcised mother to be accepted. If an unmarried woman is pregnant, we must jump on her stomach until she aborts. The mother and child may die. . . . If we bear children with an uncircumcised girl, we lose all respect in the community." Once married and "circumcised," a woman is allowed only one partner, her husband, and is allowed to bear children. Marriage cannot be disentangled from excision in legitimating reproduction.

For men, the importance of "circumcising" a bride is that it marks the woman, socially signifying that she is sexually exclusive and allowed to bear his children. As one informant described, "Circumcision is a brand. If a girl is not circumcised, she can stay with her family, and can have sex with boyfriends. We get a brand to show that she is mine, and can only be with me, and will bear my children. . . . Branding makes her mine."

When discussing the decision to "circumcise" their daughters, men also stress the economic ramifications of "circumcision." An uncircumcised girl is not socially sanctioned to marry or bear children. Excision is central in preparing a girl for marriage and entitling her family to receive large bride wealth payments. Therefore, failing to "circumcise" a daughter would have significant social and economic consequences for the girl and her entire family.[7]

When asked to describe the advantages of female "circumcision," women in particular emphasized that excision reduces a wife's sexual desire and helps her remain abstinent during the often long absences of her husband, who may leave for months at a time to take animals to the *fora* (bush) or to work in larger towns. One elderly woman explained, "If you are circumcised, your emotions (sexual desires) are reduced, and you don't have to sleep around and lose respect."

It has been debated, however, whether excised women do, in all cases, experience reduced sexual pleasure, particularly since the extent of cutting can vary considerably (see Chapter 1 of this volume for a more detailed discussion of this issue). It is often difficult to determine whether excision alters sexual response since many African women are "circumcised" long before becoming sexually active. Rendille women, by contrast, usually become sexually active prior to being excised. They therefore provide a unique perspective in evaluating the effect of excision on sexual pleasure. When asked if they experienced diminished sexual pleasure after being circumcised, responses were divided. Some women claimed to have lost all enjoyment: "Only when I was a girl did I feel pleasure. All pleasure was reduced when I was circumcised. There is now enough for one purpose—bearing my husband's children." Another informant concurred, "One disadvantage (of excision) for men is that the sexual desire of the wife is reduced. In a way it is good because you don't go to other men. In a way it is bad because you are not interested in him." Other women claimed to experience fulfilling sexual pleasure after marrying. In response to a question about differences in sexual enjoyment before and after excision, several women insisted that sex was actually better *after* being circumcised, a finding also reported by anthropologist Anne Beaman (1981:321–322). As one informant told anthropologist Elliot Fratkin (1991:70) in what he described as consciously contradictory terms, "But you know, the men like to see us circumcised. They think we won't see other men if we are circumcised. But they are wrong," she laughed.

Although women certainly play a central role in promoting the practice of excision, the interests of men are not irrelevant. The importance of engenderment for women cannot be separated from the fact that they are oppressed by men throughout their lives. Rendille women have very low status in terms of control over economic resources or decisionmaking about events in their life or household affairs. Although they play an important role in economic production, women own no independent property and are thus dependent upon their husbands or, when widowed, upon their sons. Male dominance over women expresses itself in ideology, economic control, and behavior. One elderly female informant explained, "When a man has married, he takes control of you. You must follow his rules. . . . If you make a mistake—if he thinks that you have gone to another man, or that you did not care for the goats—he can leave you without animals, and without food and water, and he can beat you." "Circumcision" transforms a girl into a bride, and she becomes property that is transferred upon payment of bride wealth. Women receive their status of full wife upon bearing a child, emphasizing the importance of fertility in defining a woman's role. Without being excised, a woman can never bear legitimate children or achieve the full status of womanhood in Rendille society.

Recent Changes in Attitudes and Practice

As noted by Lori Leonard in Chapter 9 of this volume, descriptions of the cultural context of female "circumcision" promote the idea that the tradition is deep-seated and unchanging. It is important to recognize that the practice of female "circumcision" is a response to complex social concerns, but it is also necessary to realize that social conditions are dynamic and consequently so is the nature of this practice.

By conducting questionnaires among women and focus groups and in-depth interviews with men and women across a broad range of ages, we were able to identify intergenerational differences in the practice of and attitudes toward female "circumcision." These changes are not the product of anticircumcision campaigns, since none have been implemented as yet in Marsabit District.[8] Rather, changing attitudes and practices reflect the rapid social transformations accompanying settlement and development in Rendille communities.

According to the "development and modernization" approach to eliminating female "circumcision," as societies experience dramatic social change in the process of development, traditional values erode, and adherence to the practice of "circumcision" declines (see van der Kwaak 1992). What is not clear is how great these social changes need be, or whether educational campaigns are required to initiate a public discourse questioning the value of female "circumcision."

Throughout the Rendille community, the manner in which female "circumcision" is performed departs little from tradition (Table 6.2). In the vast majority of cases, excision is performed by a *kamaratan* at the mother's

Table 6.2   Characteristics of Female Genital Cutting Among the Rendille
            (n = 900)

	%
Type of genital cutting performed	
clitoridectomy	0.0
excision	99.6
infibulation	0.4
Location of the operation	
clinic	0.7
bush	0.7
mother's home	98.6
Training of the circumciser	
traditional circumciser (*kamaratan*)	86.6
traditional birth attendant	12.2
trained nurse	0.2
doctor	0.0

home. Across communities, the prevalence of excision among women ages fifteen and over is very high (97.8 percent), and is universal among ever-married women in all communities except Marsabit (Table 6.3). Although we hypothesized that the practice of female "circumcision" would decline in settled communities, particularly in Marsabit Town and Songa, the practice shows no sign of diminishing in Songa, even in the younger cohort. In Marsabit, however, 5 percent (n = 7) of married women were not "circumcised." All these were Rendille women married to men from an ethnic group that does not circumcise either males or females. Abandonment of female "circumcision" in cases of interethnic marriage has been reported elsewhere (see, for example, Chapter 4 in this volume) and demonstrates the importance of cultural constructs of marriageability in determining whether or not the practice is retained. In communities in which lifestyle changes are so recent, changes in attitude would be expected to herald changes in behavior. Therefore, a more telling indicator might be to consider women's intentions for their daughters. Of women with unmarried daughters, we found that 98 percent intend to "circumcise" their daughters and that the preferred type of "circumcision" is still excision. Together, these findings indicate that, except in cases of interethnic marriage, there appears to be no decline in the demand for traditional excision in settled Rendille communities.

Although the demand for excision remains high, the circumstances surrounding the practice are changing. In settled Rendille communities the tradition of arranged marriage is eroding. As it becomes increasingly common for girls to attend school, a rising number of girls elope without the consent of their families, some without being excised. Whereas male elders express dis-

Table 6.3   Prevalence of Excision Among Rendille Women

	Nomad (%)	Korr (%)	Karare (%)	Songa (%)	Marsabit (%)	Total (%)
All women ages 15–17 (n = 920)	88.8	97.5	98.5	99.1	95.4	97.8
Ever-married women (n = 843)	100	100	100	100	95	99.2

approval of this departure from arranged marriage, women most often tacitly approved, recalling their own unhappiness with this tradition. Commonly recounted were feelings of distress over being forced to marry an old man and becoming separated from their friends. However, men and women alike expressed deep concern over a girl initiating childbearing without being excised. A woman of any age is regarded as a "girl" if uncircumcised and as unable to legitimately bear children. The solution to avoiding childbearing by uncircumcised girls has been to uncouple "circumcision" and marriage. One informant explained: "We now circumcise schoolgirls before they marry so they can go on with their education. . . . At school, a girl may decide to marry without parents' permission. It is bad to go with a husband if you are not circumcised. This mother will bring shame to her family. Somalis circumcise early, and our schoolgirls want to do this also. A girl's blood is shed in her mother's house so she can go on with her education."

Our survey results confirm this trend. Overall, the mean age of "circumcision" is seventeen years and in most cases corresponds to the age of marriage. However, in the most recent generation, "circumcision" is preceding marriage by an average of two years. Additionally, among never-married women, 88 percent (n = 77) were already excised. These unmarried "circumcised" women were all attending school.

The most obvious recent change in the practice of female "circumcision" has been the gradual adoption of medical treatment to prevent infection. Each of the settled communities are served by mission-sponsored dispensaries staffed with trained nurses. These health practitioners have encouraged families to bring girls and boys to the clinic to receive an antitetanus injection and antibiotics the day before being circumcised, and families are instructed to purchase a new sterile razor blade. In focus groups among both married and unmarried men and women, we found a consensus that the health hazards arising from "circumcision," particularly infection and hemorrhage, are considered to be serious problems. Among informants there was a widespread sense that medical interventions have been effective and that further education and certain efforts to minimize the health risks would be welcomed. Although men expressed willingness, even eagerness, to adopt changes that would decrease the pain and health risks associated with excision, women were divided. Most women supported the idea of providing training for traditional circumcisers, but there was considerable debate over other suggested innovations: using anesthesia, decreasing the extent of cutting, employing a trained nurse to perform the excision, and performing the excision at a clinic. The suggestion to stop practicing excision was adamantly opposed by all women. In a discussion among recently married men, one informant was open to this idea but received very little support from other participants:

> HUSBAND 1: We know that women bleed and die. I think we should stop this practice if everybody agrees.
>
> HUSBAND 2: No, if it killed too many women, we would have stopped long ago. Nobody complains much about it, so it is good. To some communities it is bad, but to us it is good.
>
> HUSBAND 3: There is no way to stop female "circumcision," but we can help it. It is our custom, and we cannot abandon it. We can try training circumcisers or going to the clinic, just like with traditional birth attendants and delivering babies.

The rest of the group agreed with this view.

Health Consequences of Excision

A clear understanding of the extent and nature of health consequences of female genital cutting is warranted, since health outcomes form the basis of anticircumcision educational campaigns and inform policy decisionmaking. An enormous body of literature has been devoted to describing the medical consequences of female genital cutting, yet serious gaps in knowledge exist. After extensively reviewing the literature on health outcomes, Carla Obermeyer (1999:92) reported that, in actuality, only eight studies systematically assessed health complications. Attempts have been made to quantify the range and frequency of "circumcision"-related complications from clinic and hospital records (e.g, Aziz 1980; Rushwan 1980; De Silva 1989). However, because these data suffer from selection bias, they need to be interpreted with caution. Women are often reluctant to seek medical attention because of cost, modesty, and in rural settings, inaccessibility of health services. Consequently, complications tend to be reported only if they are severe and prolonged. Furthermore, in some regions such as the Sudan, certain types of genital cutting are illegal, and women hide medical complications for fear of legal repercussions (El Dareer 1982; Toubia 1993).

The best information available on the incidence of various complications comes from a few case-control studies as well as several large-scale popula-

Table 6.4   Percentage of Excised Women Reporting Specific Short-Term
             Complications

Type of Complication	%
Infection	9.9
Pain	9.1
Hemorrhage	8.1
Tetanus	4.2

tion-based surveys, the first of which was conducted by Asma El Dareer
(1982) in northern Sudan. However, self-reported retrospective survey data
also suffer from a number of limitations. Recall error on details surrounding
events that occurred many years ago is inevitable. Moreover, since many
women may have been cut as infants or very young children, it may be impossible to remember immediate adverse health outcomes. Questionnaire design must take into account that informants' concept of illness or abnormality
may be different from that of medical researchers. For example, Hanny Lightfoot-Klein (1989:59) reported that women who claimed to have no difficulty
with urination also indicated that it took up to fifteen minutes to empty their
bladder. This condition was considered normal in a community where all
adult women were infibulated. Self-reported retrospective survey data also
suffer from selection bias in that they are limited to women who survived
genital cutting.

Despite these limitations, survey data currently provide the best information on health risks associated with genital cutting. Unfortunately, the many
reports fail to distinguish between medical complications associated with different types of genital cutting. Furthermore, the conditions under which the
procedures are conducted and the medical support available are not considered.

Data from the Rendille Maternal and Child Demographic and Health Survey allow us to examine the range and frequency of complications associated
with excision. Additionally, we can evaluate the effect of medicalization in reducing these risks. In order to estimate the prevalence of immediate short-term
postcircumcision complications, women were asked whether they experienced
any symptoms within one month of being cut. Overall, 16 percent of women
reported experiencing at least one complication.[9] As set out in Table 6.4, the
most commonly reported condition was general infection (9.9 percent), followed by extreme pain and hemorrhage. In addition, 4.2 percent of respondents specifically reported contracting tetanus following the procedure.

Women were also asked to report chronic long-term health problems. Although a small fraction of women in our study suffered from primary or sec-

Table 6.5   Percent of Procedures Performed with Medical Assistance[a] in Each Community

Nomad	Korr	Karare	Songa	Marsabit	Total
0.0	8.9	16.1	17.4	13.3	12.2

Note: a. Sterile razor, antitetanus injection, and prophylactic antibiotics.

ondary sterility, it is unclear that the cause is excision rather than other factors such as sexually transmitted diseases. None of our respondents reported dermoid cysts or chronic problems with urination or menstruation.

Among all excised women, 12.2 percent received medical assistance in the form of receiving an antitetanus injection, prophylactic antibiotics, and use of a new, sterile razor (Table 6.5) This occurred only in settled communities, all of which are served by dispensaries. To evaluate the effect of medical assistance on the risk of short-term complications, several variables were examined as predictors of complications arising within one month of being excised. These include the use of medical assistance, location of the operation, and community. In a logistic regression analysis (Table 6.6), the use of medical support was found to have a significant effect on the outcome of the operation. Women who received no medical assistance experienced 3.1 times higher risk of developing complications following the procedure. Stated the other way, women who received medical assistance experienced nearly 70 percent lower risk of short-term complications.

For decades debate has continued as to whether excised women experience elevated risk of obstetrical complications (Epelboin and Epelboin 1981). It has been suggested that delayed healing due to infection results in the for-

Table 6.6   Logistic Regression Analysis of Use of Medical Support as a Predictor of Complications Within One Month of Excision

Outcome Variable: Complication[a]

Predictor Variable[b]	Coefficient	Odds Ratio	95 percent CI for Odds Ratio	Excess Risk
Medical Assistance[c]	−1.367	0.321	(−2.149, −0.585)	3.1 percent

Notes: a. No complication was used as reference category.

b. Location of the operation and community were not significant covariates and were removed from the final model.

c. Assistance was used as reference category.

mation of fibrous scar tissue that is nonelastic, contributing to obstructed labor. Tearing of the scar tissue is also reported to result in an elevated risk of hemorrhage (Mustafa 1966; Sami 1986). Among respondents who had at least one live birth, we examined the association between delayed healing due to short-term complications and problems during the last labor and delivery. Overall, 20.4 percent of women reported excessive bleeding following their last labor and delivery, and nearly 40 percent reported prolonged labor. A history of complications following excision was examined as a predictor of prolonged labor (labor lasting more than twenty-four hours) while controlling for other potential causes and confounding factors: maternal age at delivery, parity, short stature (< 150 cm), training of assistant during labor and delivery, location of delivery, and presentation of the baby (breech or normal). None of these factors is a significant predictor of prolonged labor among Rendille women.

We also examined complications during healing from excision as a predictor of excessive bleeding while controlling for other potential causes. The results of a logistic regression analysis (not shown) reveal that breech births are associated with a 6.1 times greater risk of excessive bleeding, whereas short-term postcircumcision complications do not have a significant effect.

These results demonstrate that delayed healing and scarring from excision in this study sample are not associated with the types of complications during labor and delivery commonly found among infibulated women. It may be the case that obstetrical complications, such as tearing and hemorrhage, are more common during first births. Since our study is retrospective, there may be underreporting of complications because of recall bias. Therefore, this issue would be better analyzed through a prospective study of first pregnancies. Our survey did, however, reveal that excision is associated with significant risk of short-term complications, including infection and hemorrhage, particularly when the procedure is performed without preventive medical support. When the excision procedure was performed with sterile cutting instruments, antibiotics, and antitetanus injections, the risk of subsequent complications was substantially reduced.

Conclusion and Policy Implications

The Rendille case illuminates several key issues that arise in debates surrounding the practice of female genital cutting. First, development and social change, at least on the level experienced by the Rendille, do not by themselves lessen the demand for excision. Although the nature and meaning of the practice has changed, the new context of excision does not undermine its importance for Rendille people. Second, excision is not associated with the types of long-term obstetrical complications reported among infibulated women, although it is associated with serious, potentially life-threatening short-term complications. And finally, even minor levels of medical intervention dramatically reduce the risk of developing immediate complications. Given these findings, we must at least consider medicalization as an intermediate solution to improving the health and welfare of women.

Opposition to all forms of medicalization is central in international efforts to eliminate female genital cutting. In 1982, the World Health Organization issued a statement declaring it unethical for female genital cutting to be performed by "any health officials in any setting—including hospitals or other health establishments" (WHO 1982). In 1994, the International Federation of Gynecology and Obstetrics passed a resolution that calls on all doctors to refuse to perform FGM, and the federation was joined by many other major organizations, such as the American College of Obstetricians and Gynecologists, the United Nations International Children's Emergency Fund, and the American Medical Association (ACOG Committee Opinion 1995). Additionally, in response to threats of withholding international aid and World Bank loans, ministries of health in many African countries have issued similar statements.

This staunch opposition to medical intervention rests on one central assumption: that medicalization will counteract efforts to eliminate female genital cutting. This assumption is not based on empirical evidence, however, and deserves critical examination. Our role as scholars is to assess whether (and if so, how) medicalization influences anticircumcision efforts. Regardless of legislation or international opinion, female genital cutting is and will continue to become increasingly medicalized throughout sub-Saharan Africa. Therefore, we must determine whether medicalization is best viewed as one in a series of steps in improving women's health or as an impediment to change.

Among the Rendille, efforts to change the practice must take into account the sociocultural situation in which the people are enmeshed and the socioeconomic hardships that families who try to change the practice would experience. Excision is an integral part of marriage and gender identity. Performed as part of the marriage ceremony, it prepares a bride for her future husband, transforming her from a girl to a woman who is ready to assume the rights and responsibilities of marriage and childbearing. Awareness of the fact that female "circumcision" is associated with adverse health consequences is widespread, yet the Rendille view the risks as worth taking in light of the implications for marriageability. Marriage and children are a central part of a woman's role in society, and not being "circumcised" would define a woman as an outcast and render her unmarriageable. Although women are economically active, participating in livestock production, agriculture, milk marketing, and more recently, wage employment, their cultural identity and economic well-being are embedded in large family production units, in their role as a wife and mother. Men also stress the economic consequences of female "circumcision." A daughter who is not excised is not marriageable, and the family risks losing the large bride wealth and social ties gained through marriage. It may surprise outsiders that genital cutting is not simply imposed on women by men but also perpetuated by women themselves, despite their awareness of the pain and serious health risks involved. However, the motivation for this practice is best understood in terms of its social and economic ramifications for men and women and in terms of its wider cultural meaning. In this case, ritual "circumcision" entwines the issues of gender identity, cultural heritage, marriageability, and socially sanctioned childbearing. Efforts to discourage female "circumcision" will need to consider these issues and help seek alternative solutions to these social concerns.

Until acceptable alternative solutions to female "circumcision" are found, Rendille women are women without choices. A woman who is not excised cannot marry or bear children and is ostracized if she does become pregnant. Yet Rendille society is rapidly undergoing change, and one can hope that the demand for female "circumcision" will decline as educational and economic opportunities improve, particularly for women, and as educational campaigns highlight the disadvantages of excision and encourage members of the community to seek alternative practices. Yet this process is slow, and interim solutions for improving women's health need to be at least considered. In this chapter we have shown that even small steps in improving the septic conditions for excision significantly reduce medical risks for the women involved. If improvement in women's health is truly targeted as a priority, intermediate solutions, including the improvement of medical conditions for female "circumcision," merit careful consideration.

Notes

This research was supported by funding from the Andrew W. Mellon Foundation and the John D. Rockefeller Foundation. Helpful comments on an earlier draft of this paper were given by Dr. Solomon Katz, Dr. Susan Scrimshaw, and Dr. Lynn Thomas. Permission for this research was granted by the Office of the President of Kenya, permit number OP 13/001/25C 282/5. Logistical support in planning this research was kindly provided by Dr. Elliot Fratkin. We wish to thank our team of research assistants, particularly the field managers, Larion and Anna Marie Aliayaro, for their dedication, patience, and humor during data collection. We also thank the many Rendille people who generously shared their time, insights, and opinions. Correspondence may be addressed to the senior author at the University of Washington, Department of Anthropology, Box 353100, Seattle, WA 98195-3100.

Dr. Aziza Kamil, who is quoted at the beginning of the chapter, is the leader of the Cairo Family Planning Association's project on "female genital mutilation" and is quoted in Toubia (1993:16–17).

1. As this manuscript was going to press, a paper by Obermeyer (1999) appeared, making a similar point.

2. This reference was kindly provided by Lynn Thomas: Bancroft Library (Berkeley), 96/49 Fadiman Collection, English translation of M. Pick. (1961). "Il piu grande amico delgli africani, Paolo Chiono medico missionario." E.M.E. Torino.

3. See Obermeyer (1999) for a recent critical review of empirical data supporting or contradicting the assertion that the prevalence of FGC declines with improvements in economic status and female education.

4. In Chapter 13, Gerry Mackie describes a case in which, after community members took a pledge not to circumcise daughters, the practice was eradicated in several Senegalese communities virtually overnight. We would like to stress that efforts preceding the pledge, that is, introducing the concept to a community and obtaining support, will take varying amounts of time in different social settings. In southeastern Nigeria (described in Chapter 4 of this volume), this process may be rapid since marriageability is the main factor blocking elimination of the practice of female "circumcision." Among the Rendille (described later in this chapter), the notion of abandoning the practice was deemed entirely unacceptable by most informants. Clearly, change efforts could take much more time in this community.

5. Classification of economic status (poor versus not poor) is a relative measure in each community, based on livestock holdings (total livestock units), garden size, and other income sources.

6. Traditionally, bride wealth among the Rendille is fixed at eight camels, but this can be paid over many years. According to Beaman (1981), usually no more than half of the bride wealth is paid at one time. There is more variability in the amount and form of bride wealth payments in the settlements, particularly when the bride elopes.

7. In Chapter 13, Mackie emphasizes the importance of recognizing the link between female genital cutting and marriageability and argues that eradication efforts must assist in developing a forum in which uncircumcised women retain marriageability.

8. Although central Kenya has a long history of anticircumcision campaigns (see Chapter 7 of this volume), the remote Rendille community has not yet been targeted in these campaigns. According to Kratz (1994:342), "In Kenya . . . debates about circumcision began almost as soon as missionaries arrived, and were framed within the question of whether (and which) local customs violated standards of Christian behavior and had to be condemned and eliminated." In the 1920s and 1930s, moral arguments gave way to medical arguments, and a health approach is still emphasized in current campaigns. For example, the Kenyan women's group Maendeleo ya Wanawake Organization is distributing pamphlets to schoolgirls entitled "The Dangers of Female Circumcision: Female Circumcision Is Harmful to Women's Health." Therefore, it is of interest to determine whether the health message delivered will ring true when it eventually reaches Rendille communities.

9. In an attempt to estimate the degree of recall error in reporting complications, we compared the frequency of reported complications among women "circumcised" within the past ten, fifteen, and twenty years. Not surprisingly, the frequency of reported complications declines with time lapsed since "circumcision." Therefore, these figures reflect underreporting at an estimated rate of 6–10 percent.

7

"*Ngaitana* (I Will Circumcise Myself)": Lessons from Colonial Campaigns to Ban Excision in Meru, Kenya

Lynn Thomas

Those of the iron-wedge knife (ciorunya)*, stay at the side, you.*
Do not abuse those of the razor blade (ciokaembe)*, you.*
A circumcised girl without water in the stomach when guarded by the
  Government.
A circumcised girl without water in the stomach when guarded by the
  Government

—Veronica Kinaito

In the mid-1950s, recently excised girls in Meru, an administrative district on the northeastern slopes of Mt. Kenya, sang this song as they performed punitive hard labor for defying a ban on clitoridectomy. The Njuri Ncheke of Meru, an officially sanctioned local council of male leaders, unanimously banned clitoridectomy in April 1956. Today, people in Meru recount how news and defiance of the ban spread quickly and widely. Former Chief M'Anampiu of Mikinduri remembered returning in the evening from the Njuri Ncheke council meeting, only to find that "all the girls had been circumcised" (interview, May 10, 1995). In the three years following the passage of the ban, more than 2,400 girls, men, and women were charged in African courts with defying the Njuri's order.[1] Interviews suggest that thousands of others who defied the ban paid fines to local Njuri councils and headmen.

As adolescent girls defied the ban by attempting to excise each other, their initiations marked a profound departure from the past. They also differed from earlier practices by forgoing the preparations and celebrations associated with initiation and the instruments typically used. Although *atani* (singular *mutani*), the older women specialists who performed excisions, had previously used special triangular iron-wedge knives, *irunya* (singular *kirunya*), these girls of the mid-1950s simply used razor blades purchased at local shops. These departures caused some from Meru, both then and now, to doubt the legitimacy of these initiations (interview, Celina Kiruki, June 30, 1995; University of Nairobi presentation, November 8, 1995). The song is, in part, an appeal by these girls to older age grades, "those of the iron-wedge knife," to stop abusing them and to recognize their initiation as proper. Similarly, the Meru name—*Ngaitana*, "I will circumcise myself"—given to these girls by older men and women mocks the girls' determination and highlights these elders' sense of the absurdity of their undertaking. Today, mention of the name in Meru draws chuckles or, on occasion, head-shakes of knowing disapproval from those who can recall the time of *Ngaitana*. For those younger than forty-five years of age, however, the name most often elicits perplexed faces and queries.

The song and the name of *Ngaitana* also suggest the political exigencies of the mid-1950s, namely the Mau Mau rebellion and ensuing State of Emergency. Although the ability to remain calm and brave—"without water in the stomach"—when being detained in a headman's camp or police station would have been a feat for an adolescent girl at almost any time during the twentieth century, such courage took on special significance during the Mau Mau rebellion, when Africans were often tortured or killed by government personnel. The name *Ngaitana* also conveys many adults' reluctance to defy the ban for fear that their homes would be burnt or that they would be fined or imprisoned. In the face of parents and *atani* who refused to assist them, some members of *Ngaitana* apparently proclaimed, "I will circumcise myself." Others who received assistance from parents or *atani* refused to implicate their co-conspirators, claiming before headmen and African court personnel that they had "circumcised themselves."

Current international debates about female genital cutting originated during conferences organized as part of the United Nations Decade for Women (1975–1985). Deploying the term "female genital mutilation," some feminists such as Fran Hosken (1993) denounced these practices, claiming that they ravaged women's health and underpinned patriarchal structures. Mary Daly (1978) posited these practices as one instance of the "Sado-Ritual Syndrome" structuring "planetary patriarchy." Human rights activists (e.g., McLean 1980) and feminist medical doctors Nawal El Saadawi (1980) and Asma El Dareer (1982) exposed female genital cutting as medically dangerous practices intended, among other things, to control female sexuality. At international conferences, however, some African women protested these calls for eradication as a neocolonial intrusion that drew attention away from more pressing development issues (Dorkenoo 1994:62–63). Anthropologists accused by Hosken and Daly of a "patriarchal cover-up" (Lyons 1981:500) responded by drawing attention to the racist underpinnings of earlier campaigns against both male and female circumcision and by elaborating how processes surrounding female genital cutting often are "the primary context in which women come together as a group, constituting a ritual community and a forum for social critique" (Kratz 1994:347). Drawing on poststructuralist theory, others criticized eradicationists for their discursive construction of a decontextualized, passive, and oppressed "third world woman" (Kirby 1987; Hale 1994). Eradicationists responded to these critiques by strengthening networks with African women's and health organizations engaged in anticircumcision campaigns (Koso-Thomas, 1987; Dorkenoo, 1994). The controversy continues in Europe and North America today as debate turns to the threat of female genital cutting as grounds for political asylum and the legality of these practices among African immigrant populations.

A historical analysis of the 1956 ban in Meru demonstrates the limitations of universalist discourses of sexual oppression, human rights, and women's health as well as poststructuralist deference to "the Other" for an understanding of the social complexities of female genital cutting. Whereas the international controversy has largely cast girls and women as victims, examination of adolescent girls' efforts to excise each other situates girls and women as central actors. Patriarchy, "the manifestation and institutionalization of male dominance over women and children in the family and the extension of male dominance over women in society in general" (Lerner 1986:239), clearly structured familial and community relations in 1950s Meru. Yet to reduce adolescent girls' belief that excision would transform them into adult women to patriarchal conspiracy would be to ignore how the institution of female initiation regulated relations among women as well as between men and women. Observers of female initiation have long noted that girls and women tend to defend the institution more vigorously than their male counterparts. Colonial officials and missionaries attributed female adherence to female genital cutting to the inherent "conservatism" of women, but contemporary anthropologist Janice Boddy (1989:319), more insightfully, has explained such adherence as women's efforts to preserve "bargaining tools with which to negotiate subaltern status and enforce their complementarity with men." In Meru in the 1950s, where adolescent initiation of males and females constituted the pivotal moment in the construction of an influential age grade system, female defense of excision must also be viewed as an effort to maintain processes that differentiated females of various ages (see also Bledsoe 1984; Robertson 1996). Initiation transformed girls into women and mothers of initiates into figures of authority within the community. Evidence suggests that although members of *Ngaitana* associated female initiation with the disciplining of sexual desires as well as notions of fertility and cleanliness, they did not fully anticipate the physical severity of excision. The reluctance of older age grades to accept *Ngaitana* initiation as legitimate thus added insult to injury.

Earlier Efforts to Regulate Excision in
Central Kenya, 1920s–1950s

As early as 1906, Protestant missionaries, the most vocal European opponents of excision, denounced the practice as "barbaric." During the 1920s, as their medical work expanded and cultural relativist thought gained influence in colonial circles, these missionaries began to ground their opposition to excision in health concerns instead of accusations of "barbarity." They argued that scar tissue resulting from excision lead to impaired urination, menstruation, intercourse, and, most importantly, complications during childbirth. Although some physicians in Kenya doubted that the ill effects of excision were so severe, the moral force of mission critiques captured official attention.[2] Moreover, opposition to excision grounded in arguments about infant and maternal mortality resonated with colonial officials' concern over low population growth rates in East Africa prior to World War II (Thomas 1997:chap. 3).

In 1925 and 1927, administrators in Nairobi encouraged local native councils, bodies of elected and appointed African men presided over by a British district commissioner with veto powers, to pass resolutions restricting excision. The Meru Local Native Council complied, passing resolutions prohibiting excision without a girl's consent, limiting the severity of the "operation," and requiring the registration of all female circumcisers.[3] These resolutions proved largely ineffectual. As one administrator noted, "public opinion does not seem to be in sympathy with the cause" (Murray 1974:114). Believing that excision, as part of female initiation, transformed girls into women, most Africans ignored the resolutions. According to E. Mary Holding (1942), a British Methodist missionary with anthropological training, people in Meru viewed female initiation as preparation for marriage and procreation: it marked the end of sexual freedom, affirmed parental authority and filial duty, protected one against the dangers of sexual intercourse, and ensured fertility as well as ancestral blessings.

The years 1929 to 1931 mark what has been termed within Kenyan historiography as the "female circumcision controversy." During this period, Protestant missionaries engaged London-based humanitarian and feminist groups in their campaign. Female parliamentarians and women's rights organizations argued before the House of Commons that excision should be banned because of the dangers it posed to infants and mothers during childbirth (Pedersen 1991). Within Kenya, renunciation of female initiation became the subject of declarations of Christian loyalty at Protestant mission stations, whereas support of the practice became a platform issue for the Kikuyu Central Association. The Methodist Church of Meru, for example, instituted a loyalty declaration in early 1930; within weeks their membership dropped from seventy to six (Nthamburi 1982). Popular protest against the missionaries' antiexcision campaigns spread with young men's and women's performance of *Muthirigu*, a dance-song that chastised missionaries, government officers, and African elders by name for corrupting custom, seducing young women, and stealing land. Although the Nairobi administration moved quickly to ban performance of this critique of colonial authority, they were reluctant to enact colonywide antiexcision measures (Murray 1974). Intervention, though, continued at the local level.

Considered to be on the political margins of central Kenya, local native councils in Meru and Embu Districts passed further resolutions in 1931–1932, restricting the severity of the "operation" and providing instruction for circumcisers in the newly authorized procedures.[4] The impact of these measures varied. District Commissioner H. E. Lambert recorded personally instructing the "operators" in the new procedures, and his wife remembered, when interviewed in 1969, that she used to "inspect" recently initiated girls to determine whether they had been cut in accordance with the local native council regulations.[5] Other sources suggest that Methodist missionaries also participated in these efforts to modify and medicalize the practice. In 1931, the Kenyan director of medical services assured a Methodist doctor in Meru that it would not be a breach of medical ethics to either instruct circumcisers in less severe forms of excision or lend them scalpels to perform the procedure (on medicalization elsewhere, see Gwako 1995; Bell 1998; and Chapters 4, 5, and 6 in this volume).[6] Interviewees Esther M'Ithinji and Julia Simion (interview, October 14, 1990) recalled how, in the late 1930s and early 1940s, *atani* carried permits on their walking sticks certifying that they had undergone an official training. Methodist missionaries, however, recorded witnessing the illegal and more severe form of excision in 1938 and 1939.[7]

In an effort to eradicate the "widespread" practice of preinitiation abortion, administrators in Meru also worked to lower the age of female initiation. Officers attributed the apparently high prevalence of abortion in Meru to the late age at which excision took place. Whereas elsewhere in central Kenya, female initiation took place prior to puberty, in Meru it was a prenuptial rite. Officers observed that as "custom" prohibited uninitiated females from bearing children, unexcised girls who became pregnant most often obtained abortions. To eliminate the possibility of a girl being sexually mature but unexcised, administrators enforced measures requiring girls to be excised before puberty. Under the supervision of government police and without any warning, prepubescent girls were rounded up and excised en masse. These measures clearly contravened central government policy of refusing to condone— let alone enforce—any form of excision (Thomas 1998).

During the early years of the Mau Mau rebellion, administrators in Meru restricted initiation ceremonies and in some cases required that "fees" of five shillings or fifty rat tails—in contribution to public health campaigns—be paid (interview, Tarsila Nikobwe and Margaret Mwakinia, September 20,

1990). Between the 1920s and 1950s, the timing and form of initiation under-went significant change. Not only did most initiations occur at puberty rather than just prior to marriage, but few initiates chose to have abdominal tattoo-ing (*ncuru*) performed or large earholes pierced. But apart from a few dozen girls from strong Christian families, girls in post–World War II Meru antici-pated excision as the transformative moment in their passage to womanhood.

Passing the Ban

Documentary evidence suggests it was District Commissioner J. A. Cumber who first introduced the topic of a ban on excision at a meeting of the Meru African District Council (formerly, the local native council) in March 1956. He opened the meeting by stating how the governor's recent decision to cre-ate a Meru Land Unit, apart from the Kikuyu Land Unit, meant that the "Meru people had now gained independence from the Kikuyu." He proceeded to suggest two measures by which the Meru African District Council could express its appreciation and affirm its cooperation with the government: the introduction of a coffee tax and a prohibition on female "circumcision." Cum-ber contended that in passing such a ban, "the Meru would be setting a good example to other Tribes in Kenya who persist in the enforcement of this iniq-uitous Tribal Tradition." Later in the meeting, the medical officer of health explained how he could not, in good conscience, follow the 1931 resolution and provide permits to circumcisers because none of them practiced the oper-ation in a clean and hygienic manner. The medical officer proposed that boys should be circumcised between the ages of six months to one year instead of at adolescence, and female "circumcision" should be abandoned entirely be-cause it resulted in complications during childbirth.[8] Reportedly, the council "wholeheartedly welcomed the suggestion" regarding female initiation and referred the matter to the Njuri Ncheke for a final decision. The following month, the Njuri Ncheke issued an edict forbidding excision within Meru, and the African district council passed a by-law endorsing it.[9]

Although District Commissioner Cumber strongly supported the ban, provincial and central government officials raised serious doubts about it. Provincial Commissioner Lloyd pressured the Meru African District Council and the Njuri Ncheke to exempt the more "backward" locations of the district from the ban. The central government also prohibited the ban from being pub-licized in either the vernacular press or Meru language broadcasts for fear that it would incite further unrest in areas of Mau Mau activity.[10]

Oral sources cast doubt as to whether male leaders supported the ban as uniformly as expressed in official reports and suggested by the Njuri Ncheke's unanimous vote at Nchiru. On the one hand, former Senior Chief Naaman M'Mwirichia (interview, September 18, 1995), a former Methodist teacher and member of Njuri Ncheke who worked very closely with colonial officers and missionaries, contended that the Njuri Ncheke strongly supported the ban. Similarly, former Chief Daniel M'Iringo (interview, June 25, 1995) recalled favoring the ban after hearing a presentation by a British medical doctor on the dangers of excision. But former Chief M'Anampiu (interview, May 10, 1995) and former Subarea Headman David M'Naikiuru remembered that many at Nchiru disagreed with the ban. M'Naikiuru explained:

> You know, it was during the bad times of the Emergency. No one could argue with the authority then. Because the rule came through the District Commissioner to Njuri, they [Njuri Ncheke] could not oppose it. . . . In my opinion, they decided to ban it during Emergency because they thought, then, no one would go against it. (interview, April 29, 1995)

A letter complaining of the ban, written by Gerald Casey, a white settler from a nearby area, to Member of Parliament (MP) Barbara Castle corroborates the Njuri Ncheke's ambivalent position. Casey wrote, "The ordinary tribesmen I talk to say: 'It is not our will. If we ask the *Njuri* they say it comes from the Government. If we ask the District Commissioner he says it comes from the *Njuri*.'"[11] Casey also claimed that African mission adherents working for the government, if not European missionaries themselves, played central roles in the orchestration of the ban.

> I would agree that it [the ban] may represent the will of the Government servants and mission-influenced Africans who are a minority and separated by a psychological gulf from the more primitive and illiterate tribesmen. I was assured by officers of the administration that the missions have taken no part in the matter. The ordinary tribesman tells me the missions have very much to do with it but keep in the background. It is at least certain that the great majority of Africans holding any position of authority in the Reserve are mission-trained and under strong missionary influence.[12]

Corroborating Casey's assertion, interviewees with the closest ties to the Methodist mission station, Stanley Kathurima and Naaman M'Mwirichia, expressed the strongest support for the ban. As Methodist mission–educated young men in the 1950s, Kathurima and M'Mwirichia served, respectively, as secretary of the Njuri Ncheke and as a headman and played crucial roles in the formulation of the ban. Although no documentary evidence yet reveals the direct involvement of missionaries in the formulation of the prohibition, they could not have been far removed from official discussions. Although Presbyterian and Methodist missionaries had both long been interested in the elimination of excision, the Presbyterians maintained a more strident position than the Methodists, expelling all schoolgirls who underwent initiation (Macpherson 1970; Nthamburi 1982). In 1953, Clive Irvine of the Presbyterian hospital at Chogoria undertook his own initiative against excision, only to provoke, in the words of the district commissioner, "a violent re-action in the Reserves."[13] And in 1955, Irvine argued against the administrative policy that all government employees become members of the Njuri Ncheke on the grounds that the Njuri Ncheke still condoned the practice of excision.[14] When the Njuri Ncheke passed the ban in 1956, the Presbyterian and Methodist mission societies received the news with prompt congratulations.[15]

Women's voices were notably, if not surprisingly, absent from the passage of the 1956 ban. An ethnographic account written by Methodist missionary E. Mary Holding (1942), who had worked in Meru for seven years, recognized female initiation in Meru as an affair of women. Holding stated that women's councils, namely *kiama gia ntonye* (the council of entering), organized the preparation, celebration, and seclusion that comprised female initiation. Female initiation, according to Holding, not only remade girls into women, it transformed adult women into figures of authority within the community. Only a woman whose eldest child was ready for "circumcision" could gain admittance to *kiama gia ntonye* and thus a "position of authority within the tribe." By the time of the Mau Mau rebellion, the presence of women's councils, as described by Holding, had begun to fade in most parts of Meru District. Nonetheless, as defiance of the ban demonstrated, female initiation was still the women's concern and did not easily fall within the purview of the all-male Njuri Ncheke.

The African district council, unlike the Njuri Ncheke, was not an all-male institution in 1956. In line with post–World War II policies to broaden and professionalize the group of Africans engaged in administrative rule, officials in Meru appointed the first woman councilor in 1951. Martha Kanini of Chogoria joined the council at the age of twenty-six years, after completing a year of study at Makerere University. She was, most likely, among the first women from Chogoria not to be initiated. Kanini remembered how the district commissioner asked her not to participate in discussion of the ban.

> I was there alone [the only woman] and I did not even speak, the District Commissioner told me not to speak. . . . He wanted men to discuss it. Because I am concerned, I should keep quiet. . . . So long as I felt it was for their [women's] benefit, I had to keep quiet, to hear what men say. (interview, September 16, 1995)

Although Kanini recalled being present but silent at the meeting when the ban was proposed, the minutes of the two meetings at which the ban was formulated record Kanini as absent with apologies.[16] In asking Kanini either to remain silent or to refrain from attending the meetings, the district commissioner sought to place the banning of excision within the control of men.

Defying the Ban

Most adolescent girls responded to the 1956 ban on excision by defying it. Following the Njuri Ncheke meeting at Nchiru, headmen held *baraza*s (meetings) to inform people of the ban. Former Chief M'Anampiu's recollection that girls had begun to "circumcise themselves" even before he returned from Nchiru suggests that news of the ban, in some places, preceded such meetings (interview, May 10, 1995). Caroline Kirote remembers that, in Mitunguu, girls purchased razor blades and went to the bush to "circumcise each other" while their parents sat listening to the headman announce the ban (interview, June 9, 1995). Though women of the *Ngaitana* age grade recollect, in vivid detail, their defiance of the ban, few can recount the official reasons given for the passage of the ban or remember their defiance as having any connection to the Mau Mau rebellion. Between 1956 and 1959, *Ngaitana* spread from one area of the district to another. Most areas of the district experienced two or three separate episodes or "waves" of girls, of increasingly younger ages, "circumcising themselves." Charity Tirindi, of the second "wave," remembers how *Ngaitana* came to her home area of Mwichiune: "It began from Igoji [to the south] and then went to Mwiriga Mieru [to the north] so we were left in the middle alone. They used to call us cowards, abusing us, and calling us *nkenye* (uncircumcised girls) so we sat down and we decided how we will circumcise ourselves" (interview, February 10, 1995). This statement reveals how groups of recently excised girls exerted peer pressure—often expressed in song—on unexcised girls in other parts of the district to join *Ngaitana*. The first members of *Ngaitana* were probably thirteen to fourteen years old, the proper age for female initiation in the 1950s, but as the practice spread the age of initiates decreased to eight years old or younger.[17] Very few resisted *Ngaitana*. Elizabeth Muthuuri, the first girl in the Methodist schools to attain a standard seven[18] education in 1945, stated that schoolgirls did not participate in *Ngaitana* (interview, January 3, 1995). Although some school girls and their families, such as Martha Kanini, had repudiated clitoridectomy by 1956, other interviews suggest that such people were a small minority.

Ngaitana initiations were a marked departure from most previous female initiations in Meru. First of all, they took place secretly, in the bush, forest, or maize fields. In the past, girls were initiated in large open fields, surrounded by crowds of women and peering children. Initiation in the bush was reserved for those who became pregnant before they were excised. *Ngaitana* initiations also lacked the attendant ceremonies and celebrations. In the 1920s, female initiation ideally spanned three or four years, with an initiate having her ears pierced the first year, abdominal tattooing performed the next, and excision done the following year. Feasts and dances accompanied these physical procedures. A several-month seclusion followed, during which older women fed recent initiates large amounts of food and taught them how to behave like women. Initiates emerged from seclusion to travel to their new matrimonial homes. By the 1950s, female initiation had become a prepubescent rather than prenuptial rite, and practices such as abdominal tattooing and prolonged periods of seclusion had faded, but people in Meru remember *Ngaitana* as a time of profound change when female initiation was driven "underground," stripped of its attendant celebrations and teachings, and reduced to the clandestine performance of excision (interviews with Moses M'Mukindia, January 11, 1995; Jacobu M'Lithara, February 6, 1995; Isabella Ncence, October 19, 1990; Margaret M'Ithinji, October 17, 1990; Elizabeth Kiogora, October 18, 1990; Charity Tirindi, February 10, 1995; Caroline Kirote, June 9, 1995; Agnes Kirimi, June 12, 1995).

Moreover, *atani*, the older women who formerly practiced excision, performed few of the initial *Ngaitana* procedures. A Methodist missionary working in Meru at the time wrote that *Ngaitana* went "against all previous custom, some circumcised themselves, others one another and others were circumcised by their own mothers."[19] Charity Tirindi (interview, February 10, 1995), Caroline Kirote (interview, June 9, 1995), and Agnes Kirimi (interview, June 12, 1995) remembered how girls in groups of three to twenty excised each other and, later, when healing at home, were examined by *atani* and, if necessary, cut again. Isabel Kaimuri of Giantune recounted that she excised her own daughter (interview, March 20, 1995). Isabella Kajuju, who became a *mutani*, recalled that she first performed excision during *Ngaitana* when the experienced *mutani*, fearing prosecution, failed to come to excise Kajuju's niece and others (interview, March 20, 1995). In some cases, *atani* participated clandestinely in the initial cutting. Evangeline M'Iringo remembered that while she and her age mates had wondered how they would be able to "circumcise themselves," when they arrived in the forest, they found a *mutani* waiting for them (interview, March 16, 1995).

The form of excision performed during *Ngaitana* also differed from previous initiations. In 1957, the governor of Kenya reported the findings of a medical officer in Meru to the secretary of state for the colonies.

> He [a Medical Officer in Meru] has examined girls who have been circumcised by friends, from which it is obvious that they have no idea what female circumcision entails. Most are content to make simple incisions on either side of the vulva or through the skin only on the labia majora. . . . He has never seen a clitoris removed, which is the object of female circumcision when performed by a professional. The only damage done in cases he has examined has been some bleeding and occasionally secondary infection, but this is surprisingly rare, and of course pain and discomfort vary with the size of the incision. In his opinion such damage would not compare with the actual removal of the clitoris as performed by professional circumcisers.[20]

Although the medical officer attributed the less severe forms of cutting he viewed to girls' ignorance of the previous practice, *Ngaitana* members may also have been unwilling or unable to perform excision. Agnes Kirimi recounted how members of her *Ngaitana* cohort were unable to finish the operation themselves: "we could not complete, we just tried a little by cutting just the clitoris. . . . There was this other part, the remaining part to be circumcised and we did not know. None of us knew to that extent. . . . When they [our mothers] saw we had already tried, they decided to do the finishing" (interview, June 12, 1995). The amount of cutting done by the initiates may also have been determined by the instruments they used. Whereas *atani* possessed iron-wedge knives, members of *Ngaitana* only had access to razor blades. Monica Kanana recounted that the *Ngaitana* operations were less severe because of the fragility of razor blades. Kanana also recalled her mother requesting her aunt to perform a less severe form of excision on Kanana and her cohort because of their unusually young age (interview, March 23, 1995).

People were reluctant to accept the excisions that *Ngaitana* members performed on one another as proper female initiation. Celina Kiruki, who was initiated in the late 1940s, claimed that *Ngaitana* had "spoiled" female initiation by omitting the meaningful teachings and celebrations and reducing it to the cutting (interview, June 30, 1995). Members of *Ngaitana* challenged processual understandings of female initiation by positing clitoridectomy as the crux of the matter. The incisions that they performed on one another, though, revealed that they did not understand or accept what excision entailed. The second set of cutting that *atani* performed on *Ngaitana* members appears to be an effort to complete the procedure and to reassert older women's control over the process of transforming girls into women.

Drawing on their interpretations of the Mau Mau rebellion in Meru, officials explained defiance of the ban as a conflict between young and old men. In 1957, District Commissioner Cumber wrote, "It is considered that this recurrence of female circumcision is attributable to the activities of the young men, many of whom resent the varying degree of control exercised by the *Njuri* elders."[21] Similarly, before a meeting of the Njuri Ncheke, Cumber claimed that young men were encouraging girls to "circumcise themselves" so as to undermine the authority of the Njuri Ncheke.[22] Young men were a potent source of colonial anxiety during the mid-1950s. Colonial officers and Methodist missionaries in Meru established a "Youth Training Centre" to turn young men into "responsible citizens," "develop their characters," and "instill a respect for discipline and agricultural work."[23] Most young men in Meru probably did oppose the ban. According to Charity Tirindi, even educated men in the 1950s refused to marry unexcised women (interview, February 10, 1995). No evidence suggests, though, that they organized defiance of the ban. In situating young men as the "real force" behind *Ngaitana*, Cumber upheld a long tradition of colonial officers interpreting female political protest as male-instigated.

Njuri Ncheke members cited ethnic and gender as well as generational insurrection in explaining defiance of the ban before District Commissioner Cumber. Using the meeting, in part, as another opportunity to denounce their political rival within central Kenya, they claimed that it was people of "non-Meru origin," presumably "Kikuyus," who were encouraging excision. Moreover, they contended that the "tendency had sprung up recently among the women and among the government officials to disregard the *Njuri*'s authority and its existence." Turning Cumber's critique of young African men around, Njuri members denounced the insolence of Cumber's junior officers, many of whom were more skeptical than the district commissioner of the Njuri Ncheke's political worth. Njuri members also identified the prime organizers of *Ngaitana*—women.[24]

Although most men favored excision, interviewees suggested that young women, mothers, and grandmothers were the organizers of *Ngaitana*. Monica Kanana recalled how she and her age mates were "beaten thoroughly" by the first group of *Ngaitana* until they too decided to "circumcise themselves" (interview, March 23, 1995). Agnes Kirimi attributed her decision to join *Ngaitana* to her grandmother: "I remember why I got motivated. It's because my grandmother used to tell me, 'you're left here alone with your dirt.' . . . You see the grandmothers were the motivators" (interview, June 12, 1995).[25] Grandmothers' stronger advocacy for excision than mothers was attributable to the historical role that older women played as the organizers of initiation as well as to the special relationship that existed between grandparents and grandchildren, enabling them to discuss intimate topics considered inappropriate for discussions between parents and children (Holding 1942; see also Nypan 1991:54–55). In households in which parents had differing opinions on the ban, mothers most often favored excision. The fathers of both Monica Kanana and Lucy Kajuju were home guards who supported the ban. Kanana (interview, March 23, 1995) remembered her father beating her mother after he learned of her initiation, and Kajuju (interview, March 23, 1995) recalled how her mother fled following her initiation to escape her father's anger. Former District Officer Richard Cashmore recounted older women protesting the ban outside his office in Chuka. Reiterating many themes of the dance-song *Muthirigu* performed during the 1929–1931 controversy, these women sang of the ban as a government plot to make young women infertile, eliminate the "Meru tribe," and steal their land (interview, December 6, 1995).

For adolescent girls, though, *Ngaitana* was about more than maintaining a valued practice. It became a test and demonstration of their strength and determination as an age grade. Amid people being forced to live in "villages," detained and tortured in prisons, and killed in the forest, adolescent girls too confronted the colonial state. Caroline Kirote recalled how her *Ngaitana* group, on their way to turn themselves in at the headman's camp, feared the worst: "If it happened that we would be wiped out, girls would be wiped out together . . . you know because of the way the Government carried out executions at that time" (interview, June 9, 1995). Many interviewees contended that the ban encouraged rather than deterred excision. Former Subarea Headman David M'Naikiuru recalled: "Were it not for the ban they would not have circumcised such a large number because Christianity was spreading rapidly" (interview, April 29, 1995). Similarly, recollections by Monica Kanana (interview, March 23, 1995) and Charity Tirindi (interview, February 10, 1995) of being taunted and beaten by older *Ngaitana* to join their ranks suggest how *Ngaitana* became a movement, gathering even unsuspecting girls to its cause.

Although nearly all interviewees, when asked specifically, denied any direct connection between defiance of the 1956 ban and the Mau Mau rebellion, broader evidence suggests parallels, if not connections, between these two struggles. Those social groups that most vigorously participated in and supported Mau Mau—young people and women—(Kamunchuluh 1975; Kanogo 1987; White 1990; Presley 1992) were most open in their opposition to the 1956 ban. Official documents suggest that in Meru "the unmarried girl class" was particularly active in supporting Mau Mau.[26] Charity Tirindi illustrated how Mau Mau fighters themselves opposed the ban by recounting a gruesome tale of forcible excisions: "If you were not circumcised, they [Mau Mau fighters] came for you at night, you [we]re taken to the forest [and] circumcised, and you [we]re roasted for what you have been circumcised [the clitoris] and you are told to eat it" (interview, February 10, 1995). Those who supported the ban, at least publicly—strong mission adherents and male elders serving as African district council and Njuri Ncheke members, headmen, and home guards—ranked as government loyalists during the Mau Mau rebellion. Furthermore, the punishment for those who defied the ban mirrored, in part, punishments meted out to those who had taken the Mau Mau oath, with home guards rounding up suspects, burning their homes and confiscating livestock, and detaining them in headmen's camps. Veronica Kinaito recounted a song performed by her *Ngaitana* group in which they compared their one-month detention in a headmen's camp to young men's imprisonment at Manyani, the main camp for Mau Mau detainees (interview, July 5, 1995).

Enforcing the Ban

Enforcement of the ban on excision varied tremendously over its three-year duration (1956–1959) and from one area of Meru to another. In "backward" areas of the District such as Tharaka, the ban was not enforced. In other areas such as Igembe, Tigania, and North and South Imenti, *Ngaitana* cases consumed the attention of district officers, headmen, home guards, Njuri mem-

bers, and African court staff for months on end. Although all suspected trans-
gressors were supposed to be charged before African courts with contraven-
ing the Njuri's order authorized under section 17(a) of the African Courts Or-
dinance 65/51, oral evidence suggests that headmen and home guards often
contravened official policy, imposing and collecting fines themselves without
forwarding cases to the African court. Of the 2,400 individuals charged before
African courts, fathers of initiates accounted for approximately 43 percent of
those accused; initiates, 33 percent; mothers of initiates, 20 percent; and circumcisers, 3 percent.[27] Fines ranged from 50 to 400 shillings and sentences
from one month in detention camp to six months without hard labor, depending on the accused's wealth and status. Settler Casey explained the scale of
these fines: "My shepherd earns Shs. 50/- a month cash wage. He will have to
work eight months to realize Shs. 400/-. He is one of the lucky ones. Very few
old men earn half as much as he does. Some would have to work eighteen
months to two years to find the money." One district officer reportedly remarked that the African courts were "making more [money] out of it [*Ngaitana* fines] than out of all the rates put together."[28] Thousands of others paid
fines outside the African courts.

The swiftness of girls' response to the ban appears to have caught administrators unprepared. The first group of *Ngaitana* in North Imenti apparently
paid no fine. Former Chief M'Anampiu recalled sending home all the girls
whom he met on his return from Nchiru and later fining their fathers (interview, May 10, 1995). Former Home Guard Moses M'Mukindia remembered
arresting initiates as they came from the forest and taking them to the Meru
Civil Hospital to be examined by a British medical officer (interview, January
11, 1995). At Ntakira, Monica Kanana recounted how home guards burnt the
homes of an early *Ngaitana* group found healing in seclusion (interview,
March 23, 1995). Later cohorts, fearing that such punishment would be inflicted on their homes, turned themselves in at headmen's camps. Charity
Tirindi recounted why her group presented themselves for arrest: "We had
heard that those who were caught from Igoji were beaten so we might make
ourselves to be beaten for no good reason [unnecessarily] so we decided to
take ourselves" (interview, February 10, 1995).

The walk to the headman's camp, according to Monica Kanana, was not
easy as girls tried to keep their legs apart and their heads shrouded in cloths.
Upon their arrival, *Ngaitana* members responded to home guards' and headmen's queries by claiming that they had "circumcised themselves." They remained in headmen's camps from a few days to a few weeks, until their parents paid their fines. During their stay, they ate food brought by their mothers
and slept in simple shelters or on dried banana leaves. Caroline Kirote (interview, June 9, 1995) and Evangeline M'Iringo (interview, March 16, 1995) remembered that at times the camps were filled with 100 or more girls.

Headmen and home guards along with local Njuri members, who served as judicial councilors within headmen's camps, consumed all the livestock paid in fines. Fines paid varied across time and from one individual to the next. Lucy Kajuju recounted that as a headman, her father was forced to pay a double fine of two bulls and two male goats (interview, March 23, 1995). Evangeline M'Iringo recalled that she and her sister decided to be excised together, even though they were five years apart in age, so their parents would have to pay only a single goat (interview, March 16, 1995). Former Subarea Headman David M'Naikiuru remembered a gradual decrease in the fines charged: "They started with imprisoning and destroying the houses, they went down to fining cows. . . . As the number of circumcised girls increased they saw the bulls that were supposed to be eaten were too many so they started fining goats" (interview, April 29, 1995).

Fines in kind were not the only punishment meted out in headmen's camps. Many *Ngaitana* members, after healing, performed several weeks of punitive manual labor ranging from digging roads and drainage trenches to planting trees and clearing weeds to plastering floors in home guard houses. In some areas of the district, punishment involved attendance at Maendeleo ya Wanawake, state-sponsored women's groups that taught the values and practices of caring for the home (Wipper 1975–1976). A Methodist missionary recorded that most headmen regarded participation in Maendeleo ya Wanawake as a privilege and therefore, as punishment, forbade *Ngaitana* members from attending meetings for seven to ten weeks. One Christian headman, viewing such meetings as rehabilitation, insisted that "all these girls should attend classes instead of doing manual work for the location."[29] Defiance and enforcement of the ban also became entangled with sexual and marital access to initiates. Caroline Kirote recalled the following song, chastising a headman named M'Mbuju for enforcing the ban and proclaiming that he would never have sex with—"cover"—a member of *Ngaitana*:

> Yes, yes, M'Mbuju, you will die before you cover a circumcised girl.
> Yes, yes, M'Mbuju, circumcised girls have been made to dig up a road.
> Yes, M'Mbuju, circumcised girls have dug up a road, yes. (interview, June
>   9, 1995)

James Laiboni of Igembe recounted stories of two *Ngaitana* members who were betrothed to a headman and home guard, respectively because their parents could not afford the fines imposed (interview, July 23, 1995).

Interviewees remembered that individuals taken to African courts were those arrested by tribal police as opposed to home guards or those who refused to pay fines to the local Njuri. According to interviewees, people refused to pay the local Njuri because either they thought that by furthering their case to the African court, they would avoid paying a fine altogether, or, more often, they did not want to provide Njuri members, headmen, and home guards with more livestock to eat (interview, Samuel Nkure, May 7, 1995). During the Mau Mau rebellion, such consumption had taken on a particular salience as headmen and home guards confiscated and ate the cattle of suspected Mau Mau sympathizers, depriving households of wealth as well as sources of milk and meat. In collecting fines of livestock and, possibly, young brides beyond the purview of British officers, these African men pursued local political interests and masked their inability or unwillingness to prevent defiance.

Although largely ignorant of politics within headmen's camps, some European observers voiced concern over the work of African courts. Following his investigation of a *Ngaitana* case involving his shepherd, Ngarui Kabuthia, settler Casey criticized African court personnel for not allowing witnesses and arrogantly refusing appeals: "He [the court clerk] implied that the Court was infallible and no good would come of challenging it. Such a thing, he said, had never happened before."[30] In reviewing the court registers, British district officers often reduced the size of fines imposed. Central government officials, as discussed earlier, were wary of the ban from its inception. Monthly court returns from Meru reporting hundreds of people charged with defying the ban only added to their unease. In response to the April 1957 returns, listing over 200 *Ngaitana* cases, African Courts Officer Rylands wrote to the district commissioner of Meru, "Are [you] satisfied with the number of such cases so suddenly taken as a result of the Njuri's order and the severity of the fines imposed? The P[rovincial] C[ommissioner] has stressed the matter is basically one for education of public opinion." Following this memorandum, the number of cases and size of fines only increased. In July 1957, the African courts officer wrote to the provincial commissioner, "the avalanche does not slow up. . . . If this is not 'mass action through the courts' I don't know what is."[31] Central government officials, though, did not halt "the avalanche." That took a settler's letter of complaint and two parliamentary questions.

In July 1957, settler Casey's aforementioned letter to MP Barbara Castle drew her attention to the inappropriateness of the ban and the injustices perpetuated in enforcing it. He requested Castle to secure from the Colonial Office statistics on prosecutions relating to the ban. On August 1, 1957, Castle raised the issue of the Meru ban in the House of Commons before the secretary of state for the colonies. Unsatisfied with his response, Castle requested a further inquiry into the matter. In this correspondence, Castle sided with Casey: "I abhor the practice of female circumcision and certainly want to see it stamped out, but I do not think this is the right way to do it." While awaiting the governor of Kenya's comments on the subject, the secretary of state made a preliminary response to Castle's critique of the ban. He contended that if, as "it seems obvious," the ban has reduced the incidence of excision, it was justified.[32] In late December, the governor of Kenya wrote to the secretary of state, distancing central administration as well as officers in Meru from the formulation and enforcement of the ban.

> The state of affairs brought to your attention by Mrs. Castle is the result of an excessive outburst of zeal on the part of the tribal authorities and African Courts of Meru to stamp out female circumcision, which the more enlightened leaders of the tribe have come to abhor. . . . The Administration has, however, already taken steps to curb this enthusiasm and to reduce not only the number of cases being brought to court, but also to temper the sentences imposed. . . . The decision of the Njuri Ncheke, the indigenous tribal authority and the arbiters of tribal law and custom, to ban female circumcision, was taken without any influence being brought to bear on them by Government or the Missions.[33]

The governor explained that the antiexcision campaign in Meru had shifted focus from prosecutions in court to education and health propaganda. Moreover, he stated that chiefs and headmen, as government employees, would no longer prosecute cases in court; that task would be left to local Njuri members. This represented a major retrenchment in enforcement of the ban. The secretary of state forwarded the governor's letter to Castle along with notification that, on appeal, Ngarui Kabuthia's sentence had been reduced from 400 to 50 shillings.[34]

In November 1957, the Njuri Ncheke held a meeting to discuss its position on the ban. They had already begun to feel the effects of the new policy of enforcement reported by the governor. Members of the Njuri Ncheke agreed that even though the incidence of excision had only increased of late, "courts had tended to disregard hearing of circumcision cases." Speaking before British officers, they blamed the ban's failure on the weakening of their authority under colonial rule. They did not acknowledge that the ban was a largely unprecedented extension of male authority into women's affairs. Nor did they reveal how some headmen, home guards, and Njuri members used enforcement of the ban to pursue more immediate political interests.[35]

After October 1957, the number of *Ngaitana* cases decreased dramatically in nearly all the African courts. By March 1959, they had ceased entirely. Because even young girls defied the ban, it is unlikely that by 1959 there were many adolescent girls left in Meru who had not already been excised.

Conclusion

Discourses of sexual oppression, human rights, women's health, and neocolonialism structure current international debates over campaigns to eradicate female genital cutting. Analysis of the 1956 ban, though, demonstrates the significance of gender identities and generational relations to understanding the

continuance of these practices. In 1950s Meru, most people believed that excision, as a part of female initiation, remade girls into women. Through female
initiation, adolescent girls learned how to behave as young women as well as
future wives and daughters-in-law. The 1956 ban was at least as much of a
challenge to relations of seniority among women as to relations of subordination between men and women. Adolescent girls—some fearing to be denied
adulthood, others feeling peer pressure—attempted to excise each other, not
appreciating or possibly accepting the severity of the practice. Even after older
women reasserted control over the process by performing second excisions,
Ngaitana permanently altered female initiation in most parts of the district. In
appearing as a travesty of previous initiations, it lent support in some areas and
households to a growing sentiment that female initiation was no longer necessary. In other places where the practice persisted, *Ngaitana* helped to reduce
the process of female initiation to excision (Interview, Isabella Kajuju, March
20, 1995): "they are still circumcised secretly, the one who wants."[36] Today,
Meru District is reputed to have one of the highest incidences of excision
within central Kenya. Survey research conducted by Maendeleo ya Wanawake
(MYWO 1991:table 2.0) indicates that in Meru, 73.5 percent of all females
fourteen years of age or older have been "circumcised."

Yet many of the women of the *Ngaitana* age grade whom we interviewed
stated that they had chosen not to have their daughters excised because they
felt it to be an unnecessary or harmful practice. For these women and for others in Meru who have repudiated the practice, the decision of whether to excise has become tied to issues of "development," class, and Christianity. Such
people explained that excision was most common in remote or "traditional"
areas of the district, areas viewed as being less accessible by public transportation, less fully integrated into the cash economy, and with a shorter history of adherence to Christianity.[37] In Meru as elsewhere in central and eastern Kenya (Browne 1991), school education has played a key role in
changing attitudes toward excision. Protestant missionaries and teachers have
ranked among the most vocal opponents of the practice since the 1920s.
Moreover, many parents and students have gradually accepted school as a
more appropriate forum than initiation for educating girls and preparing them
for their future roles as wives, mothers, and salaried employees. For instance,
Sara Ayub explained that in her youth she and her age mates had eagerly anticipated the celebrations that initiation entailed and the status it conferred,
but girls today rightly directed their attention and enthusiasm toward school
(interview, August 27, 1990).

But opposition to excision in Meru cannot be seen as an easy by-product
of school education or the "march of modernity." Schoolgirls are often excised; at least, 38.1 percent of the women surveyed by Maendeleo ya
Wanawake (MYWO 1991:tables 1.1, 2.0) were "circumcised" and had attended some school.[38] Excision may also be experiencing a resurgence among

those who had formerly rejected it. In 1990, a social development officer in Meru, Celina Kiruki, observed that in some areas the practice had been resumed as people felt that "girls" had become "too independent and [we]re no longer submissive to the husbands or the in-laws" (Imathiu 1990:3). Worsening economic conditions in Kenya may cause still others to reconsider excision and female initiation. As families find it increasingly difficult to pay rising school fees and job opportunities for educated young men and women become ever more scarce, school may appear as a less attractive alternative to female initiation. In explaining the resurgence of female "circumcision" in northeastern Tanzania during the late 1980s, Astrid Nypan (1991) has argued that the declining economic value and social status of school education has prompted some young women—often against the will of their educated and unexcised mothers—to view initiation as a means of enhancing their social standing and marriage prospects within local communities. Thus, even within families, repudiation of excision may not be something that mothers are able to pass along to their daughters.

The history of colonial efforts to stop excision in Meru offers three main lessons for contemporary anticircumcision campaigns. Most obviously, it suggests the difficulties and even dangers of instituting and enforcing legal prohibitions.[39] Kenyan anticircumcision activists, at least, appear attuned to this dilemma. Apart from the November 1996 introduction of an ill-fated parliamentary bill to outlaw the practice (*Weekly Review* 11/2/96:15–16), most efforts in Kenya have focused on educating people on the harmful effects of excision and, in some areas, organizing alternative "rituals without cutting" (*Awaken* 1998:10–11; also see Chapter 12 of this volume).[40] Second, this history reveals the inadequacies of understanding contemporary practices of genital cutting as "traditional" relics from an unchanging past (see also Walley 1997:417–423; also Chapter 9 of this volume). In central Kenya, colonial efforts to lessen the severity of cutting, lower the age of initiation, and ultimately ban excision profoundly altered previous practices of female initiation by shrouding them in secrecy or reducing them to the act of cutting. Moreover, early colonial literature on female initiation in central Kenya (e.g., Orde Browne 1913, 1915; M'Inoti 1930; Leakey 1931; Kenyatta 1938; Laughton 1938) reveals significant variations in the timing, meaning, and practices of female initiation, suggesting that the precolonial history of female initiation was also marked by change and innovation.

Most significantly, this history of the 1956 ban in Meru reveals the importance of understanding female initiation as a process that constitutes and elaborates political hierarchies among girls and women. For initiates, excision along with its attendant teachings, ceremonies, and celebrations was an important step in transforming them into women and differentiating them from younger girls. Through their daughters' initiations, mothers heightened their own social standing, and other women, including grandmothers and those who performed excisions, affirmed their authority within the community by teaching initiates how to behave as proper women, wives, and daughters-in-law. Campaigns aimed at discouraging female genital cutting must address the reasons why some girls and women value and perpetuate these practices. Failure to consider how female genital cutting instills moral meanings of womanhood and animates relations of authority among girls and women will lead contemporary campaigns to suffer fates similar to that of the 1956 ban.

Notes

I would like to thank Henry Mutoro and David Anderson and participants in their respective history seminars at the University of Nairobi and the School for Oriental and African Studies in November 1995, as well as David William Cohen, Frederick Cooper, Nancy Rose Hunt, John Lonsdale, Kenda Mutongi, Agnes Odinga, and Keith Shear for comments on earlier drafts. Research for this piece was funded by a Fulbright-IIE Foreign Scholarship Board fellowship and an International Doctoral Research fellowship sponsored by the Joint Committee on African Studies of the Social Science Research Council and the American Council of Learned Societies in 1994–1995. For a different version of this chapter that situates *Ngaitana* more firmly in the history of post–World War II Kenya and the Mau Mau rebellion, see "'*Ngaitana* (I Will Circumcise Myself)': The Gender and Generational Politics of the 1956 Ban on Clitoridectomy in Meru, Kenya," *Gender and History* 8 (1996):338–363.

I am grateful to Carol Gatwiri, Doreen Jackson, Grace Kirimi, Richard Kirimi, Rosemary Kithiira, Sophia Mithega, Thomas Mutethia, Nkatha Mworoa, Charity Nduru, and Diana Rigiri, who at various times provided translation assistance during interviews and transcribed and translated them afterwards. The term "circumcision" is used in quoting oral sources because it is the most widely accepted translation from the Meru language.

The woman quoted at the beginning of the chapter was interviewed on July 5, 1995.

1. Kenyan National Archives (hereafter, KNA): DC/MRU/1/1/12/1, Meru Annual Report (AR) 1956; ARC(MAA)/2/9/27/II-III, MAA/7/282/-3, Meru African Court Returns.

2. KNA: Health/2/164, correspondence of the Special Sub-Committee of the Central Board of Health; Bancroft Library, University of California at Berkeley (hereafter, BLB): 96/49, Fadiman Collection, "Dr. Chiono's Opinion on Female Circumcision," translated quote from Fr. Merlo Pick, "Il più grande amico degli africani, Paolo Chiono, medico missionario," Torino, 1961:165.

3. Meru County Council Offices (hereafter, MCC): LNC/Minute Book/1, 10/12/15 and 6/2–3/27.

4. MCC: LNC/Minute Book/1, 1/29/32.

5. KNA: PC/CP/8/1/2, DC, Embu to PC, Nyeri, 5/14/31 and 7/7/31; and BLB: 96/49, Fadiman Collection, interview with Mrs. Lambert by Jeffrey Fadiman, Nairobi, 1969.

6. KNA: Health/BY/1/61, Director of Medical Services, Nairobi to Dr. Brassington, Maua, 10/29/31.

7. KNA: MSS/7, Holding papers; Grace Ovenden, letter home, quoted in Bertha Jones, *Kenya Kaleidoscope* (Devon, 1995):24–25.

8. MCC: ADC/Minute Book 6, 3/8–9/56 and 4/12/56.

9. KNA: DC/MRU/1/1/12/1, Meru AR 1956.

10. KNA: DC/MRU/1/1/12/1, Meru AR 1956; CS/1/14/100, ADC minutes, 7/3/56; MAA/1/5, Central Province, AR 1957.

11. Public Record Office (hereafter, PRO): CO/822/1647, Casey, Timau to MP Castle, London, 7/1/57. Following a request by an employee for a loan of 400 shillings to pay a *Ngaitana* fine, Casey investigated the ban, interviewing officers, headmen, African court staff, and "ordinary tribesmen."

12. Ibid.

13. KNA: DC/MRU/1/3/12, Meru AR 1953.

14. MCC: ADM/15/16/6/II, Dr. Irvine, Chogoria to DC, Meru, 5/10/55.

15. KNA: DC/MRU/1/1/12/1, Meru AR 1956.

16. MCC: ADC/Minute Book 6, 3/8–9/56 and 4/12/56.

17. KNA: MSS/7, Holding papers.

18. Standard seven in the British school system is the equivalent of grade seven in the U.S. system. Girls who entered standard one at the age of seven years and made uninterrupted progress would have been around fifteen years of age by the time that they completed standard seven. Standard seven is followed by forms one through four, the equivalent of high school in the United States.

19. Methodist Mission Society Papers at St. Paul's Office, Meru (hereafter, MMSM):1, Merle Wilde, Women's Work Report 1958. None of my oral material supports Wilde's statement that some girls "circumcised themselves," as opposed to each other.

20. PRO: CO/822/1647, Ag. Governor of Kenya to the Secretary of State for the Colonies, 12/27/57.

21. KNA: DC/MRU/1/1/13, Meru AR 1957.

22. MCC: ADM/15/16/6/III, Minutes of Njuri Ncheke, 4/15/58.

23. KNA: AB/16/6, correspondence on Youth Schemes for Meru, 1956.

24. MCC: ADM/15/16/6/II, Minutes of Njuri, 11/6/57.

25. "Dirt" appears to allude to the uncleanness associated with unexcised women as well as the clitoris itself.

26. KNA: AB/2/51, correspondence on Female Rehabilitation Centre in Meru, 9/23/54.

27. KNA: ARC(MAA)/2/9/27/II, ARC(MAA)/2/10/27/III, MAA/7/282, and MAA/7/283, Meru Court Returns 1956–1958. These percentages are estimates because it was sometimes difficult to determine an individual's status from the court registers.

28. PRO: CO/822/1647, Casey, Timau to MP Castle, London, 7/1/57.

29. MMSM:1, Merle Wilde, Women's Work Report 1958.

30. PRO: CO/822/1647, Casey, Timau to MP Castle, London, 7/1/57.

31. KNA: (ARC)MAA/2/9/27/III, Meru African Court Returns, 5/29/57 and 7/16/57.

32. PRO: CO/822/1647, correspondence between MP Castle to Secretary of State for the Colonies, 10/16/57 and 10/20/57.

33. PRO: C0/822/1647, Governor of Kenya to Secretary of State, London, 1/20/58.

34. PRO: CO/822/1647, Secretary of State, London, to Castle, Timau, 1/20/58.

35. MCC: ADM/15/16/6/II, Njuri minutes, 11/6/57.

36. See also Emily Onyango and Sheila Maina, "In Meru OP Is Done in Secrecy," *The Standard*, 9/12/90:19.

37. Because I was based near Meru town and did not have my own vehicle, my research was biased toward areas of the district accessible from Meru town by public transportation or by foot. By local standards, I worked in the less remote and more "modern" areas of the district.

38. I calculated this figure by assuming, for simplicity's sake, that all of the 26.5 percent of women who reported not being "circumcised" had also attended school. I then subtracted 26.5 percent from 64.6 percent, Maendeleo's figure for the percentage of those surveyed who had "ever attended school." On schoolgirls being "circumcised" in western Kenya, see Walley (1997:408–418).

39. On the similarly unsuccessful 1946 effort to outlaw infibulation in Sudan, see Sanderson (1981:81–95).

40. Female "circumcision" is not illegal in Kenya today. In 1982, Kenyan president Daniel arap Moi issued an administrative decree against clitoridectomy, but it did not entail legal sanctions. Only cases of "forcible circumcision," when a girl or woman is excised against her will or that of her parents or guardians, are punishable under the penal code as physical assault.

Interviews

Sara Ayub, August 27, 1990.
Tarsila Kikobwe and Margaret Mwakinia, September 20, 1990.
Esther M'Ithinji and Julia Simon, October 14, 1990.
Margaret M'Ithinji, October 17, 1990.
Elizabeth Kiogora, October 18, 1990.
Isabella Ncence, October 19, 1990.
Elizabeth Muthuuri, January 3, 1995.
Moses M'Mukindia, January 11, 1995.
Jacobu M'Lithara, February 6, 1995.
Charity Tirindi, February 10, 1995.
Evangeline M'Iringo, March 16, 1995.
Isabel Kaimuri, March 20, 1995.
Isabella Kajuju, March 20, 1995.
Monica Kanana, March 23, 1995.
Former Subarea Headman David M'Naikiuru, April 29, 1995.
Samuel Nkure, May 7, 1995.
Former Chief M'Anampiu, May 10, 1995.
Caroline Kirote, June 9, 1995.
Agnes Kirimi, June 12, 1995.
Former Chief Daniel M'Iringo, June 25, 1995.
Celina Kiruki, June 30, 1995.
Veronica Kinaito, July 5, 1995.
James Laiboni, July 23, 1995.
Martha Kanini, September 16, 1995.
Naaman M'Mwirichia, September 18, 1995.
Former District Officer Richard Cashmore, December 6, 1995.

8

Revisiting Feminist Discourses on Infibulation: Responses from Sudanese Feminists

Rogaia Mustafa Abusharaf

Few African customs have generated as much controversy and discord between African and Western feminists as has the practice of female genital cutting (FGC). Given the controversy that surrounds feminist discourses on "circumcision," in this chapter I juxtapose contrasting views: Sudanese versus Western feminisms.[1] One clarification that should be made at the outset, however, is that Western feminist discourses are not treated herein as an indivisible whole. As Chandra Mohanty correctly argues, Western feminist analysis "is neither singular nor homogenous in its goals, interests or analyses" (1991:52).

In this chapter I offer a critical reflection on one specific work, *The Hosken Report*, which not only reifies the duality of "self" and "other" but also exemplifies the shortcomings of some Western feminist discourses on female "circumcision." I have adopted an interdisciplinary approach that combines insights from anthropology, feminist theory, international law, and history in order to investigate the practice of genital cutting in the Sudanese context as well as to elucidate the views of Sudanese women on the subject. I will also discuss the current campaigns of several indigenous organizations within the Sudan to eliminate genital cutting, a practice that has officially been identified as "a basic population problem" (Sudan National Committee Population and Development Conference 1983). I conclude by describing some specific examples of the Sudanese efforts at ending the practice.

The Question of Genital Cutting Within the Sudanese Context

A thorough understanding of genital cutting requires transcending preconceived images and stereotypes of the societies in which this practice occurs.

Elsewhere (Abusharaf 1995; 1998), I have made my position on the question of genital cutting unequivocal: that the practice must end if women are to enjoy basic human rights and that understanding the cultural context of the practice does not imply condoning it.

Sudan is the largest country in Africa, covering an area of 2.5 million square kilometers, nearly one-tenth of the total area of the African continent. It is located in the northeastern part of Africa and shares borders with Egypt, Libya, Central African Republic, Chad, Zaire, Uganda, Kenya, and Ethiopia. The country is remarkable in its cultural heterogeneity. Though its population is often distinguished into binary ethnological categories such as Arabs versus Africans, its ethnoreligious composition is far more complex, and genital cutting is not universally practiced among Sudanese peoples.

Since its independence from British colonial rule in 1956, the country has experienced severe hardships: instability, poverty, and widespread human displacements. Under such constrained circumstances, priorities as articulated by Sudanese women are fundamentally distinct from those advocated by Western women, such as sexual liberation. But although hardship and suffering are common throughout all levels of Sudanese society, the situation is far worse for women. In terms of health, nutrition, food security, and access to basic social services, women's conditions are manifestly worse than those of their male counterparts. The majority of women undergo ritualized genital operations, to which they refer collectively as "circumcising," denoting in the etymological sense of the word "purification" and "cleanliness." Where genital cutting is practiced, pronounced variations exist in its prevalence, type of surgery, practitioners, and associated rites. The Sudan Demographic and Health Survey (SDHS, 1991–1992) has presented detailed statistical data on the prevalence of the practice and attitudes of women and men toward it. For instance, 89 percent of ever-married women are "circumcised." Also significant is that the operations are not carried out solely by Muslims; 47 percent of Sudanese Christian women are also "circumcised," whereas among Muslim women in the region of Darfur, 65 percent have not been "circumcised" (see also Chapter 3 of this volume).

The SDHS has also uncovered significant data on the practitioners. For example, most of the operations are found to be performed by traditional birth attendants (64 percent), whereas trained midwives perform one-third, and medical doctors perform less than 1 percent of the total operations. The health risks to girls and women range from temporary problems to life-long complications such as difficulty in passing urine and menses, infection, hemorrhage as well as a wide range of obstetrical complications, and death.[2]

In spite of its grim nature, the practice is considered a medium for transmitting multiple messages and meanings to different people who take part in it. As ritual, it rests on an opulent repertoire of diverse cultural themes regarding notions of femininity, beauty, tradition, gender, sexuality, and religiosity. Therefore, its nature, justifications, and actors have no significance apart from other dominant ideologies and beliefs. These ideologies constitute a seamless web out of which symbolic productions of rituals proceed (Abdul Fadl 1997). The practice is carried out in some regions and not in others depending on each specific region's moral philosophy. In the Sudan, not unlike in many other societies that perform genital cutting, it is considered a vital component of cultural life, a device that is essential for the construction of womanhood, "appropriate sexuality," and the achievement of adult status within the community. Among those who practice it, genital cutting is believed to preserve virginity, enhance femininity, mark ethnic boundaries, and limit women's excessive sexual desire. It is regarded at once as a vehicle for gender indoctrination, sexual sublimation, and repression and embodies a complex constellation of interrelated beliefs, values, and organizing principles of social life that must be explored (Abusharaf 1998; Kennedy 1970).

As a joyous occasion in one's life, "circumcision" in most parts of the Sudan is accompanied by ceremonies and festivities celebrating the girl's rite of passage and initiation into womanhood, thus contributing to marriageability (see also Chapter 13 of this volume). Girls are feted and regaled with gifts after the operation. One forty-five-year-old Sudanese woman told me:

> When I was little, about six years old, I could not wait to be circumcised. I recall that I used to beg my mother constantly to bring me to the midwife's place to circumcise me. I still remember that my mother used to tell me to wait till my little sister is a bit older so that we can be circumcised together. I was really thinking about the gifts and the golden jewelry, the henna and the party. Waiting was like a lifetime. Personally, I think that I would have died at that point, if my mother did not have me circumcised.

In other parts of the country, however, the practice is shrouded in secrecy. Genital cutting is a tradition safeguarded by women who undoubtedly exert considerable pressure on other women to conform to a practice that paradoxically invokes traditions associated with their own oppression and sense of inferiority as well as with psychological and physical aliments.

Preserved by women as primary socializing agents in society, these operations are believed to ensure the transmission as well as the maintenance of cultural ethos throughout a woman's lifetime. In her study of footbinding in neo-Confucian China, C. Fred Blake discusses how such a practice becomes a strategy for mothers "to inform their daughters of how to succeed in a world authored by men" (1994:676). Blake defines footbinding, which in many ways can be seen as a parallel to infibulation (see also Chapter 13 in this volume), as a "protracted discipline that mothers brought to bear upon their daughters in the name of a mother's love and a daughter's virtue"(1994:677).

Sudanese legal scholar Asma Abdel Halim points out that female "circumcision" is performed in the presence of and with the support of female kinswomen who are concerned about the well-being of the child. A child undergoing "circumcision" is believed to have the protection of angels (Abdel Halim 1995:251). Sudanese women's justifications for why they decide to "circumcise" their daughters are no different from those given by Chinese women regarding footbinding: it is a testimony to "mother's love." In a "world authored by men," "circumcision" as a practice sanctioned by "custom" touches the core of female sexuality and acts as a device to ensure virginity, without which marriage—which defines the future of the girl—becomes practically unthinkable. According to Abdel Halim:

> Closely related to the social value of inhibiting female sexual desire is the value placed on virginity before marriage. The community believes that in delivering a virgin bride to the husband, the community has preserved its honor. Female circumcision is seen as necessary both because women cannot be trusted to protect their virginity and because the community does not have the means to watch them all the time. (1995:253)

Virginity and its preservation through genital cutting becomes not only the liability and obligation of the community toward its women but emerges as an assurance of the woman's marriageability and future well-being. A Sudanese woman I interviewed in 1997 in Khartoum indicated that

> "circumcision" does ensure virginity because circumcised women do not feel the need to have sex, they don't run around looking for sex. When a man marries a virgin, she has his respect forever. He will respect her, honor their marriage, but if he married a non-virgin he will divorce her immediately, and if he doesn't he will despise her.

The Arrival of an Abhorrent Tradition? War of Visions

In addition to its sociological and cultural significance, female "circumcision" has created considerable interest in how this cultural practice obliterates the sexual pleasure and gratification of women who are subjected to it.[3] Increased awareness of this practice is a corollary of the influx of refugee and immigrant populations from African societies, many of whom practice genital cutting. It is therefore not surprising that the practice has aroused indignant horror while becoming a concern in countries such as the United States, Canada, and Western Europe, which have come to host large numbers of African refugees and immigrants. Serious concern has been expressed in the mainstream media. Especially in the U.S. media, a great deal of publicity was generated by the case of the Togolese woman, Fawzia Kassindja, who fled her home country because of her well-founded fear of undergoing the ritual. Subsequently, she was granted asylum after careful contemplation of her case and after a Harvard University legal team substantiated her claim to refugee status. With this media focus, attention was devoted to the epidemiological consequences of the operations as well as their impact on mental health. The practice has also been presented as child abuse. In her essay "Under the Knife: Female Genital Mutilation as Child Abuse," Nancy Kellner has argued that Westerners "should find female genital mutilation unacceptable" (1993:121). She proceeds to caution that clandestine mutilations of girls have taken place within Western countries and further argues:

> Evading the issue of whether or not female genital mutilation constitutes child abuse is unlikely to deter parents from engaging in a practice, which as discussed above, may be extremely harmful to their children in both physical and psychological ways. Only when the United States follows the lead of other developed countries, which have enacted legislation, either criminal or civil, only by prohibiting female genital mutilation could these children find a possible champion in the justice system for hoping to grow up in a healthy manner. (Kellner 1993:131)

According to a report issued by the Center for Reproductive Law and Policy in the United States, most anti–genital mutilation statutes were enacted in 1996, including several legislative measures that define the practice as a federal criminal offense. In addition, new legislation requires the Immigration and Naturalization Service to provide information regarding these statutes and laws when issuing entry visas to immigrants from circumcising cultures (see also Chapter 1).

There is no doubt that female "circumcision" not only has come to represent a moral dilemma but also has become a subject of heated intellectual debates. The practice has produced intense conflict between relativist and universalist paradigms (see Chapter 1). The relativist position asserts the moral equality of cultural norms around the world and sees "circumcision" from the vantage point of a ritual that signifies an important event in individual and group life. In contrast, the universalist position criminalizes those who engage in genital cutting. To many observers who subscribe to this universalist position, genital cutting is viewed as brutal misogyny, an extreme act of violence, and a violation of the human rights of women, who are in turn envisaged as downtrodden, mistreated, and disadvantaged populations. Nothing highlights this relativist-universalist antagonism more clearly than the language used to refer to the practice. Is it "circumcision," or is it "mutilation"? As we shall see below, the disharmony and conflict extend beyond semantics. But as legal scholar David Fraser points out, both positions share a discursive commonality that is "firmly rooted in the Western neo/postcolonial tradition of the identity of the other" (1995:319).

Sudanese Feminists: Talking
Themselves out of Silence

Feminism figures prominently in current questions about theory and the constitution of knowledge, and many issues raised are intimately related in some way to the inescapable impact that a feminist transformation of knowledge has had on the academy (see Weed 1989:ix). Following Weed, it can be argued that feminist knowledge and approaches to the "woman's question" should be situated within the specific histories and conditions from which they emanate. Paying attention to these histories is essential for academics and activists who work on feminist issues, ethnography, representation, and the political debates surrounding the politics and aesthetics embedded in the modification of women's bodies; whether through genital cutting, liposuction, facelifts, or breast implants.

For most Sudanese women, genital cutting is a symptom rather than a cause of women's troubles in society. To understand why these women are taking this position, a brief examination of the historical roots and sociopolitical forces that prompted women to organize for change is indispensable. As with feminist movements throughout the Third World, the history of Sudanese feminism is intricately connected to that of the nationalist anticolonial resistance and has, throughout, mirrored the broader political picture (El Bakri 1983). This history glitters with the names of pioneering feminists such as Alaza Mohamed Abdella (the wife of Ali Abdellatif, who led the 1924 uprising against the British, and the first woman to lead a demonstration against colonial occupation), Fartonata Koashie (the first nun from the Nuba Mountains), Batool Isa, Inaizi Jumma (known as Madame Anu Zeid Marajan), Medina Abdalla, Fatima Talib, Khalida Zahir, Fatima Ahmed Ibrahim, Aziza Mekki, Thoria Umbabi, and many other gifted and enterprising Sudanese women who led the march for truly transformative feminist politics.

From its inception, the politics of the women's movement in the Sudan depended on multiple alliances, recognizing and drawing upon the broader identity of women as wives, mothers, workers, and citizens. That, however, does not in any way make it "less feminist," for there is no doubt that "women's issues" and gender have played a pivotal role in shaping oppositional consciousness and in affirming the inalienable rights of Sudanese women within the household and beyond.

In her pioneering feminist text *Our Harvest in Twenty Years* (1972), Sudanese feminist leader Fatima Ahmed Ibrahim provides a thorough and compelling analysis of the "woman question." Ibrahim describes how the seed of women's organizing for change began in the 1940s; contrary to the widely held belief that the women's movement started with the introduction of formal girls' education, she argues that the feminist movement emerged in connection to the nationalist struggle against the British. Under colonial domination, women's lives were adversely affected by the colonial pursuit of economic policies, which fundamentally changed their traditional roles without providing alternatives. The oppressive British policies against Sudanese people in general and women in particular generated multiple forms of resistance. At the level of the family, social conservatism and male favoritism added a conspicuous dimension to the movement of liberating society and its most disadvantaged members: the women.

Against this background, the Sudanese Women's Union (SWU) was born, and under the leadership of Fatima Ahmed Ibrahim it led many heated battles to carve out a space for women's participatory action under restrictive and constraining conditions. Recognizing the role of the state as a determining factor in the social, economic, political, and legal status of women, Fatima Ibrahim brought to light the complex relationship between Sudanese women and the institutional state structure as a vital component of her vision of agitating for women's rights. The extent to which colonialism, militarism (after independence), and patriarchy have all collaborated in the subordination of women and their relegation to the status of second-class citizens was examined and elaborated upon. Sudanese sociologist Zeinab El Bakri and others concur with Ibrahim's analysis of the position of women under colonialism, noting that "in areas where women's subordination was clear, the British did not interfere to improve them, while in other situations where women shared equal status with men, they lost this status under the pretext of civilization. In this the colonial male bourgeois mentality played an important role" (1987:177).

My focus here on SWU emanates not only from the fact that it is the most significant oppositional movement in Sudanese women's political history but also from how the "woman question" was approached, especially as it relates to female genital cutting. The leader of the SWU saw that the problem was not merely the sexual oppression of women but rather how multiple societal configurations such as race, class, and gender intersect to mold the experience of women in the most dramatic way by forming individual and collective consciousness, social relations, and access to positions of power and privilege. For Fatima Ahmed Ibrahim and her fellow comrades in the SWU, the "woman's question" is also the man's question. Unlike feminist movements in the West, in the Sudan women's emancipation was hardly equated with sexual liberation. Instead, the broader conceptualization of women's issues taken by the Sudanese feminist movement differs fundamentally and constitutively from that of feminists in the Western world.

This in turn raises a fundamental query: just how important is sexuality to the Sudanese feminist agenda? There is no doubt that the reconstruction of women's bodies through genital cutting is intended to repress their sexuality as part of a manifestly political agenda. With Michel Foucault I argue that human sexuality is not merely a "natural" unproblematic attribute but rather a product of social forces constructed around elements that are seen as problematic by the existent power structures within a society. To understand genital cutting as a practice that touches female sexuality, it is necessary to understand specific institutionalized ideologies. Those ideologies represent a plethora of complex notions of culture, ritual, male dominance and female authority over younger generations, social behavior, and economic power.

From this vantage point it becomes obvious that female genital cutting should be squarely situated within the contexts of women's political and economic status and sex roles within the family and society (see also Chapter 2 in this volume). In an interview I conducted with Fatima Ahmed Ibrahim, she indicated the following to me:

> If our movement had focused on eradicating female "circumcision" when it started, people could have been very suspicious of our motives. That is why we tried to address fundamental questions and issues such as poverty, illiteracy, and exploitation in and outside the home and employment. "Circumcision" is a symptom, not a cause of women's subordination.

Another SWU feminist leader, Nafisa Ahmed El Amin, concurred with this view when asked about the efforts of her group to end female "circumcision":

> We never talked to Sudanese women about female circumcision or how to end it. We were convinced that there were more pressing problems facing women in our society. Our goal was to address these problems because they touch the lives of Sudanese women and their survival. Of course we recognize that circumcision is a problem, but we wanted to give women the weapons in their hands to fight it with. We emphasized education and the ability to work outside the home. We recognized from the beginning that ending oppressive practices requires basic tools that women should possess.

These two excerpts reflect the SWU's unyielding attempts to empower women to devise strategies addressing the complexities of their everyday life by challenging hereditary forms of power. Resisting patriarchal institutions, military oppression, and class oppression must take precedence over striving for sexual freedoms. Were it not for the painstaking efforts of SWU, the impact of state policies could have further deepened the exploitation and oppression of Sudanese women. To strengthen women's position in society, SWU initiated adult literacy classes and emphasized education as a primary feminist goal. According to Haja Kashif (1994), between 1952 and 1959 thirty-four night schools were established throughout the country, with the largest enrollment by residents of Omdurman; in Khartoum; and in remote regions such as Singa, Kassala, Fashir, Wadi Halfa, and Juba.

In addition to declaring its intention of obliterating illiteracy among women, SWU listed other goals for a strategy for women's liberation. Foremost among these is the liberation of women from oppressive practices within the household and on a societal level. In this regard SWU aimed at ameliorating prevailing social injustices and securing women's self-representation, political participation, literacy, legal rights, equal pay for equal work, child care, and better terms of employment, including maternal leave.

SWU's ultimate goal is achieving equality between men and women within the society and the family. The deep conviction of women's equality held by SWU activists manifested itself in attempts to ensure women's participation in public life on equitable terms. Securing women's right to vote in 1956 attested to this effort. With regard to the sphere of family, SWU succeeded in 1969 in changing existing family law, including ending the so-called obedience law.[4] An act was issued, also in 1969, providing women with the rights to be consulted before marriage, to initiate divorce, and to secure custody of their children. Other aims included the provision of health care, affordable housing, safe drinking water, and the protection of children through the prevention of child labor.

In addition, the group succeeded in 1955 in creating Sudan's first woman's magazine, *Sawt el Maraa* (Woman's voice), which attempted to explain the real issues behind female oppression and clarify the position of Islam on women's status in general and on female "circumcision" in particular. This publication helped Sudanese women to "to talk themselves out of silence" (to use an expression of the Caribbean novelist Norbesse Philips).

Advocating a general transformative change does not mean sweeping female "circumcision" under the rug. Indeed, evidence of the efforts of SWU to end the practice can be found in *Our Harvest in Twenty Years,* in which Fatima Ahmed Ibrahim wrote on June 20, 1957:

> Mr. Secretary of the Sudanese Medical Association
> Best regards
>
> We did not find an alternative besides addressing you as protectors of humanity and guardians of health care in this country, in which the humanity and dignity of women are violated. Especially recently, pharaonic circumcisions are performed on infant girls, after a rumor was spread that the Revolutionary Council will initiate a law prohibiting "circumcision" practices in a few days. Regrettably, at the Central Committee of the SWU we were informed that medical doctors are performing these "executions." Therefore, we appeal to you in your capacity as a Secretary of the Medical Association to take whatever measures you see fit to stop this practice and to save innocent children. We are ready and enthusiastic to aid your efforts by organizing workshops, lectures and community outreach throughout the country.
>
> With our deep appreciation,
> Fatima Ahmed Ibrahim, President
> The Sudanese Women's Union.

To recapitulate the position of SWU, it can be argued that SWU women were cognizant of the implications of genital cutting, through which women and men are indoctrinated into feminine and masculine social roles and subsequently into specific societal responsibilities. Under such circumstances, the female body not only emerges as "a contested terrain between competing visions of authenticity" (Khan 1995), but practices of female excision or the obligatory physical recognition of virginity are both carried out with the sole objective of "literally reconstructing women's bodies to bring them into line with what the culture considers to be acceptable sexuality in women" (Ahmed 1989:41). With this in mind, the SWU made its position unmistakable: that efforts for the obliteration of female "circumcision" have to be initiated by Sudanese women themselves. Only when we talk about social change that recognizes the existential realities of women can we talk about eradication of harmful practices. Any efforts that overlook historical and political contexts can only produce what one author has termed "a well-meaning pseudo-science" (Harvey 1989).

The Hosken Report

Some Western feminist representational discourses on female "circumcision" as a signifier for sexual oppression have come under considerable criticism for their ethnocentrism and reductionism. Varying and conflicting paradigms have generated controversy and increased polarization between some Western feminists and Africans who view their interventions and protestations as inherently paternalistic and as another incidence of veiled racism. Many commentators have concerned themselves with the question of why women who undergo an ostensibly harmful procedure tend to venerate their own mutilation. Despite well-meaning intentions, these representations have succeeded in foregrounding negative images of Africa and Africans, often portraying them as irrational and primitive savages who have nothing to do with their lives besides engage in genital cutting. Its important contribution to the literature on female "circumcision" notwithstanding, *The Hosken Report* is filled with negative statements about African societies that adhere to the practice. Hosken states, for example, that "genital mutilation is a traditional practice that reflects a social organization that is incompatible with present-day economic goals. These mutilations are an obstacle to political, social, and economic development" (1993:91).

The report attempts to discuss "circumcision" as a symbol of universal male dominance. Since this report is widely cited, often uncritically, by the most sophisticated scholars, I will use my comments on it to highlight what can be described as a Western feminist problematic. To begin, Fran Hosken describes the practice as a vehicle for the sexual mutilation of females and contends that the operation has been practiced by male-dominated tribal societies of Africa and the Middle East for many centuries (1993:8). She describes the types of "circumcision" women endure and discusses whether they are able to experience orgasm. Hosken and others who have gathered information on the subject have tended to oversimplify the complex tapestry of values that account for its resilience among a wide range of societies. She argues that Western intervention is imperative "because the myth about the importance of cultural tradition must be laid to rest, considering that development—the introduction of Western technology and living patterns—is the goal of every country where the operations are practiced today" (1981:10). By overemphasizing the effects of female "circumcision" on sexual pleasure, she has distanced herself from the socioeconomic contexts of broader violations of women's rights. Her report not only lacks a comprehensive view on the subject but also is noticeably impressionistic. The emphasis on lack of sexual gratification due to "circumcision" may be wrong-headed. A number of circumcised women I interviewed in a northern Sudanese town near Khartoum North said: "Do people think that because we are circumcised, we do not experience pleasure? We have very rewarding relationships and good experiences in our sex lives."

Hosken's inability to recognize the historical and existential realities of African societies makes her work not only ethnocentric and partial but also conveniently unconcerned with the specificity of women's experience. Instead, her intervention has focused on the universality of female oppression by patriarchal authority throughout the world:

> Though violence against women in all kinds of vicious ways goes on all over the world there is one difference: for African men to subject their own small daughters to FGM in order to sell them for a good bride-price shows such total lack of *human compassion* and vicious greed that it is hard to comprehend. But what needs to be examined is the influence such customs have on the character formation of boys who learn such behavior from their fathers. If we want peace in Africa, this kind of socialization for violence of the young must stop. (1993:16, emphasis added)

Apart from her apparent reductionist propensities, Hosken's "male dominance" thesis has political implications, for "if sexual division is assumed, then a category of sexual division is being imported into the analysis that will govern the form of questions that may be asked" (Adams and Cowie 1990:102). The assumption of a "universal sisterhood" falls short of understanding how multiple factors like class, religion, race, and sexuality converge to produce a diversity of experiences that determines the extent to which sexism will be an oppressive force in the lives of women across the globe (see hooks 1984).

In another publication, "Female Genital Mutilation and Human Rights" (1981), Hosken states that "the integrity of the human body is supreme. Any violation of the physical nature of the human person, for any reason whatso-

ever, without the informed consent of the person involved, is a violation of
human rights" (1981:10). This statement, which extends to the recent debates
on women's rights as human rights, confirms the heightened importance of
ensuring the universality, objectivity, and indivisibility of human rights concepts. Ever since the UN Fourth World Conference on Women Platform of
Action (1995) affirmed that women's rights are human rights, this concept
has raised complex issues regarding the applicability of universal laws to local sociocultural settings. According to one Nigerian scholar (as reported by
Rebecca Cook), such human rights discourses may not be productive in
Africa, where the severity of socioeconomic problems faced by women in
countries undergoing structural adjustment "may require basic needs strategy
rather than rights strategy" (Cook 1994:4). In many societies in which cultural expressions are often seen as deliberate acts of violence, dominance, and
transgression against women, such rights discourse is perceived as an ethnocentric commentary on cultural difference. *The Hosken Report* is no exception.

Although Hosken seems to advocate a postcolonial civilizing mission in
which the West should "save" African societies, she makes no attempt to address wider violations of African women's rights in the postcolonial age.
African scholars have documented in rich detail the deleterious effects of
policies such as structural adjustment on women in postcolonial Africa. According to Henrietta Moore (1988:74), "All scholars agree that colonialism
and capitalism restructured traditional economies in a way which had a profound impact on women's economic activities, on the nature of the sexual division of labor, and on the kinds of social and political options which remained open to women." Ghanaian poet Ama Ata Aidoo, for example,
describes the struggles African women face as a result of structural adjustment policies and other present-day dilemmas, which I argue can prove more
"mutilating" to them than genital cutting:

> In 1992, the African woman must cope with a "structural adjustment pro-
> gram" imposed by the International Monetary Fund (IMF) and the World
> Bank that is removing subsidies from her children's education, from health
> care, from food. Transportation to and from vital areas of her life have either
> broken down or never existed. In 1992, there is a drought and the world is
> phenomenally hot. And the African woman has already given up on the sea-
> son's crop. She is now wondering whether there will be enough water to last
> her and her children through this year for drinking, for cooking nonexistent
> food, and to keep the body minimally clean. In 1992, the African woman is
> baffled by news of a "plague that has come to end all human hopes." And
> she is afraid that she and her children might not survive this disease whose
> origins no one seems to know, and for which there is yet no cure. (1998:42)

But even advocating universalizing constructs through "traditional Western
ideals of charity and humanity" is invariably resisted by African women

throughout the continent. Numerous examples are to be found of such acts of resistance in Lillian Sanderson's 1981 book *Against the Mutilation of Women.* According to Sanderson, in colonial Africa the missionary opposition to genital cutting affected church membership and school attendance (see also Chapter 7 in this volume). And in Kenya, Hilda Stumph, an elderly American missionary, was murdered in her isolated cottage in January 1930 after criticizing the practice of female "circumcision" (1981:67). In the Sudan, a demonstration in the town of Ruffaa in Gezira region in Northern Sudan was led in the early 1950s by Republican leader Mahmood Mohamed Taha as a symbol of opposition to the ban on circumcision. To this day, numerous examples of such resistance can be found throughout Africa (see Chapters 11 and 12 this volume).

Equally significant is the fact that Hosken has failed to problematize her own position vis-à-vis Africans,which remains wholly uncomplicated and un-reflective. To echo Stanlie James's recent critique of Alice Walker, Hosken seems "possessed of the pernicious notion that she can and must rescue those unfortunate women from themselves, from their ignorance, and from their patriarchal traditions" (1998:1033). Indeed, Hosken's statement that "even now, both in the Sudan and in many areas in Africa, women are not aware that FGM is not 'necessary' and not practiced in most of the world" (1993:92) affirms her dismissal of the efforts of African/Sudanese women in extirpating genital cutting within their own communities.

The Hosken Report can be critiqued not only for its reductionism and partiality but equally for its failure to circumvent the assumption that there are "women's interests" common to all women. Obviously, this approach not only essentializes and homogenizes women's goals but also, as Moore puts it, causes gender difference to be "privileged over all other forms of difference" (1988:190). Hosken and those who adopt similar perspectives not only consolidate "the other" and contribute to "the fetishization and relentless celebration of difference" (Said 1989:213), but in so doing they affirm as well the separation of self and other, to be read as "civilization" versus "barbarism." Hosken's account further foregrounds the existing imagery and "criminalization" of "the other," who becomes at once the quintessential representation of barbarism and savagery. She has demonstrated with unmistakable clarity her failure to grasp the complexity of African women's lives in their entirety. Apart from the built-in essentializing tendencies of this approach, what it misses is the broader issue of power in society (and especially how women exercise power under specific circumstances); representation; and the larger context within which interlocking historical, cultural, and political forces combine to shape women's actions. Looking at genital cutting too narrowly as a signifier of gender oppression of women as sexed bodies not only ignores context but also continues to reproduce the privileged position that has permeated contemporary feminist analysis. This is a fact that must have limiting effects on conducting research on female "circumcision."

The way in which *The Hosken Report* was articulated not only raises important questions about the global nature of women's oppression but also brings into focus serious methodological concerns. Using "universality" as the primary epistemological stance has paramount methodological pitfalls. For example, Janice Boddy argues that "for the female ethnographer, one message rings clear: though her sex may grant her greater access to women in an alien society, it guarantees no privileged insight into what it means to be a woman in another cultural context; she and her informants may share a common biology: they do not share a common gender" (1989:56). Research on female "circumcision" not only has to take into account the place of the practice in the culture in question but also has to be foregrounded in a multifaceted analysis of the lives of those women whose genitals have become the subject of study. In her essay "When Gender Is Not Enough," Catherine Reissman sums up the crux of the matter:

> Sadly, the clash of culture is reproduced in the interview process itself. Gender congruity is not enough in this interview to overcome the ethnic incongruity. The bond between the woman interviewer and woman interviewee is insufficient to create the shared meanings that could transcend the divisions between them. As a consequence of their differences, the narrator and the interviewer do not develop a shared discourse. Confusion and misunderstanding ensue. (1987:188)

I concur with Rosalind Petchesky and Karen Judd that it is imperative to examine the varying meanings of sexual and reproductive rights from the ground up. She writes: "All of us subscribe to a view of human rights rooted in the concept of 'cultural citizenship' and the mandate that we 'listen to women's voices' in order to build a culturally appropriate definition of what reproductive and sexual rights should entail" (Petchesky and Judd 1998:2). Indeed, elucidating women's perspectives within societies practicing female genital cutting is not only a pressing political issue, but the only path for the formulation of a sound anticircumcision policy.

Ending "Circumcision" in Sudan

In almost every African country, including the Sudan, there is a long-established tradition of opposition to female "circumcision." Considerable historical evidence refutes Hosken's assertion above. In fact, *Tabaqat wad Daifallah* (a genealogy of religious and local community leaders in Sudan) contains evidence suggesting that noted religious leaders such as Farah wad Taktook and Sheikh Hamad wad Umm Marioum had launched successful anticircumcision efforts through the *khalawi* (religious schools) as early as 1860. And by 1934, other religious figures such as Sayed Abdel Rahman El Mahadi and Sayed Ali

El Mirghany urged their followers to abandon the ritual. In 1946 legislation was passed by the British administration in Sudan, prohibiting infibulation but not clitoridectomy (Sanderson 1981). In 1947 a national committee was formed, comprising religious leaders, healthcare workers, and both male and female community activists. Many people could not help but harbor deep suspicion, skepticism, and reluctance toward the ban, chiefly because these efforts were initiated and supported by the colonial administration. Despite the ban and the threat of incarceration, the majority of Sudanese people continued to practice *elkhifad El Pharoni*, or pharaonic circumcision. The fact that only fifteen people were reported to have been prosecuted for infibulating their daughters in 1948 testifies to the fact that the law did not end the practice but simply made people cling more fiercely to it.

During the late 1950s, the Sudanese Women's Union launched a pioneering campaign against FGC, with the Union's magazine *Sawt el Maraa* (Woman's voice) addressing the medical and religious dimensions of the practice. In the mid-1970s, these efforts coincided with the United Nations Declaration of the Decade of Women. An important landmark in Sudanese efforts was the 1978 seminar sponsored by the World Health Organization in Khartoum on "Traditional Practices Affecting the Health of Women and Children," at which attention was directed toward understanding the medical problems, historical roots, social roles, geographical distribution, and prevalence of the practice. Since the 1980s, a number of national agencies working toward ending genital cutting have been formed.

Today a growing number of nongovernmental organizations (NGOs), armed with extensive knowledge of local conditions, are working diligently to address elimination efforts. These include the Babikir Bedri Scientific Association for Women's Studies, the National Committee on Harmful Traditional Practices, the Assembly of Sudanese Muslim Women, and the most recent Sudanese organization to take up this issue, the Mutawinat.[5]

I conclude by pointing out that like many Africans, Sudanese women are by no means passive victims. Their painstaking struggle for social equity is well documented in voluminous writings in their native languages. In approaching eradication efforts henceforth, the perspectives of African/Sudanese women about their own realities will enrich our understanding of female sexuality, human rights, physical violence, postcoloniality, and women's struggles in society in general.

Notes

A version of this chapter was presented at the 95th Annual Conference of the American Anthropological Association in San Fransisco in 1996. I would like to thank Janice Boddy and Donald Nonnini for their comments. I owe a great debt to Fatima Ahmed

Ibrahim, the leader of the Sudanese Women's Union, now living in exile in England. Thanks to Mrs. Nafia Ahmed El Amin for sharing with me the history of Sudanese feminism. I wish to thank Mrs. Amna Abdel Rahman, the national coordinator of the Sudanese National Committee for Traditional Practices Affecting the Health of Women and Children (SNCTP) for providing valuable information pertaining to the campaign against female "circumcision."

Thanks are due to Mohamed Gaad Allah and Margaret Manoa Rawnda of the SNCTP for their help. I wish to express my gratitude to Ylva Hernlund and Bettina Shell-Duncan for their constructive comments. Last but not least, I am indebted to Mustafa Abusharaf, Fatima Mahgoub Osman, Kamal Eissa, Bakhita Amin, and Awad Bab Allah for their help and support during my stay in the Sudan.

1. I use the terms "circumcision" and "genital cutting" interchangeably. In Sudan, the term used by people who practice it, as well as by those who oppose it, is *tahur* or *tahara,* meaning literally "purification." Throughout my fieldwork in the Sudan, I did not encounter any alternative term describing the practice.

2. While visiting El Obeid town in Kordofan province, Western Sudan, I was told that an eight-year-old girl had lost her life during an operation performed by an untrained midwife.

3. I borrow Francis Deng's title *War of Visions* since it is illustrative of the tensions and the impassioned debates surrounding female "circumcision."

4. The obedience law entailed the forced return of women to their husbands in case they did not obey them and wanted to leave them. The women had to be returned to live in *Bait El Ta'a* (the house of obedience). In the initial period after the wife's return, she was forced to obey her husband's orders. To teach her a lesson, her husband was expected to treat her very harshly and refuse to have sex with her.

5. The Mutawinat group has held successful workshops and sponsored grassroots efforts at ending circumcision. Recently, they managed to issue a report addressing the importance of inclusion of female "circumcision" in education curricula, as well as report on a legal strategy.

9

Adopting Female "Circumcision" in Southern Chad: The Experience of Myabé

Lori Leonard

The "circumcision" of women is almost always assumed to have profound and deep-seated significance in those societies in which it is practiced, although the meaning of the act has, at times, been hotly contested. In reality, interpretations offered by "insiders" as well as by "outsiders" are relatively few in number and tend to cluster around the same major themes: tradition, religion, patriarchy. The picture that emerges, again and again, from the social science literature, novels, and popular media is of a relatively fixed and static practice firmly anchored in social institutions and relationships both difficult and slow to change. These narratives of female "circumcision"—outlined in greater detail in the first part of this chapter—have permeated public consciousness. Although Westerners, in particular, might find female "circumcision" difficult to *understand*, most of us, thanks to the pervasiveness of the narratives, can readily *explain* it.

One of the aims of this chapter is to destabilize—if only a little—these dominant constructions of female "circumcision" by presenting data from the south of Chad that suggest a radical departure from the usual portrayals. The data presented in this chapter were collected during two separate periods of fieldwork, the first in 1993–1994 and the second in 1998. The earlier period of study involved the conduct of a survey among urban women, in-depth interviews with key informants throughout the southern region, and an analysis of archival data from institutions in N'Djaména, Chad's capital (Leonard 1996). More recently, in 1998, preliminary data were collected for what will be a series of case studies that aim to capture, at the level of the village, the experiences of the adoption of female "circumcision" among the Sara, one of

Chad's largest ethnic groups. Findings from Myabé, a village where female "circumcision" was first practiced less than twenty years ago and one of several "cases" currently under study, make up the bulk of the second half of this chapter. The voices of village residents—circumcised and uncircumcised women, men, village leaders, the young, and the old—are juxtaposed with those that dominate current discourses on female "circumcision." The latter, however, represent the starting point for this chapter.

Narratives of Female "Circumcision"

The discourse around female "circumcision" in Africa, both in the scientific literature and in the popular media, tends with few exceptions to converge on a standard set of narratives that are used to describe and explain the practice. These accounts are characterized by several major, recurring themes.

Female genital cutting has been practiced for a very long time; it is a "traditional" practice, an "ancient" rite, a "cultural relic" (Dugger 1996; Ebong 1997; Gallo 1985; Joseph 1996; Ogiamien 1998; Ruminjo 1992; WHO 1992). Certain types of sociocultural settings are associated with female "circumcision": patriarchal societies, societies in which women are accorded "low status," cultures in which Islam or "traditional" religions figure prominently, and communities characterized by high rates of poverty and illiteracy (Council on Scientific Affairs, 1995). These environments are thought to support and even impel continued observance of the practice (Annas 1996; Constantinides 1985; Hayes 1975; Joseph 1996). In such contexts, ritual genital cutting is routinely passed from one generation of women to another, becoming over time so firmly "embedded" or "entrenched" in the culture of a group that attempts to reduce or eliminate it are stoutly resisted (Boddy 1982; Anonymous 1993; Morris 1996). Indeed, in the face of "circumcision," African women have been depicted as "prisoners of ritual" (Lightfoot-Klein 1989) and as "*victims* of outdated customs, attitudes and male prejudice" (Dualeh 1982, emphasis added).

These representations are not without basis. Female genital cutting has been carried out in some parts of the African continent for millennia; artifacts from Egypt indicate that the practice antedates Christianity, Islam, and recorded history (Joseph 1996; Lane and Rubinstein 1996; Mackie 1996 and in Chapter 13 of this volume; Meniru 1994). Circumcision is oftentimes a necessary precondition for marriage, and social pressure—even force—compels women to participate in genital cutting ceremonies or, more recently, to seek asylum from them (Abusharaf 1998; Miller 1998). Similarly, religion and religious teachings are commonly invoked as motivation for the observance of female "circumcision" rituals, even though scholars of the Quran and other holy texts indicate that these sources contain no explicit endorsements of "circumcision" or injunctions to "circumcise" women (Anonymous 1993; El Dareer 1982; Lane and Rubinstein 1996; Winkel 1995). Despite trends toward medicalization of female "circumcision" in a few settings (see Chapters 4 and 6 in this volume), in many parts of Africa "circumcision" ceremonies continue to be exclusively lay and feminine events: women serve as organizers, excisers, and caretakers. For the most part, laws, mass media messages, and other intervention strategies have had an equivocal impact on the decision to circumcise (Ogiamien 1988) and in some cases have contributed to an effect opposite that desired (see Chapter 7 of this volume; Abusharaf 1998; Annas 1996; Boddy 1989).

In addition to empirical support for the various elements of the recurrent narratives, a number of theoretical perspectives underpin and are woven through these texts. Feminist theory as well as theories relating to human sexuality, religious practice, ritual, social organization, and status passage have all been used to understand and explain ritual genital cutting. Although the vast majority of the literature on female "circumcision" deals with theory only implicitly, the threads of one or more frameworks for understanding are often evident in the arguments and descriptions presented. Some of the perspectives that have been most influential in shaping the discourse on female "circumcision" are briefly summarized in the following section; their utility in understanding the practice in the Chadian village of Myabé is addressed in subsequent sections of the chapter.

Theoretical Underpinnings of the Narratives on Female "Circumcision"

The perspectives of functionalist, psychoanalytic, and feminist writers are perhaps most evident in the existing body of work on female "circumcision." A very brief synopsis of each of these strands of thought as they relate to genital cutting follows, focused in most cases on the interpretations offered by one or two prominent writers. It should be noted that these are not monolithic groupings, and each broadly defined school of thought houses divergent understandings of female "circumcision." Furthermore, although presented here as distinct bodies of work, there is a certain degree of merging and overlap among the three general perspectives.

Functionalist Interpretations: Working on the Mind

Van Gennep. In *The Rites of Passage,* Arnold van Gennep (1960) argued that "circumcision" is one of many rituals used to mark a status passage—in this case the transition from childhood to adulthood—and can only be properly understood when analyzed in that context. As part of a rite of passage, "circumcision" simultaneously separates initiates from the asexual world of childhood and incorporates them into the sexual and sex-segregated world of adulthood. Yet "circumcision" is construed as having little to do with sex per se. Rather, the function of female "circumcision" is to prepare a woman to occupy a preordained social role within the community and to serve as a potent reminder, both to herself and to others, of this, her proper place.

The act of "circumcision" therefore has little intrinsic meaning; its function in the context of the initiatory process is to "modify the personality of the individual in a manner visible to all" (1960:71). As such, it can be equated with any number of ritual acts that are used to the same end. Van Gennep compares male and female circumcision to, among other things, the removal of teeth; scarification; tattooing; the amputation of fingers or earlobes; the perforation of the earlobe, septum, or hymen; and the cutting of hair.

Critics of van Gennep have made much of these comparisons. Feminists such as Mary Daly (1978) have accused him—as well as other anthropologists, the Catholic Church, development agencies, and educated African leaders—of participating in a "coverup" and "misnaming, not naming, and not seeing" female "circumcision" for what it is: a "Sado-Ritual" and a manifestation of "planetary patriarchy." Anthropologists have countered with their own charges of "ethnocentrism," explaining van Gennep's deemphasis of the sexual aspects of "circumcision" as at least in part a reaction to the racially motivated caricatures of circumcising peoples drawn by his eugenically oriented predecessors (Lyons 1981).[1] Extended debates over functionalist interpretations of female genital cutting have also taken place within anthropological circles, notably concerning the legitimacy of equating "circumcision" (though references are generally to the male variety) with "mutilations" of other parts of the body (Vizedom 1976). Although van Gennep explicitly acknowledged the role of the clitoris as an "erogenous center" and stated that its removal "diminished sexual excitability," he glossed over these properties, contending that they were of little import to members of circumcising populations:

> Actually, semicivilized peoples did not look that far; they cut those organs which, like the nose or the ear, attract the eye because they project and which can, because of their histological constitution, undergo all sorts of treatment without harming an individual's life or activity. (1960:73)

Durkheim. Although Emile Durkheim never explicitly addressed female "circumcision" in *The Elementary Forms of Religious Life*, elements of his analysis of religious practice and ritual echo throughout current discourse on genital cutting among women. Like van Gennep, his contemporary, Durkheim also deemphasized the corporeal aspects of ritual, seeing it instead as a means of binding individuals to the collective and of simultaneously strengthening and renewing the larger group. These processes are described as internal and cerebral rather than physical, "act[ing] on minds, and on minds alone." Ritual activity such as genital cutting is again framed as an instrumental practice, but this time in the service of the collective rather than the individual consciousness, a point on which Durkheim and van Gennep disagreed (Vizedom 1976). For Durkheim, rituals serve not only to periodically remind individuals of the importance of the collective but to ensure its continued existence by engaging members in common efforts to reshape, renew, and reenergize the group. Informants' claims that they carry out a particular ritual because their ancestors did so were taken by Durkheim as evidence for his thesis.

Psychoanalytic Interpretations: "Normalizing" Women

Dual Sexuality of Women. In contrast to anthropologists' functionalist interpretations of female "circumcision," psychoanalytic explanations center on the psychological needs, desires, and impulses of individual actors. Although this lens, like others, has more frequently been trained on male than on female ceremonies, a handful of influential psychoanalytic accounts relating to female "circumcision" dot the literature. These include two volumes by Felix Bryk, *Voodoo-Eros* (1964) and *Circumcision in Man and Woman* (1934), both drawing on fieldwork conducted in East Africa, and chapters by Marie Bonaparte ("Notes on Excision"), a student of Sigmund Freud, and Bruno Bettelheim ("Girls' Rites") at the conclusions of their longer works, *Female Sexuality* (Bonaparte 1953) and *Symbolic Wounds* (Bettelheim 1955). Each author favors a different interpretation of female genital cutting.

Bryk (1934), echoing Freud's theory of the dual nature of female sexuality (Freud 1931), argued that female "circumcision" promotes the transfer of the erogenous zone from the clitoris to the vagina, the sine qua non of "normal" sexual development and "mature" sexuality in women. According to Bryk, removal of the clitoris, women's most sensitive sexual organ, serves as both a facilitator and a symbol of the shift in women's sexuality that occurs around the time of puberty. This shift involves the privatization of women and their sexuality; once "common property," the young uncircumcised, sexually unrestrained, and clitoridal girl becomes the "private possession" of her husband. As such, her sexuality, now vaginal, comes under social control, with reproduction as its intended aim.

Others, including psychoanalytic writers, have challenged Bryk's thesis. Bettelheim, for example, noted the implausibility of "primitive men" knowing about the dual nature of women's sexuality and, in addition, questioned whether removal of the clitoris effectively shifted orgasmic response from the clitoris to the vagina. Freud's pupil Marie Bonaparte also expressed reservations, noting that although male partners of "circumcised" women reported that their partners could achieve orgasm, these reports need to be interpreted with caution as, in her opinion, men are easily "deluded by women in such matters, helped by their vanity and their indifference" (1953:192). Nevertheless, influenced by conversations with Freud in which he apparently concurred with Bryk, stating that "circumcision" could not inhibit women's orgasmic response—"otherwise the Nandi men would never have allowed a custom which deprived them of mutual participation in voluptuous pleasure, which all men prize in all climes" (1953:192)—Bonaparte details her exploration of this question. On the basis of interviews with "circumcised" European and Egyptian women, several of whom retained clitoral sensation despite excision, Bonaparte concluded that female sexuality was not likely to be altered by ablation of the clitoris and that the operation did not achieve the objective of "feminizing" or "vaginalizing" women. Rather, she saw female genital cutting as equivalent to the mental or "psychical intimidations" imposed on European girls in response to masturbation; the objective was to thwart adolescent sexuality. Whereas such a goal was accomplished using verbal tactics in certain settings, more "primitive" peoples, whose instincts are "stronger" and "harder to curb," resorted to physical violence to attain the same end.

A Reaction to Envy. Bettelheim's analysis breaks from previous psychoanalytic accounts in its emphasis on positive, ego-based motives for the practice rather than on the destructive and at times vengeful id-based arguments put forth by his predecessors. Although acknowledging the interpretive challenges posed by the practice of female "circumcision," he nevertheless offers two interrelated explanations. The first has to do with men's ambivalence toward female sexual powers; the second is simply that women copied men's initiation ceremonies. In *Symbolic Wounds*, Bettelheim's thesis is that boys, lacking a physical marker of sexual maturity such as the onset of menstruation, seek through ritual "circumcision" and subincision to acquire the reproductive powers of women. For women, however, Bettelheim argues that the actual physical changes occurring around puberty are far more remarkable than the rites concocted to mark them. In fact, he questions whether the rites might not be an "afterthought," a reaction to men's "awe," "anxiety," and even "envy" in the face of women's mystical metamorphosis. That girls' ceremonies are almost universally described as less complex and less important than those of boys is taken by him as further evidence in support of the notion that female rituals sprang up as parallels or copies of male rituals.

Feminist Interpretations: A Manifestation of "Planetary Patriarchy"

Feminist scholars, whose stance on genital operations pervades the public health literature, have generally interpreted clitoridectomy and other female genital operations as attempts by the patriarchy to control women, their bodies, and their sexuality. This work often portrays the operations as violent,

cruel, and oppressive and highlights the physiological significance and consequences of the practice. In *Gyn/Ecology* (1978), radical feminist Mary Daly
catalogs "African genital mutilations" alongside Indian suttee, Chinese footbinding, European witch burnings, and U.S. gynecology in her list of "Sado-
Rituals." Her analysis of genital cutting is laced with descriptors that signal a
stance distinct from those occupied by functionalist or psychoanalytic writers.
Women's genitalia are "mutilated," not circumcised, excised, or cut. The
practice is "barbaric," an "unspeakable atrocity," a "massacre" "inflicted" on
women. Female "circumcision" is constructed as both a reflection and rein-
forcement of a social and moral order—the "phallocracy"—in which women
are expected (or, in this case, physically forced) to be silent, subservient, virtuous, faithful, and pure.

The fact that women themselves are most often the ones to carry out the
"mutilations" poses, at least on the surface, a problem for feminist analysis.
Daly, however, argues that women's involvement is made possible through a
process of mental numbing; indeed, a common feature of the Sado-Rituals described by Daly (part of what she terms the "Sado-Ritual Syndrome") is to silence the mind, to distract women from reflexive activity or contemplation of
"Self." "Circumcision" deadens and deflects critical thinking by keeping
women preoccupied with the pain of their "mutilation." Thus, Daly characterizes women's role in ritual genital cutting as "passive" and "instrumental."
Men are the real, though hidden, "perpetrators." Substantiating evidence includes male refusal to marry uncircumcised girls and the "reconstruction" of
the female vagina to conform to the shape and size of the future partner.

Daly attacks both functionalist and psychoanalytic writers, among them
van Gennep, Bryk, and Bonaparte, accusing them of producing "patriarchal
scholarship." Indeed, another feature of the Sado-Ritual Syndrome is the use
of "objective" research to obfuscate what Daly calls "the facts"—the patriarchal underpinnings of the practice—and in so doing to legitimate and "mis-
name" "atrocities" like female "circumcision." She depicts Bonaparte, in particular, as having fallen victim to the "phallocracy"; like "circumcised"
women, she has been "mentally castrated" and is therefore unable to see "circumcision" for what it really is. Critics, however, counter that Daly and other
feminist scholars and activists interpret female "circumcision" out of its socioeconomic, political, and historical context, use inflammatory and distancing
language, "other" poor and culturally distant women, and thereby effectively
alienate precisely those women whom they purport to help (Abusharaf 1995;
Gruenbaum 1996; Lyons 1981; Robertson 1996; Chapter 14 of this volume).

Alternative Interpretations

Though the bulk of current discourse on female "circumcision" reflects functionalist, psychoanalytic, or feminist thought, a handful of accounts depart

from these frameworks as they are explicated above. Three examples are noted here. The summaries of these works are extremely cursory, meant only to acknowledge and provide some sense of the types of alternative interpretations found in the literature.

Structuring relations among women: Circumcision in central Kenya. The descriptions of female "circumcision" in central Kenya in the current century, particularly in the post–World War II years, offered by Lynn Thomas (1996 and Chapter 7 of this volume) and Claire Robertson (1996) reveal multiple possible interpretive layers. One is highlighted here. Both authors link genital cutting rituals to the establishment and maintenance of female age sets and to the structuring and enactment of intergenerational relations among different groups of women. Women in the older age sets wield power over their younger counterparts in multiple and even seemingly contradictory ways; "circumcision" illustrates this complexity well. For example, members of older age sets reinforce men's preferential status through the initiatory ritual. Robertson notes the incorporation of certain "cosmetic alterations," notably scarification of the pubis, that supposedly enhance men's sexual gratification. At the same time, however, the ceremonies are occasions for forging solidarity among members of the age sets and the newest one in particular and for garnering support for the all-women structure itself.

In the years 1956–1959, when young Kenyan girls defied en masse a ban on "circumcision" imposed by the British colonial government, missionaries, and associations of older men, their actions were interpreted, at least in part, as an effort to maintain this age-based system of organization. In explaining why thousands of adolescent girls circumcised themselves and each other during this three-year period, Thomas (1996 and Chapter 7) argues that "circumcision" "became a test and demonstration of their strength and determination as an age group" (1996:351). Similarly, the actions of older women, who often "recircumcised" girls who participated in the resistance movement, in many instances because the latter had underestimated the extent of cutting required, are placed within the same interpretive framework. Members of the older age sets sought to reassert the hierarchy and to regain control over their positions within it. Robertson's analysis traces the subsequent decline of female "circumcision" and initiation to the restructuring of women's collectivities; in the postwar period the age-based structure has been gradually replaced by groupings organized around economic and class-based interests. The paradox, as she points out, is that declines in "circumcision"—a boon for women's health—have been accompanied by the erosion of an organizational structure that provided women with a more predictable measure of security, support, and status than the market-driven collectivities that have followed.

Socializing fertility: Infibulation in a Sudanese village. In her 1982 study of a northern Sudanese village, Janice Boddy also locates women as central and strategic actors, but this time in the practice of infibulation rather than cli-toridectomy. She interprets genital cutting and covering or closure as sym-bolic acts that serve to foreground women's fertility by de-emphasizing their sexuality. Infibulation defines and perhaps even creates women as potential mothers rather than as sex partners. This analysis is developed through the ex-plication of a number of symbolic associations, including those having to do with "enclosedness," "purity," "smoothness," "whiteness," and "cleanliness," that are too complex to be detailed here. At the crux of her argument, how-ever, is the notion that by purifying, smoothing, and cleaning women's outer surface and by enclosing and safeguarding the womb, infibulation and the re-infibulation that is conducted periodically throughout a woman's reproduc-tive life accomplish the goal of asserting her fitness and her capacity for reproduction.

The ability to produce children and particularly to cofound a lineage sec-tion is what makes Sudanese women in the village Boddy studied "socially indispensable." It is this indispensability that infibulation underscores. The production of children, and apparently sons more than daughters, also gains women status and respect. Reproduction is sanctioned, however, only in the context of marriage, which is in turn predicated on infibulation. Therefore, in-fibulation as the crucial first step in the trajectory toward relative privilege and position can be interpreted as an "assertive" and "strategic" act on the part of village women.

Deodorizing female herders: A historical interpretation of infibulation in So-malia. A third example is found in the work of Pia Grassivaro Gallo and Franco Viviani (1992), who put forth an evolutionary hypothesis for the prac-tice of infibulation among women in mixed-herding populations in Somalia. Although admitting that confirmation of their thesis is practically impossible, they present data to suggest that infibulation was, at least historically, a prac-tical solution to the need to control body odors, particularly those produced by menstruation, given off by female herders. By preventing odor, infibula-tion protected women, whose husbands were away tending larger livestock and who normally lived with their children in a tent surrounded only by a fence of brambles, from wild animal attacks. For the same reason it also made women's presence "less disquieting" to sheep and goats, which, according to the authors, have been shown in experimental studies to avoid menstrual blood. In the harsh Somali environment, where women and their children were dependent on the herd for sustenance, infibulation thus enhanced the probability of survival.

The differences and the tensions across and within the theoretical schools and alternative sources highlighted above belie a commonly shared core assumption: female "circumcision" is almost everywhere invested with great significance. Functionalist, psychoanalytic, and feminist accounts all argue that female "circumcision" works to channel women into prescribed social roles or to place limits on their behavior. Disagreements are largely confined to the question of *how* this is accomplished: Through a process of socialization? In reinforcing the collectivity (and the relations it entails) and individuals' ties to it? By facilitating "normal" psychosexual development? By means of blatant violence and physical "mutilation"? The handful of writers who have infused the literature with different perspectives have also portrayed the practice as deeply meaningful or at least extremely practical.

In the second half of this chapter, I explore how the narratives of female "circumcision," the theoretical perspectives that underpin them, and the common assumption of significance relate to the experience of female "circumcision" in southern Chad. In particular, can the existing frameworks help us to understand the recent adoption of female "circumcision" in the Sara village of Myabé? This "case," and others in the region like it, is perplexing in that it runs counter to current trends. A growing number of reports attest to a diminution of the practice elsewhere on the continent and link measures of "modernization," such as women's increased access to education, with the decline (see Chapter 4 of this volume; Caldwell, Orubuloye, and Caldwell 1997; Crossette 1998; Knudsen 1994; Meniru 1991, 1994). In July 1998, as fieldwork for this study was under way, the United Nations bestowed its Population Award on the Sabiny Elders Association, a group in eastern Uganda, for their work in reducing the incidence of female "circumcision" by more than one-third (Crossette 1998). Opposition to the practice on the part of international bodies, such as the World Health Organization (WHO) and the United Nations Commission on Human Rights, and in the form of declarations and resolutions from international, regional, and national forums appears to be coalescing (Abusharaf 1998; Annas 1996; Dorkenoo 1996). How, then, is the recent adoption of female "circumcision" in Myabé to be understood? To provide context for the data presented, I turn first to brief descriptions of the Sara, the research setting, and the history of female "circumcision" in southern Chad.

The Sara, the Sara Kaba, and the Village of Myabé

The Sara number slightly more than 1.7 million and constitute between one-quarter and one-third of Chad's total population (Bureau Central du Recensement 1995a). Though they are usually spoken of as a collective, the Sara are actually an amalgamation of at least twelve smaller ethnic subgroups that share a cultural heritage and speak similar languages (Chapelle 1986; Fortier

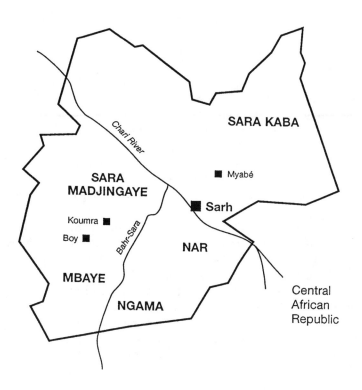

Map 9.1   The Moyen-Chari Region

1982). The Sara Kaba, with an estimated population of 80,000 (Ngoussou n.d.), are one of the largest of the Sara subgroups and, as residents of the village of Myabé, are the focus of much of this chapter.

The Sara's homeland is the Moyen-Chari, one of Chad's fourteen administrative regions, or prefectures, situated in south-central Chad and forming a portion of the country's border with the Central African Republic (see Map 9.1). The Sara Kaba inhabit the northeastern corner of the Moyen-Chari region, which includes the village of Myabé (population 1,069), located about 60 kilometers to the north and east of Sarh, the regional capital. The village serves as the *chef lieu*, something like a county seat, for approximately ten smaller villages in the area. The 1993 census enumerated a total population of 495 males and 574 females divided among 188 households (unpublished data).

The village economy, like that of other Sara villages, is centered almost exclusively around agricultural production and, secondarily, fishing and hunting. Cotton culture, introduced and made compulsory under French colonial rule, is the principal source of revenue for most families. Millet, sorghum, peanuts, and a local legume called poids de terre (earth peas) constitute the staples of the local diet.

In terms of social organization, the group is both patrilineal and patrilocal. Descent is traced to a common ancestor known as the *gir ka*, around whom the village is constituted (Magnant 1977). Marriage is exogamous, women are acquired as marriage partners via the payment of a bride-price, and polygamy is practiced, although it is relatively rare among the Sara Kaba (Ngoussou n.d.). Basic sociodemographic statistics are not yet available for Myabé because more structured surveys are planned for a later phase of this ongoing work and existing census data cannot be disaggregated at the level of the village.

The overall impact of Christian missionaries on the Sara has been far-reaching, even though their influence in Myabé has been minimal. American Baptists settled in the Moyen-Chari in 1925 and were followed a decade later by French Catholic orders. According to the 1993 census, fully 85.2 percent of Sara are Christian: 51.9 percent Catholic and 33.3 percent Protestant. Animism remains the religion of 5.2 percent of all Sara; few (1.7 percent) have adopted Islam. Priests and pastors from larger regional centers visit Myabé once or twice a year, and residents estimate membership in the village's Catholic and Protestant congregations to range from twenty to fifty men and women.

As an aggregate, the Sara have some of the highest rates of literacy and primary school attendance in Chad. The national literacy rate stood at 10.8 percent in 1993, the last census year, whereas the rate among the Sara was nearly 50 percent higher, at 15.1 percent (Bureau Central du Recensement 1995b). An even greater gap exists with regard to primary school attendance, which is not compulsory. Less than one-third (31.8 percent) of all school-age girls and boys in Chad were enrolled in the primary grades in 1993, compared to nearly three in five (57.5 percent) among the Sara. Important gender and urban-rural differences on both measures are observed in all areas of the country. In Myabé, two hangars erected at the edge of the village are used to teach first- and second-grade classes. Primary school instructors have been difficult to recruit and retain; courses are currently taught by a newly arrived civil servant and by a volunteer from the village. Sporadically filed enrollment records obtained from the regional department of education in Sarh indicate that attendance over the last decade has fluctuated between thirty-two and 140 for the two classes, with boys outnumbering girls by an average ratio of approximately five to one.

Non-Western forms of education, notably male and female initiation ceremonies, are a prominent feature of Sara life. Male initiation (*yo-ndo*) is a rite

of passage from childhood to adulthood practiced by all of the Sara subgroups, including the Sara Kaba. Ethnographers have speculated that Sara
men have been initiated for at least two centuries and perhaps for as many as
four or five (Fortier 1982; Jaulin 1967). In contrast to the male equivalent, female initiation, variously called *bagne* or *gadja*, has a much shorter history.
The centerpiece of the female initiation ceremony is the practice of female
"circumcision"; indeed, the practices of initiation and "circumcision" are
nearly synonymous. Prior to the adoption of female "circumcision," female
initiation was virtually nonexistent. Only women belonging to the family of
the *mbang*, the Sara's supreme spiritual and religious leader, participated in a
form of initiation called *gor*. During the twentieth century, however, female
initiation and "circumcision" diffused throughout Sara territory and have become an important feature of life in the vast majority of villages in the region.

A Brief History of Female
"Circumcision" Among the Sara

No definitive history of female "circumcision" in southern Chad exists. However, oral accounts provided by older Sara men and women indicate that the
"circumcision" of women is a recent event, probably dating back no more
than 150 years, to the middle of the nineteenth century. According to local
folklore, "circumcision," of the *sunna* or Type I variety (Toubia 1994), was
originally practiced in Boy, a small village outside Koumra (see Map 9.1),
and was performed by a single woman who alone had knowledge of the operation (Leonard 1996; Négué and Kemoral 1997). Girls from surrounding
communities were brought to Boy to be "circumcised," an event captured in
the lyrics to songs still sung by older women in the area.

Some investigators (Négué and Kemoral 1997) have speculated that "circumcision" was introduced in the Moyen-Chari in conjunction with the nine-
teenth-century *razzias* (slave raids conducted by the Arab empires to the
north). Although the timing is plausible, no evidence exists to either confirm
or dispute the link. Oral accounts and linguistic evidence suggest the possibility of multiple, simultaneous influences from the south as well as from the
north. Certain of the Sara subgroups, notably the Ngama, refer to female "circumcision" as *gadja* and claim to have "copied" it from their neighbors in the
Central African Republic, who use a similar term, *ganza*, for the procedure
(Eustache 1952; Maran 1921). Others use the term *bagne* and cite the Sara
Madjingaye, the largest of the Sara subgroups, as the source. Some of the
older women interviewed recalled a time when distinctions between the two
traditions, *bagne* and *gadja*, were meaningful but acknowledge that these lines
have since been blurred and that the practices are now entirely equivalent.

From Boy and, perhaps, the Central African Republic, female "circumcision" has gradually diffused across the Moyen-Chari region. During the twentieth century, an increasing number of women in an increasing number of villages experimented with the practice, developing around it, in many places, a form of female initiation. The Sara's adoption of female "circumcision" does not represent the revival of a dormant or dying practice, as has been documented among other African groups (e.g., Nypan 1991). Rather, female genital operations are an entirely novel addition to the Sara's cultural repertoire. Only a few isolated pockets remain, notably in some of the Sara Kaba villages in the northeast and in a handful of Mbaye villages in the south, where genital operations are not performed on women. As a subgroup, the Sara Kaba are the most recent adopters; oral accounts indicate that Sara Kaba women were first "circumcised" around 1950 (Leonard 1996; Ngoussou n.d.), and in some villages, including the village of Myabé, adoption is much more recent.

Until the current decade, relatively little was written about female "circumcision" among the Sara. Most of the works of explorers, colonial officers, Christian missionaries, historians, and ethnographers make no mention of female initiation and "circumcision," and although a number of unpublished manuscripts touch on the subject, they do so in a cursory manner (Aerts 1954; Anonymous 1963; Chaine and Meynier 1951; Dagoma 1990; Doh, 1984; Kogongar n.d.; Kameldy 1964). In the 1990s, a handful of descriptive studies relating to female "circumcision" appeared, documenting the prevalence of the practice, the attitudes and opinions of Sara men and women toward "circumcision," and the reasons they provide for carrying it out (Chaine and Saidel 1992; Leonard 1996; Nabia 1991; Négué and Kemoral 1997). Read as a whole, these generally broadbrush accounts reveal the major features of the practice. Approximately 80 percent of Sara women are "circumcised," most between the ages of eight and twelve. Clitoridectomy is the most commonly practiced procedure, with only rare instances of more severe forms of cutting. Women are generally "circumcised" outside their natal village, with others belonging to the same age cohort and by nonmedical personnel. The ritual is followed by a prolonged period of recuperation sometimes accompanied by education, typically lasting about one month and culminating in a public "coming-out" ceremony.

Beyond these general contours, however, important variations in practice are found. The intent of this chapter is not, therefore, to represent the experience of female "circumcision" for all Sara or even for all Sara Kaba. The focus is instead on the narratives of men and women in a single village, which raise important questions about the meaning and practice of female "circumcision" in this setting, some of which have yet to be explored. More importantly, they represent a clear break from the narratives outlined at the start of this chapter. The section that follows comprises a brief historical overview of the village's experience of "circumcision," followed by the interpretations of the practice offered by some of its residents.

Adopting Female "Circumcision": The Village of Myabé

Genital operations have been practiced in Myabé for less than twenty years; although estimates vary by several years in either direction, most villagers concurred that the first girls to be "circumcised" attended the ceremony around 1980. Since that time five cohorts of young women, probably no more than fifty or sixty girls in total, have participated in the ceremonies. With very few exceptions, mothers, grandmothers, parents, and religious and spiritual leaders in the village are not advocates of female "circumcision" and do not organize or carry out "circumcision" ceremonies. In fact, most of them express strong opposition to female genital operations, and some have actively sought to block infiltration of the practice. The impetus for the adoption of this innovation comes instead from adolescent girls. Young women in Myabé organize themselves to undergo the procedure and actively seek women from outside the village to conduct the operations and to care for them in the period of recuperation that follows. Some girls attempt to enlist parental support, whereas others obtain the necessary materials (i.e., razor blades, clothes, fees, food items) on their own and surreptitiously and sometimes describe sneaking away from the family compound on the morning of the ceremony to join their friends and age-mates. Adolescent girls insist that their participation is "voluntary" and use neither religion nor "tradition" to bolster their claims that "female circumcision is good." The narratives of these girls as well as those of other village residents suggest that female "circumcision" in Myabé is anything but a "traditional" practice forced upon passive, young victims as a result of patriarchy, centuries-old custom, or religious doctrine. Instead, genital cutting is more like a fashion statement; it is a thoroughly "modern" thing to do.

Zaki

Now they imitate modernism. Circumcision is modernism. It came from somewhere else. I don't know where it came from. People say it came from the Sara Madjingaye but I don't know.

—Zaki

Zaki did not know her age, saying only that she was born "before the whites came." She was perhaps the oldest resident of Myabé, was nearly blind, and lived by herself in a small hut close to the center of the village. In the early

1920s, when Chad was still part of French Equatorial Africa, Zaki's husband was recruited to assist in the construction of the *chemin de fer,* the railroad linking Brazzaville in the Congo with Pointe-Noire on the Atlantic coast (Fortier 1982:123; Comby 1984). Because she was newly married and had no children, Zaki was taken along to do road-clearing work, "sweeping," in the morning and to prepare food for the men in the afternoon. She described the journey from Myabé to Brazzaville as long and extremely arduous. The recruits were put in neck chains and taken to Sarh, where they were loaded into vehicles and later into boats. She remembered that no one would stop to pick up luggage that had fallen over the side of the truck and that the bodies of those who died en route were left by the roadside or were thrown overboard.

At the time she was recruited for the work in Brazzaville, Zaki, like other women in Myabé, wore lip plates, a practice specific, even among the Sara, to the Sara Kaba. Prior to marriage, a woman's fiancé would pierce her lips with a pointed object, and the holes would be gradually stretched as the woman, over time, inserted successively larger pieces of polished wood or dried gourds, called "calabashes," into the openings. N. Ngoussou (n.d.) reports that the lip plates weighed as much as 20 to 30 grams and sometimes measured 10 to 30 centimeters in circumference. The size of the plates "disfigured" women and made it difficult for them to speak, eat, or even retain saliva. Although some writers have speculated that the practice served to repel slave raiders by "damaging" women, making them look "monstrous" and "ugly" and reducing their value on the market (Aerts 1954; Ngoussou n.d.), Zaki described lip plates as doing the obverse. For her, the plates, like body scarring, ear piercing, and tooth removal, were a means of beautification.

Only a slight trace of a scar remained where Zaki's upper lip had been pierced; the "white people" had forced the women to remove their lip plates as well as their earrings upon arrival in Brazzaville. Zaki didn't know why; she and the other women "were afraid to ask," but she speculated that the white people found their calabashes beautiful because they confiscated them and "took them all for themselves." When Zaki returned to Myabé after two years of work on the railroad, she noted that those who had stayed behind were still wearing the lip plates but that the practice stopped shortly thereafter. In fact, the *femmes à plateaux* or *manda sundu,* as the women who wore lip plates are called, were few in number, limited to the area of the Moyen-Chari around Myabé, and almost exclusively women of Zaki's generation.

In making sense of female "circumcision" and the actions of village girls, Zaki reflected on the past and on the practices of her own generation. In her view, young girls in Myabé are no longer interested in lip plates or body scarring; these and other practices have virtually disappeared, and only the oldest members of the community bear their traces. Instead, adolescents are experimenting with novel practices, "copying modernism." Yet unlike most of the village elders, Zaki did not find these changes disturbing; she did not find girls' involvement in the "circumcision" ceremonies problematic and was not opposed to the practice. In her judgment, "female circumcision must be good, because if it wasn't good people wouldn't copy each other."

Nabia

I imitated my friends. I saw the dance of Fatimé and I thought it was good. . . .We call people who didn't do it "sato." We just call each other this and it's sure that if your friends call you "sato" you'll go.

—Nabia

The most common answer given to the question of why girls in Myabé have started to attend "circumcision" ceremonies has to do with "imitating" or "copying" others. The first women from the village to be "circumcised" say they "saw it" elsewhere and "it interested [them]" or they "thought it was good." More recently "circumcised" women, like Nabia, talk about imitating their friends and neighbors. When women describe what it is they see and judge favorably, their narratives center almost exclusively around the coming-out ceremony; for example: "What I thought was good was the moment when they came out from the circumcision and danced."

Once the "circumcision" wounds are healed, generally about a month after the procedure, the girls take part in a public dance that is widely attended by village residents. As part of that ceremony they wear strings of multicolored beads, cover their faces with masks, and paint their bodies with kaolin and *karité* oil to give it a reddish sheen. Both men and women comment on the aesthetic appeal of the performance:

When they come out and dance and wear kaolin they are beautiful.
—male, about twenty

I was in Sarh and I saw it among the Sara there. I saw it here in Myabé too before going. People appreciated it a lot and that is also what pushed us to go.
—"circumcised" female, about twenty-five

I can't see [the "circumcision"] but I can see the way they dress and how they look when they come out.
—male, about twenty-five

The appeal of the public coming-out ceremony is not, however, linked with the operation that precedes it. Girls talk about participation in the dance, but not in the "circumcision" ritual itself, as enhancing their ability to attract boys. Their allure is depicted as ephemeral and as concentrated in the moment of the dance when "we wear what we wear" and "the kaolin we put on our bodies makes us attractive." Paradoxically, being "circumcised" is said to benefit women little, if at all, in terms of their ability to attract and sexually satisfy a member of the opposite sex. Men and women alike forcefully assert that female "circumcision" is not a necessary precursor to marriage. In fact, many of the young men in Myabé express a preference for uncircumcised sexual and marriage partners, and many of the women know and reiterate this preference: "Men say that circumcised women, it's not good to be having sex with them. They take everything off. They don't leave even a piece of the clitoris so men make fun of them."

In addition to the aesthetic appeal of the public coming-out ceremony, girls like Nabia say they are motivated to "copy" or take part by peer pressure and the desire to do what their friends do (see Chapter 12 of this volume). A variety of epithets, among them *koy*, *kara*, and *sato*, are reserved for uncircumcised women. None of these epithets are Sara Kaba, and their use in Myabé seems to be selective, infrequent, and relatively time-delimited.[2] Moreover, none of the girls or women in the village knew the meanings of these terms. *Koy*, from the Sara Madjingaye, means "owl," a bird that is both feared and despised by the Sara. Owls, like the spirits, circulate at night; they are thought to be harbingers of bad news or bad luck, and the Sara attempt to avoid them or keep them at a distance. *Koy* is also a term of derogation used to refer to the uninitiated who, like owls, are disdained, ignored, and marginalized (Leonard 1996). The other terms, *kara* and *sato*, were identified by informants in Sarh as derived from the Rito, a small ethnic group in the Central African Republic, though their meaning in the Rito language is not clear. One "circumcised" woman from Myabé said that "when you quarrel with your friend you'll call her *kara*, but if you do you'll be sure to [physically] fight with her. Otherwise there is no reason to do this." Another young woman, this one uncircumcised, said that her friends used to come to her house and tell her that her clitoris was long, but they have since stopped. She has no regrets about not going to the "circumcision" ceremony, and her husband (she is now married and has one child) doesn't care that she is not "circumcised."

"Copying" is spoken of in a similar manner in relation to other common practices like tooth removal and facial scarring that, for women in Myabé, are independent of the initiation ceremonies. The majority of men and women in Myabé (based on an eyeball estimate, perhaps three-quarters of the adult population), have removed either two or four bottom teeth, mostly because friends have done the same:

> If your friend did it and it looks good you'll do it too.
> When you've seen your friend take out her teeth you'll do the same thing.
> Before I had my teeth out my friends made fun of me and said I had too many teeth. I did it at age nine with one other person after my friends started making fun of me.

One woman drew a direct parallel between tooth removal and genital cutting:

> It's not parents who take our teeth out. It's like "circumcision"; the parents will accept it if you do it even if they don't want it. I did it by myself. I went to an old man. My friends had done it first and made fun of me when I didn't have it done. It hurt, but I had to do it.

Munikir

> *There isn't a goal, but it is for pleasure. You go, you get circumcised, they buy you a head scarf and clothes and you find lots of money. . . . We did it for pleasure only. For new clothes and oil on our bodies and people pay us. I was happy.*
>
> —Munikir

Munikir was in the third or fourth group—she couldn't remember which—of women from Myabé to be "circumcised." She said she had seen other girls from the village do it—the dance they did afterwards, the new clothes they wore—and had asked her father if she, too, could go. He didn't want her to go, but she asked him many times and told him that all of her friends had been "circumcised," and he finally accepted. When she came out, he and other family members bought her new clothes and gave her money.

In other parts of the Moyen-Chari region, female "circumcision" is associated, to varying degrees, with initiation into adult society. In some areas the theme of death (of the child) and rebirth is symbolically played out by replacing initiates' material possessions, such as clothes, with new ones, giving them a new name, and sometimes even constructing new living quarters for them within the family compound (Leonard 1996). These practices are minimally evident in Myabé; some of the girls describe receiving new clothes or a small gift at the time of the public ceremony that signals the completion of the ritual, others say they received nothing at all. Yet, even when they are observed, these practices are often cast quite differently. One woman described the acquisition of new clothes in the context of paying the *handa gadja*, the woman who cares for the newly "circumcised" girl in the interim between the "circumcision" operation and the coming-out ceremony, for her services:

> Those that have been circumcised pay the *brodjoro* and the *handa gadja*. The *brodjoro* gets 6,000 CFA and the *handa gadja* gets 3,000 CFA and the clothes that you left the house with go to the *handa gadja*. They take that from you in the bush.

Both during the "circumcision" ceremony and in the coming-out period, women remarked not only on the possible material gains but also on the attention they received and on the special or different things they got to wear or do:

> They put leaves over my face when I walked back here. I laid on a bed and they washed me with hot water and put oil on every day. . . . We get to wear skirts with medallions on them.

> People didn't do it here. We went to [another village] and then they brought us back here. People accompanied me and gave cries of joy and applauded. . . . They accompany you, put leaves on you, and are singing with you. . . . They teach you songs and how to dance and then they make you come out and dance so that people can see you. . . . Circumcision is something people admire a lot; when your friend sees you he is really happy. You cut your clitoris, put on kaolin and medals.

Kadja

> *Here in the village you can do it if you want to but you don't have to if you don't want to. There are even young boys who haven't been circumcised. There are old men who still aren't circumcised. They went to initiation and everything!*
>
> *When we got to the* brodjoro *certain women were afraid and they ran away. But I did it since it was my wish.*
>
> —Kadja

Before going to the ceremony, Kadja had a vague sense of what to expect. She said she knew she was going to be cut; in fact, all girls in the village, whether "circumcised" or uncircumcised, know that the *brodjoro,* the woman who acts as the exciser, cuts something called a clitoris. When they get to the "circumcision" site, the *brodjoro* tells them what the clitoris is and at the same time tells them not to tell others, not "even your own daughter." According to Kadja, if women want to know what "happens there," they just have to go and find out for themselves, and "if it hurts you or not that's your problem because you've gone voluntarily."

Although Kadja and other women talk of "copying" and peer pressure and are mindful of the insults reserved for uncircumcised women, their narratives also hint at personal agency, individual choice, and respect for the choices of others:

> You don't have the right to say anything to your sister because you yourself went voluntarily, so you shouldn't come back and say anything.
>
> —Fatimé, "circumcised"

Everything is voluntary. I didn't go, and if my friends make fun of me it means little to me. I'm already old. Maybe my daughter will go, but I won't force her.

—Albertine, uncircumcised

Nanda, Chief of the Land

My grandparents didn't do it and it keeps it from raining. Young girls don't listen. They go somewhere else and do it and bring it back here. I tell them not to go somewhere else and do it. It is commerce. . . . For me it is ignorance, it is not beauty or anything. It disturbs things in the village. I get angry all by myself. There is nothing I can do. The older people obeyed me and the younger people don't. It hurts me.

—Nanda, chief of the land

Nanda is the *chef de terre*, the "chief of the land," or the supreme religious and spiritual authority, in Myabé. There are actually three *chefs de terre* in the village, each in charge of separate functions, but Nanda is widely regarded as the most important and the most powerful. In talking about female "circumcision," many village residents mentioned the chief's opposition to the practice, though their comments reflected different interpretations of his stance. Some thought he was "jealous" of the *brodjoro* because he received none of the profits such as money, locally made beer and whisky, or chickens from the ritual. The *brodjoro* were described by a variety of informants, including the chief, as *commerçants*, or businesswomen, who travel throughout the region drumming up business for their services.

By his own account, Nanda is vehemently opposed to female "circumcision" because it is not a tradition of the *kaka* (ancestors) and has never been practiced in Myabé. He said he tells young girls not to do it because it brings "nothing good"; instead, shedding blood on the ground "disturbs things." Until now, Nanda has been relatively successful at keeping "circumcision" out of Myabé itself and, to a lesser extent, in preventing girls from having the operation done. Four of the five groups of girls who have been "circumcised" had the operation performed in neighboring villages, at distances ranging from 7 to 14 kilometers. The *brodjoro* and the *handa gadja* have almost always been outsiders, in large part because the women who play these roles have to be "circumcised." The one time the wife of a Myabé resident organized a "circumcision" ceremony, Nanda said he "kicked her out" of the village and forced the girls to stay clear of Myabé until their wounds were completely healed.

The "disturbance" associated with female "circumcision" that Nanda talked about most was the lack of rain. By the end of June, fully two months into the rainy season, it had only rained twice in Myabé, the cotton was not yet planted, and all of the crops were well behind schedule. People were talking about the rising prices and diminishing reserves of grain, where the crops stood last year at the same time, and whether they could afford to buy seeds to replace those already lost to the drought. In addition to claiming that female "circumcision" caused "disturbances," including a lack of rain, in the village, Nanda talked about it as a symptom of more pervasive and deep-seated change that he finds difficult to deal with and highly disconcerting. Older residents used to listen to him, but the younger generation no longer does, and he "get[s] angry all by [himself]."

Parents

Most parents, mothers as well as fathers, expressed confusion, anger, and dismay at the arrival of female "circumcision" and at the participation in the rituals of young girls and, notably, their daughters. To date, female "circumcision" in Myabé is a first-generation phenomenon; there is no case of a "circumcised" mother with a "circumcised" daughter, and only one or two "circumcised" women have daughters at or approaching the age of "circumcision." Therefore, mothers with "circumcised" daughters have no firsthand knowledge of the practice, having been prohibited access to the girls during the cutting and caretaking periods. One "circumcised" woman said her mother only "saw what was cut" when she gave birth because her mother needed to take care of her postpartum "wound."

Although parents in Myabé are largely opposed to female "circumcision," their comments reveal the first hints of potential change. The views of Marie and Kutu (appearing last in the following sequence of quotes), both "circumcised" mothers, signal a possible shift in village attitudes:

> If there was someone in the village who was capable of doing it I wouldn't be for it. I didn't do it and so why should my children? My daughter hasn't done it. I forbid her from doing it a while ago. When I was young I went to the wrestling matches with my friends. . . .
> —Kemata, uncircumcised mother

> I had seven children, three girls, and I didn't go get my clitoris cut to spill blood on the ground. It's spilling blood. I have three girls, and two were circumcised against my wishes. I was sick and they left to do it. I didn't buy them anything. . . . I don't know what they removed from my daughters because they didn't let me in to see because I wasn't circumcised.
> —Kinga, uncircumcised mother

> I had seven girls, and only one did it. I didn't talk to them; it was the girl herself who went. After she came back she didn't explain herself. I rejected my daughter for a while—she went by herself, I had nothing to do with taking care of her. The woman who did it had to take care of her. But finally I was obligated to accept it.
> —Kemta, uncircumcised mother

We didn't do it before. The girls don't tell their parents; they organize themselves. I haven't had any children. I see that parents have to accept when
their daughters come back. . . .

—Simianda, uncircumcised, childless

Girls don't know what they are doing when they go to do the "circumcision." They see the dance and the celebration afterwards and they think they
want to be part of this.

—Celestin, father

If the *chef de terre* authorizes it I'll take my daughters, but if he doesn't I
won't. I think it's good.

—Marie, "circumcised" mother

I have a daughter in [another village] who is with her aunts. Last year she
wanted to go, but because the boys were [at initiation] they couldn't go. But
if my daughter goes I'll go with her.

—Kutu, "circumcised" mother

Toward New Narratives of Female "Circumcision": Lessons from Myabé

The experience of female "circumcision" in Myabé deviates markedly from
the descriptions and the analyses that fill the literature and circulate in public
discourse, suggesting that the practice is not as monolithic as the standard
narratives suggest. Perhaps the most striking divergence relates to the recency
of the practice; in Myabé female "circumcision" is a purely first-generation
phenomenon, dating back no further than two decades. Yet other points of
contrast are equally remarkable. Ritual genital cutting is not a mandatory element of a rite of passage for young girls (in fact, these types of ceremonies
have never been a feature of life for Sara Kaba women); it is not a prerequisite for marriage or childbearing; and it is not a practice imposed on the
youngest generation by parents, religious authorities, patriarchy, or the weight
of tradition. In fact, most parents have resisted the infiltration of the practice
by attempting to prohibit their daughters from participating and have generally reacted with anger, disgust, confusion, and—finally—resignation when
they have lost this battle. Young girls are the innovators and experimenters.
Their adoption of female "circumcision" raises wide-ranging questions, including questions about the meanings of genital cutting; the dynamism of culture and cultural practices like female "circumcision"; and the form, timing,
and focus of strategies for change.

Village narratives suggest that the theoretical frameworks used, whether
implicitly or explicitly, to make sense of genital cutting provide little insight
into the events unfolding in Myabé. It is difficult to argue that female "cir-

cumcision" marks a status passage for village women or that it serves to rein-vigorate the group. Rather than reinforcing the social and moral order, female "circumcision" is interpreted by many as an unwelcome departure from the ways of the ancestors and as evidence of a growing rent in the social fabric. No shifts in girls' status, role, or social position succeed the "circumcision" ceremony, and it has little symbolic content suggestive of transition.[3] Female "circumcision" is not about "vaginalizing" women (the location and function of "what is to be cut" or "what they removed" is usually vaguely understood) or parental repression of adolescent sexuality. Although elements of the fe-male ceremony resemble male initiation, a practice dating back centuries, women are more intent upon copying each other. Standards of beauty, shaped and upheld by both men and women, contribute to the appeal of the coming-out ceremony. Yet men have little direct hand in the adoption of female "cir-cumcision" in Myabé, and girls are by no means forcibly, violently, or aggres-sively being made to conform to patriarchal ideals through this act. The attainment of womanhood is still tied, unequivocally, to reproduction. As one respondent indicated, "A woman is a woman once she has a child."

In addition to missing the mark, the interpretations of female "circumci-sion" offered by functionalist, psychoanalytic, and feminist writers seem, at least with reference to Myabé, overdrawn. At present, female "circumcision" has no great sexual, social, or symbolic significance in the village. Although adolescents exert pressure on each other to attend the "circumcision" cere-monies, their attempts at persuasion are described as rather mild, unorga-nized, and short-lived, and the voluntary nature of girls' participation is widely recognized by their peers. When adolescent girls talk about "circumci-sion," the usual themes of tradition, religion, and patriarchy are notably ab-sent from their narratives, and different clusters of meaning emerge. Girls are saying that "circumcision" is little more than a fashion statement, a fad, something that is fun, rebellious, and cool. Village narratives force us to ask not what it means, but, rather, whether it means anything at all. At least some residents think not. One informant, tired of my questions, said "You are look-ing too hard—there is nothing!"

Yet although fads often fade away, the future of female genital cutting in Myabé is less than clear. Data gathered in other Sara villages (not presented in this chapter) where female "circumcision" was first experimented with in the 1930s (fifty years earlier than in Myabé) indicate that significance has ac-crued, rather than waned, and it has done so quickly. The narratives of the first women in those villages to be "circumcised" echo, almost exactly, those of the much younger girls and women who are the pioneers in Myabé today. Within the last half-century and the lifetimes of many of the initial adopters, however, the practice has taken on a very different cast. In these villages rit-ual genital cutting is now universally practiced and is considered a prerequi-site for marriage. It has become a highly organized ceremonial event initiated by girls' parents, the *chef de terre*, and other village elders and is well on its way to becoming "embedded" or "entrenched" in the life of the group. Thus, within the space of two generations, the practice of female "circumcision" has undergone a radical transformation.

For those approaching the issue of female "circumcision" with an eye to prevention, these findings suggest a unique but potentially short window of opportunity. They also present interventionists with a number of paradoxes. The standard narratives would suggest that parents, religious and spiritual leaders, village authorities, and elders are the key agents of change; that as educational and other opportunities become available to girls and to women, the attraction of female "circumcision" will fade; or that young girls are passive victims, caught in a train of events dating "from time immemorial" over which they have little control. The "case" of Myabé challenges all of these assumptions, forcing us to expand our view of female "circumcision" and to develop new frameworks for understanding and for action.

Notes

Research for the fieldwork conducted in Myabé was funded by the National Science Foundation (SBR-9811074). An earlier study of female "circumcision" among the Sara, from which some of the background information presented in this chapter is drawn, was funded by a J. William Fulbright Fellowship from the Institute for International Education (IIE). The name of the village (Myabé) and the names of all male and female informants living there have been changed.

1. Daly contends that Western critics are intimidated by accusations of "racism" and argues that even though these accusations may stem from ignorance, the effect (that is, fear, intimidation, and a failure to label female "circumcision" as mutilation) is to uphold the patriarchy.

2. In addition to being the name of a Sara subgroup, Sara Kaba is also the name of the dialect spoken by its members.

3. Vizedom (1976) has noted that initiation is not always succeeded by clear shifts in status, role, or social position; thus, the absence of a notable change in girls' status postinitiation is not unique to Myabé.

10

Handing over the Knife: *Numu* Women and the Campaign Against Excision in Mali

Claudie Gosselin

As part of the campaign against excision[1] in Mali, some nongovernmental organizations (NGOs) have established programs for traditional excisers, who are mostly women of the potter/blacksmith "caste" or socioprofessional group (in Bamana,[2] *numu,* plural *numuw*). These programs generally start by convincing these women to abandon the practice of excision and often culminate in a public ceremony during which they hand over their knives. Subsequently, the excisers are offered training in other income-generating activities because the underlying assumption is that the main incentive for these women to practice excision is economic. From April 1997 to March 1998, I was engaged in a collaborative research project with a women's association in Mali that has pioneered such programs, the Conseil Malien pour la Promotion de la Femme (CMPF).[3] The association's leadership has publicly stated that the success of its campaign against excision is largely due to its innovative approach working with traditional excisers.

Using ethnographic data, in this chapter I explore the complexities lurking behind such seemingly straightforward programs. First, some background numbers will be given on the current prevalence and practice of excision in Mali. Then I situate the traditional excisers, *numu* women, within the Mande caste system. An understanding of the structure and ideology of this dynamic social system is crucial to an analysis of the programs targeting *numu* women. Aid donors, foreign feminists, and human rights activists working to end excision often do not have the benefit of this knowledge. Such an understanding, however, allows one to apprehend the local meanings associated with the practice of excision and the social status of those who perform it.

Next, I present and discuss a recent ceremony during which *numu* women handed over their excision knives. The analysis of the "female patronage system" developed by Rosa De Jorio (1997) in her dissertation on women's associations in Mali illuminates aspects of the ceremony such as the public transfer of money. I also discuss underlying discourses on health and "evolution" that reflect current ambivalent attitudes toward modernity as the caste system and the logic behind traditional medicine are eroded by social change and imported worldviews. *Numu* women find themselves in a difficult mediating position as owners of non-Western medical and ritual knowledge. At the same time, several of them have proven very enterprising in accessing the capital made available as a result of the appeal that the antiexcision campaign has for Westerners. In conclusion, I reflect on some issues that influence the effectiveness of programs that work with traditional excisers.

Overview of Excision in Mali

In 1997–1998, my assistant Mariam Diakité and I interviewed 223 women fifteen years of age and older, selected at random in the towns of Segu, Mopti, Kayes, and Sikasso, four regional capitals in Mali. Of those 223 women, 214 (nearly 96 percent) said they were excised. This percentage is consistent with the results of the national Demographic and Health Survey published in Mali in 1996: having surveyed 9,704 women between ages fifteen and forty-nine across the country, the researchers found that 94 percent of them reported having been excised (Coulibaly et al. 1996:185). More precisely, 52 percent of those said they had undergone clitoridectomy, 47 percent said they had undergone excision (in this case defined as ablation of the clitoris and the labia minora), and less than 1 percent declared having been infibulated. There was no marked difference in rates between younger and older women.

Except for one Bamana woman in Segu, all the women in my sample who had not been excised came from groups who have not historically practiced female genital cutting (FGC). Similarly, in the national Demographic and Health Survey, the women who had not undergone cutting predominantly came from the Timbuktu and Gao regions, which are dominated demographically by people who generally do not practice excision (the Tuareg and most Songhay groups). In fact, Salif Coulibaly and his colleagues concluded that ethnic origin was the only factor that significantly affected the prevalence of female genital cutting in Mali, since only 17 percent of Tuareg women and 48 percent of Songhay women said they had been excised (Coulibaly et al. 1996:187). Education levels and religion were not found to significantly affect prevalence.

Although the median age of excision in the Demographic and Health Survey was found to be 6.3 years (Coulibaly et al. 1996:189), there is a steady decline in the age at which excision is practiced, as frequently noted in most

African areas where female genital cutting takes place.[4] For women forty-five
to forty-nine years old, the average age at "circumcision" was 8.8 years; for
those ages thirty to thirty-four, 6.7 years; and for the youngest bracket in the
survey, women between fifteen and nineteen years of age, it was 4.3 years
(Coulibaly et al. 1996:189). This decline is even more dramatic when we look
at the age at which the daughters of the interviewees were excised: for 72 percent of them the operation took place in the first four years of their lives
(Coulibaly et al. 1996:189). It was also found that the age at excision is significantly lower in urban centers and among daughters of educated mothers
(Coulibaly et al. 1996:192).

Parallel to the lowering of the age at which excision takes place, we observed a certain transfer of the practice from traditional operators to medical
personnel (on the medicalization of FGC, see also Chapter 1, as well as Chapters 5 and 6 of this volume). In my survey, women and men in all cities except
Segu reported a high level of medicalization. To the open-ended question
"Who practices excision in your town?" 23 percent of respondents in Kayes
answered "medical personnel," and another 21 percent answered "*numuw* and
medical personnel." In Sikasso, 39 percent of women and men interviewed
identified medical personnel as the operators, and another 11 percent said that
both medical personnel and *numuw* perform excision. In Mopti, 15 percent
said that medical personnel perform the operation, and 9 percent responded
both "doctors"[5] and traditional excisers (in this case not just *numuw* but also
Fulani *maabo* weavers and *Fulajonw*, literally, descendants of captives of the
Fulani). The case of Segu was different: there, according to 61 percent of my
respondents, the practice is firmly in the hands of the *numuw*.

Coulibaly and his colleagues (1996) found a much lower level of medicalization when they asked the women in their sample who had excised
them. One out of ten women did not know, and 82 percent said they had been
excised by a "traditional exciser," 6 percent by a "traditional midwife," and
only 2 percent by medical personnel (Coulibaly et al. 1996:192). In urban areas, the number of excisions performed by medical personnel was slightly
higher (Coulibaly et al. 1996:193–194). The researchers also found that medicalization of daughters' operation increased with mother's educational level:
19.5 percent of women with a secondary education or higher had their daughters "circumcised" by medical personnel (Coulibaly et al. 1996:194). The differences between my results and those of Coulibaly et al. (1996) indicate that
medicalization of the procedure has increased since 1980.

The *Numuw* in the Mande Caste System

The term "Mande" refers to a cultural and linguistic group in West Africa and
the largest ethnolinguistic grouping in Mali. It includes the Bamana, Malinke,

and Jula, three ethnic groups representing approximately 40 percent of the Malian population (Traoré 1980:27), as well as smaller Mande groups including the Somono and Bozo fisherfolk and the Khasonke and Soninke (Sarakole, Maraka), who have their roots in the Kayes region.

Recent historical work by Tal Tamari (1991) gives support to the common view that the Mande caste system developed in the thirteen century with the founding of the Malian empire (McNaughton 1988:1). Caste systems are currently found among more than fifteen West African peoples, including the great majority of groups present in Mali: Mande people as well as Dogon, Songhay, Tukulor, Senufo, and most Fulani and Tuareg groups (Tamari 1991:221). On the basis of linguistic and historical evidence, Tamari (1991) argues that all these caste systems developed from the Mande model, through migration, conquest, and cultural borrowing.

Bokar N'Diaye (1970) provides what has become the standard description of the Mande pattern of social organization, presented as a three-tiered, ranked caste system in descending order of social status:

- the *hòrònw* (noble or free people), including farmers, ruling lineages, warriors, and religious leaders—in fact, the great majority of the population;
- the *nyamakalaw*, endogamous socioprofessional groups including principally the *numuw* (potters/blacksmiths), the *jeliw* (praise-singers), and the *garankew* (leather-workers); and
- the *jonw* (slaves or captives).

Even though slavery was abolished during colonization, this social division of society is still very meaningful in Mali, although recent anthropological work has shown the model to be more fluid than what has become codified (see Conrad and Frank 1995).

Much of the current academic debates centers around the social status of the *nyamakalaw*, who were portrayed very negatively in most of the colonial and early ethnographic literature as outcasts, beggars, or malignant sorcerers (Conrad and Frank 1995:2; McNaughton 1988:7–8). The etymology for the word *nyamakala*, published by N'Diaye (1970:14), certainly did not help to portray them in a more positive light. He noted that *kala* means "stalk" or "handle," and *nyama* means "manure" or "garbage." Although this is one of the possible meanings of the word *nyama*, I prefer to use the etymology given by Patrick McNaughton (1988:18–19, 152) and Sarah Brett-Smith (1994:38) who, following Dominique Zahan (1963:127), stress another meaning of *nyama*. This analysis helps us to understand the ambivalent attitudes of Malians toward *nyamakalaw*, including the *numu* women who perform excision. *Nyama* has been eloquently discussed by McNaughton (1988:15):

> At sorcery's base lies a phenomenon that generates its own fair share of am-
> bivalence and disquiet among the Mande. It is perceived as the world's basic
> energy, the energy that animates the universe. It is the force the Mande call
> *nyama*, which I refer to as special energy or occult power. . . . The Mande
> believe that in concentrations, especially when they are massive and uncon-
> trolled, this force is potentially dangerous, even deadly. People can learn to
> control it through sorcery, however, and thereby harness it to help them
> carry out their activities.

The *nyamakalaw* are therefore literally "handles of *nyama*." Brett-Smith describes them as "human instruments for contacting and mastering this unpre-
dictable energy" and points out that among them, "the blacksmith-sculptors
are the supreme instrument for controlling *nyama*" and often regarded as
"necessary but dangerous" (Brett-Smith 1994:38).

In fact, *nyamakalaw* are more than necessary. They are also respected
and admired for their technical and esoteric expertise and have often served
as advisers, mediators, and spokespeople for Mande rulers and chiefs. They
have important roles in Mande religion: *numu* men, notably, are priests of the
important *kòmò* male initiation society. As noted by David Conrad and Barbara Frank (1995:2), the ambivalence in perception of *nyamakalaw*, alternatively despised and respected, partly stems from the social position of the
speaker: informants tend to emphasize negative aspects of *nyamakala* behavior, such as their perceived lack of shame or modesty (cf. Grosz-Ngaté
1989:170), whereas *nyamakalaw* themselves, while often acknowledging
their shamelessness, tend to stress society's dependency on their products and
services.

Gender is another sphere in which informants' location greatly influences
perceptions and depictions of reality, but ethnographic work from the point of
view of women is rare in studies of Mande *nyamakalaw*. Studies of potters
tend to be mostly technical, the work of ethnoarcheologists (see, for instance,
Gallay et al. 1996; La Violette 1995). Conrad and Frank inform us only that
numu women "are said to share some of the respect and caution accorded
their husbands," who are "respected and feared for their knowledge of the occult" (1995:1). McNaughton (1988), who wrote what is still the definitive
work on Mande blacksmiths, devotes only four passages to women, in which
all we learn is that *numu* women own the rights to pottery making and that
there may be a parallel women's association to the *kòmò* male secret society
(McNaughton 1988:7, 22, 34, 130).

Nambala Kanté, a Malinke *numu* born in 1952 in Narena, a Malian village near the border with Guinea, provides us with a rare glimpse of the ritual
and medical roles of *numu* women (Kanté and Erny 1993). He tells us that in
Narena, *numuw (les forgerons*—gender unspecified) are responsible for four
secret cults addressed to *jinn* (spirits), including the ritual for the extraction of

clay. The goal of this ritual is to insure that the *jinn* who own clay will allow the work of potters to proceed safely. Most people in Mali fear the *jinn*, and ancestor spirits suffuse the Malian imagination. Blacksmiths play the important part of mediators, negotiating "treaties with a complex of spirits through ritual" (McNaughton 1988:18). The "union thus created give the blacksmiths access to the powers of the spirits" (McNaughton 1988:18), and the relationships that *numuw* have with spirits "add tremendous mystique to [their] work" (McNaughton 1988:20).

Numuw are among various experts on traditional medicine in Mali. Kanté (1993:143–144) lists the problems in which they tend to specialize and tells us that although *numu* men treat adult men, *numu* women treat women and children. Among the illnesses listed by Kanté are problems of reproductive health: impotence, sterility, and problems related to menstruation. Anthropologists Younoussa Touré, Yaouga Félix Koné, and Tiéman Diarra (1997:24–25) write that *numu* women have "occult" powers that help facilitate birthing and are called upon both to prevent and solve problems during parturition. Their assistance is seen as invaluable in offsetting the risks of giving birth—the maternal mortality rate is extremely high in Mali, at 1,200 deaths per 100,000 live births, according to UNICEF (1998:34). This rate, according to Touré, Koné, and Diarra (1997), is one of the reasons people hesitate to abandon excision: they fear that *numu* women would refuse to help a nonexcised parturient. Kanté (1993:144) reports that his mother acted as a midwife, even though there were a health center and a maternity ward in his village, and candidly comments that "this was certainly because my mother's treatments were effective and free" (Kanté and Erny 1993:144, my translation).

Arguably the most important function of *numuw*, however, is *bolokoli:* excision of girls and circumcision of boys. Whereas the *numu* men with whom McNaughton worked considered circumcision to be one of their most important social responsibilities, most had refused to learn how to perform it. They explained to him that "completing the operation successfully was the most difficult and potentially dangerous enterprise in their profession" (McNaughton 1988:70). There are dangers for the children undergoing the operation as well as for the operator. McNaughton was told that "just learning the medicine and the sorcery required would take an entire year" (McNaughton 1988:70). Smiths have at their disposal various herbal medicines to treat problem cases. They also use preventative measures: for instance, Habibatou Diallo points out that excision of girls never takes place in the heat of the day, in order to prevent heavy bleeding (1990:36). Children are also at risk of sorcery attacks because the extreme physical and spiritual stress at the moment of the cutting makes them particularly vulnerable. Here, the smith's knowledge of procedures for countering such threats is critical (McNaughton 1988:68). However, *numuw* do not always succeed. Kanté (1993:184) writes that "previously," deaths of newly circumcised boys due to tetanus or other diseases were attributed to sorcerers. In my own fieldwork I found that, although all the nine excisers I interviewed claimed never to have lost a girl, several other informants knew of cases of deaths, generally caused by excessive bleeding.

In the traditional Mande view, operators are also at risk (see also Chapter 11 of this volume). According to McNaughton (1988:69) high levels of *nyama* are released at the moment of incision:

> The escaping energy is said to be potent enough to blind a smith who has not mastered all the techniques of the surgery, and a really clumsy smith could actually be killed. To protect against this power, blacksmiths utilize secret speech constantly. They also have at their disposal lotions with which they can cover their entire bodies to serve as a shield against the energy.

Female operators face the same risks and also use protective devices. Diallo (1990:35–41), who observed four excision sessions in four different villages, notes the use of "incantations," including some directed toward female sorcerers. Germaine Dieterlen (1951:188) reported that Bamana *numu* women protected themselves from the negative energy emitted during excision by wearing bracelets and amulets and using an ointment on their eyes. In September 1997, a *numu* exciser in Kayes explained to Mariam Diakité and me that only women from certain *numu* families practice excision because "in some families in the past some women (after excising) became ill in their eyes and in their fingers—up to seven of them. So people saw that excision wasn't good for their families." The same woman told us that excessive concentrations of *nyama* in women's genitals was at the origin of the ancestral practice of excision and related this story:

> In the past there was a woman with a lot of *nyama*. When her husband wanted to touch her, he would see light like fire coming out of his wife's sex. So he couldn't take her but he wanted her so badly that he lost weight. People asked him what he was suffering from. They sent a *jon* (slave), Bilal, to ask him what he was suffering from. The man explained and told Bilal: "If you really want to know you stay close by tonight and I will try to touch my wife." Bilal stayed. When the man tried to lift his wife's skirt, the *jon* saw. He told the old men and the old women. They returned the woman to her parents. The elders said: "In order to fix this [go to] Dufalo [the ancestor of the smiths], since smiths know how to fix things. Take the woman to Dufalo." So Dufalo's wife, Mariam, she cut the *nògò* [the "dirty thing," a phrase used to designate the clitoris]. Once she had cut the clitoris she threw it and "pfft!" it caught on fire. The woman returned to her husband. After that the husband did not have any problems. After that Mariam said that men who want to marry a woman shouldn't do it unless the woman has been cut.

Handing over the Knives

The discussion above presented the roles and powers of *numuw* in the Mande social system. It is with this context in mind that antiexcision programs targeting traditional excisers must be analyzed and evaluated. In this section I will discuss one such program in Mali, focusing on a ceremony that I was permitted to record in June 1997.

The Ceremony

In May 1997, the head office of CMPF in Bamako received a letter from the Association des Exciseuses de Mopti (Mopti's Excisers Association), which read:

> Madam President,
>   Since the year 1993 after a [CMPF] Seminar during which we learned and understood the damages excision causes for girls and women, we have hung our blades, little knives used as tools for excision.
>   However since this practice is the source of our livelihood, then Madam we come to you in order to find us a means of subsistence for the well-being of our families.
>   Any means, whether material or financial, would be perfect for us.[6]

As a follow-up to this letter, the CMPF national office, in collaboration with volunteer members in Mopti, organized a ceremony with the excisers. This event was purposely scheduled to coincide with the visit of delegates from one of the association's international donors, a Canadian NGO, which had sent one staff member and one filmmaker as part of a tour of Asia, Latin America, and Africa to film the activities of the women's groups that it funds. The footage would then be edited into an educational and promotional video for Canadian television.

What follows are some excerpts from this public ceremony, held in an outdoor cinema on the morning of June 10, 1997. The ceremony took place in Bamana, with some parts, mostly songs, presented in the Fulani language. The Canadian NGO visitors did not have the language skills to allow them to understand what was said or sung. Having only been in Mali for six weeks at that time, I understood very little myself but was able to have the Bamana portions of the tapes transcribed and translated afterward.

The two main themes of the ceremony appeared in the opening speech of the event, given by one of the local organizers. The first is the economic opportunity offered the excisers and personified by the presence of the Canadians. The woman pointed out their presence: "The collaborators are those *Tubabs* [white people]. Everything that can advance this business at hand, they too will help her [the president of CMPF] with." The second theme is the notion of progress or development, which French-speaking Malians usually call "evolution." Explaining why *numu* and CMPF women were gathered there, the presenter said it was "because what the knife could bring them before, there's none of that now; because our children know a lot of things which we don't know," implying that times have changed and more knowledge is now available.

After this introduction the microphone went to the president of CMPF, who started by stressing two of her social relationships with the audience: first she called Mopti residents her *burankaw* (affines to whom respect is owed), and then she pointed out her *sénénkùnya* relationship, as a Fulani, with the *numuw*.[7] After establishing the fact that she was there at the request of the excisers and exhibiting their letter as proof, she thanked Allah that this initiative corresponded with the visit of her Canadian NGO friends, explaining:

> They come from Canada, we have worked together for five or even six years. This means that they trust me, because if they trust you, if they help you, if you don't do good, they leave. . . . In the world they have gone to five countries; in Africa, it is Mali that has been chosen, and in Mali it is [CMPF] that has been chosen. So this is a great honor for us [applause]. It is an honor but also a responsibility. If we can honor our name, it will be a very good thing; otherwise, they will never come back to Mali.

I was also introduced, as a student who had come "to learn our way of life and what girls' excision is."

Next, reference was made to the 1993 local CMPF Seminar on Violence against Girls and Women, during which, she said, "those who were there, they [the excisers] told us that they do it because it gives them something with which to survive [and] because they have inherited it." Then she said that she and her supporters had not come to tell people to stop excision but only to give information. "The women who practice excision," she continued,

> they are the ones who must now show—say that "now that we have had information on this, we have stopped." This is why the women of Segu, they were the first to send us a paper and say "we have understood," and to say that between the Fulani and themselves there is a *sénénkùnya* . . . that is older than ourselves. So because of this prohibition they have sworn that they will never take back the knife, because if they ever take back the knife. . . .[8]

Next the president reviewed the negative consequences of excision. After stressing that girls' "circumcision," as opposed to boys', is not required by Islam, she presented the adverse health effects of female genital cutting, more or less as they have been presented in the international activist literature on "female genital mutilation," outlining, in order: obstetrical difficulties, hemorrhaging, tetanus, and difficulties during sexual intercourse. She then argued that nowadays excision has lost its meaning, for two reasons. First, although the practice is supposed to guarantee virginity at marriage, now there are numerous excised young women who become pregnant before marriage. Second, the cutting is no longer part of an initiation into womanhood, since it is now practiced on babies within the first forty days of life. "Hence," she said, "we have moved beyond all these ancient things."

After recalling once again the sacredness of an oath between Fulani and *numuw*, the president explained to the assembled women why it is so important for the *numuw* women to hand over their knives:

> Up until now it has not been possible to raise the 5 million CFA.[9] But we cannot get the 5 million if those who give don't come to see us. What is the proof? The tools with which you do it, you put them in the basket, then they will take a picture, [and] we will keep the knives. . . . They are here to be our witnesses. The things we will bring to Bamako now [i.e., the knives], they will be in front of them. That way they will believe us.

She closed her speech by recalling one more time the sacred link between *numuw* and Fulani and then invited the excisers to speak. The president of the excisers' association took the microphone:

> You have well spoken. [If] Allah wills it, you can do it, the will is Allah's. Everything that is in our power, we tell you. Excision, we are the ones who had said that we had received it as an inheritance. Before, the problem that is here now, it did not exist before. It is something that we don't like either. Everything that makes us good, that gives us a name, that is what we ask from Allah. We also will stop excision today. Allah willing, we give you our word of honor that we will last. We will stop excision today. But we are asking you: our life is linked to that excision. If we stop today, we are giving you our word, when we say that we have stopped, we will never start again. Allah willing, everything that you want in life, we do it [applause].

The organizer coached her on: "So, what Fanta[10] said, you repeat it. You have to tell her." The *numu* women's representative continued:

> What she has asked us we are aware of. We have reached an agreement: excision is something that has no advantage. We are moving backwards, and everything that makes us go backwards, we do not ask Allah for. [Recording unclear for a few seconds.] So, we gave you our word yesterday, we said that if Allah allows you to set foot in this city, we will cease excision. We are giving you our knives; our life is linked to those knives. Allah willing, you can do it, the will is Allah's: may you be able to help us as much as you can to facilitate our livelihood.

The organizer concluded: "We can't add to this. I think that you have just said your last word. If she has said her last word, we will applaud. You said your last word, so you go first, you get up first and you give your knife."

One at a time, the seven women ceremoniously handed over their knives to the CMPF president, who was obviously very touched and thanked them, on the verge of tears. Some of the excisers also had tears in their eyes. Women in the audience applauded; some cried. The camera was rolling. It was a very emotional moment.

Afterwards, the ceremony continued with the public offering of 250,000 CFA[11] in cash, given by the president of CMPF to her counterpart of the Excisers Association, as a token of goodwill on the part of CMPF. The woman representing the Canadian NGO, visibly uncomfortable, asked the CMPF president whether she wanted the giving of money to be filmed. The president insisted that it be on film. She then told the *numu* women that they were expected not to divide up the money, but to jointly invest in an income-generating project, explaining: "because now if you don't help yourself they don't help you. If you send them a project for 5 millions, they ask: 'What have you done?' They don't just take the money to give you. They help you so that you can help yourself." To close, she asked the excisers to involve their daughters in their new enterprises in order to prevent them from taking over the practice of excision and to send their granddaughters to school so that they will not learn how to perform it at all.

At the end of the ceremony, the *numu* women seemed happy. One was so awestruck by such a large number of bills that she asked that they be spread out on the table to be better admired. Then the *numu* women spontaneously started a dance during which the women squatted and made cutting gestures. This was happening in a general spirit of fun and pride, and male musicians who had been in attendance joined in. At one point, one French-speaking woman came to me and spontaneously offered an explanation: "You see, this is what we used to do when we excised: you take the little girl. . . ." She left her sentence unfinished, instead pointing to the center of the dance, where the *numu* women were miming an excision.

Economic Redistribution, Hòrònya, Development, and Evolution

At one level, the ceremony just described involves a small-scale transfer of capital from rich to poor countries. As measured by conventional economic indicators, Mali is one of the poorest nations of the world. Feeding one's children is a very real problem for a large number of Malians. In this context, foreign official development assistance (ODA) is an important source of capital, and the international development business is ubiquitous in the country. Indeed, one of the characteristics of the Malian economy is an "extreme reliance on foreign financing of official budgets" (Brigaldino 1997:129). In 1996, Mali received U.S.$505 million in net ODA (OECD 1996:140), and its (real) gross domestic product was estimated by the World Bank at U.S.$2.61 billion (1997:17).

People in Bamako and in the small cities where I worked know that foreign NGOs and embassies have money to offer. In fact, at times it seems that everyone is trying to start a development "project," a word that, to borrow De Jorio's phrase, has almost acquired magical connotations (1997:213, 254). The plethora of formal Malian women's associations formed in the aftermath of the 1991 events that ended Moussa Traoré's autocratic one-party state compete almost ruthlessly for this capital. Many of their leaders, through their knowledge of the international women's movement and their contacts with various actors in the foreign aid sector, have become aware that money has been made available for programs against excision. For those women's organizations such as CMPF who have long campaigned against excision, this funding enables them to continue their programs, since the current Malian government so far has not made funds available to women's associations.

At another level, the handing-over-of-the-knives ceremony operates within the structural context of Malian women's associations so insightfully analyzed by De Jorio. It is quite common for new members, such as the women of the Mopti excisers association, to join a women's group for economic purposes. In fact, De Jorio concludes that money is one of the main motivations for most women, who expect the leader(s) of the association to assist them financially. In addition, De Jorio states, "given the preferential relationship that . . . women's groups have established with [various development agencies], the leaders . . . have represented the mediating channel between international capital and the local population" (1997:326).

When the president of CMPF insisted that the Canadian team film the giving of money to the *numu* women, she was also exemplifying a behavior that De Jorio has found to be characteristic of women leaders in Mali. Women leaders acquire prestige and large followings by establishing patron-client relationships. In fact, leadership is impossible without redistribution (De Jorio 1997:268), which has been expected, in the form of aristocratic largesse, from Mande political leaders since precolonial times (see Bagayogo 1987). This economic redistribution, however, maintains very unequal relationships between women's group leaders—generally literate and from the relatively wealthy bureaucratic class—and their largely poor and illiterate constituencies (De Jorio 1997:279). The cultural structure of the Mande caste system creates this class division, as De Jorio explores in her analysis of two types of ceremonies currently dominated by women, naming ceremonies and weddings (De Jorio 1997:285–322). During such ceremonies, women's public redistribution of wealth takes place in the form of gifts in kind and in cash. The public giving of money, especially to "casted" people such as *jeliw* and *jonw*, is seen to enhance the "nobility" (*hòrònya*) of the giver.

A final theme to emerge from the ceremony is "evolution," no doubt a legacy from the "civilizing" project of French colonialism. The autobiography of Aoua Kéita (1975) testifies to the extent to which the Malian bureaucratic elite had assimilated this attitude by the time of independence in 1960. Although the discourse of "evolution" exemplifies the problematic African rapport with modernity,[12] it can also allow *numu* women to avoid losing face when publicly abandoning a practice that has been so central to their social identity and status.[13] One example of this is the organizer's comment: "since our children know a lot of things which we do not know." It is also apparent in the speech of the representative of the *numu* women, when she says, "the problem that is here now, it didn't exist before," and later, "everything that makes us go backwards, we do not ask Allah for."

Reflections on the Effectiveness of Programs with *Numu* Women

Several months after the ceremony described above, Mariam Diakité and I conducted interviews with the Mopti exciser who had spoken at the ceremony and with eight other *numu* women in three other cities (Segu, Kayes, and Sikasso) where activities with excisers had also been conducted by CMPF. From these interviews it appears that the operation is no longer the monopoly of *numuw*. In fact, the only exciser who agreed to talk to us in Sikasso was a sixty-two-year-old Bamana *hòròn* woman. She explained how she and her co-wife came to practice excision: "Since my husband is a health professional, he circumcised boys and traditional circumcisers did the girls and each time there was hemorrhaging, they would be taken to hospital and since my husband was a surgeon, he had to fix it, so he decided to show my co-wife how to do it, and myself I hold the child." They started ten years ago, and ask 1,000 CFA (about U.S.$2) to perform a clitoridectomy.

This shift is quite distressing for *numu* women. One forty-five-year-old *numu* woman in Kayes told us: "Since I was born, I had only seen *numuw* doing it [excision]. But currently it is changing: *hòròn, jòn, siyaw bee b'a ke*" (all the 'races' do it). Later she added: "Even the nurses at the hospital do it, but some come to me: some prefer *numuw*." In this distress there is obviously a question of technical, ritual, and economic monopoly being lost, but there is also a more profound malaise. Just ten years ago, McNaughton wrote about boys' circumcision: "As with iron working, no one else in traditional Mande society is qualified to do it, and it is virtually inconceivable that anyone but a smith would try" (1988:66). Currently, however, as I outlined at the beginning of this chapter, an increasing number of girls are being operated upon by Western-trained health personnel, and anecdotal evidence suggests that even more boys are circumcised in clinics or hospitals. This change reflects the steady Islamization of Mande and Malian society, which has led to the loss of the initiatory aspects of circumcision and excision that were rooted in traditional religions (Kanté 1993:183). Imams and Muslim religious leaders we interviewed, as well as those who have made public statements in the Malian media, have all called for the medicalization of the practice.

Numuw's loss of monopoly over circumcision and excision also reflects a larger phenomenon in Mali, particularly urban Mali: processes of boundary maintenance between the various "castes," although they were probably always more flexible than reflected in early writings, have in the last few decades been strained to the verge of collapse.[14] Under the heading "Fluidity of Society, Disintegration and Enlarging of the Caste System," a UNESCO social scientist analyzing the incipient process of democratization in Mali wrote a few years ago: "The living conditions brought about by the encounter with the outside world have disorganized the exclusivity of hereditary transmission of socio-professional functions. In order to survive, children of uncasted families have had to accomplish certain tasks previously strictly restricted to casted people" (Talbot 1992:n.p., my translation). For her, it is a positive development: "This frees creativity and makes society more fluid, because it causes the crumbling of the caste system and of gerontocracy"(Talbot 1992). Whether the transfer of the operations of circumcision and excision from *numuw* to the medical profession is a positive development, however, creates great controversy, both in Mali and in the international community (see Chapters 4, 5, and 6 in this volume).

In the case of excision, some see this lack of respect for the prescriptions and proscriptions of the caste system as affecting the spiritual status and ritual capacity of *numu* women to perform the operation safely, as explained to us by another *numu* exciser in Kayes:

NANSA FANÉ:[15] In ancient times, each *hòròn* had his/her *numu*, so when a *hòròn* had a baby girl, the one who shaved the baby's head, she also excised her.

C.G.: But what about now?

NANSA FANÉ: Now there are few *numu* women who practice excision because those who practiced before, they did not have intimate relationships with *hòrònw*. If you have intimate relations with *hòrònw*, for example, friendship[16] or marriage, you can no longer excise. For example, if I am a *numu* and I have a relation with a *hòròn* man, I cannot excise. If somebody comes to me for an excision, I have to refuse. And now there are more and more *numuw* who have relationships with *hòrònw*.

C.G.: Why can't you excise, if you have a relationship with *hòrònw*?

NANSA FANÉ: Only Allah knows this. Before, the grandmothers who excised, they had incantations that they did in water, and then they poured the water on the genitals of the girls, and immediately the blood would stop. But if a *numu* violates the interdiction, she will not be able to stop the bleeding. Only Allah knows why.

A friend of the *numu* woman interjected: "What, the exciser will be damned!"

Here the social malaise due to the disintegration of the caste system gets reinterpreted through the idiom of illness. However, the increased fluidity of the caste system benefits some upwardly mobile *numu* families, which could create another motivation for *numu* women to hand over their excision knives. De Jorio (1997:307–308) gives an example of a wealthy *numu* family, one of the richest families in Segu, whose members have adopted *hòròn* behavior in their efforts at social climbing. As evidence of this, she reports that the women of the family have stopped performing services such as excision and the shaving of babies' heads during naming ceremonies.

From the perspective of the *numu* women interviewed, the ignorance of non-*numu* who have recently taken up excision explains why there are now so many cases of complications, which they say were extremely rare in the past. These non-*numu* people do not know the proper ritual procedures, how to prevent complications, or how to heal those who do have problems. As the Mopti *numu* woman who had spoken at the ceremony later told us: "We can say that it [excision performed by health personnel] is not efficacious because it is not the same thing. When we excise, we do *kilisi* [secret ritual speech]; the nurses, they use medication—it is not the same thing." The problem that was most often discussed was that of hemorrhaging, and in this respect, *numu* women were adamant in their answers that their knowledge was superior to that of male-dominated Western medical knowledge. This statement by a *numu* exciser in Kayes is typical:

> Now health agents do it [excision]. Traditional excisers have been told not to do it, that it is bad if they do it, that their knives are dirty. . . . "Doctors" do it. When there are problems, the "doctors" come to my door. Myself I refuse but they knock on my door. "Doctors" go and see the parents when there is a birth [to offer their services as excisers]. Allah be praised, with what Allah has given me in terms of secrets, I do my best.

The same woman later told us that "men" (doctors? nurses?) who now perform excision had asked her for her "secrets" to stop excessive bleeding, but she had answered that she would never reveal them.

To determine the effectiveness of targeting *numu* women in order to bring excision to an end, then, activists should monitor the extent to which those who hand over their knives are simply replaced by entrepreneurial health personnel. Even if they are replaced, however, one could claim that declarations by *numuw* in favor of the abolition of the practice, considering their social roles and status, ought to have influence over the public perception of excision. In order to evaluate the impact of the June 1997 ceremony described above, Mariam Diakité and I conducted interviews in March 1998 with 100 people chosen at random in three adjacent neighborhoods of Mopti, including the neighborhood where the ceremony had taken place. We spoke with sixty-five women and thirty-five men aged fifteen and older, from seventy-eight different households (compounds, *duw*), and found that almost none had heard about the ceremony. When asked whether they had followed campaigns against excision, forty-six women and twenty-three men (69 percent) answered in the affirmative. When those sixty-nine people were asked to describe the campaign, forty-eight of them (69.5 percent) described television or radio programs targeting excision. Only three women described meetings that may have been the CMPF ceremony I attended.

Another part of CMPF's strategy for the eradication of excision consists in organizing former excisers to carry out follow-up public educational activities on the health hazards of excision. Based on the results of our interviews, however, I am doubtful whether the message that *numu* women will take back home is the one the women's association would like them to spread. The woman who spoke at the June ceremony in Mopti, for instance, gave this answer to the question "What did CMPF teach you about excision?":

ARAMATO SISSOKO:[17] They have not taught us anything. We have learned nothing. We had a seminar for three days, and then we left. Teach us what?

C.G.: For example, what doctors say about the negative consequences of excision.

ARAMATO SISSOKO: Yes, they showed us pictures.

C.G.: What are the consequences of excision?

ARAMATO SISSOKO: Today there is no advantage in excising.

Later on, she mentioned "the negative consequences" of excision, but never explained them in detail for us. Most of the other excisers shared the view that the association has not taught them anything new about excision. "How could they?" they asked, "they are not *numuw*!" Such answers indicate that older *numu* women have not adopted the "scientific" medical discourse used by antiexcision activists as theirs, because it challenges their authority as practitioners of traditional medicine and also because it is largely foreign to their worldview.

The medicine that *numu* women practice is based on principles that are at odds with Western scientific medicine. McNaughton reminds us that in Mande cosmology, illness can be caused by the malevolent acts of people or spirits or by "unguarded proximity to unbridled occult energy" (1988:42). Therefore, when *numu* women say that hemorrhaging or other complications after excision are due to the actions of sorcerers, I believe that they are doing more than discharging responsibility for their acts, as some activists cynically remark—they are also expressing a common and current belief about possible causes of illness and injury in their society. The identification of the causes of illness can be at odds with Western medicine, but traditional remedies are also based on different principles. The logic behind traditional treatments is based on analogies: treating like with like, as Kanté puts it (1993:154).

Campaigners' presentations on the negative health consequences of excision do not seem to have been particularly well understood or at least not well retained. In Mopti, for instance, when asked "What are the consequences of excision?" 23 percent of our sample of 100 women and men answered that there were no consequences, 20 percent believed that the consequences were positive, and 20 percent did not know. The next most common answer (9 percent) concerned unspecified "problems" or "illnesses." These responses are consistent with interviewees' personal experiences: only one of the fifty-eight excised women we interviewed in Mopti reported having experienced health or sexual problems that she attributed to excision.

The message is not entirely lost, however. It seems to resonate more with educated women of the bureaucratic class. For instance, a thirty-two-year-old professional woman who is a member of CMPF-Mopti told me that she had been convinced of excision's negative consequences by the speech given by the president of the association at the knives ceremony. She added that this could inspire her to educate other women "on the problems [excision causes] when giving birth, infections, all of that." A young man we interviewed in the survey of the three neighborhoods said that he had been convinced of the need to stop excision by his aunt, head of the local CMPF chapter. My evidence overall suggests that, in general, local CMPF members, for the most part Western-educated and professional, have been much more actively involved in public education than "converted" *numu* women. Even so, there appears to be a need to clarify the message. During our interviews in Mopti, we happened upon an elderly Fulani woman who told us that she had recently stopped excising. When asked why, she said: "Because I have heard that if you do it the authorities will arrest you. I got scared. Also, I am old." Currently, no legislation specifically outlaws excision in Mali, but it appears from our interviews that some CMPF members believe that there is, and they have been giving women this message.

The inexactitude of the health information offered by local campaigners may also have contributed to the campaign's failure to convince the majority of the population, including *numuw*. There is a tendency, on the part of activists, to exaggerate the rate at which complications are known to occur, and sometimes the information is based on untested claims from the international anticircumcision literature, which tends to extrapolate from case studies of the consequences of infibulation (see also Chapters 6, 7, and 12 in this volume). This is dangerous because, as Bettina Shell-Duncan, Walter Obungu

Obiero, and Leunita Auko Muruli point out in Chapter 6, "the dissemination of distorted, exaggerated, or incorrect information to target communities undermines the credibility of anticircumcision campaigns." In my own work, I encountered a significant number of people who felt insulted by the statements of anticircumcision activists because the information presented contradicted their own knowledge and common sense. Many seemed to have taken the antiexcision message to mean that excision causes all women to have difficulties at each parturition—a claim easy for them to dismiss based on their own experience. *Numu* women who also act as traditional midwives are particularly irritated by the claims of activists. At the end of our interview with a very knowledgeable *numu* woman in Kayes, she demanded to know "how is it possible that *bolokoli* [in her practice, clitoridectomy] can cause problems during menstruation or birth? I only cut the clitoris that stands up; it has nothing to do with the vaginal orifice."

When *numu* women are presented with concrete evidence of damages caused by excision, however, they can be convinced to abandon the practice. When I asked the representative of the Mopti *numu* women why she had agreed to give up her knife and her admittedly lucrative practice (see below), she answered: "They showed us the consequences and they told us that if we abandoned excision they would give us something [in return]." What she did not explain was that the local CMPF leadership took a senior *numu* exciser to the local hospital, where they visited thirty-five "victims of excision, women who have been divorced because of this" (probably fistulae cases).[18] It was the CMPF-Mopti representative who made this information public at a national seminar on excision in Bamako a few weeks after the knives ceremony in the cinema, adding that the excisers "were convinced and the depositing of the knives was spontaneous."

One final aspect of the programs, which is problematized by research findings, is the assumption that the main motivation behind the practice of excision is economic. In fact, for most excisers we interviewed, excising girls is a social responsibility. Many said they would be willing to abandon the practice, especially in favor of a more lucrative occupation, but that when people bring them their daughters, it is their duty as *numuw* (and sometimes they say, as Muslims) to excise them. In Mali, the social stigma attached to nonexcision is still very strong.

For most, the revenues from excision are important not as their sole source of income but as one revenue among others in the typical poverty-driven strategy of diversifying income-generating activities. When asked if the revenues from excision allow them to earn a living for the whole year, only two out of nine excisers answered "yes." One of them was the *numu* representative at the ceremony in Mopti, who explained that in only one day she could excise forty girls, for each of whom she would receive 2,000 CFA (about U.S.$4). The other woman making a living from the practice of excision was from Kayes, and she explained that she was called to excise in other villages, which pays very well.

Conclusion

The discussions of antiexcision programs with traditional excisers revealed a gap between indigenous knowledge and Western scientific knowledge—a conclusion often reached by anthropologists analyzing development discourses and programs (Grillo 1997). It is my hope, however, that I have avoided the common problem of presenting indigenous knowledge as "complete, accomplished, and hence static and unchanging" (Grillo 1997:25). In fact, the ceremony I have described exemplifies processes of change, which are nevertheless embedded in a historically produced, specific social and economic context.[19]

For example, when several women cried at the ceremony, foreigners might have thought that the emotion was linked to the pain of the practice—symbolized graphically by the knives—which would now come to an end. Pain and overcoming it, however, are valued in Mande society, and I think that the emotion came more from witnessing the courage and humility of *numu* women publicly surrendering the instruments of a practice that had been so central to their collective identity.[20] Unlike the Westerners present (including myself at the time), the CMPF members in attendance understood the magnitude of the social and ideological significance of this act.

In this chapter, I have discussed some aspects of the situation in which *numuw* now find themselves in Mali. The traditional religions in which they were respected leaders are losing followers to increasingly more orthodox forms of Islam. The medicine they practice, although still largely appreciated and used, is increasingly challenged by administrators and medical personnel. An ever-growing number of urban people are taking their sons and daughters to Western-trained *dòkòtòrow* for circumcision and excision, causing or threatening to cause *numuw* to lose income and prestige. At the same time, imported manufactured goods are competing with the products historically sold by *numuw*, including pottery. In the context of the extreme poverty and the dearth of economic opportunities outside of subsistence agriculture and animal husbandry, trying to access foreign development funds is a sound strategy—perhaps even a question of survival, in some cases.

In order to access this capital, however, *numu* and most other women need to go through NGOs or formal women's associations, which have become intermediaries between foreign donors and the population. In this exchange, patron-client relationships are established. Such vertical relationships are historically rooted in Mali (see Amselle 1992; Bagayogo 1987; De Jorio 1997) and are not necessarily to be equated with "corruption." As Jean-Loup

Amselle (1992:641) explains, such an analysis is a modernist and moralizing projection on phenomena based on entirely different logic. I agree, however, with De Jorio that such redistribution within women's associations maintains the status quo in all its inequality. As such, clientelism is at odds with the stated goals of the international feminist and human rights movements. Nonetheless, the clients (in this case, the *numu* women) reap immediate economic benefits, and the patrons acquire prestige, increased social status, and power, since in Mali power comes from the ability to mobilize followers. The emotion felt by the CMPF leadership at the ceremony, which obviously reflected pride in the advancement of the antiexcision cause, probably also came from the leaders' success at mobilizing a large number of women (around fifty), including figures as respected and feared as elder *numu* women.

Although this chapter has demonstrated that programs with *numu* women can benefit both women's group leaders and excisers, it is doubtful that they will significantly contribute to ending the practice of excision in Mali. First, my findings indicate that a significant number of medical personnel have replaced *numu* women in performing the operation, at least in the cities of Kayes, Mopti, and Sikasso. This shift might increase because most of the Muslim religious leadership in Mali has been lobbying for the medicalization of the practice. With this shift in practice from *numuw* to *dòkòtòrow*, "conversions" of *numu* women may not reduce prevalence as much as originally hoped. Second, even if changing social and economic circumstances have made some excisers willing to publicly renounce their work, to enlist them to actively campaign against the practice is perhaps unwise or unrealistic. *Numu* women in general still see themselves as experts on excision and are unlikely to relay the message that abolitionists want to reach the population. Further, when people bring their daughters (sometimes classificatory) to *numu* women and insist that they be excised, many still feel that it is their social responsibility to do so.

It is important to stress that activities targeting excisers represent only one of several strategies within the campaign against excision in Mali and that some local activists and intellectuals doubt whether these activities should be continued.[21] Although it is important to continue to involve *numu* women and other traditional excisers in the campaign, I believe that programs need to be reviewed and reoriented. The category "excisers" should be expanded to include nurses, doctors, and midwives, who should be targeted more actively. The quality of the public health education messages needs to be improved and the information presented in ways that acknowledge the knowledge and experience of local experts and residents. First and foremost, the specific consequences of locally practiced forms of cutting should be discussed (see also Chapters 6 and 12 in this volume). Second, organizations that have planned to use "converted" traditional excisers to carry out follow-up public education activities need to review this part of the program. Although these long-term activities are important, to reach and convince a larger segment of the population, they must be improved. If *numu* women are to be responsible for these activities, they must be better trained, given on-going support, and paid. To expect women to volunteer their time for activities that bring no economic benefit and may even erode their social capital is unrealistic, considering the poverty in which most find themselves.

Ultimately, however, in Mali as elsewhere, the prevalence of excision will decline only when the demand for the practice subsides. Programs with excisers address the supply side of the equation and as such can only have a limited impact (for a related discussion, see Chapter 13 in this volume). Considering their role and status in society, however, it is important to continue to involve *numu* and other traditional excisers in a broader, community-based strategy against excision. Otherwise, they might join the active and possibly growing pro-excision movement in Mali.

Notes

This research was made possible by funding from the International Development Research Centre (Young Canadian Researchers Award no. 96-0800-11), from the Social Sciences and Humanities Research Council of Canada (Doctoral Fellowship no. 752-95-02005), and from the Associates of the University of Toronto Travel Grant Fund. Field research was authorized by the Centre National de la Recherche Scientifique et Technologique in Bamako (authorization no. 41/CNRST/1997). For their help in various capacities, I would like to thank Janice Boddy, Fatoumata Siré Diakité, Ylva Hernlund, Bettina Shell-Duncan, Mariam Diakité, Geeta Narayan, Faris Ahmed, Oumou Suco and her family in Kayes, Mme. Sidibé Diaba Camara, Mme. N'Diaye Aminata Sall, Mme. Yatassaye Badiolo Fofana, Mme. Magasuba Doussou Traoré, Mme. Niangado Fanta Koné, Mme. Coulibaly Kady Bagayoko, Mme. Dembélé Kadiatou Diarra, Ami Kouyaté, Mme. Cissé Djénéba Maïga, Mme. Konaté Binta Bah, Agna Samassékou, Kama Kanté, Younoussa Touré, Molly Ruth, Michael Lambek, Marcia Brown, Roland Pirker, David C. Conrad, and all those women and men in Mali who generously shared their time, knowledge, and opinions with me.

1. Clitoridectomy and all other forms of female genital cutting are most commonly called "excision" by Malians who speak French. I have decided to use the term in this sense, except in the discussion of the prevalence of different forms of cutting, where it refers to a particular type of operation, as outlined in Chapter 1 of this volume.

2. The Bamana people and their language also appear in the literature as "Bambara." Here I follow recent scholars in using the indigenous term as opposed to the colonial one.

3. This is a fictitious name.

4. Some groups, however, such as the Soninke (also Sarakole or Serahule) and some Fulanis (also Fulas) have for as long as we know excised girls as babies, usually on the seventh day after birth (in Chapter 12, Ylva Hernlund discusses this subject with regard to the Gambia).

5. In Bamana, *dòcòtorow*, which could also mean nurses and other health personnel.

6. I feel that this letter is now part of the public domain, since the Canadian team (see below) filmed its contents for a video to be aired on television.

7. *Sénénkùnya* is a hereditary alliance between two ethnic, caste, or lineage groups that involves a license to joke and tease but also an obligation to assist and be truthful to the other partner. It also involves certain prohibitions, especially against inter-marriage.

8. It is a common feature of Bamana speech to leave the second part of a sentence unspoken when it is assumed that the audience knows how to finish it. In this case I was not sure what the implied threat was, but a few months later the president told me that one of the *numu* women who had sworn to stop excision had suddenly died. The women of Mopti who related the news to her, she said, were adamant that the death was due to the fact that the woman had broken her pledge and resumed excising.

9. At the time, 5 million CFA was worth 50,000 French francs, roughly U.S.$10,000—a very large amount of money in Mali, where a professional civil servant in 1997 earned less than U.S.$100 a month. Presumably this was the amount the *numu* women had requested in exchange for handing over their knives.

10. This is a pseudonym.

11. Approximately U.S.$500.

12. See Appiah (1992), for a recent and excellent essay on this most celebrated theme in African studies.

13. Touré and Koné (1997:38–42) relate a conversation with an exciser during which she blamed changes in diet for what she saw as the current greater incidence of complications and the lesser capacity of young generations to withstand the pain of excision. Touré and Koné see an opportunity to use this argument, that is, to highlight changing circumstances, in designing a more culturally sensitive campaign against excision that would not insult *numuw* or elders. See also the discussion of "ritual without cutting" by Hernlund in Chapter 12.

14. A well-known example is the case of the singer Salif Keita, who is not only *hòròn* but a descendant of the Keita rulers of the Mali Empire and who was ostracized by his family for taking up a "casted" occupation—singing—properly the monopoly of *jeliw*.

15. This is a pseudonym.

16. This was most likely a euphemism for pre- or extramarital sexual relationships.

17. This is a pseudonym.

18. A fistula is an opening between the vagina and rectum or the vagina and urethra, causing an involuntary leakage of feces or urine, respectively.

19. For an example of the flexibility of "traditional" knowledge and practices, see Chapter 12 in this volume for a discussion of the conscious manipulation of ritual.

20. On the importance of withstanding the pain of "circumcision" in other African societies, see also Chapters 6, 7, and 12 in this volume.

21. I will discuss the campaign as a whole in a forthcoming publication.

11

Becoming a Muslim, Becoming a Person: Female "Circumcision," Religious Identity, and Personhood in Guinea-Bissau

Michelle C. Johnson

Many studies conducted by anthropologists have focused on initiation rituals and have addressed female "circumcision" in a cursory manner as part of these rituals (e.g., MacCormack 1979; Boone 1986; Kratz 1994).[1] More recent studies as well as media attention on the subject have moved in the opposite direction, focusing on excision practices as extracted from their wider sociocultural contexts. Here, I argue that female "circumcision" practices among the Mandinga of Guinea-Bissau must be understood in relation to the overarching ritual of girls' initiation and to the construction and transformation of religious identity and personhood. The relationship between female "circumcision" (the physical act of genital cutting) and initiation (the educational period and rituals that traditionally accompany it) are currently undergoing change and constitute a site of significant controversy. Much of the discourse surrounding female "circumcision" practices, their changing relationship to girls' initiation rituals, and campaigns to alter or end the practices in Guinea-Bissau centers around the issues of religious identity and personhood. I suggest that exploring this discourse in terms of these two issues can provide a lens into understanding the internal debate surrounding female "circumcision" in Guinea-Bissau.

My approach is twofold. First, I explore the meaning behind female "circumcision" both inside and outside the context of girls' initiation rituals, in particular its implications for religious identity and personhood. I argue that personhood and religious identity frame much of the local discourse surrounding female "circumcision" and efforts to alter or end it in Guinea-

Bissau. Second, I explore the changing nature of female "circumcision" practices in relation to the overarching ritual of girls' initiation. I argue that these changes must be understood both in terms of external factors such as the recent national and global efforts to alter or eliminate female "circumcision" practices in Guinea-Bissau and throughout the world and of internal factors such as urbanization and modernization that are taking place somewhat independently of—though alongside—these efforts.

Throughout this chapter, I have attempted to include perspectives on who supports or opposes female "circumcision" and for what reasons. These views provide invaluable insight into the internal debate (which is only in its nascent stages) surrounding female "circumcision," initiation rituals, and religious identity and personhood in Guinea-Bissau. In focusing on the internal debate, I also explore the relationship between excision and sexuality, how the factors of gender, class, age, and religion come into play in the global debate surrounding female "circumcision," and how these issues are currently being understood in local contexts.

Female "Circumcision" in Guinea-Bissau: Ethnographic Background

In Guinea-Bissau, there are three ethnic groups that practice female "circumcision": the Mandinga, the Fula, and the Biafada. Since all these groups are Muslim, female "circumcision" in Guinea-Bissau is considered to be a Muslim practice and is often a principal means through which Muslim groups define and identify themselves in relation to their non-Muslim neighbors. When compared to neighboring countries such as Senegal and Gambia, Guinea-Bissau is unique in this respect.[2]

It is estimated that approximately 50 percent of Guinean women have experienced some form of female "circumcision," although no official statistics are currently available for the country.[3] The two most common forms of female "circumcision" practiced in the country are incision (a "nick" in the prepuce of the clitoris) and clitoridectomy (ranging from partial or full removal of the clitoral prepuce or of the clitoris itself).[4] In addition, healthcare workers contend that excision and infibulation are practiced among some Fula groups in Guinea-Bissau, although these forms are thought to be far less common (Burema Njaai 1997, personal communication). The difficulty of pinpointing the physical practice by its name is compounded by the fact that all the practices are termed "excision" (excìsão) in Portuguese and "initiation/circumcision" (fanadu) in Kriolu (for a similar example in French, see Chapter 10 in this volume). The more precise terms "incision" and "clitoridectomy" do not have common counterparts in local languages.

As in many other parts of the continent, the age at which female "circumcision" is performed varies according to the ethnic group and context. It is also important to note that where female "circumcision" takes place in Guinea-Bissau, it is controlled, organized, and encouraged primarily by women. To term female "circumcision" a women's practice, however, does not mean that men do not play a part. Several studies have shown, for example, that influential women such as traditional circumcisers and initiation "owners" often owe their leadership roles and statuses in part to their kinship or affine ties to influential men (Schaffer and Cooper 1987; Bledsoe 1984).

In this chapter, I focus almost exclusively on the Mandinga context, since it is the one with which I am most familiar. I do, however, include non-Mandinga perceptions for purposes of comparison. In 1996–1997 I conducted eleven months of ethnographic research in Guinea-Bissau, spending the first half of my research working with Mandinga men and women in several *bairros* (neighborhoods) in the capital city of Bissau, including Pilon, Sintra, and Bairro Militar. For the second half of my research, I lived in the Mandinga village of Bafata-Oio in the country's northern Oio region. During this time, I was also able to make frequent trips to work in the neighboring villages of Kapatris, Biriban, Medina, and Farim.

The Mandinga people are the third-largest ethnic group in Guinea-Bissau. They number approximately 122,000 people and make up 12.2 percent of the country's total population of 1 million (Forrest 1992:118). They trace their origin to the Manding heartland, located primarily in present-day Mali. Mandinga in Guinea-Bissau emphasize their "oneness" with other Mande groups in neighboring Gambia, Senegal, and Guinea, and their difference from non-Muslim ("animist") groups in their home country. They speak Mandinga, a language belonging to the Northern Mande language group (which includes the closely related Bamana and Dyula). Although they can be found in most regions of the country, the Mandinga are most concentrated in the Oio region of northern Guinea-Bissau, where they are subsistence farmers engaged in the production of rice, manioc, corn, millet, and peanuts. Although some Mandinga keep cattle and sell milk products in nearby villages and towns, they engage in herding activities significantly less than neighboring Fula and Balanta groups do, and their identity is based more on farming than on herding. In addition to the Oio region, there is also a sizable Mandinga population in the capital city of Bissau, concentrated in the *bairros* of Pilon, Sintra, and Bairro Militar.

To contextualize female "circumcision" practices among the Mandinga, I suggest that they must be understood in relation to the overarching ritual of girls' initiation in which they are traditionally situated. Among the Mandinga in this region, the physical act of genital cutting (the removal of the foreskin of the penis in the case of boys and clitoridectomy for girls) traditionally took place within the context of initiation rituals. For both boys and girls, these rituals marked the passage from childhood to adulthood. They included the building of a thatched structure in the forest, a seclusionary period during which initiates learned initiation songs and rules of etiquette governing intergender and intergenerational communication and behavior, circumcision or excision by ritual specialists, and public, celebratory "coming out" rituals following a brief healing period. The Kriolu (the national language of Guinea-Bissau) term *fanadu* (*fanadu di mindjer* for girls, and *fanadu di omi* for boys) further reflects this association because it refers both to "circumcision" (the physical act of genital cutting) and the initiation rituals that accompany it. In the Mandinga language, the term for *fanadu* is *kwion* (*musakwion* for girls and *kekwion* for boys), which refers to the traditional palm thatched structure built by the initiates.

When I initially went to Guinea-Bissau, I planned to study initiation and the accompanying practices of female "circumcision" as rites of passage that transform young girls into women in particular and adult members of society in general. Studies of female "circumcision" occurring both within and apart from the context of initiation in African societies have commonly emphasized the symbolic links among the physical act of genital cutting, gender identity, and adulthood. In her study of Sande initiation among the Mende of Sierra Leone, Sylvia Boone found that the blood shed during excision "causes" the symbolic death of the *kpowa* (uninitiated girl) and marks her new status in the community by transforming her into a woman and making her eligible for marriage (Boone 1986:65–66; see also Chapter 6 of this volume for a discussion of the relationship between excision and marriage among the Rendille of northern Kenya). Similarly, in a comprehensive study of Okiek girls' initiation in Kenya, Corinne Kratz found that after being excised, Okiek girls were no longer children but adult women because their genitals were made "smooth" and "clean" (1994:114). In the Somali context, as described by Anke van der Kwaak (1992:782), infibulation marks the first step in initiating the segregation of the sexes and the construction of gender identity, removing a girl's "hard male parts" and making a woman forever soft and feminine. Similarly, Janice Boddy (1988, 1989), working in nearby Sudan, found infibulation to be a crucial facet of the cultural process of genderization, symbolically associating women with the overarching concept of "enclosure." In the Sudanese context, infibulation is said to prevent the loss, contamination, or misappropriation of a woman's blood; it preserves virginity and constructs morally appropriate fertility by deemphasizing a woman's sexuality.

When I arrived in Guinea-Bissau to begin conducting ethnographic research on the topic of initiation rituals, I expected to find similar associations between female "circumcision," gender identity, and social adulthood. I soon discovered, however, that these same meanings did not hold for Mandinga in Guinea-Bissau. In the first place, "circumcision" and excision for both sexes sometimes takes place well before puberty (ages six to eleven for boys and from six months to eleven years for girls) and do not bear any direct relationship to marriage as in other African contexts, although it is clear from Antonio Carreira's (1947) descriptions that this was not always the case. Whereas in the past initiation occurred shortly before marriage, nowadays girls are often "circumcised" long before they are married. When I inquired about the link between initiation and adulthood, Mandinga informants did not associate initiation with the creation of "men" and "women." The transformation from childhood to adulthood in the Mandinga context is accomplished for both sexes after the birth of a woman's first child in the final stages of marriage (when the wife has moved from her natal compound to reside with her husband in his compound). Instead, Mandinga linked circumcision for boys and clitoridectomy for girls first and foremost to religious identity—a factor that has been significantly less explored in the ethnographic literature on the subject.

Becoming a Muslim: Female "Circumcision" and Religious Identity Among the Mandinga

When asked to explain the reasons behind clitoridectomy, Mandinga informants assert that it is a cleansing rite that defines a woman as a Muslim and enables her to pray in the proper fashion, both of which are defining features of Mandinga identity. As one elder woman from Bissau explained:

> The Pepel, the Mankanya, the Bijugos, many groups do not go to *fanadu*; just the Muslim groups, the Mandinga, the Biafada, and the Fula, because we have to pray. If you don't go to *fanadu*, you will have an odor there [in the genital region] and you will not be clean. If you cannot pray, then you are not a Muslim, and Mandingas are Muslims.

This need for cleansing or purification fits with Muslim ideas concerning gender and the life cycle. As women progress through the life cycle, changes in the body affect changes in purity and hence in religious participation. Often, changing bodily states have contradictory effects on women's public and private religious lives. Physical maturation can have a positive effect on religious practice and identity. As Susan Rasmussen notes for the Tuareg of Niger (1997), women begin to take part in religious observances such as obligatory prayer and fasting upon their first menstruation. At the same time, however, as women mature physically they come into contact with polluting substances such as menstrual blood, the blood of childbirth, and bodily emissions of young children, all of which limit women's involvement in religious activities such as prayer and going to the mosque (see also Delaney 1988). Among the Mandinga, clitoridectomy is considered to be at least a partial solution to the problem of compromised purity associated with physical maturation.

Recent campaigns to alter or eradicate excision practices in Guinea-Bissau that have been led by foreign aid organizations, local and foreign healthcare workers, and government agencies have responded to this explicit link between female "circumcision" and religious identity as perceived by many in Guinea-Bissau. Focusing on educating women about the negative health consequences associated with the practice, these activists started by trying to convince women that Islam does not advocate female "circumcision," nor does the Quran prescribe it. In my research with Mandinga men and women, however, I discovered that the relationship between female "circumcision" and Islam extends beyond what is explicitly stated (or not stated) in Islamic texts. Whether others claim that Islam does not advocate the practice for women is not the issue, since many Mandinga with whom I spoke are fully convinced that it does. After discussing this issue with a medical doctor in Bissau leading the campaign against "excision" in Guinea-Bissau, I decided to engage Mandinga men and women more actively on the connection between female "circumcision" and Islam.

When I asked how female "circumcision" began and why the Mandinga first started practicing it, several women (and some men as well) told me the following story, which they claimed comes from the Quran. The version that I cite here was taken from a recorded interview I conducted with an elder Mandinga woman who lives in Bissau and whose grandmother was a *ngamano* (traditional circumciser). She explained:

> It was from the side of Mohammed that we took this thing [female "circumcision"]. Mohammed took a wife who was very old—so old that she couldn't have a child. They wanted to have children so they looked for a way around this problem. Mohammed adopted a young girl who would become his second wife and who would give them a child. Now, as time went on, his first wife began to realize that Mohammed was growing to like the young girl more than his first wife. She quickly became jealous of the young girl, who soon became pregnant. When Mohammed went on a trip—and he traveled a lot in those days—the old woman took the young girl into the courtyard[5] and slit [pierced] her earlobes. Because in those days only slaves [war captives] had their earlobes pierced, the old woman hoped that Mohammed, upon his return, would reject the young girl. When he arrived and saw what had happened, he said nothing. Mohammed was a powerful man and had many intermediaries who helped and advised him. Many of these men received direct messages from God. One of them heard about the incident and came to Mohammed. He said that God had spoken to him, telling him that Mohammed should not be angry, that soon all women would begin to slit [pierce] their earlobes just like his young wife. Mohammed bought some gold pieces and put them in his young wife's earlobes. She looked more beautiful than ever. All of the women in the village came to see just how beautiful she was. They all went home to slit [pierce] their own ears and collect gold pieces to put in

them. Mohammed's first wife did the same. Mohammed left for another trip, and this time he was away for three months. Again, he left his first wife in charge of the house. Since the old wife was still full of jealousy and spite for the young girl, one day in the early morning she took her into the courtyard and cut her little thing [clitoris]. When Mohammed returned from his trip and wanted to sleep with her, the young girl was afraid and refused him. Mohammed asked her, "What is it?" The young girl explained that she hurt down there. The old woman was content, since she knew that the young girl would not sleep with her husband because of the pain she was feeling. Mohammed prayed to God. A friend came to him and told him that he had received a message from God that Mohammed should not be angry. He said: "That little thing—now removed—will make your young wife even more beautiful and pure." Since the young girl was circumcised and God was content, the Mandinga put the idea of female circumcision into their heads, and that is how it all began.[6]

Alice Walker (1997:58) discusses a similar story told to her by an imam (Muslim spiritual leader) in Bolgatanga in northern Ghana, involving Abraham, his wife Sarah, and his concubine Hagar. In this version, Sarah seeks revenge upon Hagar for having borne Abraham's son. To appease Sarah, Abraham offers to "destroy" Hagar's beauty, which traditionally involved cutting a woman in three places—on her nose and on each earlobe. Sarah feels sorry for Hagar and instead asks that she be "circumcised." Rather than cutting her earlobes off, she asks that Hagar's ears simply be pierced. Hagar then wore gold earrings. Walker's informant stressed that this story is not found in the Quran, but rather in the "secret book" of the Muslims. In contrast, all Mandinga with whom I spoke assured me that this story can be found in the Quran itself. Unable to locate the story after reading the Quran, I decided to bring my dilemma to a well-known Muslim holy man and quranic scholar (*muro*) in the capital city of Bissau. Presenting the *muro* with a customary offering of five kola nuts, I explained the problem and listened to the intermediary repeat my words to the old man in the typical fashion. The *muro* smiled and answered in a partly frustrated and partly amused tone: "You have learned our language, read our texts, and now you think you can see everything! I have been reading the Quran for more than 30 years and I still cannot see such a sacred passage." According to this *muro*, even experts are not always perceptive enough to see or understand all the mysteries of the Quran.

Walker's reference to the "secret book" (which she suggests may also hold clues to other "oppressive" customs such as purdah)—evidence that there is no "real" religious/textual basis for female "circumcision"—overlooks the overarching importance of secrecy in African societies. Much of the ethnographic literature on African societies reveals the widespread existence of hidden, deep, or "secret" meanings beyond the readily visible or apparent. As Zahan (1979:53) points out, the former is often culturally valued over the latter, as it is considered to be "truer and more profound." Indeed, secrecy in

African contexts should not be seen as subversive and antisocial but instead as a key to the understanding of African politics, religion, and social relations.

The *muro*'s response to my question also highlights the link between secrecy and the text in African contexts. In an insightful study of literacy in Sierra Leone, Caroline Bledsoe and Kenneth Robey (1986:202) argue that the Mende of Sierra Leone (who are linguistically related to the Mandinga) value writing both for its technical function (its role in transmitting information and conveying meaning) and its social function (its role in creating a hierarchy of knowledge and in gaining power and dependents). As the authors state, writing is "a mode of access to other secret domains of knowledge whose meanings are dangerous to those without legitimate social and ritual qualifications" (1986:204). Not only is this reminiscent of Zahan's general point concerning secrecy, but it also underscores the fact that many Mandinga informants explained that the passages in the Quran discussing female "circumcision" are so sacred that they cannot be seen (and should not be looked upon) with the naked eye. This principle holds in the practice of initiation ceremonies. Many Mandinga women and men told me that anyone who is not a ritual specialist should not look directly at the "circumcision" knife—a sacred object that wields power—for fear of damaging one's eyes even to the point of blindness. "Capturing" the image of the knife or of the new initiates with a photographic flash is said to lead to insanity on the part of the perpetrator. It is also said to attract witches to the initiates, thus leading to their harm.

Becoming a Person: Mandinga Girls' Initiation and Personhood

Aside from being linked to religious identity, girls' initiation among the Mandinga is also inherently tied to the cultural construction of personhood.[7] After explaining the link between female "circumcision" and religious identity, Mandinga with whom I spoke asserted that initiation (including circumcision for boys and clitoridectomy for girls) also constitutes an important process whereby one comes to "know the eye" (*kunsi udju* in Kriolu; *nya lon* in Mandinga). This term refers to the moral and educational components of initiation, whereby young children are taught their position in society and the correct way of acting in a variety of social situations relative to their gender and age.[8] To "know the eye" also involves being socially graceful, being perceptive, and possessing the ability to anticipate the thoughts and actions of others and the knowledge to react accordingly. Among the Mandinga, the uninitiated (uncircumcised) person is considered to be reckless, disrespectful, and unrefined. In their words, he or she is a "foolish person" (*bulufu*) who "doesn't have a head." Whereas initiation for the Mandinga does not itself officially mark the onset of adulthood as it does elsewhere in Africa, the idea of "knowing the eye" suggests that it may be considered to be an important step along the way (cf. Ottenberg 1989).

Placing the physical act of genital cutting within the context of initiation rituals also reveals another aspect of Mandinga personhood: an important part of "knowing the eye" is learning how to "suffer." Adults often tease uncircumcised children, boys and girls alike. Playfully showing them kitchen knives and yelling "*no bai fanadu!*" ("let's go to the circumcision bush!") almost inevitably sends them running away. Although children look forward to initiation as an important step in their lives, it is also a source of considerable anxiety since stoically enduring the cutting—which is performed without any anesthetic—is one of the most culturally valued displays of strength and courage. In recalling their own initiations, many of the women with whom I spoke stressed their bravery in "suffering" the pain or the relative ease of the operation compared to what they had expected. One Mandinga woman from the village of Fambanta told me that she was disappointed during her initiation when her "circumcision" (during initiation) simply did not involve the "suffering" that she had anticipated.

> When I was circumcised, I wasn't afraid and it didn't even hurt. When the *ngamano* [traditional circumciser] cut me, I asked her, "Is that it?" I asked her to cut off the tip of my pointer finger because I didn't feel anything. To this day, the old woman still smiles at me when she greets me.

Among the Mandinga, pain and suffering endured during initiation play a transformative role that extends beyond the ritual context of initiation into everyday life. Mandinga say that a baby cries when he or she is born because the child knows that life will be hard and that suffering is an inevitable part of it. From the pain of childbirth to the death of a relative to the backbreaking work of clearing the fields before planting, people are said to learn and to grow with each event that they are made to "suffer." Circumcision for boys and clitoridectomy for girls are no different—to endure the pain of the cutting is to accept one's path to self-enhancement and, eventually, adulthood (see also Sargent 1989, and Chapter 6 of this volume).

In exploring and documenting the meanings associated with female "circumcision" in the context of initiation rituals, however, I confronted a classic anthropological problem: a notable disparity between theory and practice. Although nearly all Mandinga with whom I worked claimed that the practice of female "circumcision" is inseparable from the ritual context of girls' initiation, this did not always hold true in practice. Once I began to question women about the details of their initiation, I discovered that about half the women with whom I spoke were excised in the context of initiation ceremonies, but the other half were not. Indeed, in Guinea-Bissau nowadays there is often a disjunction between the physical act of excision, termed *fanaduz-*

inu, or "small initiation" in Kriolu, and the rituals of initiation, termed *fanadu garandi,* or "big initiation" in Kriolu (see also Chapter 12 of this volume for a parallel case in the Gambia). Whereas traditionally these two events took place together for girls who were anywhere from eight to twelve years old, girls today are more commonly "circumcised" at a younger age (anywhere from six months to eleven years old), but the *fanadu garandi* may be scheduled for a later time in life or may not even take place at all.

When I interviewed Mandinga women and men regarding this change, explanations seemed to converge on a few factors. First, almost everyone made reference to the recent campaigns to end excision practices. Although the government has not yet officially outlawed the practice, it does support and encourage those organizations that are working to end it. This is not the first time that Guineans have experienced government intervention in traditional practices. During Guinea-Bissau's 11.5-year war of liberation, the African Party for the Independence of Guinea-Bissau and Cabo Verde (PAIGC, started by Amilcar Cabral) worked toward the liberation of women while leading the struggle against Portuguese colonialism. Under the direction of Cabral, the PAIGC made the practices of polygyny, forced marriage, and denial of divorce rights for women illegal in the liberated zones because they considered these customs oppressive to women. As Stephanie Urdang notes (1979:186–188), however, clitoridectomy was not banned along with these practices because women themselves did not consider it oppressive. Instead, the PAIGC waged an educational campaign aimed at the younger generation concerning the practice. They argued that clitoridectomy was unnecessary, that it was linked to infection, and that it was not a precondition for the attainment of true adulthood. As during the war of liberation, recent government intervention, however indirect it may be, is leading to both fear and resentment on the part of many Mandinga, especially elders and ritual practitioners. I was told that female "circumcision" and the rituals of initiation that accompany it, once a semipublic ritual (although never to the extent of the boys' rituals), are now more often done behind closed doors. Second, many Mandinga informants discussed the financial difficulty associated with the *fanadu garandi.* Not only do mothers have to buy expensive items such as cloth and cowry shells for their daughters, but they must purchase daily meat and oil to send to the girls while secluded. One Mandinga woman from the village of Fambanta was planning to send her eight-year-old daughter to a "traditional" initiation at the beginning of the dry season. She told me that her mother was planning to sell a cow to finance her initiation. During the time of my research, the price of a large cow was approximately 8 million Guinean pesos, or about $200 U.S. dollars. This is a considerable cost, given that the annual per capita income in the country is about U.S.$180.

The recent campaigns against female "circumcision" in Bissau encourage women to retain the educational and ritual aspects of initiation and do away with the physical act of genital cutting (Burema Njaai 1997, personal communication)—an option gaining popularity in several countries in East and West Africa (see also Chapters 1 and 12 of this volume). Mandinga women with whom I spoke, however, seemed strongly opposed to this option because they claim that the actual cutting of the clitoris is the most important part of girls' initiation. Many had opted to have their daughters "circumcised," postponing or putting off altogether the accompanying rituals. As one Mandinga woman in Bissau asserted:

> If people tell you that girls' initiation is about drumming, dancing, and eating, they are wrong. That is just spending money. The important thing is that when you give birth to a girl, once she is 10 or 11 you circumcise her. The rest is not that important. It is just an opportunity to show everyone that your daughter has been initiated and so everyone can be happy. But if you don't want to do this part, you can just take your daughter into the courtyard and circumcise her yourself. Put the traditional medicines on her, and when she heals it is all over.

Other recent changes in initiation have more to do with urbanization and modernization than with the recent campaigns to end female "circumcision" practices directly. A number of informants explained that girls' initiation has changed simply because there are fewer *ngamanolu* around today to conduct the rituals. When asked why, women asserted that they no longer "have the head" for such work. By this, they mean that there has been a recent loss of traditional knowledge and skills required to perform female "circumcision" and its associated ceremonies in the "traditional" or proper manner. Mandinga explained that the recent "head loss" is due to the fact that the *ngamano*'s job is a difficult one. A *ngamano*—coming traditionally from a line of blacksmiths—is said to "have head" (*tene kabesa* in Kriolu), which means that she possesses an extraordinary connection to the supernatural world (see also Chapter 10 of this volume for a discussion of knowledge of blacksmiths in Mali).[9] With this connection comes an enormous responsibility that many women choose not to bear. *Ngamanos* must wage a constant battle with *fitseiros* (*buwa* in Mandinga), or witches—invisible to the eyes of the average person—who smell the freshly shed blood of the initiates and come for an easy kill at the time when the girls are most vulnerable (see also Chapter 14 of this volume).

A witch who kills a young initiate during or shortly after her "circumcision" is said to be a "king witch," and a *ngamano* is said to suffer greatly in the rare case that a child dies in the *baraka* (circumcision bush).[10] The *ngamano* must therefore take every possible precaution so as to avoid this scenario. Her cuts must be quick, precise, and controlled, and she must never allow the initiates to see the circumcision knife. In short, the hand of a good *ngamano* should be "easy to suffer." As a Mandinga elder explained:

A *ngamano's* work is very hard and there is no money in it. This is why there are fewer people who do it today. My grandmother was a *ngamano* her whole life. When she became too old to work, she buried her circumcision knife in our courtyard. When I was a child, I found it, which meant that I was the one who should take up the knife after her. You see this thing is handed down through the generations. But to accept the knife, you can't be any ordinary person. You must have the head for it. If you don't want to accept the knife, you can refuse. I didn't want to take it. I told my grandmother that I did not want the responsibility and that I preferred to be a businesswoman.

This woman currently operates her own business in Bissau. With the help of her eldest daughter, she travels to Dakar, Senegal, about once every two months to purchase the latest clothing styles. She brings them back to Bissau, where she sells them to local women out of her home, a career that she envisions to be more economically profitable and less exhausting than initiation.

The Internal Debate Surrounding Female "Circumcision"

In attempting to uncover the internal debate surrounding female "circumcision" in Guinea-Bissau—how Guinean men and women are thinking reflexively about the practice both in response to and independently of the global debate surrounding it—I engaged many different people (women and men from a number of ethnic groups) about their views on initiation and the recent campaigns to end female "circumcision" in Guinea-Bissau. I spoke to many men (both Mandinga and non-Mandinga) and many non-Mandinga women who supported either altering or ending the practice, but I did not encounter a single Mandinga woman during the time of my research who opposed the practice. Overall, Mandinga women's views on the current debate surrounding female "circumcision" were strongly in favor of retaining the practice. I later discovered that when I first told members of the Mandinga community in Bissau that I had come to conduct research on the life cycle that included initiation rituals, most women thought that I had come to try to end female "circumcision." It was only after four months that I finally managed to convince the community that this was not the case. When I asked Mandinga women about their opinions concerning the recent attempts to eradicate female "circumcision," most would shake their heads and say, "I kana pudi kaba ku kila" ("they won't be able to end that"). Even the Mandinga woman who refused to *toma faca* (literally, "take up the knife" and become a traditional circumciser) so as to start up her own clothing business made it clear to me that clitoridectomy is crucial for being Mandinga and for becoming a Muslim and that the government and foreigners have no business telling Mandinga women otherwise. She then explained that it is primarily the *kris-*

tons (literally "Christians," this Kriolu term was often used to refer to non-Muslims in general—whether actually "Christian" or not) who want the Muslim groups to stop circumcising women:

> They [*kristons*] say that *fanadu* causes problems with childbirth. I am a circumcised woman and I gave birth to eleven children without ever going to the hospital. It is not *fanadu* that is causing health problems but the small iron piece that people put inside of them.[11] That is what is causing all of the problems.

Research on the internal debate in Guinea-Bissau also revealed contradictory opinions on the relationship between female "circumcision" and female sexuality. In addition to the negative health consequences associated with many forms of female "circumcision," Western critiques of the practice have centered around the assumption that the practice (no matter what the degree) compromises or totally inhibits women's sexual pleasure—defined as clitoral orgasm—which is considered to be a fundamental human right and a key to women's liberation. What this critique has explored less thoroughly, however, is the variation in the physical practices and their differing effects on female sexuality, as well as differing definitions of sexual pleasure (see Shaw 1995: chap. 1). Some common negative health consequences of the practice that are featured in much of the literature on "female genital mutilation" (FGM) are sexual dysfunction, psychosexual problems, and loss of sexual desire (WHO 1996; Hosken 1993; Dorkenoo and Elworthy 1992). These same studies list protection of virginity and the prevention of promiscuity in women among the reasons for female "circumcision" practices around the world. However, as interviews in Guinea-Bissau with men and women, Muslims and non-Muslims alike, suggest, the correlation between female "circumcision," sexual activity, and sexual sensitivity may be much less clear than is automatically assumed in the West. When asked to share their views regarding female "circumcision" practices in Guinea-Bissau, most non-Muslim men and women thought that it was a bad practice that should be stopped. This group readily identified a relationship between female "circumcision," sexuality, and morality. One woman from Bissau who defined herself as a Catholic linked female "circumcision" to sexual promiscuity and even to prostitution in Bissau:

> When women are circumcised, sex doesn't feel good for them. They hear other women talking about how much they enjoy sex, so they think that the problem lies with their husbands or lovers. They look for other men to sleep with until they find ones who can satisfy them.

Even a few Muslim men living in Bissau shared these views. As Burema Njaai—the Mandinga physician quoted earlier—explained:

A common consequence of female "circumcision" is a decline in or absence of pleasure during sex, which can lead to two things: either a total lack of interest in sex or the opposite, an insatiable sex drive. A woman may want men too much. She may talk to women who say that they have a great time during sex. The circumcised woman may wonder why she doesn't and may think it is the man's fault. She will seek out sexual relationships with men until she is satisfied.

A young Mandinga man living in Bissau explained that female "circumcision" is not good because "it makes women crazy to the point that all they want to do is be with different men." Other Mandinga men with whom I spoke, however, claimed the exact opposite, that the practice "tames" women's sexuality. As one Mandinga man and quranic scholar from Bissau explained: "*Fanadu di mindjer* is a good thing because it calms women down and makes them more faithful to their husbands. Why do you think you never see Muslim prostitutes in Bissau?" Similarly, another Mandinga man in his mid-thirties living in Bissau and working as a *jila* (seller) at Bissau's tourist central market asserted: "'Circumcision' is a good thing for women. I have been with many women who are uncircumcised and it is not good because when you have sex with them, they scream."

This statement must be explained in terms of Mandinga discourse concerning loud noises such as screaming and whistling. Mandinga equate these with wild animals, witches, and nonhuman agents such as spirits, and they consider them to be negative and dangerous. Because of their association with the nonhuman (and often amoral) realm, parents actively discourage their children from making these noises from a young age. They are considered to be most inappropriate in the village (the realm of humans proper) and at night—the time when sexual activity takes place—so as to avoid improper mixing of these worlds. Screaming during sex—associated with sexual pleasure—is a highly inappropriate mixture of these human/nonhuman realms and is thus considered to be dangerous.

Whereas all these people readily identified a link between female "circumcision" and decreased sexual sensitivity, the above accounts reveal that the latter has varied and often contradictory social consequences. Unlike most men and non-Muslim women, however, Muslim women themselves never brought up the issue of sexuality unless specifically asked about it. They preferred to speak about the religious aspects of female "circumcision," how it defines them as Muslims and allows them to pray.

Mandinga and non-Mandinga opinions on female "circumcision" practices and recent campaigns to end them point to the importance in considering the intersection of factors such as gender, class, age, and religious identity. I found that middle-class, urbanized Guineans were more likely to oppose excision practices than were those of the lower classes or those living in the villages. Exposure to Western media, proximity to educational campaigns, and study abroad in Europe (usually Portugal or Spain) seem to have shaped the viewpoints of many people living in Bissau. Whereas most Mandinga men and women provided me with clear reasons (usually religious) for why they support female "circumcision," a few people in Bissau mentioned the more vague notion of "tradition" as a primary reason for the continuation of the practice despite recent efforts to end it. Discussions with many people about the importance of "tradition" point to an ideological rift between older and younger generations. One young Mandinga man who owned a small neighborhood shop in Bissau brought up this issue during an interview:

M.J.: There are some people in Guinea-Bissau who say that *fanadu di mindjer* is not a good practice and that it should be stopped. What do you think about that?

B.S.: I think that it should be up to the women what they want. If some women want to do it, that is fine. If they don't, they shouldn't have to. But it is not easy for a woman if she doesn't because the elders will say that she cannot get married unless she is circumcised. They will think, "We gave birth to you and now you want to tell us that what we tell you is wrong?"

M.J.: Would you ever marry an uncircumcised woman?

B.S.: I have been with [i.e., had sex with] many woman who are not circumcised. For me it is not a problem. But my older relatives would never agree to it. I would have to ask the woman if she would be circumcised, and if she refused, then I wouldn't be allowed to marry her.

In addition to age and social class, gender is another important factor in the internal debate surrounding female "circumcision" practices in Guinea-Bissau. To focus entirely on women and women's viewpoints on the subject neglects another side of this multifaceted debate. I found that, in general, Mandinga men had an easier time than women discussing all sides of the debate. Ironically, they were more inclined to think critically about the practice, less convinced of the necessity of the practice, and generally more open to discussing the possibility of change than were their female counterparts. I would argue that this is due in part to the parallel debate taking place in the case of boys' initiation, which has received no scholarly or media attention to date. I found that although most women spoke positively about their own initiations, men more often spoke negatively about theirs. Many recounted horror stories of their own initiations, including their experience of what they considered to be unnecessary beatings, hunger, and painful circumcision. Instead of sending their own sons to traditional "bush" initiation ceremonies, many men in Guinea-Bissau are now opting instead for hospital circumcisions, which they claim are safer, more economical, and less traumatic. As one Mandinga man explained:

> I was circumcised with 120 boys and we spent three weeks in the bush. I was the youngest boy in the group so the older boys beat me. When it was time for me to be circumcised, I was made to sit on a cold stone. When he cut me it hurt very badly. When the men came to dress the wound, I felt pain all over my body and my legs started shaking. If I have boys, I will have them all circumcised in the hospital. Bush "circumcision" is wicked business.

Since hospital "circumcisions" for women are not performed in Guinea-Bissau, women's choices are more limited than are men's. Many women assured me, however, that if given the option of hospital "circumcisions," they would not be interested because "the cutting is not the same." On the issue of medicalization of genital cutting, the factor of gender is again compounded by age and location, with younger men living in the city being more open to discussing alternatives to both girls' excision and boys' circumcision than are older men living in villages, most of whom still support "traditional" procedures as strongly as women do. Indeed, members of this latter group of men were very much opposed to hospital circumcisions for boys and blamed much of Bissau's social problems such as theft and drug use on the improper initiation of youth.

Religious affiliation is perhaps the most readily apparent factor in the debate surrounding female "circumcision" in Guinea-Bissau. As I mentioned previously, all the women with whom I spoke who were opposed to "circumcision" for women were non-Muslims. These women mentioned health complications, decreased sexual pleasure, and problems during pregnancy as primary reasons for their views. They often told me that Muslim women "have a hard life." Muslim women explained to me that non-Muslims oppose the practice because they are trying to take away their right to pray. This discourse points to the growing tension between Muslims and non-Muslims as they are faced with the challenge of living closely together in the city and tolerating each other's contrasting lifestyles. For example, my Muslim neighbors often complained that shortly after a *chur* (animist funeral ceremony) the entire compound smelled of cashew wine and "spoiled" their quranic study and prayers. The non-Muslims in the neighborhood often complained that the Muslim chants sung throughout the night on important holy days were noisy and kept them awake. Many women in the Muslim community told me that the current debate surrounding female "circumcision" is just a way for non-Muslims to make money working for nongovernmental organizations (NGOs) in Bissau (see also Chapters 10 and 12 in this volume). Expressing frustration over non-Muslim women's involvement in a practice concerning Muslim women, one woman asserted: "They carve poles out of trees, call them their fathers, and pray to them—how could they ever understand us?"

Members of the educated elite class in Guinea-Bissau tend to be from non-Muslim groups or foreigners, and Muslims blame this group for the recent negative attention to their traditional practices. Although many Mandinga women responded to the recent campaigns to end female "circumcision" with secrecy and silence, others chose a more aggressive path to resistance. Toward the very end of my stay in Guinea-Bissau, women in the town of Mansoa held what the news report broadcast nationally in the country called the largest girls' initiation ceremony in the history of the Oio region (for a discussion of similar backlash reactions, see Chapters 1 and 12 in this volume). For the women of Mansoa, the event was an act of protest directed toward the government, foreign aid organizations, and local and foreign healthcare workers who, in launching anti-FGM campaigns, had refused to take their views into account.

Conclusion

In the current debate surrounding the varied practices of female "circumcision," discussions around the world have centered on cultural relativism, human rights activism, and cultural forms of domination. This focus has led to a gap that is only recently beginning to be explored by scholars: How are these discussions currently being understood by people in local communities, and what effect have the global debates had on local peoples' everyday lives?

In attempting to explore such internal dynamics among the Mandinga of Guinea-Bissau, I have argued that female "circumcision" is linked to the construction of religious identity. Women claim that the physical act of "circumcision" enables them to pray, thus making them full-fledged Muslims. It is at this point that religious identity becomes fused with ethnic identity, as becoming a Muslim is an important aspect of being Mandinga. Female "circumcision" and girls' initiation in this context are also linked to personhood, the development of social sense termed by Mandinga as "knowing the eye."

I have suggested that female "circumcision" in the Mandinga case must be examined—however problematically—in relation to girls' initiation rituals. As I have attempted to show, the recent disjunction between the two must be understood in terms of both external factors such as recent global efforts to alter or end female "circumcision" and internal factors such as the loss of traditional knowledge brought about by the processes of modernization and social change. Among the Mandinga, "knowing the eye" is linked more to the educational aspects of initiation rituals than to the physical act of cutting. When asked to comment on the recent disjunction between the physical act of cutting and the rituals of initiation and its implications for Mandinga personhood and religious identity, most women considered the cutting to be most important. Women assured me that whereas parents can, and do, teach their children to "know the eye," a mother cannot give her daughter the right to pray—making her a true Muslim—without having her "circumcised." Ethnographic explorations such as these can provide explanations for why current campaigns to alter or end female "circumcision" may be failing and may suggest alternative, more productive channels to take.

The Mandinga case thus sheds light on a number of important issues in the study of female "circumcision." First, it underscores the fact that religious identity is constructed in locally specific ways that often differ from global doctrines and texts. That there is no textually founded basis for female "circumcision" does not undermine the centrality of the practice for religious identity among the Mandinga. Second, although there has been a physical disjunction between the physical act of cutting and initiation rituals, this does not imply that the meanings associated with the latter are no longer relevant. Whether performed within the context of initiation rituals or not, female "circumcision" in the Mandinga case remains central to personhood and to the social and moral development of children. Finally, whereas the physical and psychological consequences of female "circumcision" for sexuality may be firmly established and consistent in the West, dissenting voices from Mandinga men, women, Muslims, and non-Muslims point to the reality that elsewhere, these consequences are often perceived as variable and contradictory.

Notes

This research was funded by an International Predissertation Fellowship from the Social Science Research Council and was the first stage of a long-term project concerning personhood, religious identity, and the life cycle among Mandinga of Guinea-Bissau and in Portugal. I would like to thank Dr. Karibe Peter Mendy, director of Bissau's Instituto Nacional de Estudos e Pesquisa (INEP), for making this research possible. I am also grateful to the Mandinga people of Bissau and the village of Bafata-Oio for sharing their knowledge and experiences with me, especially Adja Djiba Mané, Tai Njaai, and Dr. Burema Njaai in Bissau, and Alihadj Fodimaye Tur, "Numo" Tur, Idrissa Saidy, and Binta Njaai in Bafata-Oio. *A baraka!* I also benefited from insightful comments and suggestions from Bettina Shell-Duncan and Ylva Hernlund at the University of Washington, Eric Gable at Mary Washington College, and Alma Gottlieb at the University of Illinois at Urbana-Champaign, all of whom read earlier versions of this chapter. Last but not least, I would like to thank my husband, Edmund Q. S. Searles, whose unwavering support and thoughtful criticism were invaluable both in the field and during the write-up of this chapter.

1. Here I do not mean to imply that all female "circumcision" practices can always be examined in relation to rites that accompany them. In some parts of North and East Africa (e.g., Egypt, Sudan, and Somalia), the practices may not be accompanied by any major ritual.

2. An exception to this is the case of mixed marriages. Several non-Muslims claimed that a non-Muslim woman who marries a Muslim man will most likely undergo female "circumcision." Although I found these marriages to be rare in general, I did meet several Muslim men who were married to non-Muslim women who had not been "circumcised."

3. In Guinea-Bissau, all estimates have been calculated based on the percentage of Muslims in the country at the time. In 1979, Urdang estimated that about 30 percent of the population practiced female "circumcision"; the recent higher estimate of 50 percent reflects the growth of the Muslim community and Islamic conversion (Burema Njaai, personal communication, November 27, 1996).

4. Urdang notes that the most common form of female "circumcision" in the country, as far as she could ascertain, was partial clitoridectomy (1979:185–186). In his colonial ethnography of the Mandinga ethnic group, Carreira documented that "genital mutilation" for women consisted of excision of the tip of the clitoris (1947:82). This is, for the most part, consistent with my own research on the subject; I found, however, that whether part or all of the clitoris was removed seemed to be an issue among Mandinga from different regions.

5. The exact word that Musokeba Mane used was *kintal*, a Kriolu term referring to the women's quarters located outside the house and used for socializing, cooking, and working. I have translated this into English as "courtyard" for lack of a better term.

6. This interview was recorded in both Mandinga and Kriolu, and I later translated and transcribed it into English. Although I heard this story many times during my stay in Guinea-Bissau, it often sparked dispute among both men and women whether the first girl to be "circumcised" was a second wife or daughter of the Prophet Mohammad or the second wife or daughter of the Prophet Ibrahim.

7. Following ideas proposed by the anthropologist Meyer Fortes, I consider personhood to include "the distinctive qualities, capacities, and roles with which society endows a person" and "how the individual, as actor, knows himself to be—or not to be—the person he [or she] is expected to be in a given situation and status" (1973:287; see also Jackson and Karp 1990).

8. This concept is similar to Paul Riesman's (1992) and Audrey Richards's (1982[1956]) use of "social sense" for the Fulani of Burkina Faso and the Bemba of Zaire, respectively.

9. Although many *ngamanolu* in Guinea-Bissau today are from the *numo* (blacksmith) group of artisans, several women explained that midwives and people "with a head" can also become circumcisers if they decide to dedicate themselves to the job. In the Mandinga case, "having a head" seems not to be restricted to any particular group of people.

10. Although this Kriolu term may appear to come from the Arabic *baraka,* meaning "blessing," it actually is derived from the Portuguese *barraca*, meaning "hut" or "tent."

11. This woman was referring to intrauterine devices (IUDs), a common form of birth control practiced by many women in Bissau. Most of the Muslims I talked to were opposed to this method.

12

Cutting Without Ritual and Ritual Without Cutting: Female "Circumcision" and the Re-ritualization of Initiation in the Gambia

Ylva Hernlund

The small West African nation of the Gambia has in recent years become the stage for an intensive debate surrounding the practice of female "circumcision," as well as a great deal of change in both the practice itself and the discourses that surround it. The controversy over "female genital mutilation" (FGM) in the Gambia today is far more than a public health issue; it has become a locus for contested views of "culture." Although historically many Gambian girls were "circumcised" in the context of coming-of-age pedagogy and celebration, it has in recent decades become increasingly common for very young children to undergo a primarily physical procedure with little or no accompanying ritual or transmission of "traditional" knowledge. In response to this globally growing pattern of cutting without ritual, some Gambian women activists have embarked on a project focused on ritual without cutting: the revitalization of girl's adolescent initiation minus the element of genital cutting.[1]

In this chapter I examine one such "alternative ritual" within the context of the local, national, and international debates framing the controversy in the Gambia today. Short of proposing replacement rituals as universally appropriate, I will suggest that in the particular context of the Gambia, such community events may not only contribute to the elimination of female genital cutting (FGC) but can also provide a powerful avenue for women's empowerment while allowing individuals and communities to avoid the accusation that to give up female "circumcision" is to give up one's "culture."

This material is drawn from several research trips to the Gambia during the 1990s. Throughout my research I have conducted extensive interviews with men and women of all ages in the urban area of Bakau regarding their experience with and attitudes toward the practice of female "circumcision," as well as their reactions to attempts at its elimination. In addition, interviews were conducted with nurses, doctors, and traditional birth attendants (TBA), government officials and lawyers, anticircumcision activists, and circumcisers. Archival research focused on newspapers, government records, and materials from nongovernmental organizations (NGOs) in order to trace the history of public discourse on the issue; and I attended workshops, training sessions, and conferences organized by each of the organizations campaigning against FGC. In 1997–1998 much of my focus was on participant observation with the Association for Promoting Girls' and Women's Advancement in the Gambia (APGWA) during the planning of their first alternative ritual. I interviewed staff, attended workshops and meetings, and worked as a volunteer teacher at one of the organization's skills centers. Finally, I participated in and videotaped the Basse youth camp where girls were first "initiated without circumcision."

The Place and the Practice

The Gambia is a narrow strip of territory surrounding the Gambia River, covering a mere 10–16.5 miles on either side of the river but stretching more than 300 miles into the interior. With a short coastline on the Atlantic Ocean, the Gambia is surrounded on three sides by Senegal. The land borders the Sahel and experiences an increasingly long dry season as well as a brief time of rains. At the time of the 1993 census, the population of the Gambia was estimated at just over 1 million, a steep increase from 687,000 ten years earlier. After being colonized by Britain, the Gambia became an independent member of the Commonwealth in 1965 and a republic in 1970, experienced a bloodless military coup in 1994, and held free elections again in 1997. The nation seemed doomed from the moment of its independence to rely on foreign assistance for its survival and is today still one of the poorest in the world, although rapid development has been taking place in recent years.[2]

The population of the Senegambia area is the result of a series of voluntary and involuntary migrations that took place over the past 2,000 years. In the thirteenth to seventeenth centuries, the Mali empire expanded into Senegambia, where a number of Mandinka kingdoms were founded along the river. The largest ethnic group in the Gambia, the Mandinka (elsewhere called Mandingo, Manding, Mandingka, or Mandinga) comprise roughly 40 percent of the population, followed by 20 percent Fulanis (in Gambia called Fulas).

Other major ethnic groups include the Wolof, Jola, Aku, Serer, Serahule (Soninke), and Bamana.[3]

As is true elsewhere, the origins of female "circumcision" in the Gambia are not entirely clear. Gambians generally report that the practice is old, "we found it from our grandmothers," but rarely offer suggestions as to where or why it may have originated. In Chapter 13, Gerry Mackie has proposed a diffusion theory of FGC that, if correct, would situate the Gambia in the outlying area practicing "incidental" circumcision, not necessarily as part of a chastity/fidelity complex. Among the Mandinka, Serahule, Bamana, and Fula—all groups believed to have migrated to the area from the east—female "circumcision" is nearly universal, although this is also true of the Jola, who are believed to be indigenous to the region.[4] The Wolof, thought to have come from the north, did not practice female "circumcision" in the past, but estimates put the number of Wolof females "circumcised" nowadays at about 30 percent (this figure was widely quoted to me by doctors, activists, and others, but I have been unable to find its source and assume it to be an estimate based on anecdotal evidence).

Official statistics on the overall frequency of genital cutting in the Gambia vary: local studies, invariably based on extremely small samples, report that 79 percent (Singateh 1985) to 83 percent (*Knowledge, Attitude, and Practice Study*, Women's Bureau of the Gambia 1991) of all Gambian women have undergone some form of genital cutting, whereas others use the Hosken report's estimate of 60 percent (Touray 1993). Several organizations are in the process of collecting new data on the practice of female genital cutting throughout the country.[5] Based on my research, however, a few current trends can already be identified concerning the practice of, attitudes toward, and discourses surrounding female "circumcision" in the Gambia.

Changing Talk and Action

The way that female "circumcision" is talked about in the Gambia is changing rapidly and dramatically. Prior to the 1980s, the topic was seldom publicly addressed; it was considered *kulloo* (secret).[6] Recent years, however, have seen intense media coverage of FGM in newspapers, on the radio, and in the past few years, on television. Gambians are not only consumers of international media that often have treated FGM in a sensationalist manner but have also repeatedly become the subjects of such reports, and there is widespread awareness that this "local practice" has become part of a global debate. In the 1980s and 1990s, an increasingly intense dialogue has emerged between those Gambians who perceive a need to eradicate "female genital mutilation" and those who seek to preserve female "circumcision" as an integral part of culture.

These perspectives are reflected in the terminology used to describe the practice. The Mandinka language has a number of expressions for female initiation and its accompanying genital cutting. According to my informants, *nyiaka* is a contraction of *nyiama* (grass or weed) and *kaa* (to cut clean) and refers to the genitals that must be cut clean, just as farmland must be weeded. *Barango* comes from *baa* (mother) and *ring* (little) and refers to the initiates as the little (i.e., future) mothers. Other expressions are more subtle, such as *kuyango*, used for both male and female initiation (meaning "the affair," but also referring to the shed that is constructed for the initiates), *wulakonota* (to go to the bush), and simply *musolula karoola* (literally, "the women's side," but meaning more generally "that which concerns women").

"Female circumcision" is an expression commonly used when Gambians discuss the procedure in English. Although "circumcision" implies a less severe operation than that which is commonly performed in the area, this term is seen by many Gambians as less judgmental and provocative than "female genital mutilation" (for a more extensive discussion of the dilemma of terminology, see Chapter 1 of this volume). I will use this term, but with cautionary quotation marks, alongside the somewhat neutral "female genital cutting." It must be noted, however, that most Gambian activists working for the eradication of female genital cutting *do* use the term "female genital mutilation" and that the acronym FGM is widely recognized among Gambians in general. There is some ambivalence about the term, however. As one representative from a local NGO involved in a "sensitization" campaign against the practice told me: "When you say 'mutilation,' it disturbs people. It sounds like they just cut, and cut, and cut."

Those who campaign against FGC in the Gambia have made ambitious attempts to document local "rationales" for the practice. Several research efforts, starting with the 1985 Women's Bureau study, have asked survey respondents to choose from a limited set of broad answers like "culture," "cleanliness," and "religion." In my own research I have found the most commonly and strongly stated reasons for practicing female "circumcision" to revolve around the maintenance of "tradition" and the pressure of conformity. In Chapter 13, Mackie argues that marriageability lies at the root of all female genital cutting but agrees that "in some places the association with marriageability may have been lost" and overshadowed by secondary sources for the maintenance of the practice.

In the Gambia, I rarely heard an explicitly stated concern with marriageability, and intermarriage between all the ethnic groups—whether or not they practice FGC—is common and comparatively unproblematic. Instead, Gambians more generally draw attention to the relationship between female "circumcision" and ethnicity, religion, proper childrearing, and the maintenance of tradition and "culture." Although, as Mackie points out, the perception of female "circumcision" as an ethnic marker may be "a consequence, not a cause" of the practice, over time the two become mutually reinforcing, and in the Gambia today many people identify themselves as belonging to groups whose "ways" include female "circumcision" in contrast to others with different traditions. Religion, as well, has become associated with FGC, although not unequivocally so (Gambia is about 97 percent Muslim). Many Gambians, including several powerful Muslim leaders, argue that Islam supports or even requires female "circumcision," but many others disagree (cf. Chapter 11 of this volume for an account of Mandingas in Guinea-Bissau, among whom the practice appears far more closely linked with Islamic identity). Anti-FGC campaigns have focused much of their efforts on disputing the notion that FGC is a religious injunction, and a number of imams have spoken out against the practice. Also, Gambian Mandinkas seldom argue that in order to be a good Muslim one has to practice female "circumcision" because it is generally thought that the Wolof are "as good Muslims as anyone," despite their generally not practicing FGC.

In addition, respondents often mention cleanliness (both literal and spiritual), the control of female sexuality (see also Chapter 1 of this volume for a discussion on FGC and female sexuality), aesthetics, and greater ease in childbirth. Others point to the importance of proving oneself able to withstand the physical pain (see also Chapters 6, 10, and 11 of this volume) and, when referring to "traditional" initiations, stress the importance of learning socially acceptable behavior and respect for elders.

The reason for practicing female "circumcision" most strongly stated by Gambians, however, is respect for tradition and conventional norms of behavior. Those who are not "circumcised"— as well as those who "act like they are not"—are contemptuously insulted as *solema*. This extremely powerful invective means not only "uncircumcised" but also rude, ignorant, immature, uncivilized, unclean—"someone who does not know herself." The fear of being labeled as *solema* acts as an extremely strong motivation for a woman to "join" herself or her daughter with those who are "circumcised"; it is not unheard of for young Wolof girls to defy their families and join their Mandinka friends in "circumcision" (see also Chapters 7 and 9 of this volume) and for Wolof wives in Mandinka compounds to tire of the taunts of co-wives and agree to undergo the procedure as adults.

As elsewhere, female "circumcision" in the Gambia is generally seen as "women's business" and in no small part is perpetuated by women themselves, although males are becoming increasingly involved in the debate. It is also true that perhaps equally important to the status change of the initiates is the way older women's authority is bolstered by the process of initiation (see also Thomas 1996 and in Chapter 7 of this volume). What cannot be emphasized too strongly, however, is the complexity and fluidity of the current debate. It is just as common, for example, to find an elder woman who opposes the practice as it is a young man who supports it.[7] Knowing that Gambian "traditions" have come under intense scrutiny in such contexts as Alice Walker's film *Warrior Marks* and several U.S. network news "specials," many Gambians have an acute awareness that the practice of female genital cutting will, for better or worse, be talked about worldwide and that increasingly these local debates have become entangled with national and international discourses about FGM.

In urban areas, few individuals are unaware of local campaigns to convince people of the need to eradicate "female genital mutilation." In rural areas, as well, many communities have been contacted by fieldworkers from groups trying to abolish FGC, either as a single issue or as part of a broader mandate (for example, a 1994 GAMCOTRAP study carried out in ten villages scattered over two districts and including responses from 300 individuals showed that 72 percent overall had heard about the campaign against female "circumcision"). The Gambian campaigns can be traced back to the mid-1980s, when a small group of urban, educated women, all of whom are to this day involved in work against FGC, began an organized effort to abolish genital cutting. It all started through the Women's Bureau, which represented the Gambia at the 1984 meeting in Dakar organized by the Senegalese government and the Working Group on Traditional Practices (and cosponsored by the World Health Organization, United Nations Children's Fund, and the United Nations Population Fund) at which the Inter-African Committee (IAC) was formed. Due to the perceived need to address FGM separately from the broader goals of the Women's Bureau, the Gambia Committee of the IAC was then created, and in 1992 its name was changed to Gambian Committee on Traditional Practices Affecting Women and Children (GAMCOTRAP). Later other groups were formed, such as the Foundation for Research on Women's Health, Development, and the Environment (BAFROW) and APGWA.

As elsewhere, the campaign in the Gambia has primarily focused on FGC as a threat to the health of women and children. It has not, however, been well documented what type of genital cutting is most commonly performed in the Gambia. The 1985 Women's Bureau (Singateh 1985) study defines the common term "excision" as "removal of all *or* part of the clitoris *and/or* all *or* part of the inner labia" (my emphasis), thus collapsing into a single category several different procedures. My interviews with Gambian women who have been "circumcised" indicate that physical and psychological effects vary significantly depending on the extent of the cutting and that the issue of "how much is taken" is a salient one in many women's subjective accounts. Although sources generally list the most frequently performed types of genital cutting in the Gambia as "clitoridectomy," followed by "excision," some women activists I spoke with claimed that the reverse may be true. In reality, they insisted, many Gambian women have had all or most of their outer genitalia excised. Surveys, these women argue, have nonetheless yielded the frequent response "clitoridectomy" both from circumcisers, who seek to minimize the extent of cutting that they perform, and from "circumcised" women themselves, who are often "ignorant of their own bodies" and the exact nature of the procedure they have undergone. As an illustration, two of these activists related to me how each one of them had always thought that she had had a "clitoridectomy." Each woman later came to realize that she had been excised; one by being told by her husband that "everything is gone," the other by examining herself with a mirror after seeing pictures of the various types of FGC.

If the goal is to eliminate FGC because of the danger it poses to the health of women, then more research is needed on the medical consequences of the practice. Knowing the type of cutting most frequently practiced locally and avoiding excessive reliance on outside sources such as *The Hosken Report* will affect the credibility of any campaign approaching FGC as a health issue (see also Chapter 6 of this volume). Young people I interviewed after they had attended anti-FGM workshops with video screenings of an infibulation in Ethiopia said that their reaction had been: "But this isn't what we do here in Gambia!"[8] Clearly, if a campaign primarily focuses on the argument that FGC can cause obstructed labor, this is likely to be more salient to women who have undergone extensive excisions or infibulations, as opposed to partial clitoridectomies.

A number of Gambian women told me that they could not see how "circumcision," as they practice it, can have such an effect on childbirth and insisted that they themselves had given birth to "many children without any problems" (see also Chapters 7, 10, and 14 of this volume). Gambian activists recognize this fact, and several clinic- and hospital-based studies are currently being implemented that seek to determine the exact nature of the practice as well as any negative health effects suffered by Gambian women as a result.

Female "circumcision" in the Gambia rests, as well, at the nexus of an ongoing debate over national identity and ideas of "culture," as African nations come under increasing pressure to show efforts to eradicate FGM. Although many neighboring countries have legislated against FGC, including Senegal in January 1999, the Gambian government is unlikely to consider such a move. In May 1997, the then newly elected Gambian government issued a decree that banned the broadcasting on state radio and TV (the only TV station in the country is controlled by the government) of any programs "which either seemingly oppose female genital mutilation or tend to portray medical hazards about the practice." After massive protests—in particular from GAMCO-TRAP, aided by an international letter-writing campaign organized by New York–based Equality Now—the decree was lifted, although with so little publicity that many people remained unclear on what is and is not legal to broadcast. Vice President Isatou Njie-Saidy, herself a women's health activist who has previously been involved in the campaign against FGC, was soon thereafter quoted as stating that the government's policy will be to "discourage such harmful practices" and that NGOs will not be prevented from working against the practice (*Forward with the Gambia* newsletter, July 7, 1997). President Yaya Jammeh, in his 1997 annual address marking the 1994 July 22 military takeover, restated the government's position as being opposed to FGC but stressed that any campaign must be conducted in a culturally sensitive manner. More recently, in reaction to the Senegalese ban, the president publicly criticized anti-FGM campaigns, arguing that "female circumcision is a choice" and warning that women's activists "cannot be guaranteed that after delivering their speeches, they will return to their homes" (*The Observer*, Gambian daily newspaper, January 25, 1999). The vice president has since then reiterated that the government supports ongoing "awareness programs" but that "you can't legislate culture and tradition" ("The Gambia: A Special International Report Prepared by the *Washington Times* Advertising Department," February 18, 1999). There is every indication that the local and national debate is becoming more polarized and acrimonious.

Much of this tension is surely rooted in "reactance" (see Chapter 13 of this volume) to international pressures. A recent influx of increasing amounts of aid money earmarked for the eradication of FGC has led to a number of symposia, workshops, and conferences addressing the issue.[9] Interviews I conducted in 1996 and 1997–1998 showed mixed reactions to this sudden increase in discourse, ranging from relief that outside help is speeding up the elimination of genital cutting to rage at what is perceived as imperialist meddling in what should be an internal matter. Among both supporters and opponents of the practice, however, there is a recognition that the way female "circumcision" is practiced today in the Gambia has changed a great deal from the way it was "traditionally" done, particularly in regard to the ritual context—or lack thereof—in which genital cutting is performed as well as the age at which girls are taken.

Cutting Without Ritual

Historically, genital cutting in the Gambia was carried out as part of girls' coming-of-age ritual and accompanied by a lengthy seclusion that served as both ordeal and education. It is, however, becoming more common for girls in the Gambia to individually undergo only the cutting itself, in the context of little or no teaching or celebration. Although many individual Gambians say that they wish girls, like boys, would have access to "safer" clinic "circumcisions," girls in the Gambia are never taken to hospitals and clinics to be "circumcised," and the Gambian Medical Association strongly condemns the medicalization of FGC, as do all the groups campaigning against the practice.

Many of the young women I interviewed related their own experiences of having been "circumcised"—alone or with a few other girls—in a compound in town with little or no training and ritual. Various reasons were given for this: the expense of lavish celebrations can be avoided if the girls are taken quietly and privately; schoolgirls "circumcised" during holidays had to return to school and thus had no time for a lengthy seclusion; in a few cases girls were taken against their will and those of their mothers, and no celebration followed (especially if the girls were considered "too old," as in one case involving a fourteen and a seventeen year old); and in one instance "circumcisions" were performed in secret by a circumciser who had agreed to cease the practice (for a discussion of the sensitization and retraining of circumcisers, see below). In addition, some families and entire communities who adhere to a more orthodox interpretation of Islam insist on "cutting without ritual" because they consider traditional "circumcision" rituals un-Islamic (cf. Chapter 10 of this volume).

The trend of a decrease in ritual is supported by much of the literature. In a survey of cross-cultural coming-of-age rituals, Simon Ottenberg writes that there is "a worldwide trend toward the decreasing importance of traditional initiation rituals—ending, shortening and secularizing them" (Ottenberg 1994a:353). Efua Dorkenoo agrees that, in many African societies, "ceremonial aspects are falling away" (Dorkenoo and Elworthy 1992:40). Dorkenoo and Elworthy argue further that these days the child's role in society generally does not change at all after the procedure, a claim bolstered by the findings of Astrid Nypan's research among the Meru of Tanzania, where "circumcision does not confer the status of adult woman on a girl as it did when it was part of, or in preparation for, marriage" (Nypan 1991:56).

Another related development in the Gambia, as elsewhere, is the tendency to "circumcise" girls at a younger and younger age (see also Chapter 10 of this volume).[10] Ottenberg writes that, worldwide, "children are initiated at a younger age, when they are less capable to comprehend the nature of the experience" (Ottenberg 1994a:353). Representatives of several Gambian women's groups suggested in interviews in 1996 and 1997 that in the Gambia, this trend may very well also be in part a twofold reaction to campaigns against the practice.

On the one hand, people's fear that a law will be passed making the practice illegal can result in communities seeking to "circumcise" all girls before it is "too late."[11] The 1986 Special Report of the UN Working Group on Traditional Practices (henceforth referred to as Special Report) agrees that the age at which FGC is done varies according to "whether legislation against the practice is foreseen or not" (UN 1986:10). As in the reported coercive mass initiations into secret societies that took place in Sierra Leone in 1997 in apparent reaction to external pressures against FGM (Leigh 1997), a backlash was reported in the Gambia as well (see Chapter 11 of this volume for a similar incident in Guinea-Bissau).

On the other hand, another factor contributing to the lower age of female "circumcision," these Gambian activists argue, is that younger girls are seen as less capable of "fighting back." Nowadays, many believe that the younger the girl is, the "easier" the procedure will be for both her and the circumciser. One circumciser I interviewed told me that she herself will no longer "circumcise" older girls because it is "too difficult" for them. She said that "cir-cumcisions" used to be performed on prepubescent girls as a rite of passage, but that these days people prefer to have their toddlers, and even babies, cir-cumcised. Now that there is so much talk about the dangers of female "cir-cumcision," she said, the older girls try to fight back, and it is "just too painful," for both her and the girls.[12]

When older girls are "circumcised," it appears that they are kept in seclu-sion somewhat longer, and people often explained that this is because it is harder for the "big ones" to heal. Others insisted that the age at which a girl goes does not affect the pain she experiences. As one young woman com-mented: "At any age there is pain. A body is a body." It was also pointed out to me by health professionals and activists that, ironically, the increasingly young age at which girls are "circumcised" may be contributing to more se-vere excisions—and even "accidental infibulations" resulting from excessive bleeding and clotting—being performed, as cutting with any degree of preci-sion becomes exceedingly difficult on the tiny genitals of a very young child.

The age at which a girl is "circumcised" obviously affects the extent to which she undergoes a period of cultural education in addition to the physical procedure. The Special Report succinctly argues that any rite performed at in-fancy is "deprived of its initiatory value given the intellectual ability of the child to take part consciously in the ceremonies" (UN 1986:13). Supporters of female "circumcision" in the Gambia often argue that without undergoing the procedure, young girls will not know how to "deal with people," nor how to show proper respect for elders. Several young women and men involved with BAFROW's Youth Advocacy Group argued in a discussion in 1996 that the practice has already become "completely meaningless." "What kind of cul-ture," they asked trenchantly, "can you teach a two-month-old baby?" A num-ber of people pointed out to me that, although girls these days may be "circum-cised" at a very young age, they will go back and join their peers in subsequent years to continue learning in a gradual process. Nonetheless, there is wide-spread agreement that young people these days "just don't know the traditions like they should." As with the trend of "cutting without ritual" in general, the often younger age at which girls undergo genital cutting seems to support the conclusion that the three elements of female "circumcision"—the genital cut-ting of the initial day, the seclusion during which training takes place, and the celebration through which the girls are returned to their communities—have already in many cases become conceptually separated from one another.

Ritual Without Cutting

In this context, groups and individuals involved in working against FGC in the Gambia strive to operate within "culturally appropriate" parameters. Campaigns are often seen by proponents of the practice as rooted in outside influences, leading to comments like these: "These people who say they are against female circumcision are just trying to get *tubaabo* [white person] money"; "Those who are working against female circumcision are trying to destroy our culture. They want us to become like Americans, who have no culture." Thus, campaign workers, as well as individuals who are known in the community to be outspoken opponents of female "circumcision," admitted in interviews to being put in the position of having to defend their cultural loyalty. Typically these women and men told me: "I am just as good a Mandinka as those people. You can get rid of this one thing and still have your culture."

It becomes crucial, then, for those involved in efforts to abolish FGC to clearly demonstrate that they oppose only this one harmful element of "tradition" and are not rejecting "the culture" as a whole. At times speakers at anti-circumcision meetings employ the metaphor of the *tentengo* (sieve or winnowing basket), which allows one to guard that which is beneficial in the culture while letting that which is harmful fall away. For example, each of the Gambian groups involved in the campaign understands the need to reach out to circumcisers (*ngansingba*, sing.; *ngangsingbalu*, pl.), attempting to convert and retrain them while letting them retain—or regain—their important roles and high status in their communities.

Some are experimenting, as well, with the introduction of various forms of "replacement rituals" that seek to compensate for the culture that is seen as sacrificed if female "circumcision" is discontinued. For instance, a training manual published by BAFROW in the summer of 1996 encourages communities to return to holding prepuberty rituals for young girls while stressing "traditional" values such as virginity before marriage and respect for elders. In 1997 these replacement rituals had not yet been performed, however, because representatives of BAFROW stated that no community was yet deemed "ready." GAMCOTRAP, stressing the importance of preserving positive traditional practices while working to eliminate those that are harmful to women and children, has in the past worked toward a public ritual project in which *ngansingba* women publicly "put down the knife" (for similar ceremonies in Mali, see Chapter 10 of this volume). And in one recent case, which I discuss in the next section, the idea of "alternative" ritual was actualized as noncutting initiation.

Ritual Negotiations and Cultural Compromise: The Basse Youth Camp

Recently incorporated as an NGO, APGWA was formed in May 1992 by a group of female farmers, professional women, and businesswomen in the informal sector, with the main objective of "assisting less fortunate Gambian women and young girls" (APGWA pamphlet, as well as personal communication with Director Binta Sidibeh). APGWA has a staff of twenty-five and is supervised by a board of directors and an advisory committee. Funds come from various donor agencies and private individuals in Germany as well as from the association's local fund-raising schemes. The organization's stated goals are to contribute to the welfare and empowerment of women in all aspects of their lives. Although one explicit goal is to campaign against FGM, the group also aims to "engage people in cultural programmes to promote awareness and appreciation for the traditions of the Gambia and the sub-region" (APGWA pamphlet).

APGWA operates one urban skills training center and three village multipurpose centers, each of which includes a skills training center, a kindergarten offering free tuition and free lunch, an administrative center, and an income-generating project activity such as fish processing, gardening, raising poultry, or operating cooperatively owned shops. Health care for women and their children is provided through a visiting nurse-midwife. These general activities aimed at women's welfare cannot be separated from the group's campaign against FGC. Circumcisers are not directly paid for not cutting, but material benefits distributed to communities that agree to discontinue the practice are seen as one element contributing to the success of the campaign.[13] As in Mali (see Chapter 10 of this volume), a powerful system of "female patronage" operates in the Gambia, and the APGWA director is seen as a conduit channeling external funding to needy communities.

APGWA works through already existing groups and associations, such as an urban market women's association that recently became involved in a fish-selling program. This way, "you can talk to them about FGM while they're selling fish, instead of pulling them away from gainful work to have a special meeting," laughed the director in a 1997 interview. Anti-FGM workshops are also conducted in cooperation with local women's groups, including the traditional barren women's societies—*kanyeleng kafo*—whose irreverent jokes, songs, and dances combine with drumming, feasting, and speeches from traditional *griot* women to create a "sweetness" that otherwise is experienced by these often desperately poor and heavily overworked women only during events such as "circumcision." "It is an outlet from daily stress, abusive husbands, fights with co-wives and malicious gossip," said the director, arguing that the group tries to provide the same feeling of community, women's empowerment, and sheer enjoyment as do "traditional" circumcision ceremonies.

After several months of preparatory workshops and meetings, in May and June 1998 APGWA conducted a Youth Camp on Traditional Practices in Basse, a modestly sized trading and administrative town in the far eastern region of the country (according to the 1993 Census, Basse and environs had a population of less than 16,000). The Basse event, the first one of its kind held in the Gambia, included fifty-six girls from Basse and seven surrounding villages. The girls ranged in age from nine to twenty years old, with an average age of 14.6 years—one goal of the project was to push the age of initiation up to where the girls are "old enough to understand."

Each initiate (*ngansingo*) had been selected by local women leaders, and all were briefly interviewed during the first day's registration to get an idea of their backgrounds. All had previously been "circumcised." When asked at what age, most of the girls answered "as a baby," but some remembered the exact age of their "circumcision," which ranged from five to thirteen years. APGWA staff hope that this will be a transitional group: that these girls will choose only noncutting initiation for their own future daughters and that subsequent events may "catch" girls who have not yet been cut. Of the fifty-six girls, twenty-seven had attended Western schools, three only "Arabic" school, and twenty-six indicated that they had had "no" formal education. Some of the girls left the camp for a few hours a day to attend their regular schools. In the course of the training period, it became apparent that none of the girls had had much training at the time of their "circumcisions" and that they were often hearing songs and proverbs for the first time.

The "youth camp" teachings covered a range of topics, some "traditional" and others not: marriage, pregnancy and childbirth, breast-feeding, safe motherhood, family planning, food and nutritional taboos, traditional/ herbal medicines, public speaking methods, "female genital mutilation," sexually transmitted diseases including HIV, the role of the *ngansingba* and other leading women, "positive and harmful traditional practices," and various types of skills training. The trainers included five traditional circumcisers and several herbalists/TBAs and local women leaders in addition to APGWA representatives. The latter included a female *griot*, these days described as a "traditional communicator," who repeated in song the speeches of the director and representatives from communities previously reached by APGWA's projects. The girls and their guides were Mandinka, Fula, and Serahule, and both the language of instruction and the information transferred blended these traditions.

Although the participants left to sleep elsewhere each evening, roughly twelve hours a day were spent in a *jujuyo* (circumcision hut), which had been constructed in the back of the large compound of one of the local women's leaders. This square wooden structure with a straw roof and low, partial reed walls provided shade—if not privacy—for the girls, sitting closely together on straw mats on the ground, their legs stretched out straight in front of them and their faces downcast. The elder women sat on benches and folding chairs around a *djetango* (waterdrum), a large calabash floating upside down in a basin of water and beaten with a stick by women, who are "not supposed to beat real drums." All teaching was done in the traditional manner of songs, dances, questions and answers, recitation, and repetition. Although there was no corporal punishment, trainers did symbolically cane and reprimand girls for lapses in obedience and respect.

The camp lasted for two weeks, starting with a large public event during which the girls were brought together as a group and the general public informed about the project. In his enthusiastic opening speech, the local commissioner stressed the role of these rituals in reviving tradition, preserving "culture," and adding much-needed discipline to the education of youth. "A country without culture," he told the large crowd, "gives you no possibilities." He elaborated on the present situation in which youth no longer understand the things they ought to have learned in the bush: hints, proverbs, gestures, "the eye" (cf., Chapter 11 of this volume); and he urged the community to support this new initiation ritual. "Our culture is in your hands," he concluded.

Later that evening, a traditional masquerade was brought out: a male dancer completely enveloped in green leaves sang in a tinny voice songs of admonition and advice for the initiates, as is done in this region before actual circumcisions. A large group of people stayed awake throughout most of the night as the initiates and their mothers danced for many hours, partially illuminated by the headlights of a parked pick-up truck. The following morning, everyone gathered in the courtyard where the circumcisers were honored with songs and dances praising the blacksmith caste and the traditional circumcision knife (for more on the *numu* caste, see Chapter 10 of this volume). A dialogue of sorts unfolded as the APGWA director made a forceful speech about the importance of preserving and honoring positive cultural practices and discarding harmful ones, while one *ngansingba* sang: "The way I did it before, it wasn't bad. People say if you cut too much, the girl will lose her life. But it is because it was her time to die, not because of the cutting." As the girls were taken in to the *jujuyo*, the praising of the senior women continued, with the younger APGWA staff members approaching the seated circumcisers on their hands and knees, singing songs thanking them for not letting the girls come to any harm.

At the conclusion of the two weeks, an alternative *ngansingbundo* (coming out of the initiates) was held. In the morning of the last day, the initiates were taken through the streets and market to the spot by the river where girls are normally "circumcised." Under a huge kapok tree, the girls sat for several hours with heads covered, while the senior women encircled them, waving fresh tree branches, singing, and dancing. In the afternoon an elaborate public ceremony was held at the outdoor Community Center, the girls proudly emerging in matching cloth and traditional hair ornamentation of cowry shells and red and white beads. The initiates performed songs and dances, many of which they had not known prior to the camp. In addition, there were speeches by various community leaders and the presentation to each of the girls and women involved of a Certificate of Participation. After an all-night celebration of singing, dancing, drumming, and feasting, the girls were returned to their families the next morning, but only after making a semipublic pledge: "I promise never to circumcise my daughters."

Throughout the course of the youth camp there arose, spontaneously, remarkable instances of compromise, flexibility, and ritual creativity. The girls and their elders engaged in a constant process of negotiation on what to keep, what to change, and what to discard. For instance, the organizers had preferred that the girls not eat in the traditional way: when food is brought out the initiates all crouch on their knees and stomachs on the ground, hovering with downcast faces over a communal bowl of food. The girls themselves insisted on keeping this element, although Binta Sidibeh felt that such behavior is demeaning to women. On the last day by the river, shrunken to extremely low levels by a long dry season, it was discovered that the steep banks made it nearly impossible to have the girls enter the water for their ritual bath. Instead, plastic basins were promptly filled with river water and each girl instructed to wash her face, arms, and feet in a symbolic ablution.

When the circumcisers were honored in song and dance, they were thanked and praised for having cut the girls without causing any damage, although no one was actually cut. This is in complete contrast to "fake rituals" elsewhere that actually try to deceive people into thinking that girls have been cut when they have not (Abusharaf 1998; Kere and Toposiba 1994). Here, instead, the girls were symbolically pronounced "circumcised" and the circumcisers allowed to retain their authority.

Conclusion

Ritual, it has been suggested, is ascribed with the power of preserving past traditions. But in varied contexts around the world, people are also asking "to what extent ritual is capable of dealing with the new and 'present' world" (Coville 1989:104). At the present time, a number of individuals and communities in the Gambia have come to question the need for female genital cutting, and many others are aware that the practice has come under global assault as an alleged health hazard and human rights violation. Some of them hope that revitalized ritual, operating within culturally appropriate ideas of "tradition," will prove effective in providing such a way of "dealing with the present."

Of course, not everyone agrees that the ritual is more important than the cutting. Some people I interviewed thought the idea of "ritual without cutting" nonsensical. "What is there to celebrate if they haven't been cut?" said a few individuals. Others, males in particular, argued that the rituals are un-Islamic and inappropriate in the first place, and still others complained that these lavish celebrations are a waste of money and should be discouraged (see also

Chapters 11 and 13 of this volume). In addition, the content of initiation pedagogy is no longer uncritically accepted: one activist from another Gambian
group stressed that she not only opposes the genital cutting itself but is also
against retaining the "training" phase. In her opinion, what is taught to the girls
during this seclusion is "based on patriarchal values" and geared at "turning
them into submissive wives and mothers." This concern was partially addressed in the APGWA camp: the curriculum included information on the legal
rights of women and advice on vocational training in traditionally male profes-
sions, in addition to ancient proverbs, songs, and dances teaching "proper
womanhood." When asked about this, the director told me: "Western women
often think that all of this is about the oppression of women," but in her opinion only the cutting part is. "The rest," she argued, "is actually very empowering to women" and must not be lost (see also Chapter 14 of this volume).

Only time will tell whether the people of Basse and the other communities participating in APGWA's "ritual without cutting" will keep their collective promise and refrain from "circumcising" their daughters in the future and
whether these "new rituals" will continue being performed until they too are
thought of as "tradition" (see Chapter 9 of this volume).[14] Perhaps it is, as
Mackie suggests, the elements of education, public debate, and declaration
which must be credited if these events turn out to contribute permanently to
the abandonment of FGC in the Gambia. Because all the participants had previously been "circumcised," the 1998 camp cannot properly be considered a
"replacement" ritual, and it still remains to be seen whether upcoming camps
will start to include previously uncircumcised girls as well. What was revealed in Basse, however, is that more than simply the abandonment of FGC
is at stake when African women engage in what the author of one recent article describes as "developing their own communities of resistance" (James
1998:1045). The event contributed to community cohesion and solidarity
among and between young women and their female elders and strengthened
existing women's groups that will continue to administer resources infused
into the community. The initiates reported feeling that they had learned a
great deal about their "tradition" in the two-week camp; and the senior
women were allowed to regain their status as elders, respected for their ritual
knowledge, without the stigma of performing a "traditional practice" increasingly under siege. By reviving what is perceived as a tradition in danger of
being lost, minus the element of genital cutting, the youth camp served to
counteract the argument in some quarters that to give up female "circumcision" is to give up one's "culture." Perhaps alternative rituals are not broadly
applicable, but in the Gambia this experiment deserves serious consideration
as one strategy not only to influence the practice of genital cutting but also to
more broadly contribute to women's empowerment and aid in the maintenance of what is perceived as positive traditional practices while defusing often volatile debates over cultural autonomy and authenticity.

Notes

The research on which this chapter was based was carried out during several time periods. After brief stays in the Gambia in 1988 and 1989, I conducted independent research there in 1993 and, in 1996, a predissertation study sponsored by the University of Washington, Department of Anthropology. Dissertation research was carried out from August 1997 to June 1998, with the support of the Wenner-Gren Foundation for Anthropological Research (Grant #6186) and by Paul Bariteau. These sources of support are all gratefully acknowledged. I also wish to thank those individuals and organizations who have made this work possible: research assistants Lamin Touray and Lamin Darboe; the staff of GAMCOTRAP, in particular Isatou Touray, Mary Small, Amie Bojang-Sissoho, and Amie Joof-Cole; the APGWA staff, in particular Mrs. Binta Sidibeh and Awa Mbye, as well as the *kanyeleng* women of the APGWA campaign and all the initiates, circumcisers, and families who allowed me access to the alternative ritual in Basse.

I am grateful to Mr. Bakary Sidibeh and the National Council of Arts and Culture in the Gambia for approving and facilitating my research. For their friendship and support, I extend a warm thank you to Sainabou Joof, Elin Kvaale, and the Saine/Joof and Saho families of Bakau. I also want to thank those people whose comments and insights have helped me develop this chapter, including Bettina Shell-Duncan, Sidia Jatta, Bassirou Drammeh, David Spain, Claudie Gosselin, Lynn Thomas, Michelle Johnson, Simon Ottenberg, Svea Wülfing, Heidi Skramstad, Gerry Mackie, and Fuambai Ahmadu. Finally, I wish to thank the many Gambian women, men, and children who have shared with me their opinions and thoughts on this topic.

1. In this particular context I use a definition of "ritual" that refers primarily to the ceremonial and collective aspects of the practice. In reality, of course, things are less clear-cut. Even when girls are taken alone and "circumcised" without much ceremony, there is always some degree of ritualized elements present (such as consulting with marabouts to pick an auspicious date, the applying of herbal medicines and holy waters to promote healing, as well as a number of spiritual preparations made by the circumcisers). Nonetheless, the distinction of "with or without ritual" seemed to make immediate sense to most Gambians who spoke to me. I am grateful to Fuambai Ahmadu for her assistance in thinking about this.

2. According to the 1993 census, the infant mortality rate is 91.5 per thousand and life expectancy at birth fifty-five years (up from forty-two in 1983). The literacy rate is 54.4 percent for males and 26.4 percent for females, and according to the 1993 Household Economic Survey, per capita earnings are D5640 for males, versus D1418 for females (10 Dalasi were in 1998 equivalent to U.S.$1). In addition to the monocropping of peanuts for export, the Gambian economy depends increasingly on tourism.

3. Although this is the term currently favored in the literature, the older word "Bambara" is what is generally used in the Senegambia area.

4. Among the Jola, who will not be specifically discussed in this chapter, circumcision for both males and females generally takes place in the context of elaborate initiations. For a further discussion of the origins of FGC, see Chapter 1.

5. Of particular interest is an extensive Participatory Rapid Appraisal research project being conducted by GAMCOTRAP as part of a UN Children's Fund pilot project for the subregion. Seventeen communities in two divisions in 1998 selected two local individuals each—ideally one male and one female—to be trained to conduct research on FGC in their own communities. These research findings, it is hoped, will not only contribute to a greater understanding of FGC as it is practiced in this area but will help develop community-based initiatives to eradicate the practice.

6. Gambian Mandinka does not have standard spellings of words, and these terms may be spelled differently by others.

7. The scope of this chapter prevents a more detailed discussion of these local debates, which will appear in a forthcoming publication.

8. In Gambia there are cases of "sealing." This is a variation of infibulation in which the vagina is not stitched shut but sealed by allowing blood to coagulate in the opening, creating what amounts to an additional hymen that is indeed intended to prevent loss of virginity (Singateh 1985:48–49). It is difficult to determine the proportion of cases of genital cutting that involve sealing; the Women's Bureau study's estimate was 6.5 percent of total cases of FGC in the Gambia.

9. In this chapter, I focus in detail on just a few of the NGOs conducting anti-FGC campaigns. Other organizations and individuals are involved, as well, either directly or by providing funds. Some of the major funders of anti-FGM programs in the Gambia include UNFPA, UN Children's Fund, Action Aid, Global Fund for Women, and the World Health Organization. Also, Rainbo, Equality Now, Save the Children, Anti-Slavery Society, Foundation for Women's Health, Research, and Development (FORWARD), and a number of smaller European women's groups and individual philanthropists support or have in the past supported anti-FGC projects in the Gambia.

10. In discussing this change in the Gambian context, I focus primarily on Mandinkas. Serahules have historically "circumcised" their daughters in the first week of life, and some Fulas, as well, are said to "circumcise" their girls when very young.

11. As discussed above, it is becoming less likely that, in today's political climate, any such law will be passed in the Gambia. It was pointed out to me by legal scholars, however, that existing child abuse laws make it possible to bring charges of assault when FGC is carried out without consent. Indeed, some people told me that "if anyone tries to take my daughter, I will take them to the police," but I know of no such cases having actually been pursued in a court of law. For a further discussion of legal approaches to the cessation of FGC, see also Chapter 1 of this volume.

12. Her stated discomfort with inflicting this sort of pain stands in stark contrast to the circumciser in Alice Walker's film *Warrior Marks*, who emotionlessly says: "I can't hear them scream."

13. This strategy has been tried by others before, but many think that it merely encourages dishonesty because circumcisers accept the money but also continue cutting. See also Chapters 1 and 13 of this volume.

14. As of February 1999, another five communities had conducted similar events, involving approximately fifty girls each.

13

Female Genital Cutting:
The Beginning of the End

Gerry Mackie

In 1996, I published a more or less complete, although condensed, "convention" theory of female genital cutting (FGC), which attempted to account for the origins, distribution, maintenance, and possible abandonment of this perplexing practice. In that article I did what social scientists often preach but seldom practice: I made a prediction. I predicted that the formation of a certain kind of pledge association would help bring FGC to an end. If there is some critical mass of individuals (it definitely need not be a majority, and also the more genuinely influential the individuals, the fewer that might be needed), within a group of people whose children marry one another, who have come to the point that they would like to abandon FGC, a public pledge among such individuals would forever end FGC for them and also quickly motivate the remainder of the intramarrying population to join in the pledge and abandon FGC as well. Also, both the overlap of a successfully pledging group in neighboring marriage markets and the empirical example of successful abandonment might inspire neighboring groups to undertake their own pledges, so that the process would be contagious within some larger collection of overlapping groups.

The practice of footbinding of women in China was swiftly ended by such pledge associations. I showed precisely why the Chinese reform tactics succeeded so well, and I explained why FGC is in essentials equivalent to footbinding, such that local adaptations of the Chinese reform tactics might work in Africa. In the summer of 1998, I learned that some villages in Senegal had invented, reinvented actually, the pledge technique, that the pledge had succeeded unequivocally in Malicounda, that nearby villages had after periods of deliberation devised their own pledges, and that the pledge idea was spreading further, all just as I had hoped. The reformers in Senegal were not aware of my article or of its theory, but once we exchanged information it was clear that there is a tight correspondence between the convention theory and the practice unfolding in Senegal.

For a more formal and detailed account of the theory, the reader is directed to the original article, "Ending Footbinding and Infibulation: A Convention Account" (Mackie 1996). In this chapter I give an informal summary of the theory and provide some information about convention shift in Senegal. Then I offer some considerations on reform strategy based on a more fine-grained examination of the African case.

The Convention Model

FGC has persisted for generations, is nearly universal within the groups where it is found (Carr 1997:61), and in some areas is becoming more widespread (Leonard, this volume) or extreme. Many insiders emphasize that the practice is so deeply embedded that change will be very slow. An educated Sudanese woman said it will take 300 years to bring it to an end (Lightfoot-Klein 1989:135), and the casual observer would likely agree that it would take a very long time to erode such a fundamental cultural trait.[1] However, it turns out that within an intramarrying group, if FGC ends, it will only end quickly and almost universally. Furthermore, without the right sort of reform program, FGC might take many generations to end, regardless of the degree of economic development or cultural internationalization. Fortunately, after a period of credible nondirective education about its health consequences, the way to end FGC is almost as simple as the formation of associations whose members pledge to abandon the practice.

Why do I say that FGC must either persist indefinitely or end rapidly? Before proceeding with an explanation, we must listen to what the people who practice FGC say about it. Almost all say that FGC is required for a proper marriage, and many say that it is required for the virtue of the woman or for the honor of her family. Moreover, many have been unaware until recent years that other peoples do *not* practice FGC, and many have believed that the only people who do not do FGC are unfaithful women or indecent people. Like many other outsiders I find FGC horrifying to imagine, but for an insider FGC is more like dentistry than it is like violence.[2] Americans subject their children to painful and frankly exotic dentistry practices, and not to provide dental care to one's child is to damage his or her chances in life and marriage. Imagine that some foreigners come along who claim that dentistry is dangerous and leads to fatal diseases in middle life (a few people claim that mercury fillings represent just such a danger). American parents would find it very difficult to believe that there is a problem, and after they independently confirmed the information they would find it difficult to give up pretty teeth for their children if other parents didn't give them up too.

FGC is a matter of proper marriage. An individual in an intramarrying group that practices FGC cannot give it up unless enough other people do too.

FGC is a certain kind of "Schelling convention": what one family chooses depends on what other families choose. To understand, imagine that there is a group that has a convention whereby audiences (at the cinema, at plays, at recitals) stand up rather than sit down. Sitting has been forgotten. Standing is both universal and persistent. An outsider comes along and explains that elsewhere audiences sit. After the shock of surprise wears off, some people begin to think that sitting might be better, but it would be better only if enough other people sit at the same time. If only one person sits, she doesn't get to see anything on the stage. If only one family abandons FGC, its daughter doesn't get married (because of the belief that only unfaithful women forgo FGC). However, if a critical mass of people in the audience can be organized to sit, even just a column of people who are less than a majority, they realize that they can attain both the ease of sitting and a clear enough view of the stage. This critical mass then has incentives to recruit the rest of the audience to sitting, and the rest of the audience has incentives to respond to the recruitment. Similarly, if a critical mass of people in an intramarrying group pledge to refrain from FGC, then the knowledge that they are a critical mass makes it immediately in their interest to keep their pledges and to persuade others to join in and, after persuasion, makes it in everyone else's interests to join them. Without an understanding of the underlying mechanism, the abrupt end of such an entrenched practice by means of a mere public declaration would seem to be nearly miraculous.

A peculiar characteristic of a convention like female "circumcision" is that even if each individual in the relevant group thinks that it would be better to abandon the practice, no one individual acting on her own can succeed. One way to do this is to declare a public pledge that marks a convention shift. Every family could come to think that FGC is wrong, but that is not enough; FGC would continue because any family abandoning it on its own would ruin the futures of its daughters. It must be abandoned by enough families at once so that their daughters' futures are secured.

Is this speculation? No: I have shown that the convention model explains the binding of women's feet in China, both the former universality and persistence of footbinding and its sudden demise. The practice began when the girl was about eight years old, bending the toes under the feet, forcing the sole to the heel, and tightly wrapping the girl's foot so that as she matured her feet remained tiny, perhaps a mere 5 inches in length. Footbinding was painful, dangerous, and disabling, but the Chinese did it to ensure a proper marriage, the virtue of the woman, the honor of her family. Footbinding and FGC are essentially equivalent practices and originate from similar causes (see also Mackie 1996). They persist because of the same convention mechanism. Footbinding lasted for a thousand years, was universal among all "decent" Chinese, and was undented by liberal agitation and imperial prohibition in the nineteenth century. The most optimistic reformers in 1899 thought that it would take several generations to end. However, footbinding had ended for the vast majority by 1911, when a legal prohibition was enacted. Moreover, in localities where it did end, it ended quickly and universally, just as the convention model predicts. Therefore, the methods used to end footbinding in China, properly adapted, should work to end FGC in Africa.

The work of the antifootbinding reformers had three aspects. First, they carried out a modern education campaign, which explained that the rest of the world did not bind women's feet. The discovery of an alternative is necessary but not sufficient for change. Second, they explained the advantages of natural feet and the disadvantages of bound feet in Chinese cultural terms. New information about health consequences, again, is necessary but not sufficient for change. Third, they formed natural-foot societies, whose members publicly pledged not to bind their daughters' feet nor to let their sons marry women with bound feet. The problem is that if only one family renounces footbinding, their daughters are thereby rendered unmarriageable. The pledge association solves this problem—if enough families abandon footbinding, then their children can marry each other.

The first antifootbinding society was founded in 1874 by a local mission for its converts, who accidentally discovered the effectiveness of the public pledge. This local success went unnoticed until it was rediscovered and advocated on a national level in 1895 by the newly founded Natural Foot Society. The pledge societies and the cessation of footbinding spread like a prairie fire. By 1908, Chinese public opinion was decisively against footbinding, and footbinding of children was absent from urban populations by 1911. Other Chinese marriage practices, such as arranged marriages and early female age of marriage, changed slowly over many decades. Notice that cultural regularities do not all behave in the same fashion. In the United States there are campaigns to breastfeed babies rather than feed them formula. Change has been incremental; what one family does about infant feeding does not depend on what another family does. Footbinding and FGC, however, are each a special kind of convention; one family's choice does depend on another family's choice.

Convention Shift in Senegal

In September 1996, women involved in the Tostan basic education program in Malicounda Bambara in Senegal decided to seek abolition of FGC in their village of about 3,000 people.[3] The women went on to persuade the rest of the village—other women, their husbands, and the traditional and religious leaders—that abolition was needed to protect the health of their female children and to respect human rights. On July 31, 1997, Malicounda declared to the world its decision to abandon FGC and urged other villages to follow its example. Although some members of the Bambara ethnic group had stopped

FGC on an individual basis, no village had ever made a public and collective commitment to stop the practice. The commitment worked: public opinion continues to resolutely oppose FGC, and villagers say that deviators will be identified and punished. This is the first unequivocal collective and contagious abandonment of FGC on record, and the event supports the convention hypothesis of FGC.[4]

Their decision was controversial among those who had not worked through the Malicoundan's reasoning on the issue, and some neighboring Bambara, Mandinka, and Sosse people, both men and women, were angry and sent hostile messages to Malicounda. The women were hurt and depressed, yet defended their position, and even traveled to the villages of Nguerigne Bambara and Keur Simbara to discuss their commitment with women there in the basic education program. On November 6, 1997, the women of Nguerigne Bambara decided to renounce FGC forever. On November 20, 1997, the president of Senegal decried FGC and called on the nation to emulate the women of Malicounda. At the same time, the people of much smaller Keur Simbara decided that they could not stop FGC without consulting with their extended family that lived in ten villages near Joal. Their decision to consult also supports the convention hypothesis: the Keur Simbarans were aware that a change would have to involve the population among whom they commonly intermarried. Two men, one a facilitator in the basic education program, the other a sixty-six-year old imam who had been a student of the basic education program, went from village to village over eight weeks to discuss FGC. The men were at first afraid of being chased out of the villages for talking about such a sensitive and controversial topic, but the fact of the Malicounda decision provided an opening for discussion. I infer that the demonstration effect was important: that the Malicoundans had succeeded at a collective abandonment and had avoided bad consequences.

Three representatives (the village chief and two women) from each of the ten villages gathered in Diabougou on February 14 and 15, 1998, along with delegations from Malicounda Bambara, Nguerigne Bambara, and Keur Simbara. These fifty representatives of 8,000 people in thirteen villages issued the "Diabougou Declaration":

> We . . . declare:
> Our firm commitment to end the practice of female "circumcision" in our community.
> Our firm commitment to spread our knowledge and the spirit of our decision to our respective villages and to other communities still practicing female "circumcision." . . .
> We make a solemn appeal to the national and international community to quickly mobilize their efforts to assure that girl children and women will no longer suffer the negative health effects associated with female "circumcision."

The ten villages had not gone through the basic education program; rather, they had been persuaded by the emissaries from Keur Simbara, but the ten villages petitioned in the declaration to have the basic education program brought to them as well. U.S. first lady Hillary Clinton received the women of Malicounda in Senegal on April 2, 1998. They explained everything that had happened, and Mrs. Clinton congratulated them on their courage. President Bill Clinton also greeted and congratulated the Malicoundans.

The Wolof of Senegal do not practice FGC, are generally prestigious, and are also considered to be good Muslims, so perhaps it helped Malicounda, a Bambara village, to know that the natural alternative is imaginable. It has been further suggested that abandonment was motivated by a desire on the part of the Bambara, a minority in the region, to assimilate to the Wolof, a majority in the region. There is no evidence for this assimilation hypothesis. No such motivation was cited by the Malicoundans, who did cite negative health consequences as a motivation. Further, if all Bambara wanted to assimilate, why was it that nearby Bambara who did not possess credible information about negative health consequences were hostile to the Malicoundan decision?

Next, eighteen villages in the region of Kolda in southeastern Senegal (beyond the Gambia), led by the village of Medina Cherif, which had completed the basic education program, followed the example of Malicounda. Among this ethnic group, the Fulani, the regional prevalence of FGC is about 88 percent, and there are few Wolof in Kolda, which permits rejection of the hypothesis that abandonment is motivated by a desire to assimilate to a majority. On June 1–2, 1998, three representatives from each village (the village chief and two women), health workers, the imam of Medina Cherif, and representatives from government ministries met, and they issued the "Medina Cherif Declaration":

> We . . . have made the conscious decision to definitively renounce the practice of female "circumcision," which is a source of multiple health dangers and constitutes a violation of the fundamental rights of our girls. We have taken this decision in order to assure the respect of girl's rights to health, bodily integrity and human dignity. With this historic decision, we hereby join the great movement to end female "circumcision" which began in Malicounda Bambara.

The decisions put forth in the declaration, both in content and in style, emphasize that from this moment forward, the future shall be different from the past.[5]

Credible new information, the opportunity for a critical mass to form, a period when the critical mass conducts persuasion among the remainder of the population climaxed by a coordinated decision on abandonment, the news that a positive alternative can be safely attained, followed by replication of the process among neighbors: all these developments parallel Chinese events and support the convention hypothesis for FGC. I have not mentioned the most important factor, however: the fact that these events originate with women who participated in the same basic education program designed and implemented by Tostan (which means "breakthrough" in the Wolof language), a nongovernmental organization (NGO) supported by the UN Children's Fund (UNICEF) and the government of Senegal, among others. The basic education program includes literacy training but goes well beyond that. The program is oriented toward women, but men are not excluded. There are six modules of learning, and each module contains twenty-four two-hour sessions carried out over two months. The six modules are distributed over eighteen months; there are also additional modules beyond the basic six (Tostan's new women's empowerment program, six months in total, is proving effective in trials). The first module concentrates on problem-solving skills, the second module on health and hygiene, the third on preventing child mortality caused by diarrhea or lack of vaccination, the fourth on financial and material management for all types of village projects, the fifth on leadership and group dynamics, and the sixth on how to conduct a feasibility analysis to predict whether proposed group projects would result in net gains. Reading, mathematics, and writing are introduced in parallel, partly motivated by the substantive topics. The pedagogy uses local cultural traditions and learner-generated materials, including proverbs, stories, songs, games, poetry, and plays. Technique and content are regularly tested and evaluated.

Tostan is organized somewhat like a virtuous pyramid scheme. Tostan's trainers, all of them Senegalese, first recruit village facilitators approved by the community of participants; one trainer helps prepare and monitor facilitators operating in ten or so adjacent villages. Graduates are encouraged to transfer the basic education program to new villages; former learners become new facilitators in the vicinity, and excellent facilitators might become permanent trainers. Once the program is demonstrated in a pioneer set of villages, neighboring villages want the basic education program and are willing to pay moderate fees in advance for its operation.

One key to Tostan's success is the trustworthiness of its message. Rural Africans regularly encounter novel factual claims: from various salespeople, missionaries, the radio, and elsewhere. Just like us, they must evaluate the credibility of information coming from clearly interested or unknown outside sources. From the outset of its education program, Tostan provides useful skills and information in an explanatory context that participants test in their daily lives. It earns a reputation among participants for providing accurate and beneficial information, and participants gain individual and group confidence that further encourages change. Participants say that a consequence of the program is that one is able to *tiim sa xel* (to look down upon one's mind). Finally, the program is nondirective. People are *never told what to do*. The nondirective approach is essential for success because of "reactance," a concept I will explain below. It also expresses a proper respect for others.

It has been observed that Europeans and Americans are peculiarly selective in expressing concern about the public health aspects of FGC while neglecting activism on behalf of more basic public health efforts in Africa such as prevention of infant diarrhea, vaccinations, and so on. When I hear that comment, I think, that's right, but does one improvement always have to exclude another? It comforts me that the Tostan program provides a background of skills and information that facilitates autonomous and multiple improvements in health, education, and welfare. Indeed, an important lesson from the Tostan project, some other FGC projects, and some family-planning interventions is that a multidimensional approach is more effective than a single-issue approach. Obviously, a multidimensional approach is more efficient, but the neglected point is that its message is more trustworthy: outsiders who show up with concern over only one item stir justifiable suspicion.

To return to Malicounda, the thirty-nine Tostan participants embarked on module 7, on women's health. Their facilitator was from the Wolof, an ethnic group that does not practice FGC. When this facilitator brought up FGC, the participants refused to take part and began speaking in Bambara. After several days of effort, the women started responding to the questions and comparing experiences. In the process they discovered a connection between FGC and negative consequences that had been attributed to other causes, realized that individuals believed that negative consequences were isolated because they had not been publicly disclosed, and thereby concluded that the negative consequences were not normal but avoidable. For example, a woman from a nearby village came who had once been a cutter but had stopped thirty years ago because her own daughter was almost killed by the procedure. The women were free to choose their own village projects, or none, and it was they who decided that stopping FGC would be their first project. Then there was the question of the religious propriety of FGC. The village imam ruled that FGC is not a religious obligation and revealed that he had not had it performed on his daughters. The nexus of causal information, private experiences and attitudes made public, and the larger context of the education program created a critical mass of women who then went on to persuade others in the village.

News of the first declarations spread around Senegal and then around the world. The government of Senegal enacted legislation prohibiting female genital cutting on January 13, 1999. Delegations from the Tostan villages contributed to parliamentary deliberations. The law is mixed in effect: it promotes reaction and defiance and at the same time adds an argument for local abandonment (it would be counterproductive for the government to enforce the law harshly at the moment). The women's caucus of the parliament encourages international funding to promote local declarations in another 1,000 villages. On June 19, 1999, delegates from twelve more Bambara villages representing some 13,000 people met near Thies and enacted the "Baliga

Declaration" in the same pattern as those of Malicounda and Medina Cherif. More such mass declarations are pending elsewhere in the country: 100 more villages are expected to abandon before the year 2000. Tostan seeks funds to organize more mass declarations within Senegal and to train organizers from other countries in the Tostan process.

How does the basic education program compare to programs for the cessation of FGC? A striking difference is that the Tostan program did not directly intend to end FGC. Its purpose is to provide skills and information that help people better define and pursue their own goals; it also creates a forum in which women can safely engage in free and equal deliberation about real problems. Unlike some campaigns, it does not accuse people of intentionally doing wrong to their children. The nondirectiveness of the education and the buildup of trust and confidence as the program proceeds seem to be factors in its success. In addition, the process is not limited to women; rather, women go on to persuade husbands, religious figures, elders, their entire village, and later nearby villages of the rightness of a change. Unlike compensate-the-cutter programs (see Chapter 10 of this volume), participants pay to obtain a basic education. Under the Tostan program, the former cutters do not ask for money or new jobs but forgiveness for having participated in a mistaken practice. Further, participants say that the basic education program takes the place of the initiation ritual. Apparently, it was the instructive and celebratory aspects of former initiation rituals that people valued more than their occult aspects.

Conventions Regulating Access to Reproduction

Transmission of Footbinding

Correspondences between footbinding and FGC are numerous: Both customs are nearly universal where practiced, are persistent, and are practiced even by people who oppose them. Both control sexual access to females and promote female chastity and fidelity. Both are necessary for proper marriage, are believed to be sanctioned by tradition, and seem to have a past of contagious diffusion. Both are supported and transmitted by women.

The origins and transmission of footbinding are relatively clear. There is documentary evidence that footbinding arose in the imperial court during the Sung Dynasty (960–1279). The practice expanded along three dimensions over several centuries. First, it spread from the imperial palace to court circles to the larger upper classes and then to the middle and lower classes; eventually, the higher the social status, the smaller the foot. Second, it became more exaggerated over time; a practice supposedly originating among dancers eventually made dance a forgotten art. Third, it radiated from the imperial capitals to the rest of the empire. It was clearly the normal practice by the Ming Dynasty (1368–1644), if not before. In the nineteenth century, all Chinese women had their feet bound except for those too poor to avoid the dishonor of natural feet. Footbinding was universal and persistent for 1,000 years.

An explanation of the origins of a cultural practice such as footbinding requires some preliminary considerations. With a few understandable exceptions, men and women prefer expending their life effort on closely related children rather than on unrelated children. Women are almost always certain that a child is their own. Men, however, are more or less uncertain that a child is their own. Men promise to support the children, but women are more or less uncertain about whether a man will keep that promise. In the standard case, the female requires assurances of resource support for bearing and rearing children, and the male requires assurances that the children are his own. If children are desired, then each party prefers marriage to nonmarriage. The institution of marriage is intended to exchange and to enforce these assurances. Under conditions of resource equality, monogamy, and reliance on trust as to paternity and child support, humans compete in conveying the many signs of trustworthiness to possible marriage partners.

Suppose, however, there was an ancient empire with a rich capital and a poor countryside and thus with extreme resource inequality between families. Sociologists draw stratification diagrams to display the inequalities in a society. An egalitarian society would be represented by a horizontal line; a society with equal numbers of rich, middle, and poor would be represented by a rectangle; and an inegalitarian society ruled by an emperor would be represented by a pyramid—one rich man at the top; some nobles in the next rank; a number of officials in the next rank; merchants, farmers, and then a mass of poor in the bottom rank. When resource inequality reaches a certain extreme, a woman is more likely to raise her children successfully as the second wife of a high-ranking man than as the first wife of a low-ranking man (polygyny, or the practice of having plural female consorts). Thus, there are few men and many women at the top, and few women and many men at the bottom. The higher the male's rank, the greater the resource support he offers, the greater the number of consorts he attracts, the greater his costs of controlling the fidelity of his consorts, and thus the greater the competition among families to guarantee the fidelity of their daughters. These families will advertise the honor of their lines, the purity of their females, and their members' commitment to the values of chastity and fidelity, the so-called modesty code. An emperor will support several thousand women, and the interests of his consorts will be to seek insemination from men more available than he. It is then in the emperor's interest to inflict costly methods of fidelity control: enclosure, guarding by eunuchs, hobbling, the honor and modesty code, and so on.

The next lower stratum will compete to provide wives and concubines to the apex of the pyramid and thus will imitate and exaggerate fidelity-control practices so as to gain economic, social, and reproductive access to the palace. The vacuum of women in the first lower stratum will be filled by women moving up from the second lower stratum, who in turn will adopt the fidelity-control convention and so on, all the way down. As women flow up the stratification pyramid (hypergyny, or the practice of women marrying up), conjugal practices flow down.

Thus, a practice almost arbitrarily adopted in the imperial seraglio as a physical constraint on artificially confined females over time radiates from that center down the classes and across the empire and becomes exaggerated to the physical limit. What is now the sign of modesty, chastity, and fidelity had its origins in the lewdest of circumstances; what is now the sign of highest distinction had its origins in imperial female slavery. In Chapter 11 of this book, Michelle C. Johnson reports from the Mandinga of Guinea-Bissau an origin story in which a jealous older wife of Mohammad inflicted pierced ears and FGC on a younger wife, the signs of a slave, in order to displace her from the household. Mohammad accepted the alterations as beautiful, and then all the other women in the village copied them to become beautiful as well. A similar tale about Abraham, his Egyptian slave-concubine Hagar, and their son Ishmael was recorded in the twelfth century among the Egyptian Copts. The jealous Sarah expatriated Hagar and Ishmael to Egypt. Ishmael became beautiful in the eyes of women, but when approached about his possible marriage, Hagar said, "We are a circumcised people, both the men and the women of us, and we do not marry, except with the like of us." The local women were then "circumcised," Ishmael married them, and "circumcision spread in that country and in that which was neighboring to it" (Meinardus 1967:391).

Now that it is the sign of decency, necessary for a proper marriage, no one family can escape from it. Moreover, the average husband with one or two wives has no real problem of fidelity control, and because of the damage mutilation inflicts, both male and female would be better off without it, but again they cannot escape. Women are even more vigilant in perpetuating the mutilations because that is how they do best by their daughters under the constraints they face. After a while, people in this culture begin to draw the false inference that women must be excessively wanton to require such scrupulous guarding of their honor:

> Such is the nature of women; they are insatiable as far as their vulvas are concerned, and so long as their lust is satisfied they do not care whether it be with a buffoon, a negro, a valet, or even with a man that is despised and reprobated by society. . . . Women are demons, and were born as such. No one can trust them, as is known to all. (Shayk Nefwazi, quoted in Hicks 1996: 78)

Even when the empire is long dead, all the originating conditions are absent, society has changed, and modernization is apace, still the convention persists because it can only be escaped by a collective action. At first, it will rarely occur to anyone to want to escape because the natural alternative is forgotten and the mutilation is done by everyone and thus is normal.

Except for the assumption of an originating period of extreme resource inequality, the details of the origin story need not be correct for the convention account to succeed. However the custom originated, as soon as women believed that men would not marry an unmutilated woman, and men believed that an unmutilated woman would not be a faithful partner in marriage, the convention was locked in place. A woman would not choose nonmarriage and not to have her own children; a man would not choose an unfaithful partner and not to have his own children.

Marriageability is primary, but an independent and secondary source for the maintenance of a practice such as footbinding or FGC is peer pressure. Judith Harris (1998:183–217) makes a powerful case that much transmission of culture is from child to child peer rather than from parent to child. One must be careful in appealing to a conformity motivation because the parent-to-child version was too loosely applied in the past so as to explain all cultural patterns. Here, the peer pressure motivation is evident from reports of untreated girls begging to be made the same as their friends or untreated women undergoing the knife to escape the ridicule of co-wives. The motivations are distinct: the parent (or in a few places the young woman herself) wants FGC done in order to establish marriageability; the child (or young woman) may want FGC done for the sake of conformity. The conformity motivation is strongest at adolescence and may itself be rooted in reproductive drives (an organism with median qualities is most adapted to the local environment and hence is most attractive). A merely conformist cultural trait is much more fragile, as evidenced by the evanescence of fads, than a marriageability convention. Fortunately, a public pledge should work just as well to overcome peer pressure as it does the marriageability problem, but it is important to note that the audiences are different: for conformity it is one's peers, for marriageability it is the potential parties to marriage.

Transmission of FGC

As a conventional sign of marriageability, FGC becomes universal within an intramarrying group. Because of its connection to marriageability, FGC will remain persistent within a source group even if originating conditions of polygyny and hypergyny become ancient history. FGC is contiguously distributed and contagious. It spreads across groups as more resource-endowed males encounter less resource-endowed females in circumstances of inequality. It will continue within a less resource-endowed group even if that group does not share the obsessions with chastity and fidelity that inspired FGC in the source groups, and it will continue even as the less-resource-endowed group over time improves its fortunes in the world. In the source groups at or near the center of the distribution, not only FGC but also the entire honor and modesty code persists. In some groups closer to the edges of the distribution only FGC obtains, but not the honor and modesty code.

Many authors have listed the stated reasons for FGC, which differ from place to place but often include references to chastity and fidelity and almost without exception include references to marriageability. That FGC is necessary for a proper marriage is the common factor across heterogeneous groups. Far from its zone of origin, FGC is practiced by some populations whose cultures lack the originating obsessions with chastity or fidelity. In these populations, FGC is still the conventional sign of marriageability. Among the Rendille of Kenya, for example, women are free to engage in premarital sexual relationships but must undergo FGC upon contracting marriage. According to an informant husband, "If a girl is not circumcised she can stay with her family, and can have sex with her boyfriends. . . . ['Circumcision' shows] that she is mine, and can only be with me, and bear my children" (see Chapter 6 of this volume).

Marriageability is the vector of transmission, which does not require that marriageability be the most important association with FGC. The bite of an infected mosquito is the necessary vector of transmission of malaria, but the bite is not the dramatic part about malaria. Malaria is also associated with wetter areas, warmer weather, lower latitudes, and so on, and was once thought to be caused by swamp miasmas. In Senegal, I am told, it was believed that mangoes cause malaria, because the mango season and the malaria season perfectly coincide. However, it was the discovery of the one common factor across localities, the bite of the infected mosquito, that provided understanding of the mechanism, explanation of the distribution, better strategies of amelioration, and so on.

Marriageability is also the main engine of continuation. According to the author of the most thorough survey research on FGC, the vast majority of women state that they favor its continuation because it is custom or tradition (Carr 1997:27). This response perplexes outsiders, who suspect that the appeal to custom is merely obscurantist. However, the respondents are completely correct: FGC is a certain type of convention involving reciprocal expectations about an interdependent choice, and that is exactly why it continues. Whether to drive on the right-hand side of the road or on the left-hand side of the road is another convention of this type, and whether most people speak English or most people speak French in a locality is another. You can try driving on the wrong side of the road, or not speaking the local language, but you will pay the price. If you asked American respondents why they continue to drive on the right, and why they continue to speak English, they would think you a bit funny and then provide the obvious answer, "Be-cause that is the custom here." The custom explanation inspires some authors to explain footbinding or FGC as somehow motivated by ethnic differentia-tion. Such conventions, especially those connected to marriage, come to be seen as ethnic markers, but this is a consequence, not a cause, of the practice. Further, if ethnic differentiation were a cause and not a consequence, then FGC would be distributed noncontiguously, but it is not. Why adopt a sign of ethnic differentiation that makes you resemble nearby ethnic groups?

FGC is distributed more or less contiguously across a zone running from Senegal in the west to Yemen in the east and from Egypt in the north to Tan-zania in the south. With explainable exceptions, FGC is unique to that zone. The two axes intersect in the Sudan in the general vicinity of Nubia and the west coast of the Red Sea, where the most intense practice, infibulation, reigns today. The earliest documented evidence of FGC 2,200 years ago re-ports infibulation at the same site in the Sudan on the west coast of the Red Sea (and clitoridectomy in Egypt, cited in Agatharchides 1989)—the hypoth-esized source of origin. The FGC zone includes a vast heterogeneity of cul-tures, economies, and ecologies, and thus environmental explanations are not supported. There are, however, plausible mechanisms of diffusion, and there is sufficient opportunity for and evidence of requisite contacts within the zone. Thus, single-source diffusion is the most likely hypothesis.

I now believe that the transmission of FGC was similar in principle to but much different in detail from the transmission of footbinding. Ancient Nubia, Kush, or Meroe in the territory of today's Sudan and also ancient Egypt were highly stratified empires of the type that can prompt costly methods of fi-delity control at the imperial apex that diffuse contagiously from higher-resource families to lower-resource families throughout the territory of the empire. In China during the relevant period, there was usually a single cen-tralized empire. Male access to material and reproductive success was gov-erned by an imperial examination system based on a single written canon. Marriage traditions were generally exogamous. These factors contributed to the comparative homogeneity of Chinese society in the second millennium C.E. (compare Diamond 1996). Societies in the FGC zone are comparatively heterogeneous. Marriage traditions tend to be more endogamous. There was never a single centralized empire spanning the FGC zone. Thus, although FGC has been contagious from group to group within its zone of distribution, at the same time it is highly variable in form and meaning from group to group.

Diffusion as a general assumption is deservedly in disrepute because early social science incorrectly explained cultural development as a matter of invasion and conquest from some single advanced Caucasoid source. I aim to avoid these errors. It is necessary to distinguish three mechanisms of diffu-sion of cultural traits (neither exhaustive nor exclusive): (1) demic diffusion, in which for one reason or another a population thrives and expands in numbers; (2) technological diffusion, in which one population copies techniques witnessed in another population; (3) hypergynous diffusion, in which prestigious or powerful apex groups (not just in the settled capital of some empire but, alternatively, wandering traders and raiders) with greater control of crucial resources pull females from groups with lesser control of resources, and thus traits diffuse down stratification chains. Demic diffusion and technological diffusion are more familiar concepts, hypergynous diffusion less so. Footbinding spread within the Han population by hypergynous diffusion from an imperial apex, and the Han population also expanded, resulting in demic diffusion. Because of its persistent nature, FGC expanded demically as practicing populations grew and segmented. FGC expanded hypergynously in three different manners: by pastoralist clientelism, within a number of sudanic empires similar to the Chinese case, and by unequal interethnic contact. There is necessarily an element of technological diffusion as well.

One source of extreme resource inequality in Africa was the fact that sudanic pastoralists sometimes enjoyed a military superiority complementary to their pastoralist specialization, which permitted their establishment as a noble apex to a hierarchy of client groups engaged in service and agriculture, and a broad geographic mobility that scattered such influences. If such nobles practice FGC, it diffuses down the status hierarchy and becomes locked into the client populations. This is empire in miniature.

The early civilization of the Middle Nile (Nubia, Kush, Meroe) in the eastern sudanic belt thrived from the second millennium B.C.E. into the beginning of the first millennium C.E. (Adams 1977). The Meroite civilization lay at the center of the distribution of FGC (in today's Sudan where the most intense FGC, infibulation, is practiced) and engaged in what I call imperial female slavery. Further kingdoms and empires studded the sudanic belt in the first and second millennia C.E., from east to west: Meroe, Darfur, Kanem, Bornu, Songhai, ancient Mali, and ancient Ghana (Edwards 1998). The notion that these states were the consequence of Egyptian or Meroitic contacts is overly simplistic; they were indigenous, but surely they learned some social technologies from one another. Evidence suggests that there were no large migrations or conquests across these states, but there was long-distance trade in elite goods, especially female slaves, even some trades with Egypt (Last 1985), and also ample diffusion of agricultural technology such as domesticated plants and animals (Murdock 1959). I conjecture that an imported female who was genitally cut was likely accompanied by discourse about the fidelity-promoting purposes of the treatment, which inspired technological imitation in the importing seraglio. The sudanic states share a number of common features: for example, "the ruler is invariably surrounded by a large number of wives and concubines" (Murdock 1959:38). Some of these features are common to all empires, some are attributable to the material conditions of the sudanic belt, and some are likely due to diffusion within the sudanic belt.

Another source of extreme resource inequality in sudanic Africa and its margins was interethnic contact, especially as a group with more impressive material, military, or cultural resources expanded its influence through trade, raid, or travel. Because of its tight connection to successful reproduction and by way of its hypergynous vector, FGC can diffuse while leaving only traces of other cultural, linguistic, or genetic evidence. The mechanism is demonstrated by a documented recent instance of the diffusion of infibulation.

> The Baggara [who are distributed from Lake Chad to the White Nile], whose original home is in the west formerly practiced the "sunna" [milder] form of circumcision, but the "pharaonic" method [infibulation] gradually came into use through the influence of traders and other inhabitants of northern Sudan with whom they came in contact. The Messeria, being the most easterly of the tribes in question, were the first to adopt this practice, *and after it had become universal among them, they passed it on to their neighbours*, the Fellaita section of the Homr, whence it made its way to the Agaira section of the same tribe. At the time of my first visit to Muglad, in 1917, I found that the Agaira were still practicing the "sunna" method, and made every effort to convince the Nzir Nimr Ali Gulla of the atrociousness of the pharaonic custom and the damage and suffering which it inflicts on the women. I earnestly advised him to use all his influence to prevent it from spreading among his section. He appeared to be convinced by my arguments and promised to do his best; I regret to say however, that during my next visit in 1918, I found that the "pharaonic" custom had made its appearance there and was given a hearty welcome. The reasons given for the adoption of this form of "circumcision" are (1) that it is supposed to be a protection against untimely pregnancy, and (2) that it is regarded as rendering the victim more attractive to men. (N. Yuzbashi, quoted in Hicks 1996:238, emphasis added)

In this example, infibulation is adopted in order to make oneself attractive to prestigious resource-bearing outsiders, diffuses through the enriched contact group until universal there, and then diffuses through overlapping groups. Notice that infibulation had already taken Messeria and Fellaita, and thus because of intramarriage connections was inevitable in Agaira. There is also an element of technological diffusion here.

Presently in Darfur, the Sudan, it is the more highly educated women who favor the continuation of FGC:

> Traditionally, many ethnic groups in Darfur, which is in western Sudan, did not practice genital cutting. Overall prevalence in the region (65 percent) is still the lowest in the country. The association of these practices with higher socioeconomic groups, however, may be contributing to the positive reception of cutting among educated women in Darfur. In her fieldwork in Sudan, Gruenbaum observes that the Arab-Sudanese commonly consider western Sudan's ethnic groups "socially inferior," with some regarding infibulation as

a sign of "ethnic superiority." Toubia notes that after Sudan's independence in 1956, the expansion of various government services into the western region by northern elites led to the adoption of genital cutting among some ethnic groups that had not previously performed the procedure. (Carr 1997:61)

FGC is contagious from higher-resource to lower-resource populations and once passed on is persistent down generations.

The reasons for the *origin* of the practice in fidelity control are distinct from the reasons for the *maintenance* of the practice as a conventional sign of marriageability. A practice such as FGC is the best alternative only for a male who is attempting to control sexually a large number of females. It is not best for the controlled female, but under the circumstances, it is better for her than the alternative of nonmarriage. Imperial polygyny (Betzig 1986) is different from everyday agricultural polygyny (Boserup 1970). For the average husband with one or two wives, the practice is damaging to the interests of the husband and the wife (although they may not realize this if they are not aware of the unmutilated alternative), but they are trapped by the convention. The stone was thrown in the pond under some originating conditions. The ripples spread away from the source of impact over millennia not as mass migrations but as a practice hypergynously and technologically traversing heterogeneous populations. In each of the new populations, the practice combines with other local practices and meanings that do not necessarily resemble the practices and meanings prevalent under originating or source conditions.

In present-day Egypt and the Sudan, the hypothesized source of origin of FGC, not only is it a matter of marriageability, but it is also associated with the virtue of the woman and the honor of her family within a comprehensive and exaggerated modesty code, as was footbinding in traditional China. However, by its contagious and adhesive nature and merely as the conventional sign of marriageability, FGC has entered cultures elsewhere that lack the obsessive honor and modesty code. In some places there is a concern with *pragmatic chastity*, a desire by the parents to avoid the problem of an untimely pregnancy by their adolescent daughter, but the modesty code is lacking. Here, typically, if present, FGC is said to reduce the chances of an untimely pregnancy, and girls are also married shortly after menarche due to the same concern. Where there is a high incidence of polygyny and extended postpartum abstinence, at any one time the large majority of men lack a sexually available wife, women in the large polygynous households lack sexual attention and lifetime marital security, and here an attitude of *relaxed fidelity* may be found.[6] People are expected to remain nominally faithful and to keep up appearances, but extramarital relations are tolerated within understood boundaries, and premarital relations are tolerated if they are discreet and incomplete and do not result in pregnancy (see Caldwell, Caldwell, and Orubuloye 1992). Here, typically, if present, FGC is said to ease the temptations of women constrained by polygynous marriage or by postpartum abstinence (see Dorkenoo 1994:35).

FGC might have been adopted in some of these places as a matter of technological diffusion. For an analogy, consider that the original idea of a written language was rare or perhaps unique, but peoples are known to have invented completely innovative scripts merely upon hearing of the idea of a written language. Between, but not within, intramarrying groups, there is high variation in the form and meaning of FGC: a group might perform it at infancy, before puberty, at puberty, with or without initiation rites, upon contracting marriage, in the seventh month of the first pregnancy, after the birth of the first child, and so on, but it is always linked to marriageability. In some places the association with marriageability may be lost altogether, and here the applicability of the convention account is limited: if the practice is maintained as a matter of peer conformity, a public declaration among peers may help.

Strategies of Melioration

Modernization

Someone might object that what matters is how to end FGC, not whether one theory of FGC is better supported than another one. However, different theories of FGC can and do entail different strategies of melioration. Further, if a theory recommends a strategy of melioration and that strategy fails in practice, that counts as evidence against the proposed theory. Unfortunately, reports of cessation are rare and often dubious. Worse, there is evidence that FGC has instead been on the increase in the modern era, in its demographic expanse and sometimes in its physical intensity (for example, see Chapter 9 of this volume). There is a family of modernization theories that predicts, generally, that with increased urbanization, education, mass communication, and economic development, traditional practices eventually would be abandoned. In Chapter 6 of this book, Bettina Shell-Duncan, Walter Obungu Obiero, and Leunita Auko Muruli show that development does not in and of itself reduce the demand for FGC among the Rendille. A more specific version of modernization theory might suggest that these factors weaken the old family structure, draw women from their natal family to the labor market, and both expose them to new influences and increase their independence such that their bargaining power in general and in the marriage contract is improved.

Such a theory assumes, however, both that women are willing and are individually able to abandon FGC. Generally, women more actively perpetuate FGC than do men (as is illustrated by several chapters in this volume), and so it does not automatically follow that increased economic independence would reduce FGC. Detailed cross-country survey research does not show a relationship between economic independence and attitude toward continuation of FGC (Carr 1997:25).[7] Further, the convention hypothesis maintains that in the absence of a collective shift, FGC would persist indefinitely even if every individual wanted to abandon the practice. It is important for all concerned with FGC to understand that, because it ends with a relatively sudden convention shift, reform activity might result in major attitude change within a population in the complete absence of behavioral change. For example, in Eritrea, 95 percent of women are "circumcised," and 90 percent of mothers report that their eldest daughter is cut. Yet, the continuation of FGC is opposed by half of those between ages 15 and 24, most urban dwellers, and most of those with any education (Carr 1997:52, 71–72): "The findings suggest that these traditions can prevail even among the offspring of mothers who say that they disapprove of cutting" (Carr 1997:54).

In Chapter 4 of this volume, I. O. Orubuloye, Pat Caldwell and John Caldwell could be read to support a modernization theory of cessation because they observe 13 percent absence of FGC in a Yoruba urban (and educated) location as compared to 3 percent absence of FGC in a Yoruba rural location, but I believe that their findings better support a convention theory of cessation. As to why the Yoruba "circumcise" females, the overwhelming response falls in the category "tradition, culture, social conformity," which means that people "should not expect their daughters to bear the brunt of breaking the social consensus. . . . Their fears center on whether an uncircumcised girl would be marriageable. . . . Most parents of daughters . . . fear to be the first innovators." Those who have abandoned FGC did not act spontaneously but were influenced directly by the organized campaign of cessation or indirectly by local discussion prompted by the campaign. The mothers of uncircumcised girls do not expect their daughters to have worsened marriage chances; they believe that, in town anyway, society is changing and will change much more. Finally, the authors say, "many mothers who continue to 'circumcise' their daughters say that they would desist if only that message were much stronger, thus guaranteeing that uncircumcised girls were in the majority. They feel that it is unfair of the government to promote change without doing it very loudly and clearly." In sum, "the major reason that the practice persists is the fear that their daughters will be penalized in the marriage market. . . . At the present rate of acceptance of the message not to 'circumcise,' full change would take several generations. It is probable, however, that change will begin to snowball." The consistency of these observations with convention theory is self-evident.

Orubuloye, Caldwell, and Caldwell identify three factors associated in their data with absence of FGC. One is an uncut mother, which they say may reflect inclusion of ethnic subgroups that do not perform FGC. The second is education, not education in general but precisely that the more-educated respondents are more likely to have heard the message of the cessation campaign than are the less-educated respondents. The third and strongest is an urban-rural differential, independent of education. The authors offer the explanation that townspeople can go their own way with less interference than in rural areas. I offer an alternative explanation, that urbanization enlarges marriage opportunities so much that in an urban area, the number of uncut families can become large enough that their children can marry one another. To be the one family that does not cut in a village of 100 families means that marriage for the daughter is unlikely, but to be among the 100 families that do not cut in a city of 10,000 families means that suitable marriage for the daughter is more likely. I think that the abandonment of footbinding began in the cities of China for the same two reasons: because the cities had larger marriage pools and because that is where the abolition campaigns were logistically easiest to carry out and most likely to be heard. However, urbanization is not a necessary condition of change. In Senegal, due to the accident that the pledge technique originated in a rural location, it looks like change might begin in the country and move to the city.

Compensation for the Cutters

Functionalist explanation used to dominate the social sciences, and although thoroughly discredited, its influence lingers. Structural functionalism analogized society to a biological organism, such that every cultural practice functioned to promote the survival of that organism. Functionalism assumes that all social phenomena have beneficial consequences that explain them (Elster 1995). This is unobjectionable with respect to so-called *manifest* functions, for example, that a family practices FGC with the intention to establish the marriageability of the daughter, but falls into difficulty with respect to *latent* functions, for example, that FGC is maintained *because* the midwife-cutters are paid one way or another for performing the operation.[8] The strategy of functionalist substitution recommends listing the functions that a practice fulfills and then substituting alternatives that fulfill the functions of the practice to be displaced. Thus, such a strategy might recommend that midwife-cutters be paid not to perform the practice:

> Consideration must also be given to compensation for the midwives and women who perform the operation because they often depend on the income for this service for their livelihood. Any approach to eradicate female "circumcision" that ignores the dependency of people on the practice will not be successful. (Slack 1988:485)

Programs to compensate the cutters (primarily by retraining them) have been funded in a variety of locations, and apparently they have failed to reduce the prevalence of FGC: "Some evidence suggests that this approach in relation to a service that is highly in demand may benefit the supplier but may not improve the overall situation since the same suppliers may continue despite alternative training or, even if they stop, other suppliers will step in to fill the demand" (Toubia 1998:47).

One reason for the popularity of this suspect strategy is a heuristic found among all peoples that seeks to explain negative outcomes with the question, who benefits? If I break a leg, it's because of the evil eye of my envious neighbor. If we lose the war, it must be because the financiers profit from war loans. If there is a plague, it must have been concocted by the pharmaceutical companies. Painful and dangerous FGC persists because cutters benefit from the practice, and so on. However, the fact that someone benefits from a negative outcome is not *itself* evidence that she caused the outcome. A causal connection must be traced from the benefit to the outcome. The umbrella seller in the plaza did not cause the rain. The doctor's office did not cause my influenza. True, female genital cutters immediately cause female genital cutting, but they do not cause parents to want FGC for their children and thus do not cause the continuation of the practice. Oddly enough, it is the daughters who are both the primary and intended beneficiaries of FGC because inside the convention trap FGC advances their marriageability, and this benefit causes the continuation of the practice. To illustrate the fallacy of this kind of approach, consider that functionalism would claim that people have babies *because* obstetricians are paid to deliver them, so that if you wanted to reduce the birth rate you should pay obstetricians not to deliver babies. People have babies for many obvious reasons, but to keep doctors in business is plainly not one of them. If people have fewer babies, there will be fewer obstetricians, but making fewer obstetricians will not make for fewer babies.

Even assuming that cutters comply, they will not often constitute the critical mass sufficient to tip the practice into abandonment. The local status of cutters varies. In many places they belong to less prestigious castes or outgroups, and in such places their conversion would not be persuasive to the rest of the population. In some places the cutter has no special status, negative or positive. In some places, the cutter might be the extremely prestigious leader of a secret society. In these latter circumstances, of course, the genuine conversion of such cutters through nondirective education would be crucial. But a program to convert the cutters might work only accidentally, that is, only insofar as it provided information that an alternative exists, offered credible information about negative health consequences, and mobilized a critical mass sufficient to provoke an abandonment. Draining the swamps works to reduce malaria, not because swamps cause malaria, but rather because it reduces bites by infected mosquitoes.

Generally, paying people to change their attitudes does not work. This is shown by the forced-compliance experiments of the cognitive dissonance theorists. Cognitive dissonance theorists had experimental subjects perform a very boring task and then had the subjects convince another person supposedly waiting outside to do the same task that its performance was quite fun and interesting. Subjects reduced the consequent cognitive dissonance between believing the task to be boring but telling someone it was not boring by actually changing their attitudes to believe that the task was fun and interesting. However, another set of subjects, who were in addition well paid to convince the waiting person that the boring task was not boring, did *not* come to believe that the task was fun and interesting. These latter subjects did not have to change their attitude about the task because they were able to tell themselves that they were being paid to lie. The experimenters showed that the more money is paid, the less the subjects' attitudes changed (Manstead and Hewstone 1995:106). One can purchase many things in this world, but it is common sense that genuine attitude change is not one of them.

Alternative Initiation Rites

The convention theory admits and attempts to explain between-group heterogeneity in form and meaning of FGC. This heterogeneity has implications for program design. For example, outlying cases probably exist for which a strategy of public declaration would be of no use. Another strategy of cessation is to provide alternative initiation rituals that do not include FGC.

The most queried point in my original article on footbinding and infibulation was my assertion that these practices are generally not associated with initiation rites. The audience tends to assume that footbinding was an initiation ritual, maybe because they are personally acquainted with painful initiations and assimilate the unfamiliar practice to this familiar experience. But it was not. The anthropologist Hill Gates has organized interviews with thousands of women who encountered footbinding in their youth:

> Footbinding, which girls and their mothers had endured for centuries, was extraordinarily unelaborated, virtually empty of "culture" in its ideational/ritual sense.
>
> "Did your mother do anything special on the day that she bound your feet?" we asked. "No."
>
> "Did she choose a good day, or burn incense and pray to ask for success, or make special food, or put medicine on your feet?" "No."
>
> "Where did she bind your feet, and who was there?" "In the house, no one was around. It wasn't anything special."
>
> "Were there any customs?" "No." . . .
>
> By contrast with all this negativity, when we asked about marriage customs, or birth customs, or how people worshipped "in the old society," we got the usual range of . . . answers. . . . Everyone knew *something*. (Gates 1998)

In Chapter 11, Johnson writes that when she went to Guinea-Bissau she planned on studying FGC as an initiation rite. But as she began her research among the Mandinga there she discovered that "circumcision" sometimes took place well before puberty and had no "direct relationship" to marriage (although it had at one time), but was now most associated with Muslim religious identity.

FGC, especially near its hypothesized source of origin, is often not an initiation ritual. According to Rose Hayes, "infibulation is not a rite of passage among the Somali, nor do my data indicate that it is in Sudan, and according to Kennedy it is not so in Egyptian Nubia" (Hayes 1975:621). Further, the age at which FGC is done varies between groups. In more than a few it is done in infancy, and elsewhere it can be done as late as after the first child. FGC clearly is not an initiation ritual at those ages. I would guess that the average age of treatment across cultures is about eight, which is several years short of puberty, and genital cutting at this age may or may not imply initiation purposes. However, in some places, especially near the fringes of its distribution, FGC is sometimes associated with initiation rites. In coastal West Africa, from Senegal to Nigeria, FGC is associated in a number of groups with elaborate initiation ceremonies at puberty, which in a subset of those groups also involves entrance into a women's secret society (Murdock 1959:263, 269). In the East African highlands, a number of groups are organized into age-grades entered by initiation, usually at adolescence and associated in a subset of those groups with "circumcision" (Murdock 1959:337, 345). Historically, if a group with a tradition of an initiation ritual later adopts FGC, then FGC might be integrated into its initiation ritual.

Initiation, especially among those secret societies that cut across local groups, might carry such a freight of other purposes and meanings that the supposed connection between "circumcision" and marriageability is secondary or even absent (see also the description of forcible initiations including FGC by secret societies in Sierra Leone in Dorkenoo 1994:109–110). Among the secret societies, for example, "Male youths belonging to societies not practising ['circumcision'] have been known to undergo the rite with the novices of a strange and distant society, and women, sometimes advanced in years, have come from far distances to submit to the operation" (Butt-Thompson 1929:123).

Incidentally, there is often an association between male circumcision and the man's marriageability. Associations are highly variable between groups. In northern Nigeria, for example,

[male] circumcision is generally, but not always, closely associated with initiation rites by which boys are formally admitted to membership of the tribe. . . . That circumcision is not a necessary feature of initiation is apparent from

the fact that whereas most tribes [here] hold initiation rites, only some circumcise, while among other tribes which practise circumcision the initiation
rites are kept totally distinct from those of circumcision. (Meek 1925:84)

In some places the states of *adulthood* and *marriageability* might be distinct,
such that the elements of the initiation ritual that establish adulthood are not
sufficient to establish marriageability, which requires the separate step of
male or female circumcision. In other places the states of adulthood and marriageability might be indistinct, so that retaining initiation ritual but abandoning FGC might be a feasible strategy. However, it would be a mistake to over-
generalize such a strategy to groups that distinguish between adulthood and
marriageability or to groups that do not practice initiation rites.

A properly placed alternative initiation rite offers the advantages of perhaps being sufficient to halt a practice sustained only by peer conformity; being immune to criticism that reformers are betraying tradition; and being likely
to launch a process of education, discussion, and convention shift. I have reservations about the applicability of this strategy, however. In Chapter 11, Johnson reports that although the Mandinga in Guinea-Bissau among whom she
worked claimed that initiation and FGC are inseparable, half of respondents
were cut without any initiation ceremony. In Chapter 12, Ylva Hernlund reports that it is becoming increasingly common for girls in the Gambia to be cut
with less ritual and at younger ages and argues that this is part of a general
trend. The same tendencies are reported for groups in Mali (Assilan Diallo,
cited in Dorkenoo 1994:40) and Kenya (Ng'ang'a 1995:35). Efua Dorkenoo
(1994: 39–40) suggests that the trend to less ritual and younger ages undermines the hypothesis that FGC is explained as an initiation rite. If initiation is
fading, but FGC stubbornly remains, perhaps that is evidence that they are separate entities and that initiation is much more weakly persistent than is FGC.
The participants in the "Diabougou Declaration" adamantly and unanimously
opposed alternative initiation rituals. One said, "We need to do away with
these rites altogether. We need a means of controlling what goes on and if you
have the drumming and singing, it will be associated with cutting. People will
use this pretext to cut in secret. This must end." Another said, "Let's be honest,
we were cutting our girls at 2 weeks to 3 months over the past years so this was
not even part of the ritual any longer. This is a romantic notion you westerners
have and want to impose on us now!" (Melching 1999).

In summary, because the popular understanding subsumes all FGC to initiation although FGC is often not initiation, because when FGC is found with
initiation the two might yet be distinct practices, because the results of the alternative initiation strategy are as yet unclear, and because positive results
might be due to convention shift rather than to rite substitution, I urge caution
about deploying the strategy too broadly.

Medicalization

Most often, FGC is opposed because of its negative health consequences. Having FGC performed by nurses and doctors would reduce the negative health consequences, but medicalization is opposed on the argument that it would help perpetuate FGC. In Chapter 6, Shell-Duncan, Obiero, and Muruli urge that opposition to medicalization be reconsidered, arguing that it is an empirical question whether medicalization would be an additional contribution to the perpetuation of FGC. I acknowledge that this question is not easy in its normative aspects and that it is worthy of discussion. Here, I want to comment only on its positive aspects.

Shell-Duncan, Obiero, and Muruli suggest that what I call modernization has not had much effect on FGC, and I agree. They say that change in other values, such as reducing high fertility, has been genuine but slow. Thus, they propose that medicalization be reconsidered as an intermediate solution to improve the health of affected women. If the convention hypothesis is correct, some considerations follow. If, as I have argued, neither profit for the cutters nor the availability of FGC services sustains the practice but rather the marriageability problem, then medicalization in itself should not augment the persistence of FGC.[9] However, for FGC to end, attitudes have to change, but everywhere in the world attitude change depends on information from authoritative figures, and the most authoritative sources on the negative health consequences of FGC are the attitudes and practices of the medical profession. Thus, medicalization might slow or stop attitude change. Recall the Yoruba mothers interviewed by Orubuloye, Caldwell, and Caldwell: they wanted the government's message to be loudly and clearly in favor of change, so that the whole population would be made ready for a definitive end. Perhaps there is a program design that satisfies these diverse concerns.

Propaganda and Prohibition

Bullying from outsiders breeds defiance or sham abandonment. Social psychologists have developed the concept of *reactance*: a motivational state directed toward the restoration of freedom. People are accustomed to a range of free actions, and when freedom to act is threatened or actually denied, reactance motivates attempts to protect or to regain the freedom of action. If a man's mother-in-law tells him that it is too hazardous to drive in the rain, he will more than ever want to drive in the rain. If a father tells a son to take a warm coat, he won't. The motivation has been demonstrated in controlled human subject experiments. It has been shown that the greater the pressure to comply, the more that one wants to defy, and that the more important the freedom, the greater the resistance. A daughter's marriageability is one of the most important issues in life, and the pressure to abandon FGC is at times severe. Threats to outlaw FGC have often been met with increases in FGC. In Chapter 7, Lynn Thomas details such an instance of reactance.

There is a moral dimension as well. If some outsider tells you that you are a bad person because of a family tradition you follow, and you follow this tradition just because you are a good person, then will you abandon the practice and thereby confirm the outsider's ignorant judgment that you are a bad person? I think not. Molly Melching of Tostan writes,

> You know, some words that never come up in development jargon and academic papers are love and respect. But the truth is that one of the main reasons our program works is because of the mutual love and respect between villagers and Tostan. When people have another agenda—let's end FGC—let's get people doing this or that—it often boomerangs because it implies that all you care about is changing people, which means you don't accept them the way they are. Whereas when one loves and respects and trusts others to make the right decision it happens quite naturally.[10]

Nondirective education works. Harsh propaganda backfires. The example of footbinding suggests, however, that it is appropriate in some circumstances for outsiders to state their opposition to FGC, but only if such opposition is factual, understanding, and respectful.

Suppose that a law professor is charged with the task of eliminating automobile usage in Los Angeles and proposes this strategy: legal prohibition enforced by serious penalty. Because the professor has provided no alternative method of transportation, no one can stop driving. Because no one is able to stop driving, police and prosecutors will not waste their time picking out some poor Joe Blow for punishment. But there will be black marks on a white page to satisfy the irate Oregonians and Bangladeshi who demand that the Angelenos stop their destructive driving habits. Criminal law works because thieves and murderers are a minority of the population that the state can afford to pursue with the cooperation of the majority of the population. It is not possible to criminalize the entirety of the population or the entirety of a discrete and insular minority of the population without the methods of mass terror. Reactance complicates the problem. The example of footbinding shows that legal prohibition is most appropriate at the climax of the national process of abandonment, not at its beginning. Legal prohibition that is not the expression of local popular will on the subject is ineffective, if not undemocratic. Europe and the United States have every right to prohibit FGC among their inhabitants, however, because FGC is a mistaken practice and also because the children of the immigrants aspire to participate in their uncut host societies (see Dorkenoo 1994:123–124 for tragic examples and thereafter for strategies beyond mere legislation).

Conclusion

The convention theory, as reflected by events in the Senegalese villages, suggests a tripartite strategy of abandonment: basic education, public discussion, and public declaration. Educational information must be from a credible source and must be nondirective. During public discussion, a motivated core carries information to ever broader audiences. Information and discussion are standard techniques. What this approach adds and explains is public declaration within the local pool of marriage eligibles, and results are promising.

Campaigns of broad publicity should continue because it is important that international, national, and local attitude change should continue to amass. Although it is not possible to explain why here, the critical mass definitely need not be as large as a majority. Nevertheless, some sufficient proportion of attitude change is required prior to convention shift, and it begins with broad publicity. Abandonment once begun is potentially contagious, which has implications for reform planning. It is contagious because if one marriage pool successfully abandons FGC, that directly raises the issue to overlapping marriage pools, and additionally abandonment demonstrates to similar populations that the beneficial shift can be made safely. Thus, it may be worthwhile to sharply concentrate efforts on attitude change and then convention shift among some exemplary groups and, after success, among their kin and neighbors and then among their coethnics. Concentration can operate at neighborhood, local, provincial, country, and regional levels.

Generally, women more actively perpetuate FGC than do men. It is women's business. It may be possible to concentrate initially on women because if they are won over, they will persuade husbands, grandparents, and religious and political figures. It is also effective to win over local political and religious leaders with genuine authority. Obviously, it is desirable to expand as rapidly as possible the declarations in Senegal. If the Senegalese process continues to deliver dramatic results, then proven techniques should be extended to coethnics in neighboring countries. Further, it may be easier initially to inspire attitude change and convention shift in countries or regions where there are respected ethnic groups that have never practiced FGC, as in Senegal. Another criterion for concentration is if many practice FGC but many also are against the practice, as in Eritrea (unfortunately, trapped in tragic warfare at the moment). Additionally, it may be easier initially to trigger change in groups where FGC is *shallow*, that is, in groups toward the edges of the distribution without the exaggerated emphasis on chastity and fidelity, than in groups where FGC is *deep*, that is, in groups at the center of the distribution that are strongly connected to the modesty code.

It would be instructive to test culturally adapted pledge associations in an urban area where there is already a wide discrepancy between prevalence and attitudes. The larger and more educated the population, the easier it should be for those with changed attitudes to marry one another's children, provided there is a way they can find one another (it might be harder initially to reach the less educated in an urban area, however, if they are less socially cohesive there than they were in their rural homes). Further, an urban suitor may not consider that many more partners than a rural suitor, but in the urban area there are many overlapping marriage markets as compared to only a few in a rural area. Thus within a larger collection of overlapping marriage markets, if a critical mass of markets complete convention shifts, their overlap with other marriage markets can have a domino effect throughout the larger collection. No ethnic or status group anywhere should be ignored if they are ready for convention shift—successes are always more helpful for demonstration purposes than failures. But all else being equal, in an urban setting it may be most effective to concentrate on the most prestigious status groups because their shift will inspire a shift among those who aspire to join those categories. These are hypotheses, to be revised or rejected on the basis of program experiences.

The people who practice FGC are honorable, upright, moral people who love their children and want the best for them. That is why they practice FGC, and that is why they will decide to stop practicing it once a safe way of stopping is found. Since FGC will end sooner or later, it is better that we put our efforts into ending it sooner rather than later. Let's study good ways of stopping it and let the people who still practice FGC know what we and their neighbors in Africa have found out about ending it.

Notes

Discussions with many people over the last several years have improved my understanding of FGC. Generous comments by editor Ylva Hernlund helped me deepen my hypotheses in this paper, and Bettina Shell-Duncan also helped me improve my tone. I thank Molly Melching of Tostan for many enlightening discussions on practical and theoretical topics. I acclaim the people of Malicounda Bambara and Medina Cherif, Senegal, for showing the way. I am grateful to St. John's College, University of Oxford, for general support.

1. In this paper "the Sudan" with an initial capital refers to the country in northeast Africa, and "sudanic" refers to the geographical zone that runs across Africa from the Sudan in the east to Senegal in the west.

2. The dentistry analogy is adapted from Gates (1998), who came to this understanding during her many interviews with women who had undergone footbinding.

3. Bamana is now the preferred term in the literature, but the term of use in the Senegambia area is Bambara. The Malicounda women state that the Bambara tradition includes "sealing" (see Chapters 1 and 12 of this volume).

4. There are individual but collectively marginal abandonments across Africa, sometimes among the most educated and also as a consequence of various programs.

5. The writing to this point, except for the theoretical interjections, borrows from a Tostan fact sheet, "The Impact of the Malicounda Commitment to Abolish Female Circumcision," and from the texts of the Diabougou Declaration and the Medina Cherif Declaration. All documents are in the author's possession. Additionally, I conducted interviews in nine of the villages over two weeks in December 1998. See Melching 1999 for a more detailed account, and also see http://townonline.koz.com/visit/Tostan for latest news.

6. The Nupe in Nigeria do not practice FGC, but nearby ethnic groups do. The average number of wives is 2.1 per man, but a few rich men maintain many consorts, from five to 200. Here, "the starved sexuality of the women in large polygamous households strives to find an outlet" (Nadel 1942:152).

7. The relationship is mildly positive in two countries and mildly negative in two other countries, significances not reported.

8. Hayes (1975:628) appears to be the source of the notion that FGC latently functions to pay the cutters.

9. I am indebted to Bettina Shell-Duncan for suggesting an implication of my own views that should have been obvious to me.

10. Personal communication, December 16, 1998.

14

Rites and Wrongs: An Insider/Outsider Reflects on Power and Excision

Fuambai Ahmadu

The issue of female initiation and "circumcision" is of significant intellectual and personal interest to me. Like previous anthropologists, I am fascinated by the social, ideological, and religious/symbolic dimensions of these rituals, particularly from indigenous perspectives. I also share with feminist scholars and activists campaigning against the practice a concern for women's physical, psychological, and sexual well-being, as well as for the implications of these traditional rituals for women's status and power in society. Coming from an ethnic group in which female (and male) initiation and "circumcision" are institutionalized and a central feature of culture and society and having myself undergone this traditional process of becoming a "woman," I find it increasingly challenging to reconcile my own experiences with prevailing global discourses on female "circumcision."

Most studies on female genital cutting (FGC) in Africa have been conducted by "outsiders," individuals who are not from the societies they analyze and who have no personal experience of any form of the operation. The limited number of African women who have written about FGC either come from ethnic groups where female genital operations are not practiced (i.e., Efua Dorkenoo, Olayinka Koso-Thomas) or have never undergone the procedures themselves (Nahid Toubia). There is an unfortunate and perturbing silence among African women intellectuals who have experienced initiation and "circumcision." This reticence is understandable, given the venomous tone of the "debate" and unswerving demand that a definitive stance be taken—evidently, if one is educated—*against* the practice. However, "insider" voices from initiated/"circumcised" African women scholars can go a long way toward providing fresh approaches to our understanding of these practices and their continued significance to most African women.

283

In this chapter I attempt to reconcile "insider" representations with "outsider" perspectives. I seek to contextualize my own experience within the broader framework of initiation in Sierra Leone's Kono society and then contrast dominant Kono paradigms with conflicting international debates that focus on female "circumcision" as a peculiar manifestation of women's global subordination.

My main quarrel with most studies on female initiation and the significance of genital cutting relates to the continued insistence that the latter is necessarily "harmful" or that there is an urgent need to stop female genital mutilation in communities where it is done. Both of these assertions are based on the alleged physical, psychological, and sexual effects of female genital cutting. I offer, however, that the aversion of some writers to the practice of female "circumcision" has more to do with deeply imbedded Western cultural assumptions regarding women's bodies and their sexuality than with disputable health effects of genital operations on African women. For example, one universalized assumption is that human bodies are "complete" and that sex is "given" at birth.[1] A second assumption is that the clitoris represents an integral aspect of femininity and has a central erotic function in women's sexuality. And, finally, through theoretical extension, patriarchy is assumed to be the culprit—that is, women are seen as blindly and wholeheartedly accepting "mutilation" because they are victims of male political, economic, and social domination. According to this line of analysis, excision is necessary to patriarchy because of its presumed negative impact on women's sexuality. Removal of the clitoris is alleged to make women sexually passive, thus enabling them to remain chaste prior to marriage and faithful to their husbands in polygynous households. This supposedly ensures a husband sole sexual access to a woman as well as certainty of his paternity over any children she produces. As victims, then, women actively engage in "dangerous" practices such as "female genital mutilation" (FGM) to increase their marriageability (see, for example, Chapter 13 of this volume), which would ultimately enable them to fulfill their honored, if socially inferior, destiny of motherhood.

When attempting to reconcile Kono practice with dominant anti-FGM discourses, a number of problems arise, starting with the alleged physical harm resulting from the practice. Part of the problem, as Bettina Shell-Duncan, Walter Obungu Obiero, and Leunita Auko Muruli lucidly argue in Chapter 6 of this volume, is the unjustified conflation of varied practices of female genital cutting and the resulting overemphasis on infibulation, a relatively rare practice that is associated with a specific region and interpretation of Muslim purdah ideology.[2] Kono women practice excision, the removal of the clitoris and labia minorae.[3] As several contributions to this volume suggest (see Chapters 1, 5, and 6), the purported long-term physical side effects of this procedure may have been exaggerated. It can be argued, as well, that although there are short-term risks, these can be virtually eliminated through improved medical technology (see Chapter 6).

Furthermore, among the Kono there is no cultural obsession with feminine chastity, virginity, or women's sexual fidelity, perhaps because the role of the biological father is considered marginal and peripheral to the central "matricentric unit."[4] Finally, Kono culture promulgates a dual-sex ideology, which is manifested in political and social organization, sexual division of labor, and, notably, the presence of powerful female and male secret societies.[5] The existence and power of Bundu, the women's secret sodality, suggest positive links between excision, women's religious ideology, their power in domestic relations, and their high profile in the "public" arena.

The Kono example makes evident underlying biases of such culturally loaded notions as the "natural" vagina or "natural female body." The word "natural" is uncritically tossed around in the FGM literature to describe an uncircumcised woman, when actually it needs definition and clarification. Kono concepts of "nature" and "culture" differ significantly from Western ones, and it is these local understandings that compel female (and male) genital cutting. In essence, what this chapter amounts to is a critique of a profound tendency in Western writing on female "circumcision" in Africa to deliver male-centered explanations and assumptions. Scholars must be wary of imposing Western religious, philosophical, and intellectual assumptions that tend to place enormous emphasis on masculinity and its symbols in the creation of culture itself. In traditional African societies, as is the case with the Kono, womb symbolism and imagery of feminine reproductive contributions form the basis of meanings of the universe, human bodies, and society and its institutions—social organization, the economy, and even political organization can be viewed as extensions of the "matricentric core," or base of society. Female excision, I propose, is a negation of the masculine in feminine creative potential, and in the remainder of this chapter I will show how the Kono case study demonstrates this hypothesis.

This chapter is a culmination of several years of informal inquiry as well as formal research into the meaning of female "circumcision" and initiation, particularly among my parental ethnic group, the Kono, in northeastern Sierra Leone. This study constitutes an analysis of five stages: (1) my subjective experience of initiation from December 1991 to January 1992, which lasted just over one month; (2) indigenous interpretations from other participants, mainly ritual leaders and their assistants, recorded at the time; (3) later academic study, when I returned to Kono for an additional two months in December 1994 and December 1996; (4) a total of nine months conducting formal and informal interviews among Kono immigrants in and around the Washington, D.C., area; and finally, (5) approximately three months spent between January and July of 1998 traveling back and forth between Conakry and Freetown talking to Kono refugees and women activists, mainly about their more immediate survival concerns but also about "circumcision," initiation, and the future of women's secret societies. These discussions included informal interviews as well as formal semistructured interviews with three ritual officials: two traditional circumcisers, or *Soko* priestesses, and one *digba*, or ranking assistant to the *Soko*.

The cumulative data are drawn from interviews with a broad range of Kono men and women: young, old, university-educated professionals in Freetown and in the United States, as well as illiterate villagers and traditional rulers in Kono. If I have sacrificed quantification, it has been for the benefit of collecting detailed qualitative data that would enable my search for meaning and significance, both of which I felt could be best obtained through carefully selected, knowledgeable informants. What this study attempts to explain are the views, beliefs, and rationales of *supporters* of initiation and "circumcision." The extent to which these attitudes reflect those of all or the majority of Kono women is left open for future research.

My specific aims in this chapter are, first, to elucidate the significance of female initiation and "circumcision" in terms of indigenous Kono cosmology, culture, and society and to demonstrate how and why it is that bodily operations—both male and female—are viewed as necessary and important processes in the dynamics of sex and gender constructions and kinship relations. My second objective is to interrogate specific areas relating to international discourses on eradication of female "circumcision," using my own personal experience as well as Kono ethnographic data and the accounts of the experiences of individual Kono women. Finally, my goal is to discuss avenues for compromise on the "debate" about female "circumcision" and to suggest alternative strategies to current hard-line approaches.

Background to a Practice: Kono
Cosmos, Culture, and Society

The Kono are a Mande-speaking people who, according to oral historical accounts, migrated from the Guinea savannah region toward the end of the Mali Empire to their current home in northeastern Sierra Leone.[6] Kono is also the name of their geographic location and their common language. Most Kono uphold indigenous religious beliefs, although a minority proclaim Islam, and even fewer profess Christianity as their dominant faith. The subsistence economy is based on agriculture, with rice being the main crop. Diamond mining has had a major, if not disastrous, impact on Kono economy, culture, and social life. Today intense civil war rages in the diamond-rich areas (see Richards 1996 for an analysis of the full complexities of Sierra Leone's "bush war"). This conflict has driven out virtually all peasant farmers from their villages as well as traditional chiefs, professionals, and businesspeople, many of whom have also become victims of the protracted upheaval.[7]

The most salient organizing principles among the Kono are complementarity and interdependence (Hardin 1993:154–156), which are manifested in all aspects of social, political, economic, and religious life and—of particular interest to the discussion at hand—through female and male initiation and circumcision. The two institutions of paramount importance are Bundu, female "secret societies," and Poro, the male counterpart.[8] Sande is sometimes referred to as the "counterpart" of Poro by such scholars as Warren D'Azevedo (1994), who view the former as an ideological tool of patriarchy. However, D'Azevedo concedes that Sande predates Poro and that it was the women's cult that *yielded* some of its powers to men and has nevertheless been able to maintain its autonomy and distinct sources of "medicines," or power over men and other uninitiated. Politically, the separate male and female leaders of Bundu and Poro, called *soko* and *pamansu*, respectively, are all powerful. These two individuals, female and male, are considered the mediators between this world and the transcendental world of ancestresses and ancestors, other spirits, and *Yataa*, the distant Sky-God or, literally, the "One You Already Met." Bundu promulgates feminine interests: peace (through marriage alliances), sexual conduct, fertility, and reproduction. Unlike among some of their neighbors, the Poro leader among the Kono is usually the village chief, and he is responsible for masculine interests such as warfare, hunting, and arbitrating land disputes.[9] Transgression of these clearly demarcated domains by either sex is an egregious, and sometimes capital, offense.

Social organization also reflects this female-male duality. Kono lineage systems combine "public" and "domestic" into complementary and interdependent spheres of female and male influence and prestige. As Kris Hardin observed, the *bain den moe* is the matrilineage par excellence and is represented by the mother's brother and his descendants (Hardin 1993:60). The *bain den moe* embodies a "motherhood," or "one-womb," ideology, and relations are marked by closeness and familiarity (Amadiume 1987; 1997). Throughout her marriage a woman can count on her *bain den moe* as a check against her husband's *fa den moe,* where she resides and contributes her physical labor as well as her children, who will "belong" to her husband's lineage.[10] The *fa den moe*, however, is the stereotypical patrilineage, regarded with distance and formality and responsible for transmitting to individuals their juro-political status.

Both Hardin (1993:123–140) and Parsons (1964) point to the way in which female and male complementarity and interdependence also serve as the underlying principle behind the sexual division of labor. Women are responsible for the care of young children, and their share of farm work includes weeding, assisting with the harvest, and processing the harvested rice for the entire year. Men are responsible for obtaining land and rice seed, for felling trees and brush, and for sowing rice and plowing it into the ground. Al-though men "control" the land, they depend on the labor of women to make it productive, and the latter can withhold their services if they have particular grievances that need to be aired and resolved. Whereas in agriculture, men control the end product of the harvest, in indigenous cloth production women own and control the finished goods (Hardin 1993:135). As only men are per-mitted to weave, however, strict sexual interdependence is maintained in this area of production as well. There are certain "sacred" sectors of production that are exclusively male and exclusively female, such as blacksmithing (male) and ceramic pottery (female). Today, however, dramatic changes in the modern economy are resulting in women clearly becoming more and more economically and socially disadvantaged. Women are becoming more depen-dent on men for their survival as diamond mining and cash cropping and the increasing importance of cash as primary medium of exchange have led to a decline in the demand for goods traditionally produced by women.

Ritual Initiation in Kono

Initiation of girls into Bundu and boys into Poro takes place during the dry season, after the harvest, when food is plentiful and there is a significant amount of free time. This time of year is also symbolically important because it represents a new season of fruitfulness, fertility, abundance, and the possi-bilities of new life—just as initiation seeks to give birth to new, fertile, cultur-ally transformed young women and men. Thus, symbols of agricultural pro-duction and human reproduction are synthesized and given powerful meaning in initiation; but also initiation finds its meaning and justification in the per-formance of everyday farm work and sexual relations, both of which are de-fined in terms of female and male separate yet complementary contributions. The women's Bundu society and the men's Poro are severally responsible for the "creation" of female and male sociocultural beings from the raw material of nature, young children. Although some authors have stressed the symbolic negation of female reproductive powers by men, usually in reference to male initiation (e.g., Bloch 1986; Herdt 1982), it is important to note that for the Kono (and I suspect, for other initiating/genital cutting groups as well) what is negated is the biological reproduction by both male and female human be-ings, and what triumphs in initiation is the cultural creation of sexual and gen-der identity through the ritual process and the important intermediary role of the priest or priestess (as in the case of the *soko*). The imagery of female re-production is central to the ritual creation process. After undergoing a sym-bolic death, young initiates enter a metaphorical womb, the sacred grove, where they are circumcised—thus given an unambiguous sex—and then re-main in a liminal state while they receive ritual instruction. They are ritually "reborn," figuratively removed from the "vagina" of the sacred grove, as new persons with full social membership in the adult world.

In Bundu initiation, the *Soko* effects adult female identity through the act of excision and, in so doing, realizes a novice's procreative value. A young initiate's *bain den moe* are significant also in transferring fertility, that is, the healthy delivery of newborn babies. It is only through the blessing of the maternal uncle's ancestors that a newly "created" female with reproductive powers can actually, successfully procreate. Without such a blessing, a woman may certainly conceive, but her children may be stillborn or chronically ill or may not live for very long. Certainly the husband's patrilineage is desirous of healthy new members, but it depends on Bundu and any incoming bride's maternal line for its proliferation. Hence, the centrality of individual women and female ideology in controlling and manipulating the most critical resources in society: women's fertility and sexuality. What follows below is a sketchy description of my personal experience with Kono initiation. Much detail has been omitted as a result of space constraints as well as my desire to respect the secrecy and sensitivity of women's esoteric ritual and supernatural knowledge.

During the 1991 Christmas holidays, I traveled to Sierra Leone with my mother, one of my aunts, my uncle, my sister, and my cousin, my aunt's daughter. It was my final year at university in Washington, D.C., where I was born and have spent most of my life. My formative years, however, were spent in Freetown, the capital of Sierra Leone. It was during these early years in Africa that I first heard adult whispers about "Bundu society," the "Bundu Devil," and the fearfulness of initiation that, I was admonished, every girl must undergo in order to become a woman. "They're all witches! They rub you with white stuff, they mark your body and rub medicine, and then *they cut you!*" One of my female relatives, an uninitiated aunt only a few years older than I, used to taunt me with such remarks after we arrived in the United States. She would claim that she had spied on her older sister when the latter was "joining"[11] the secret society. While in school in the United States, I used to have a recurring memory of a time when my family was living in Freetown and the masked "Poro Devil" of the men's secret society was approaching, and all the women scurried to find their children to bring them inside their houses. All the doors and windows were then locked shut, and the lanterns were blown out, until the terrifying procession passed out of sight. On one occasion my brother could not be found, and I recall crying fitfully, thinking that he had been "discovered" and "swallowed" up by the devil. Although it turned out that the rascal was only hiding underneath the dining room table in our house the entire time everyone was looking for him, this did not lessen my burning curiosity to know what these "devils," "medicines," and "secret societies" were all about. So, when my grandmother, mother, and aunt all approached me, some fifteen years later, saying that it was "time," no one could have been more excited as well as afraid. My younger cousin and sister also looked forward to the promised feasting, gifts, and celebrations, as well as their first trip to their ancestral homeland.

Our first week in Freetown was spent visiting relatives who welcomed us, congratulated us for coming, and gave us gifts and their blessings. We then traveled upcountry to Kono, where both of my parents grew up. Our first stop was in Koidu, the capital of Kono, where my mother's sisters resided. Hundreds of close and distant relations came out to greet us, sing and dance, and honor our arrival and the upcoming "occasion." After several days, we traveled to Ghandhoun, my mother's patrilineal village, to pay tribute to my grandfather's tomb. He had passed away four years before. In the presence of the entire town, including fourteen of my grandfather's twenty-plus wives, my grandfather's spirit was assured that we had been brought back "home" from *Puu* (the white man's country) to carry on the traditions of our people and that his formal blessing was being sought. I was later told by a cousin that the selection of the *soko*[12] and the ritual "crier" (whose voice drowns out those of the initiates during "circumcision") also took place at this time.

After the greater part of "initiation business" (location, leaders, musicians, food preparation, and so on) was sorted out by the women, my sister and I were driven through thick forests and rough hills to my father's birthplace, Bomanjah. We were greeted by my father's relatives, and my mother was thanked again and again for bringing us. Later in the afternoon, everyone gathered in a clearing at the village center. Prayers and libations of cooked rice and fowl were offered to my father's lineage ancestors. Also, representatives were selected to attend and participate in the ceremonies in Koidu.

We returned to Koidu the following morning after traveling the entire night. The town was busy with arrangements and preparations for the "dance." I tried intently to observe everyone, every action and event taking place, although it was categorically understood that I was not to ask questions at this stage. I was concerned about my little sister, but she was enjoying being the center of everyone's attention. I "knew" what was going to happen to us, but I couldn't bring myself to tell her—perhaps like my mother could not bring herself to tell me, in her own words, "from her own mouth"—for fear of making her afraid as well. In any case, I was truly fascinated and overwhelmed by such a radically new experience. I reasoned that whatever it was I was going to endure, it would be worth the experience, the excitement of watching and being involved in the drama around me.

There was a sense that "it" was approaching. At some point we, the initiates, were isolated from everyone else. This seemed to mark the "beginning." I was more on constant alert than I was frightened. I did not want to miss anything. My female cousins/assistants were all very supportive, and I let their eyes and expressions guide my own feelings. I asked them about the pain and whether I would ever enjoy sex again, and they laughed. One very pretty twenty-one year old said to me, smiling: "When a man really loves you, he will take his time to do it, and it will be very sweet."

It must have been decided that two of my mother's sisters' homes would serve as the main ceremonial sites. The first ritual meal was prepared at the home of my mother's younger sister, Mama Yei. It was bitter and tasteless, but I was told it contained important "medicines" for our protection and was admonished to eat every grain. The initiates included myself, my sister, and a very young cousin, Sia (our American cousin who traveled with us was being initiated in her own father's village). The older women instructed us not to put anything else in our mouths; we should not accept food from anyone thereafter except from the two female elders who had been pointed out to us.

During the afternoon of this "first" day of initiation, we were taken to a river behind Mama Yei's house and bathed with special leaves and other oddities. I was given a *lappa* (wrap-around skirt), which I used to cover my body. When we were taken back to the house, our bodies and faces were painted thoroughly with white clay. We were then rushed outside into the front yard. A thin "rope" with a small amulet was attached around our waists, similar to ones worn by young children throughout West Africa for protection as well as decoration. Several women came to us and also tied various vines and leaves around our waists. I could hear the voices of some of my young male cousins singing songs about the imminent construction and preparation of the Bundu bush.

We were taken to the rear of the compound while it was still light. There was an endless stream of people dancing, singing, and waiting for us, the initiates, to emerge. When we did appear, dozens of women cried out, ran toward us, and surrounded us. Little Sia was being teased and taunted by the young boys in the crowd. She held on tightly to her grandmother's hand and turned her chin up in a subtle display of indifference. We were then led to my mother's oldest sister's compound. Although I was feeling queasy and dizzy, I could make out some familiar faces from the hundreds who had gathered to witness and partake in the ceremonies. I saw my mother, whose distance was becoming unbearable. I saw relations I used to know in the United States who had just somehow "disappeared" through the years. Elaborate indigenous country cloths were laid out across the bare ground and then on top of us. Perfumed talcum powder was tossed over us as the hairbraiding rite commenced. Ritual combs and braiders had been carefully selected. Drums were beaten as money was tossed from the crowd to the braiders. Mock battles took place between what I later understood were members representing my father's lineage, *fa den moe*, and those standing in for my mother's line, or *bain den moe*. In one such "battle" my sister, little Sia, and I were yanked up off the ground again and again and metaphorically "kidnapped" by a woman, also painted in white clay, whom I later made out was our "guardian spirit." My *fa den moe* would then attempt to take us back, but we were not released until their representatives had offered a substantial amount of money to the "guardian spirit."

Finally, I was grabbed by a different woman—extremely beautiful, elegant, almost regal. She walked my exhausted body away from the crowd, which followed behind. She explained that she was a dear friend of my mother's, that she was there to help me and to take care of me, and that she had lived and traveled extensively in Europe and the United States, so she understood what a culture shock this experience must be for me. She reassured me that my mother was okay, but that she could not be around until later, and that I should not worry because we were all in very good, skilled, and capable hands. "This is our culture," she repeated to me over and over again. The dreadful white-painted "guardian spirit" showed up again, trying to take me away in order to get more money from my father's relations, but my new "mentor" berated her and sent her away.

Later that evening—and I felt as if every moment was being closely timed—I was told by another close friend of my mother's, a registered nurse, what the "circumcision" rite entailed. She said she would give us an anesthetic injection to thwart any immediate pain and that she would also administer oral painkillers and antibiotics to prevent further pain and infection after the operation. She also pointed out that those of my relations among the audience who were medical doctors were on full alert and that there were clinics close by in case of any emergencies. I was suddenly struck by the full extent of what I had allowed myself to get into. Also, I realized that her revelations were against the "code of silence"—yet she felt obligated to inform me of what was happening, perhaps because I was a full-fledged adult or because I had been brought up in *Puu*.

We were given more "medicines," bitter-tasting, moist leaves. The celebrations went on while we were secluded inside the house. I was feeling increasingly "high" and paranoid and suspected the not-so-innocuous-looking "medicines." None of us were permitted to sleep, but we were interrupted every few minutes or so to participate in this or that prayer, blessing, or libation. At about two or three o'clock the following morning, we were made to strip by the elderly women "guarding" us. Our nether regions were shaved and we were given different *lappas* to wear. My mother appeared, her face visibly worn and drawn, and then she disappeared. An hour or so later, the noise died down.

We were rushed out, surrounded by dozens of unfamiliar older women, to another house a few yards away. We were made to sit up on the dusty cement floor, more and more women filtering in after us, one by one taking up every corner in the small room until there was no more space. Suddenly there was a knock on the door. I looked over at my sister and little Sia, both lying motionless on the ground, propped up by older women sitting among them. My mother came in with some other women, and I could see in her worried eyes that the time had come. But she did not look at me directly, and then she was gone again.

The nurse, my mother's friend, called me to her. I began to sweat as she reached into her white bag. She took out a syringe and needle and searched for the medication. The other women stared with curiosity at the nurse and her impressive paraphernalia. My sister woke up and saw the needle, and her mouth fell open. She cried out as she saw me open my legs. I was immediately hurled up and carried out by several massive, corpulent women before I could even turn to my sister. The women kicked the door open. It was dawn.

The Bundu bush is a large clearing at the site of a sacred grove sheltered from view, with "walls" made from bamboo shoots and leaves. At the center is a vast cotton tree with leaves that serve as a rooftop. I was hoisted up by four or five of these stocky women. I looked down: a large leaf had been laid on the ground directly underneath my buttocks. I looked up again. Terror finally overcame me as the women's faces, now dozens, now hundreds, moved in closer all around my near naked body suspended in mid-air. They grabbed my legs and arms apart. The women's screams, the sounds of drums, and then a sharp blade cut deep into my flesh on one side and then on the other. As I cried out in unimaginable agony, I felt warm blood ooze down between my thighs. Perhaps for the first time since I was an infant, I vomited.

I saw more, even heftier, women bring out my sister, and I tried to yell. My pleas were inaudible; I knew I had no more strength. After seconds, Sia's body was brought out, but everything appeared as a distant blur—I must have fainted. The women must have sat me down at the foot of the cotton tree because when I did come around, that is where I was, with my head resting against my mother's chest, studying the thick, bloodied piece of cloth beneath me which was tied to the thin "rope" around my waist. I felt like I was carrying a brick load between my legs. I looked for my sister—she was playing, actually running around with little Sia and some other convalescing girls in the Bundu bush. I guessed her anesthetic had been given time to take effect.

I looked up at my mother as she held me, and I begged her to take me "home," back to the United States—back to "civilized" society, I lamented at the time, where one only *reads* about this kind of thing in *National Geographic* or other exotic magazines! She kept apologizing and saying that she felt guilty. She told me that we would not stay in the "bush," that my sister and cousin and I would recover instead at my mentor's house. My mother coaxed me into participating in one more "kidnapping" rite and another special rite at the trunk of a large cotton tree, as well as a march through the town surrounded by the women, my very tormentors. We, the initiates, were once again isolated, but it was decided that the final coming-out "dance" would be suspended.

We remained in seclusion for several days or weeks—I had lost track of time. An older woman would come to us daily, bathing our wounds. She was always flanked by several other female elders. I found out later that she was our *soko*, the well-respected and revered excisor. Her entire reputation, her renowned surgical skills, her supernatural abilities, even her alleged sacred knowledge were all being tested during our excision rite. Not only were we, the initiates, the direct descendants of the ruling family in Ghandouhn, but we had come all the way from *Puu*. In these rapidly changing times of so-called development and modernization, the *soko*s are well aware of the threat to their power and authority and, worse, the challenge to their way of life and valued traditions. It was during this time, when the pain had subsided and I was assured by Bundu officials as well as by cousins my own age that my operation would in no way inhibit my sexuality, that I became relaxed enough to start inquiring into the historical relevance of initiation and why it remains important to contemporary women.

It is this older generation of women, particularly those within the Bundu traditional hierarchy, who are arguably the immediate and direct beneficiaries of female excision rites. However, from these women and the rituals they promulgate, I have learned to question my steadfast beliefs and values as a "Westernized" woman. Women of my mother's generation and now my own must weigh the benefits of such traditions against increased international concern about its physical, psychological, and sexual consequences for women. Ultimately, it is up to each generation of women to decide whether to continue or to reject this tradition without fear and coercion from outside as well as inside.

The Significance of Genital Cutting

What is the significance of such a ritual that, as described above, can be very painful and entail medical and other risks for initiates? Above I briefly examined the dual-sex structure of Kono society as a backdrop to an analysis of the relevance of female (and male) circumcision. In this section, I put aside for the moment health, sexual, and psychological issues raised by outside observers and activists against FGC, in order to consider in greater detail possible explanations and rationales for the tradition in terms of Kono worldview, dominant gender ideologies, the systemic and political influence of female ritual leaders, and, finally, individual motivations. First, I consider indigenous constructions of cosmology to the extent that these can be guessed at from documented mythologies of neighboring peoples with similar traditions and institutions. Second, I analyze local ideas regarding nature and culture and how these impinge upon human bodies and cultural constructions of sex and gender. I also consider dominant ideas regarding reproduction and sexuality and the rationale these suggest for genital cutting. Third, I discuss the ideological ramifications of female "circumcision" and its link to "matriarchal" power, as well as female ritual and sociopolitical authority. Finally, I discuss perhaps the most compelling reasons for the continuation of the practice, which, I believe, are rooted in the individual/psychological experiences of the rite. Although I treat these various "explanations" for FGC distinctly for analytic clarity, they are interconnected and mutually reinforcing and, taken together, form overwhelming unconscious and conscious motivations for the continuation of the tradition in the face of international condemnation.

Kono Cosmology

Anthropologists have for many years studied the cosmologies, or worldviews, of ethnic groups in many parts of the world who practice initiation and rites involving body modifications. A recurring theme running through creation myths of such groups is the inherent bisexuality of human beings. I believe that the Kono, or their early ancestors who came from Mali or Guinea, may have once possessed such cosmological understandings of creation, which would explain their view of humans as "naturally" androgynous beings who must later undergo rebirth (initiation) to be "made" female or male, that is, "given" an unambiguous sex. Although thus far, I have been unable to obtain such specific creation stories pointing to the intrinsic bisexuality of humans from reliable sources among the Kono, an inference can be made that similar myths may have existed in the past, based on the prevalence of such stories among neighboring groups with whom the Kono share many other cultural traits (notably, female and male circumcision as complementary processes) as well as historical and geographic links, such as the Dogon of Mali. According to the Dogon myth, excision is justified on two counts: First, the initial act of intercourse between male Sky-God and female Earth was prevented because of the presence of a protruding anthill. Only after the barrier was removed could intercourse take place and, subsequently, the conception and birth of first ancestors. Second, these first ancestors, due to a related fluke, were born androgynous—masculine elements were present in the female and feminine elements in the male. These inhibiting "cross-sex" elements had to be removed in order for men and women to be completely distinct and reproductive (see Parrinder 1996:27–28).

For the Kono, however, the role of Sky-God (*Yataa*) is much more obscure. Kono hardly refer to Earth and God and first creation, only inasmuch as the concept of *Yataa*, the "One You Already Met," is self-explanatory—the beginning and the end. Notwithstanding, autochthonous[13] creation is suggested in the widely held view of Earth as the wife of God. Also, ritual sources do recount myths of their first ancestresses accidentally severing their own clitorises, which was discovered to be a good thing, a source of power and knowledge to be kept secret from men and perpetuated in ritual. The implicit belief that the first ancestors were born from Earth, God's wife, and local mythology that depicts primordial females (inadvertently) excising themselves (usually through youthful masturbation) suggest some striking similarities to the Dogon story and a possible cosmological basis for explicit indigenous perceptions of the clitoris as an inherently masculine organ. Marilyn Strathern (1987) also postulated an "androgyny" theory to explain genital modifications among the Hagen of Papua, New Guinea. According to Strathern, indigenous views of the cosmos explain how persons are born "complete," that is, each individual contains both masculine and feminine elements at birth. Initiation is meant to engineer the deconstruction of persons into "incomplete" halves—male or female—who would then be capable of reproduction.[14]

However, the suggestion that the Kono may hold certain deep-rooted beliefs regarding the religious origin and necessity of female (and male) circumcision does not explain why the practice prevails today, particularly since local rationalizations are rarely alluded to on this level. Moreover, the fact that the layperson cannot recall such mythologies or stories about the cosmos or creation is further reason to consider other local justifications and motivations for initiation and "circumcision." Also, such worldview explanations that justify genital operations could rightly be interpreted as local ideological rationalizations that ensure the social status quo and the dominance of one group over another (e.g., Herdt 1982; Bloch 1986; see also Chapter 7 of this volume). In the case of the Kono and female "circumcision," as I will later demonstrate, ideological dimensions of female rituals ensure the power and preeminence of older women over younger women as well as over men in society. Nevertheless, myths are important because they point to origin and meaning (Bachofen 1967:70), however much history imposes its own distortions and reinterpretations (Bloch 1986:10–11). Also, the question of origin is becoming increasingly important, particularly to African women who uphold the tradition and are continually finding themselves in a position to justify the practice to outsiders and, perhaps more so, to themselves.

Nature, Culture, and "Sex" Categories

Principles of sexual complementarity and interdependence that underlie fragmented constructions of Kono cosmology and mythology are also evident in more accessible cultural notions of sex and gender and the practice of sexual operations. Unlike Western cultures, which divide human bodies into two sex categories, "male" and "female," believed to exist outside culture and therefore "natural" and immutable, the Kono have a different ontological understanding of bodies: only infants and very young children are conceived of as "natural," ontologically prior to "culture," or "proto-social," as MacCormack remarked for the Sherbro concept of children in southern Sierra Leone (MacCormack 1980:95). Like other areas that fall into the category of "nature," such as the "bush" or forest before being cleared or "tamed" and "made" into productive farmland, children must be "made" into either "male" or "female" depending on the appearance of their genitalia at birth, in order for them to be able to reproduce and become part of the world of "culture." Children and postmenopausal women, who have not reached in the first case or have passed in the second their sexually productive cycles, are given an ambiguous sex status—that is, they are seen as somehow androgynous or socially gender neutral. Initiation is the occasion for the social and cultural construction of "male" and "female" beings, and genital cutting is the key mode of effecting physical, psychological, and supernatural transformation of both sexes.

Reproduction and Sexuality

When asked about the significance of excision, ritual officials recite what are now common rationalizations for the practice (see Chapter 1 of this volume): "culture" and "tradition," cleanliness, purity, enhancement of fertility, and reduction of excessive sexual desire. The previous discussion about cosmology and cultural models of sex and gender was an attempt to explore underlying indigenous religious and cultural reasons, such as the idea of the inherent bisexuality of humans, which contribute to excision being vehemently defended as "tradition" and "culture." Local discourses on cleanliness and purity regarding excision also imply beliefs about the inborn masculinity of females, symbolized by the clitoris. Kono ideas about female fertility and sexuality also follow upon creation myths and beliefs about nature and culture as well as sex and gender, which idiomatically justify the necessity of female "circumcision."

For the Kono, sexual pleasure and reproduction are inextricably linked; the former is an incentive for the latter. The presence of the clitoris is seen to inhibit female fertility and sexuality in several ways. First, ritual officials and other Kono women adamantly maintain that if left untouched, the clitoris will continue to grow and become unsightly, like a penis; and second, leaving the clitoris untouched will categorically lead to incessant masturbation and sexual insatiability.

Like myths about the origin of excision, which invariably mention inadvertent cutting of the clitoris, the theme of masturbation is omnipresent in Kono accounts of the practice. Because the presence of the clitoris is seen as leading to excessive masturbation and excision is viewed as a condition of fertility, masturbation is logically construed as a deterrent to female fertility. It was explained to me during my seclusion period that an oversized clitoris and masturbation are inimical to fertility because the first is an obstruction and the latter an avoidance of coitus. Without coitus there can be no conception leading to human reproduction (notwithstanding modern reproductive technology, which is unavailable, if not unknown, to Kono villagers). Masturbation can be seen as preventing coitus to the extent that a young girl, discovering that she can sexually stimulate herself or be manually stimulated by others (including other females), does not desire or seek vaginal penetration by a man's penis. The clitoris is seen as parallel to the penis of a prepubescent boy—both have erotic but no reproductive value. However, according to a ritual informant, a young boy develops into an adult man, and his penis enlarges and acquires procreative value, whereas in most cases the clitoris remains relatively diminutive in size, incapable of penetration, and thus can neither sexually satisfy nor impregnate another woman. In short, the clitoris is analogous to a *dysfunctional* penis where women's reproduction and (hetero)sexuality is concerned. Thus, excision can be interpreted metaphorically and physiologically as an eschewal of undeveloped, inhibiting masculinity.

Female Ideology, Authority, and Power

However, inasmuch as a culture's sex and gender models and beliefs about reproduction and sexuality can make sense of cultural practices such as genital modifications, they are still inadequate in accounting for the widespread continuity of these practices. Thus far, I have presented Kono ideologies as if these existed in a cultural vacuum, isolated from contact with outside groups and external influences that may promulgate conflicting practices and beliefs. As noted earlier, dramatic changes have occurred, particularly within economic sectors, that have uprooted traditional life and precipitated permanent shifts in Kono society. Young Kono women, drawn to urban mining centers, are heavily influenced by new, "global" culture defined by American hip-hop, Coca-Cola, "gangsta" videos, and classic action-packed films such as *Rambo* (again I recommend Richards 1996 for an account of postmodern youth culture and the bush war being waged in Sierra Leone). Many young women are actively engaged in war, primarily as rebel recruits, exposed to and themselves committing some of the worst human atrocities in recent international history. Other Kono women have traveled, been schooled and spent most of their lives abroad. Some are national political leaders having to come to terms with heated issues such as the small yet vocal war being launched internationally to end female "circumcision." In this section I discuss the remarkable degree of continuity still found in practices of initiation and "circumcision," despite these broader changes brought on by modern developments.

Among the Kono, as Hardin has observed, power (*gbaseia*) involves above all the ability to "harness knowledge, medicines, witchcraft, and other supernatural means in socially appropriate ways" (Hardin 1993:192), and Bundu and Poro are the ultimate embodiments of female and male power, respectively. There can be no adequate understanding of the compelling force of initiation and "circumcision" without an appreciation of women's power and influence in Kono society even today. The social and cultural imperative to initiate and "circumcise" one's daughter is expressed top down through hierarchically organized categories of women. Within the women's sphere of sociopolitical and religious influence, the *soko* is the top woman, the mother of the community, the ritual intermediary between living women, their female ancestresses, and the Earth Goddess. The *soko* is also the custodian of ancient ritual secrets, particularly regarding fertility and the feminine role in creation, but she is also guardian and protector of dangerous ritual "medicines," or "leaves," which are used to protect novices during initiation, particularly from witches and other malevolent supernatural forces who "smell" the fresh blood of novices (see also Chapter 7 of this volume).

The *soko*'s "medicines" are also used to defend the sodality against intrusive men and other noninitiates who may try to steal its secrets and powers. In fact, several women ritual officials professed that the *soko* has power over all men, including those within the Poro hierarchy. Because of their secret knowledge regarding fertility, such women have the power to cause impotence in men as well as death. K. Kargbo, a Sierra Leonean diplomat and former practicing gynecologist and consultant on female "circumcision" issues, mentioned to me in an interview (August 7, 1994) that if a male politician ever wanted to commit political suicide in his country, he need only speak out against Bundu and incur the wrath of its leaders and masses of women in society.[15] The fact that the potential of witchcraft and "medicines" is accepted by virtually all sectors of society presents compelling mechanisms for social control remaining in the hands of these women.

Most important, the *soko* has the socioreligious authority to create "woman"—that most productive and reproductive asset as far as patriarchy, that is, male-headed families, compounds, villages, and lineages, is concerned. She gives religious, social, and cultural sanction to women's reproductive and productive roles: an initiated or well "trained" woman will fulfill her social responsibilities as mother and as farm laborer. Given the traditional socioeconomic primacy of marriage and motherhood among the Kono, as in most African cultures, and Bundu's paramount historical function of producing marriageable women committed to accomplishing their productive and reproductive roles, the *soko* is charged with the most credited task in society. However, the role of Bundu and its leaders in this regard has engendered some controversy among scholars. D'Azevedo (1994:342–362) and Caroline Bledsoe (1984) in particular have criticized Sande and female ritual officials as colluding with patriarchy in order to maintain the subordination of women in society. This position. however, misses the point that female subordination is much more complex and situational than Western analysis permits. What Bundu teaches first and foremost is the subordination of young girls and women to female elders: their mothers, future mothers-in-law, grandmothers, older women within the community, and, of course, female ritual leaders.

Secondly, novices are taught the *art* of subservience to some categories of men, that is, their future husbands and other male representatives of those lineages.[16] In the first instance, vis-à-vis female elders—that is, within their own sex group—initiates and younger women *are* inferior. However, cross-sex status comparisons would violate local dual-sex models, which emphasize complementarity and interdependence through sexual difference and autonomy. In the second instance, vis-à-vis their husbands and their male (and female) lineage representatives, young novices are taught to *feign* subservience—in verbal communication, body language and gestures, and the performance of domestic duties—in order to live harmoniously among their affines. But ritual leaders do not only teach subservience. They themselves are examples of ultimate female authority: wise, unyielding, and unsentimental. It is the *soko*'s responsibility to see to it that novices are inculcated with the ideals of femininity as laid down by previous ancestresses: stoicism, which must be displayed during excision; tenacity and endurance, which are achieved through the many other ordeals a novice must undergo; and, most important, "dry-eye," that is, daring, bravery, fearlessness, and audacity—qualities that will enable young women to stand their ground as adults in their households and within the greater community. Thus, the *soko* has a paradoxical responsibility of "creating" dual-natured "woman": a community-oriented and subservient person to be exchanged in marriage, as well as a defiant individual who capitalizes on the bolder qualities ingrained in her feminine identity in defending her own goals, priorities, and stakes within society.

Mothers: Upholders of Tradition

Female elders flank the upper echelons of Bundu. The next and most important category of women as far as the continuation of initiation and excision is concerned are the middle-aged grandmothers, whose critical job it is to put pressure on their daughters, who may be wary young mothers. These eminent elders have significant moral and emotional control over their married daughters. New mothers often spend a great deal of time in their natal villages under the supervision of their own mothers, particularly after the birth of and throughout the weaning period of their children. This group of older women are well aware of their importance when it comes to initiation and are often the ones spearheading the organization and orchestration of their granddaughter's ceremonies. It is incumbent on mothers to initiate their daughters properly, according to ancestral customs, in order for the latter to become legally recognized as persons with rights and responsibilities in society. Thus, there is enormous cultural demand for mothers to conform to the tradition of initiation, no matter how far their travel, the length of their absence from their local communities, and for those who are abroad in Europe or the United States, the intensity of their "Westernization."

For Kono women living in the diaspora, there is not much difference because many remain very close to their mothers. Although older women and female ritual officials put tremendous social pressure on mothers to "circumcise" their daughters, this pressure does not sufficiently explain why most women adhere to the tradition. If most women felt in some way oppressed by this aspect of culture—after all, they too were once initiates—why not then rise up individually or collectively and put an end to it? When the urgency is somewhat mitigated by distance and systematic disapproval of host countries, what are the reasons for continuation? As has been observed elsewhere in this volume, the reluctance of women to disengage from female "circumcision" could well be a result of gauging what other women will do—that is, some women may not actually support the continuation of the practice, but they do not want their daughters to be the odd ones out.

Kono women living in the diaspora explain that they want their daughters to enjoy the same legal rights as other women, and even more, they want them to "fit" into Kono society and be respected among their peers and the entire community of women. My own personal experience, which is hardly unusual, is a case in point. I am often reminded by Kono relations that had I not undergone initiation, I would not be able to be involved in meetings concerning "women's business," that I would not be able even to speak as a "woman" or on behalf of any women. Moreover, no initiated Kono woman would dare to talk to me about Bundu. In short, I would be ridiculed and maligned as an arrogant *puu moe*[17] or worse, an "uncircumcised woman," the ultimate insult against a woman. At the same time, these women do not necessarily believe that their Western-born or -bred daughters will care to be integrated in or accepted by Kono society. In fact, some admit that their daughters, if left to themselves, have no intention of visiting Kono or even Africa for that matter (given the negative image of war and poverty), let alone of marrying Kono men.

Societal coercion and pressure to conform, however, do not explain the *eagerness* and *excitement* felt by vast numbers of participants (residents in Kono as well as outside) in initiation ceremonies, including mothers of initiates, even if these same mothers also experience anxiety over the safety of their daughters. It is difficult for me—considering the number of these ceremonies I have observed, including my own—to accept that what appear to be expressions of joy and ecstatic celebrations of womanhood in actuality disguise hidden experiences of coercion and subjugation. Instead, I offer that most Kono women who uphold these rituals do so because they *want* to— they relish the supernatural powers of their ritual leaders over against men in society, and they embrace the legitimacy of female authority and, particularly, the authority of their mothers and grandmothers. Also, they maintain their cultural superiority over uninitiated/uncircumcised women.

There are numerous examples of how modernity and tradition coexist and intermingle, how initiation and "circumcision" can remain meaningful for individuals despite rapid changes in education, modernization, migration, war, and so on. Kono women engaged in altercation as far away as London and Washington, D.C., often challenge each other's womanhood—that is, the brazenness that undergoing the knife is supposed to produce and that reinforces the significance of excision as a symbol of strength and power. One female relation, who claimed to be against excision, was quick to disparage *Krio*[18] women as "uncircumcised" and "dirty" and also insisted that despite her current ambivalence, she will have her daughter "join" Bundu. In this case, excision was asserted as a symbol of cultural difference and superiority. Also, I have accompanied several female relations in delivery rooms and watched as the latter are cajoled by other female relatives to *biah*—a Krio word meaning "to endure and overcome the pain." The woman in labor is made to recall that she is a "woman," after all, a *Sandeene*.[19]

Initiation, Change, and the Impact of War

Neither modernity, global eradication campaigns, nor high-tech warfare has delegitimized initiation and "circumcision" among the subjects of this study. Rather, initiation has been changing according to exigencies of the day. The duration of seclusion has been drastically reduced, and in some rare cases, there is "cutting without ritual" (see Chapter 12 of this volume). Gone are the days when young girls spent many months and Kono boys several years in the bush, receiving cultural and religious instructions and practical training in domestic duties as well as in artistic performance, particularly song and dance. In modern times children have greater access to secular education, and so young girls enter the "bush" (sometimes the house of an older female relation) for not more than one month, sometimes just a couple of weeks, until their wounds are healed enough for their return to school. Although there was previously a limited amount of "cutting without ritual," notably among Christian Krio women who decided to marry Kono men and preferred to be "circumcised" in hospitals, today, I am told, "circumcisions" are performed on girls when they are as young as toddlers, in the fear that these children may forever forgo their Kono identities, either because of intensification and aggressiveness of eradication campaigns or because they may wind up as refugees in other, possibly Western countries as a result of dislocations caused by war.[20]

Back in Kono, other institutions co-opt and exploit the powerful symbols of secret societies for more destructive goals than "circumcision." The horrifying reality of "ritual without cutting" in war-torn Kono differs radically in intention and effect from the eradication strategy employing that concept in the Gambia (see Chapter 12). Young Kono women (and men, often young boys) engaged in bush fighting, either on the side of junta/rebels or of local traditional militia (*kamajohs*), must undergo new-age initiations and come under the influence of powerful "modern medicine" (i.e., crack cocaine) fashionable in West African warfare today. Reports from child soldiers suggest that the earlier versions of (particularly male) initiation rituals that emphasized killing, in hunting and war, and all kinds of unimaginable physical and psychological ordeals, are now primary methods used by rebel leaders in recruiting and converting young fighters, both male and female. "Circumcision" in these war campaigns would be irrelevant, if not redundant: virtually all recruits will have already gone through the "bush," but other initiation symbols are amplified, distorted, and abused for the purposes of warfare. Despite the grisliness of such facts, they reinforce the historical and religious legitimacy of initiation on a psychic level for individual women (and men) and demonstrate how these ancient rituals, originally conceived of for one purpose, may still be relevant today, even to justify additional, more nefarious ends.

The "Debate": Physical, Sexual, and Psychological Effects

Anthropologists have not been the only ones interested in initiation and female genital cutting. In the 1980s, and 1990s many others—feminists, politicians, international aid organizations, and the international medical community within and without Africa—have produced a plethora of literature and convened conferences and the like on the subject of the effects of various forms of genital cutting on women's bodies, sexuality, and psychological well-being. My intention in this section is to interrogate some of the major assumptions in prevailing international discourses on female "circumcision" in light of my own experiences and the data collected from other Kono women, primarily but not limited to immigrants residing in the United States.

First, as regards the health implications of excision, several short- and long-term risks have been associated with the practice (see Chapter 1 of this volume). I have personally interviewed several male and female Sierra Leonean gynecologists who profess that although they regard excision as "medically unnecessary," the practice does not pose any significant adverse long-term effects to women, and that, moreover, traditional circumcisers are on the whole "very well trained" and are "experts" at what they do. None had personally treated women with long-term problems related to excision, but all stated that they had come across "reports" of horror cases.

The doctors I have spoken to, irrespective of their position on the legitimacy of the practice, agree that short-term risks can be significantly reduced, if not altogether eliminated, through the use of antiseptic instruments, anesthetics to reduce pain, and skilled traditional officials. Also, it must be noted that most Kono women I have spoken to maintain that excision has existed in their society for hundreds of years, and the practice has neither adversely affected their fertility nor given their womenfolk the types of gynecological or obstetrical problems that have been associated with the operation in recent years. Thus, if some medical practitioners are saying that safe excisions are possible under the right conditions and if many Kono women do not attribute gynecological/obstetrical problems to their operations and choose to continue to uphold their tradition, a genuine case for limited medicalization can be made. As has been noted in Chapter 6, such steps may reduce the immediate risks of the operation for young girls, until such a time that women are collectively convinced to give up the practice.

Second, my research and experience contradict received knowledge regarding the supposedly negative impact of removing the clitoris on women's sexuality. Much of this taken-for-granted information may come from popular misconceptions about the biological significance of the clitoris as the source of female orgasms. It is probable that such myths evolved as a result of the heightened focus on the female clitoris during the 1960s sexual revolution and subsequent discourses regarding women's sexual autonomy (Henrietta Moore, personal communication). The clitoris has come to be seen in Western societies as not only the paramount organ responsible for women's sexual pleasure but has also been elevated as *the* symbol of women's sexual independence because the latter suited women's objectives in asserting their sexual agency and rejecting previous constraining notions of their roles as wives and mothers.

However, the presumptions that inform Kono women's values regarding female sexuality, as in other aspects of sociocultural life, emphasize sexual interdependence and complementarity, principles that are profoundly heterosexual. Western women's notions of the importance of the clitoris to female sexual autonomy can be contrasted with Bundu officials' stress on vaginal stimulation, which implies male penetration, and this emphasis glaringly suggests heterosexual intercourse, which is considered the socially ideal form of sexual relations because it leads to reproduction. My informants consider vaginal orgasm as independent of the clitoris but still fundamental to a woman's sexuality. Perhaps because women believe that the "internal" vagina is the appropriate locus of women's sexual pleasure, they profess that the clitoris is redundant and leads to excessive "sexiness." Also, because the clitoris is associated with androgyny and "nature," its presence signifies lack of self-control or self-discipline, which are attributes of "culture." Bundu officials insist that the clitoris is "no good" and that it leads to uncontrolled masturbation in girls and sexual insatiability in adult women. It is believed to be a purely superfluous erotic organ, unlike a "proper" adult penis, its sex-corollary, which at least has reproductive functions. It is thus understandable, even if one does not agree, how some Kono women can claim that although excision curbs a woman's desire for sex, the operation itself does not reduce her enjoyment of sexual pleasure.[21]

As pointed out in Chapter 1, there can be no way to "objectively" test the evidence regarding the impact of excision on women's sexuality because it is subjective and individually variable. Notwithstanding, an interesting finding in *The Hite Report* is that the external clitoris constitutes a small fraction of the total nerve endings that produce sensations for the entire appendage (see also Chapter 1). This suggests that excision does not damage most of the clitoral nerve endings because they are beneath the vaginal surface. Thus, paradoxically, even according to "objective" biological science, it is possible for a woman's sensitivity to remain for the most part undiminished after excision. This would probably explain how it is that many women who had sexual experiences *prior* to excision, the author included, perceive either no difference or increased sexual satisfaction following their operation. In any case, most contemporary, urban-educated as well as rural Kono women are just as interested in their sexuality as are their counterparts in Western countries, and they do not perceive excision as inhibiting them in any way. It is also worth noting, especially since it is usually omitted, that significant numbers of Western women, despite having their clitorises intact, experience their own difficulties in achieving any kind of orgasm, clitoral or vaginal.

Finally, with regard to the psychological well-being of young girls and women who have undergone initiation and excision, more research is needed before any credible generalizations can be made. A small but growing number of African female activists against various forms of "circumcision" have detailed the pain and trauma they underwent and the lasting impact such negative experiences have had on their lives, and they campaign against what they rightfully believe to be an affront to their human rights and womanhood. I have spoken to a few young Kono women who are adamantly opposed to initiation because of their experiences of pain, abuse, and maltreatment by female elders in the "bush." However, most women I have interviewed fervently support the practice, and my observations in the field confirm that most girls not only continue to look forward to their initiation but, further, demonstrate their ongoing support for the practice by actively participating in later ceremonies involving younger female friends and relations.

Conclusion

The question is often put to me: "How can a Western-bred and -educated African woman *support* a practice that degrades women and deprives them of their humanity?" Notwithstanding the ethnocentrism in this remark and the fact that I prefer to consider myself "neutral" in terms of the continuation of the practice, I am aware of many educated, professional, "circumcised" African women gracefully negotiating their way through culturally distinct settings. There are those, the author included, who refuse to privilege one presumably objective, scientific model of personhood over supposedly "misguided" local interpretations but rather seek to juggle "modern" and "traditional" identities according to the appropriate cultural context. Educated, "circumcised" African women, like most people of multicultural heritage, maneuver multiple identities depending on the specific circumstances in which they find themselves. Personally, I do not see any conflict or contradiction in being educated and being "circumcised" because the contexts which require each of these cultural idiosyncrasies are separate and distinct.

For me, the negative aspect of excision was that it was a physically excruciating experience, for which, given my relatively cushioned Western upbringing, I was neither emotionally nor psychologically prepared. This is in contrast to most of the prepubescent Kono girls with whom I was "joined." As with the young Mandinka girls in the Gambia among whom I am currently conducting fieldwork, they "took" excision "bonically" (a Krio term used to describe sheer human strength, strength of the flesh) and in a few hours were up, laughing and playing.[22] After one or two days, they were jumping up and down dancing the "bird dance" to the rhythm of makeshift drums in preparation for their big "coming out" dance. To impose on my research what was my own experience of "pain" would be a gross distortion of the experiences of most of the other novices and thus a certain disservice to anthropological knowledge in general.

The positive aspects have been much more profound. Initiation was the "acting out" and celebration of women's preeminent roles in history and society. Although I could not at the time put together all the pieces, I felt I was participating in a fear-inspiring world, controlled and dominated by women, which nonetheless fascinated me because I was becoming a part of it. In the years since, I have managed to make sense of much of the ritual symbolism and "acting-out," enough to understand that women claim sole credit for everything from procreation to the creation of culture, society, and its institutions, and, most important, they maintain a "myth of male dominance" so that their fundamental prerogatives are not threatened by increasing masculinization of religion, culture, and society in Africa (see Amadiume 1987).

One such prerogative is the virtual deification of mothers among the Kono (and most African societies, for that matter). Consequently, one of the greatest abominations of any African male or female, high or low, is the curse of his or her mother. This is not only symbolically important for women, but it gives them "real" power in inter- and intradomestic lineage and immediate family relations, by virtue of the moral privilege women have over sons and daughters. This could also explain the findings of Heidi Skramstad (1990:17) and Ylva Hernlund in Chapter 12 indicating that Gambian Mandinka women continue "circumcision" first and foremost out of respect for their mothers and grandmothers. Even for the few Kono women who have second thoughts about "joining" their own daughters, the idea of eradication never comes up. It is not so much that an unexcised woman is unfathomable to them, but the public defiance and condemnation that abolition campaigns require would

constitute a most unfathomable "insult" against their mothers and grandmothers.

Another feature of excision is the way in which the scar itself symbolizes women's sameness or common female identity. In effect, the operation
rite is what defines and, thus, essentializes womanhood. Unlike in Western
society, there is no confusion or fruitless intellectualizing about the definition
of "woman." Among the Kono, a woman is a woman by virtue of the fact that
she has been initiated and nothing else. But initiation also creates a hierarchi-
cal ordering of women in society. At the apex is, of course, the *Soko*, the
mother of the community, then an individual's mother, after which is her
mother-in-law, and then all other older women in the community. A woman's
equals are her age-mates, those with whom she was initiated and those falling
within the same age group. Thus, sameness is not always tantamount to
equality, and neither does it imply strict conformity to dominant values of
womanhood, such as motherhood. For example, my grandmother often nags
me about not yet having children and about the importance of motherhood to
a woman, but for her, as for the entire community, it was my initiation that
"made" me into a "woman."[23] Perhaps these ideas explain how some "circumcised" African women can be educated and Westernized and yet not view
the practice as an affront to their womanhood. In short, initiation/excision has
the positive value of creating sameness among all women and maintaining
equality within age-groups as well as a general hierarchy of female authority
in society.

Other advantages of initiation include beliefs about women's esoteric
knowledge and their monopoly over powerful "medicines." Although excision cannot be said to be a marker of ethnicity today (most ethnic groups in
Sierra Leone practice excision), what does distinguish Kono Bundu from
those of other groups are the "medicines" that are used. According to a high-
ranking Bundu official, even more important than excision itself is the
women's "medicine" used in the ritual. The more powerful a sodality's "medicine" is reputed to be, the more feared and thus influential are the women
leaders of such a group. Kono women often assert the power of their own
"medicine" and claim that this is how they dominate their men and "keep
them home." Also, it is believed that the "medicine" that is used for the
novices during initiation will protect them against all sorts of witchcraft and
other malevolent supernatural practices, which may be aimed at them
throughout their lives.

My final and more subjective point is my shared view of the aesthetics of
excision and (male) circumcision. I propose that the basis of Kono appreciation of male/female genital modifications is compatibility and harmony with
basic principles of complementarity and interdependence. These ideals underpin cosmological beliefs regarding sex and gender difference and are manifested in the dual-sex organization of culture and society. As long as there are

deeply implanted mental associations of the clitoris with masculinity, then the former will continue to be regarded as dirty, abnormal, unclean, and harmful by a culture that sees "male" and "female" as fundamentally separate and distinct moral categories.

To Cut or Not to Cut?
The Future of Excision

Although location and identity may establish who is an "outsider" as opposed to an "insider" with respect to studies on FGC, these factors do not automatically determine the position of any writer regarding abolition. For example, not a few anthropologists—who are by discipline Western scholars and often by nationality "outsiders"—have been bitterly criticized for their attempts to represent the cultural viewpoints and values of their informants. Conversely, indigenous African female activists or "insiders" fighting against FGM often promulgate the same messages contained in global discourses that link the practice to women's social, sexual, and psychological oppression. What is certain is that the future of FGC will depend on the extent to which "insiders" themselves are convinced of the purported negative effects of the practice.

The medical evidence as well as the speculations regarding adverse effects on women's sexuality do not tally with the experiences of most Kono women. It is the immediate physical pain and risk of infection that concern most mothers, and both of these hazards can be reduced, if not eliminated, through medicalization, education, and general modernization of the operation. A compelling point has been made, however, that all the eradication mechanisms, such as policies of international organizations and local nongovernmental organizations devoted to changing people's attitudes and behaviors, have already been set in place and that most likely there can be no going back (see Chapter 1 of this volume). But the virtually universal resistance to change after several decades of international and internationally sponsored local campaigning, conferencing, and legislating suggests that what is seriously needed is a rethinking of previous eradication strategies and a deeper appreciation of the historical and cultural relevance of this ancient practice and its symbolically dynamic and fluid links to women's changing sources and notions of power.

In my opinion, if eradication has become an irreversible "international" political compulsion, then the idea of "ritual without cutting" (see Chapters 1 and 12 of this volume) seems to be a reasonable middle ground. The ritual-without-cutting model positively values many cultural aspects and beliefs underlying female genital operations and initiation while attempting to eliminate the actual physical cutting. Perhaps what *is* needed to replace the physical act of cutting is an equally dynamic symbolic performance that will retain the same fluidity in associated meanings—eschewal of masculinity, womanhood, fertility, equality, hierarchy, motherhood, and sexual restraint. However, for rural Kono women in particular, the "cutting" and "medicine" are all-important. Also, as I discussed earlier, "ritual without cutting" can be very dangerous when taken out of context, such as in the recruitment and "training" of child rebels in Kono.

I continue to support, however, the goal of medicalizing and modernizing initiation and "circumcision"—not necessarily in a full sense of institutionalizing female "circumcision" or transferring the practice from the "bush" to hospitals, as in male circumcisions today, because this would reduce the power and authority of female ritual leaders and female elders but rather by making available basic, modern hygienic equipment and medications to traditional officials to use during rituals. I support change that will promote safe, sanitary environments, so that initiates are given adequate, modern medical assistance to reduce pain and the risk of infection. The position that this only legitimizes the practice is dangerously arrogant: the practice is already seen as legitimate by its proponents, who have themselves undergone excision, and denying them the benefits of medicalization only continues to endanger the health and lives of innocent young girls. Modernization should also include impartial, neutral education within primary and secondary schools.[24] Such education should detail both the positive historical and cultural significance of initiation/"circumcision" as well as its possible negative health effects. The emphasis should be on preparing young girls to make informed choices about their futures and the futures of their own female children.

What direction individual women take should be left to them and their immediate family members. Just as much as diehard "traditionalists" must relinquish their insistence that uncircumcised women are not socially and culturally "women" and therefore must be denied legal rights and dignity within society, hard-line efforts by abolitionists to coerce women to reject the practice and to stigmatize those who uphold their ancestral traditions as "illiterate," "backward," and against "women's rights" and "progress" are unacceptable. In this "debate," the majority of "circumcised" African women are unfortunately caught between a rock and a hard place, as the adage goes: either break traditional customary laws and face the consequences of "not belonging" or ignore increasing efforts to ban the practice and face possible legal penalties instigated by eradicators at the national and international level. Today, it seems that the pressure on "circumcised" African women, educated or not, is to choose between these two extremist positions—to be either "anticulture" or "antiprogress."

Change may indeed be occurring gradually, but I do not believe this is necessarily a direct result of anti-FGM campaigning. In my grandmother's days, excision was a universal rite of passage. For my educated, Christian mother who has spent over thirty years in the United States, initiating her daughters was a matter of judgment, an expedient choice to enable us to navigate easily between worlds. My generation is faced with a dramatically different and greater complexity of issues and other priorities (i.e., the complete destruction of Kono through civil war), and as a result, initiation and excision can hardly be said to be the most pressing preoccupation of young, contemporary Kono women. In the event that I ever have a daughter, I would like her to be well-informed about the sociocultural and historical significance of the operation as well as its purported medical risks so that she can make up her own mind, as I had the opportunity to do. Regarding female initiation and "circumcision" in Africa, John Mbiti has noted: "If they are to die out, they will die a long and painful death" (Mbiti 1990:129). However, through more culturally sensitive and appropriate "education" as well as limited medicalization strategies, the "death" of female "circumcision" could be more gradual, more natural, and a lot less painful for millions of future African women and girls.

Notes

I am indebted to so many people for their varied contributions to my academic and intellectual pursuits, more than I have space to mention. I would like to thank my supervisors at the London School of Economics, namely, Henrietta Moore as well as Deborah James and former supervisor Martha Mundy for their continued enthusiasm and encouragement of my research. Also, I would like to recognize the people of Kono, who are now mainly displaced refugees, for providing me with intimate, cherished details of their history, lives, and thoughts as well as the comfort of their homes in Sierra Leone and abroad. My sincerest love and gratitude to my aunty and role model, the Honorable Sia Foday-Ngongou, deputy minister, and her husband, my late uncle, the Honorable Dr. Tamba Foday-Ngongou, as well as Augusta Saidu, for their time and invaluable research assistance. My appreciation to the editors of this volume, Ylva Hernlund and Bettina Shell-Duncan, for their instructive comments and wholehearted encouragement. I would like to recognize Gambia College, particularly Dr. Bojang, Alhaji Bah, and Malik Bah for their practical and resource support throughout the completion of this chapter. Thanks to my special "daughter" Sia Kabba and "sister" Abie Tarawally for putting up with me "in the field." Above all, my deepest gratitude to those Kono women who continue to inspire me to this day: my grandmother, Gbessay Lebbie-Kokotowa, and my mothers Janet Ahmadu, Jenneh Borbor, Alice Jallow, and Manie Bah.

    1. See Strathern (1987) for an important critique of this assumption based on her work among the Hagen of Papau New Guinea. Another poignant critique of Western assumptions and models of sex and the acquisition of gender identity is offered by Atkinson and Errington (1990).

    2. "Rare" in terms of the types of procedures undergone by the total number of African women from cultures that uphold some form of female genital cutting throughout the continent.

    3. I will use the terms female "circumcision" and female genital cutting in a general sense to mean genital operations that, although rooted in cultural, historical, and

religious traditions, have no "medical" or "clinical" basis. The term "excision" will be used to describe the specific procedure undergone by Kono women.

4. This term is used by Amadiume (1997) to refer to the mother-focused structural/ideological basis of most traditional African societies.

5. I use the terms "secret societies" and "secret sodalities" interchangeably.

6. Most scholars and observers agree that the Kono (and Vai of southern Liberia) are ethnically a Mandinka subgroup who now consider themselves as a distinct cultural/linguistic group since their migration and settlement in their current geographic location.

7. The bulk of the research on which this chapter is based was collected prior to and during the gradual destruction of this area of Sierra Leone due to protracted rebel fighting. As of January 1999, Kono, a region rich in diamonds, has been completely overrun by rebels who are using the area to mine minerals, which are then used to finance the weapons and mercenaries needed for their war against the government. Kono people are currently living as displaced persons within those areas of Sierra Leone not under rebel control and as refugees in neighboring countries and in the West.

8. The women's secret society among the Kono is known as Bundu. However, among the Mende and other neighboring groups, they are called Sande. I use the term "Bundu" specifically in reference to the Kono and the term "Sande" when referring generally to secret societies in the region or to specific ethnic groups studied by authors whose work I cite.

9. See, for example, Ottenberg (1994b). Among the Mende, female chiefs are often the norm, and they are usually leaders of Sande (MacCormack 1972, 1979). These women can also be initiated into Poro and buried as "men" in the Poro bush (interview with male Poro informant).

10. See Kopytoff and Miers (1977) for an illuminating discussion of the concept of "belonging" in African lineages.

11. This term is used to signify variously becoming a member of Bundu, the initiation process itself, or the act of "circumcision," or any combination of the three.

12. Among the Kono, the *soko* is both head of Bundu and also the traditional circumciser.

13. In Greek, this term means "from the earth itself."

14. For the purposes of this study, my focus is primarily on the symbolic meaning of excision, bearing in mind that male circumcision is viewed as a necessary, complementary force.

15. An interesting parallel was recently provided in a statement by a Mandinka schoolgirl in the Gambia, where I am currently conducting research. She argued that there could never be any legal ban against female "circumcision" in the Gambia because all the male politicians are afraid of the powers of the *ngansingba* (traditional circumciser), who can strike at the seat of government in the capital of Banjul even from circumcision camps in the hinterland.

16. It is the patrilineal institution (*fa den moe*), made up of male and female members, which is regarded with such formal respect. Women have more relaxed relations with male and female members of their *bain den moe*, or maternal line. Thus, men are not automatically regarded as superior to women, if such a comparison can even be made. Status asymmetry depends on kinship/affine roles. A woman is subservient to her husband and his family, her children's *fa den moe*, but is on a par with her brother and her uncle, mother's brother, and other male members of her children's *bain den moe*. A woman's husband can also, of course, be another woman's brother or uncle, and status differentials will vary accordingly.

17. Literally, this means "white person."

18. Term used for the descendants of freed slaves who live in and around Freetown and account for less than 2 percent of the population. Although they have their own versions of 'secret societies," they do not practice initiation and "circumcision" of girls. Boys, however, are routinely circumcised in hospitals.

19. *Sandeene* is the name (a term of endearment) used for initiates. It comes from the words *Sande* and *deene* (meaning child).

20. Western aid workers report that mass initiations are taking place in refugee camps, presumably with little or no ritual.

21. This is true also of many of the Mandinka women in my current study.

22. Female participants in my initiation used this expression to distinguish modern bourgeois rituals, equipped with anesthetic and the like to numb pain, from common, traditional rites with no medications. When stoicism is displayed by initiates in the latter case, the rite is said to have been endured "bonically."

23. Like many older Kono women, she does not see my not having a husband as particularly relevant to motherhood.

24. For example, a pilot program at Gambia College, sponsored by the UN Children's Fund, trains primary school teachers in their cultural studies curricula to instruct students about the cultural and health dimensions in a "neutral" manner.

Bibliography

Abdel Halim, A. (1995) "Rituals and Angels: Women's Claim to Human Rights." In M. Shuller (ed.), *From Basic Needs to Basic Rights*. Washington, D.C.: Women, Law, and Development, International.

Abdulla, R. (1982) *Sisters in Affliction: Circumcision and Infibulation of Women in Africa*. London: Zed Press.

Abu Salim, M. I., and Y. Fadul. (1982) *Tabqat wad Daif Allah* (Book of genealogies). Khartoum: Institute for African and Asian Studies.

Abu Shama, A. O., M. A. Ali, I. Anis, J. F. E. Bloss, and H. El Hakim. (1949) "Female Circumcision in the Sudan." *The Lancet* 1.

Abul Fadl, M. (1997) "Sexuality in Islam: A Normative Perspective." Paper presented at the 96th Annual Conference of the American Anthroplogical Association, Washington, D.C.

Abu-Sahlieh, S. A. A. (1994) "To Mutilate in the Name of Allah and Jehova: Legitimization of Male and Female Circumcision." *Medicine and Law* 13:575–622.

Abusharaf, R. M. (1995) "Rethinking Feminist Discourses on Female Genital Mutilation: The Case of Sudan." *Canadian Woman Studies* 15:52–54.

———. (1996) "Revisiting Feminist Discourses on Female Circumcision: Responses from Sudanese Indigenous Feminists." Paper presented at the American Anthropological Association's 95th Annual Conference, San Francisco.

———. (1998) "Unmasking Tradition." *The Sciences* (March–April): 23–27.

ACOG [American College of Obstetricians and Gynecologists] Committee Opinion. (1995) "Female Genital Mutilation." *International Journal of Gynaecology and Obstetrics* 49:209.

Adams, P., and E. Cowie. (1990) *The Woman in Question*. Cambridge: MIT Press.

Adams, W. Y. (1977) *Nubia: Corridor to Africa*. Princeton, N.J.: Princeton University Press.

Adeneye, A. K. (1995) "Female Circumcision in South-West Nigeria: A Case Study of Owu Abeokuta." Unpublished B.S. thesis, Ogun State University, Ago-Iwoye.

Aderibige, T. (1996) "Legal Rights and Constraints for Women's Empowerment." In L. Erinosho, B. Osotimehin, and J. Olawoye (eds.), *Women's Empowerment and Reproductive Health*. Ibadan: Social Sciences and Reproductive Health Network.

Aerts, F. (1954) "Races du Tchad." Unpublished manuscript.

Agatharchides. (1989) *On the Erythraean Sea*. Trans. by S. M. Burstein. London: Hakluyt Society.

Agugua, N. E. N., and V. E. Egwuatu. (1982) "Female Circumcision: Management of Urinary Complications." *Journal of Tropical Pediatrics* 28:248–252.

Ahmadu, F. (1995) "Rites and Wrongs." *Pride* (April/May).

Ahmed, L. (1989) "Arab Culture and Writing Women's Bodies." *Feminist Issues* (Spring): 41–55.

Aidoo. A. A. (1998) "The African Woman Today." In O. Nnaemeka (ed.), *Sisterhood, Feminisms and Power: From Africa to the Diaspora*. Trenton, N.J.: Africa World Press.

Amadiume, I. (1987) *African Matriarchal Foundations: The Case of Igbo Societies*. London: Karnak House.

———. (1997) *Reinventing Africa: Matriarchy, Religion and Culture*. London: Zed Books.

Ammar, H. (1954) *Growing up in an Egyptian Village: Silwa, Province of Assam*. London: Routledge and Kegan Paul.

Amselle, J.-L. (1992) "La corruption et le clientélisme au Mali et an Europe de l'Ést: Quelques points de comparison." *Cahiers d'Études africaines* 128:629–642.

Annas, C. L. (1996) "Irreversible Error: The Power and Prejudice of Female Genital Mutilation." *Journal of Contemporary Health Law and Policy* 12:325–353.

Anonymous. (1963) "Le Tchad: Essai de classification des tribus Sara, les superstitions locales, les coutumes, les practiques de la médecine indigène dans la race Sara." N'Djaména: unpublished manuscript, CEFOD.

Anonymous. (1993) "What's Culture Got to Do with It? Excising the Harmful Tradition of Female Circumcision." *Harvard Law Review* 106:325–353.

Appiah, K. A. (1992) *In My Father's House: Africa in the Philosophy of Culture*. New York and Oxford: Oxford University Press.

Arbesman, M., L. Kahler, and G. M. Buck. (1993) "Assessment of the Impact of Female Circumcision on the Gynecological, Genitourinary and Obstetrical Health Problems of Women from Somalia: Literature Review and Case Series." *Women and Health* 20:27–42.

Assaad, M. B. (1980) "Female Circumcision in Egypt: Social Implications, Current Research, and Prospects for Change." *Studies in Family Planning* 11:3–16.

Atkinson, J., and S. Errington (eds). (1990) *Power and Difference: Gender in Island Southeast Asia*. Stanford: Stanford University Press.

Austveg, B., R. E. B. Johansen, A. H. Hersi, F. A. Mader, and S. Rye. (1998) "Kvinnelig omskjæring—veien vidare." *Tidskrift Norske Loegeforen* 27:4243–4246.

Aziz, F. A. (1980) "Gynecologic and Obstetric Complications of Female Circumcision." *International Journal of Gynaecology and Obstetrics* 17:560–563.

Bachofen, J. (1967) *Myth, Religion and Mother Right: Selected Writings of J. J. Bachofen*. Princeton, N.J.: Princeton University Press.

Bagayogo, S. (1987) "L'État au Mali: Représentation, autonomie et mode de fonctionnement." In E Terray (ed.), *L'État contemporain en Afrique*. Paris: L'Harmattan.

El Bakri, Z. (1983) "Aspects of Women's Political Participation in Sudan." *International Social Science Journal* 35:605–623.

El Bakri, Z., F. Zahir, B. Badri, TuA. Khalid, and M. al Sanusi. (1987) "Women in the Sudan in the Twentieth Century." In S. Wieringa (ed.), *Women's Movements and Organizations in Historical Perspective*. The Hague: Institute for Social Studies.

Balk, D. (1996a) "Marriage and Fertility in Northeast Africa: What Role Does Female 'Circumcision' Play?" Unpublished manuscript.

———. (1996b) *Toward a Demographic Understanding of Ritual Female Genital Practices in the Sudan*. Unpublished manuscript.

Barth, F. (1989) "The Analysis of Culture in Complex Societies." *Ethnos* 54.

Bashir, L. M. (1996) "Female Genital Mutilation in the United States: An Examination of Criminal and Asylum Law." *Journal of Gender and the Law* 4:415–454.

Beaman, A. W. (1981) "The Rendille Age-Set System in Ethnographic Context: Adaptation and Integration in a Nomadic Society." Ph.D. diss., Boston University.

Beidelman, T. O. (1997) *The Cool Knife: Imagery of Gender, Sexuality, and Moral Education in Kaguru Initiation Ritual.* Washington D.C.: Smithsonian Institution Press.

Bell, H. (1998) "Midwifery Training and Female Circumcision in the Inter-War Anglo-Egyptian Sudan." *Journal of African History* 39:293–312.

Belsey, M. A. (1979) "Biological Factors Other Than Nutrition and Lactation Which May Influence Natural Fertility: Additional Notes with Particular Reference to Sub-Saharan Africa." In H. Leridon and J. Menken (eds.), *Natural Fertility.* Liege: Ordina Editions.

Bettelheim, B. (1955) *Symbolic Wounds: Puberty Rites and the Envious Male.* London: Thames and Hudson.

Betzig, L. (1986) *Despotism and Differential Reproduction: A Darwinian View of History.* Hawthorne, N.Y.: Aldine de Gruyter.

Blake, C. F. (1994) "Foot-binding in Neo-Confucian China and the Appropriation of Female Labor." *Signs* 19:676–712.

Blakely, T., W. van Beek, and D. Thomson (eds.). (1994) *Religion in Africa: Experience and Expression.* London: James Curry.

Bledsoe, C. (1984) "The Political Use of Sande Ideology and Symbolism." *American Ethnologist* 11:455–472.

Bledsoe, C., and K. M. Robey. (1986) "Arabic Literacy and Secrecy Among the Mende of Sierra Leone." *Man* 21:202–226.

Bloch, M. (1986) *From Blessing to Violence: History and Ideology in the Circumcision Ritual of the Merina in Madagascar.* Cambridge: Cambridge University Press.

Boddy, J. (1982) "Womb as Oasis: The Symbolic Content of Pharaonic Circumcision in Rural Northern Sudan." *American Ethnologist* 9:682–698.

———. (1988) "Spirit and Selves in Northern Sudan: The Cultural Therapeutics of Possession and Trance." *American Ethnologist* 15:4–27.

———. (1989) *Wombs and Alien Spirits: Women, Men, and the Zar Cult in Northern Sudan.* Madison: University of Wisconsin Press.

———. (1991) "Body Politics: Continuing the Anti-circumcision Crusade." *Medical Anthropology Quarterly* 5:15–17.

Bonaparte, M. (1953) *Female Sexuality.* New York: International Universities Press.

Bongaarts, J., O. Frank, and R. Lesthaeghe. (1984) "The Proximate Determinants of Fertility in Sub-Saharan Africa." *Population and Development Review* 10:511–538.

Boone, S. (1986) *Radiance from the Waters: Ideals of Feminine Beauty in Mende Art.* New Haven: Yale University Press.

Boserup, E. (1970) *Women's Role in Economic Development.* London: Allen and Unwin.

Boulware-Miller, K. (1985) "Female Circumcision: Challenges to the Practice as a Human Rights Violation." *Harvard Women's Law Journal* 8:155–177.

Brass, W., and C. J. Jolly. (1993) *Population Dynamics of Kenya.* Washington D. C.: National Academy Press.

Breitung, B. (1996) "Interpretation and Eradication: National and International Responses to Female Circumcision." *Emory International Law Review* 10.

Brennan, K. (1989) "The Influence of Cultural Relativism on International Human Rights Law: Female Circumcision as a Case Study." *Law and Inequality* 7:367–398.

Brett-Smith, S. (1994) *The Making of Bamana Sculpture*. Cambridge: Cambridge University Press.

Brigaldino, G. (1997) "Managing European Aid Resources in Mali." In J. Carlsson, G. Somolekae, and N. van de Walle (eds.), *Foreign Aid in Africa: Learning from Country Experiences*. Uppsala: Nordiska Afrikainstitutet.

Browne, D. (1991) "Christian Missionaries, Western Feminists, and the Kikuyu Clitoridectomy Controversey." In Brett Williams (ed.), *The Politics of Culture*. Washington, D.C.: Smithsonian.

Bryk, F. (1934) *Circumcision in Man and Woman: Its History, Psychology and Ethnology*. New York: American Ethnological Press.

———. (1964) *Voodoo-Eros: Ethnological Studies in the Sex-life of the African Aborigines*. New York: United Book Guild.

Bureau Central du Recensement Chad. (1995a) *Recensement general de la population et de l'habitat 1993*. Tome 2: *Etat de la population*. N'Djamena, Chad: Bureau Central du Recensement.

———. (1995b) *Recensement general de la population et de l'habitat 1993*. Tome 6: *Alphabetisation–Scolarisation–Instruction*. N'Djamena, Chad: Bureau Central du Recensement.

Bureau of Statistics (Tanzania) and Macro International. (1997) *Tanzania Demographic and Health Survey 1996*. Calverton, Md.: Bureau of Statistics and Macro International.

Butt-Thompson, F. W. (1929) *West African Secret Societies*. London: H. F. and G. Witherby.

Caldwell, J., and P. Caldwell (1977) "The Role of Marital Sexual Abstinence in Determining Fertility: A Study of the Yoruba of Nigeria." *Population Studies* 31:193–217.

———. (1987) "The Cultural Context of High Fertility in Sub-Saharan Africa." *Population and Development Review* 13:409–434.

———. (1993) "The Nature and Limits of the Sub-Saharan African AIDS Epidemic: Evidence from Geographic and Other Patterns." *Population and Development Review* 19:817–848.

———. (1996) "The African AIDS Epidemic." *Scientific American* 274:40–46.

Caldwell, J. C., P. Caldwell, and I. O. Orubuloye. (1992) "The Family and Sexual Networking in Sub-Saharan Africa: Historical Regional Differences and Present-Day Implications." *Population Studies* 46:385–410.

Caldwell, J., I. O. Orubuloye, and P. Caldwell. (1992) "Fertility Decline in Africa: A New Type of Transition." *Population and Development Review* 18:211–242.

———. (1997) "Male and Female Circumcision in Africa: From a Regional to a Specific Nigerian Examination." *Social Science and Medicine* 44:1181–1193.

Carr, D. (1997) *Female Genital Cutting: Findings from the Demographic and Health Surveys Program*. Calverton, Md.: Macro International.

Carreira, A. (1947) *As Mandingas da Guin, Portuguesa*. Lisboa: Sociedade Industrial de Tipografia Limitada.

Chaine, J. P., and T. Saidel. (1992) *The Child Survival Baseline Survey*. Washington, D.C.: Devres.

Chaine, L., and A. Meynier. (1951) "Note sur le yondo des Sara." Unpublished magazine.

Chapelle, J. (1986) *Le peuple Tchadien: Ses racines et sa vie quotidienne*. Paris: Editions L'Harmattan.

Cloudsley, A. (1983) *Women of Omurman: Life, Love and the Cult of Virginity.* London: Ethnographica.

Coleman, D. L. (1998) "The Seattle Compromise: Multicultural Sensitivity and Americanization." *Duke Law Journal* 47:717–783.

Comby, M. (1984) *Documents sur l'histoire du Tchad.* Sarh: Ecole Normale de Sarh.

Conrad, D. C., and B. E. Frank (eds.). (1995) *Status and Identity in West Africa: Nyamakataw of Mande.* Bloomington and Indianapolis: Indiana University Press.

Constantinides, P. (1985) "Women Heal Women: Spirit Possession and Sexual Segregation in a Muslim Society." *Social Science and Medicine* 21:685–692.

Cook, R. (1979) *Damage to Physical Health from Pharaonic Circumcision (infibulation) of Females: A Review of the Medical Literature: Traditional Practices Affecting the Health of Women and Children.* Alexandria, Egypt: World Health Organization.

Cook, R. (ed.). (1994) *Human Rights of Women: National and International Perspectives.* Philadelphia: University of Pennsylvania Press.

Coulibaly, S., F. Dicko, S. M. Traoré, O. Sidibé, M. Seroussi, and B. Barrère. (1996) *Enquête Démographique et de Santé, Mali 1995–1996.* Calverton, Md.: Cellule de Planification et de Statistique de Ministère de la Santé, Direction Nationale de la Statistique et de l'Informatique et Macro Internatinal.

Council on Scientific Affairs of the AMA. (1995) "Female Genital Mutilation." *Journal of the American Medical Association* 274:1714–1716.

Coville, E. (1989) "Centripetal Ritual in a Decentered World: Changing Maro Performances." In S. D. Russel and C. E. Cunningham (eds.), *Changing Lives, Changing Rites: Ritual and Social Dynamics in Philippine and Indonesian Uplands.* Ann Arbor: University of Michigan.

Crossette, B. (1998) "A Uganda Tribe Fights Genital Cutting." *New York Times,* July 16.

Dagoma, A. (1990) "L'Éxcision, cette mail-aimée du Tchad." Universite de Paris X, Centre Droits et Cultures, Nanterre. Unpublished manuscript.

Daly, M. (1978) "African Genital Mutilation: The Unspeakable Atrocities." *Gyn/Ecology: The Metaethics of Radical Feminism.* Boston: Beacon Press, 153–177.

El Dareer, A. (1982) *Woman, Why Do You Weep? Circumcision and Its Consequences.* London: Zed Press.

Davies, M. (1983) *Third World, Second Sex.* London: Zed Press.

Davison, J. (1996) *Voices from Mutira: Change in the Lives of Rural Gikuyu Women.* Boulder, Colo.: Lynne Rienner.

Daw, E. (1970) Female Circumcision and Infibulation Complicating Delivery. *The Practitioner* 204:559–563.

D'Azevedo, W. (1994) *Gola Womanhood and the Limits of Masculine Omnipotence.* In T. Blakely, W. van Beek, and D. Thomson (eds.), *Religion in Africa: Experience and Expression.* London: James Curry.

De Jorio, R. (1997) "Female Elites, Women's Formal Associations, and Political Practices in Urban Mali." Ph.D. diss., University of Illinois, Urbana-Champaign.

Delaney, C. (1988) *Mortal Flow: Menstruation in Turkish Village Society.* In A. Gottlieb and T. Buckley. (eds.), *Blood Magic: The Anthropology of Menstruation.* Berkeley: University of California Press.

Deng, F. (1995) *War of Visions.* Washington, D.C.: Brookings Institution.

De Silva, S. (1989) "Obstetric Sequelae of Female Circumcision." *European Journal of Obstetrics, Gynecology and Reproductive Biology* 32:233–240.

Dewhurst, C. J. (1964) "Infibulation Complicating Pregnancy." *British Medical Journal* 2:1442.

DHS (Demographic and Health Survey). (1989) *Ondo State, Nigeria: Demographic and Health Survey 1986*. Columbia, Md., and Akure, Nigeria: Institute for Resource Development/Macro Systems and Medical/Preventive Health Division, Ministry of Health, Ondo State Government.

di Leonardo, M. (1991) "Introduction: Gender, Culture, and Political Economy— Feminist Anthropology in Historical Perspective." In M. di Leonardo (ed.), *Gender at the Crossroads of Knowledge: Feminist Anthropology in the Postmodern Era*. Berkeley: University of California Press, 1–48.

Diallo, H. (1990) *Aspects soci-sanitaires de l'excision au Mali*. Bamako: L'École Nationale de Médecine et de Pharmacie du Mali.

Diamond, J. (1996) "Empire of Uniformity." *Discover* (March): 78–85.

Dieterlen, G. (1951) *Essai sur la religion Bambara*. Paris: Presses Universitaires de France.

El Din, M.A.A.G. (1977) "The Economic Value of Children in Rural Sudan." In J. Caldwell (ed.), *The Persistence of High Fertility*, vol. 2. Canberra: Australian National University.

Dirie, M., and G. Lindmark. (1991) "Female Circumcision in Somalia and Women's Motives." *Acta Obstetrica et Gynecologica Scandinavica* 70:581–585.

Doh, N. (1984) *Faits et traditions des Day*. N'Djamena: Université du Tchad.

Dorkenoo, E. (1994) *Cutting the Rose—Female Genital Mutilation: The Practice and Its Prevention*. London: Minority Rights Group.

———. (1996) "Combating Female Genital Mutilation: An Agenda for the Next Decade." *World Health Statistics Quarterly* 49:142–147.

Dorkenoo, E., and S. Elworthy. (1992) *Female Genital Mutilation: Proposals for Change*. London: Minority Rights Group.

Dualeh, R. (1982) *Sisters in Affliction: Circumcision and Infibulation of Women in Africa*. London: Zed Press.

Dugger, C. (1996) "A Refugee's Body Is Intact but Her Family Is Torn." *New York Times*, September 11, A1, A8–A9.

Durkheim, E. (1995) *The Elementary Forms of Religious Life*. New York: Free Press.

Ebong, R. D. (1997) "Female Circumcision and Its Health Implications: A Study of the Uruan Local Government Area of Akwa Ibom State, Nigeria." *Journal of the Royal Society of Health* 117:95–99.

Edgerton, R. B. (1992) *Sick Societies: Challenging the Myth of Primitive Harmony*. New York: Free Press.

Edwards, D. N. (1998) "Meroe and the Sudanic Kingdoms." *Journal of African History* 39:175–193.

Eliah, E. (1996) "REACHing for a Healthier Future." *Populi* (May): 12–16.

Elster, J. (1995) "Functional Explanation in Social Science." In Michael Martin and Lee C. McIntyre (eds.), *Readings in the Philosophy of Science*. Cambridge: MIT Press.

Engle, K. (1992) "Female Subjects of Public International Law: Human Rights and the Exotic Other Female." *New England Law Review* 26:1509.

Epelboin, S., and A. Epelboin. (1981) "Excision: Traditional Mutilation or Cultural Value?" *African Environment* 16:177–188.

Ericksen, K. P. (1989) "Female Genital Mutilations in Africa." *Behavioral Science Research* 23:182–204.

Errington, S. (1990) "Recasting Sex, Gender, and Power: A Theoretical and Regional Overview." In J. Atkinson and S. Errington (eds.), *Power and Difference in Island Southeast Asia*. Stanford: Stanford University Press.

Eustache, P. (1952) "Notes sur l'initiation dans les groupe Oubangui: Mandjas, Banda, Gbaya, Banziri." Unpublished manuscript.

Forrest, J. B. (1992) *Guinea-Bissau: Power, Conflict and Renewal in a West African Nation.* Boulder, Colo.: Westview Press.

Fortes, M. (1973) *On the Concept of the Person Among the Tallensi: La Notion de Personne en Afrique noire.* Paris: Centre National Recherche Scientifique.

Fortier, J. (1982) *Histoire du pays Sara.* Sarh: Centre d'Études Linguistiques.

Frank, O. (1983) "Infertility in Sub-Saharan Africa: Estimates and Implications." *Population and Development Review* 9:137–144.

Fraser, D. (1995) "The First Cut Is Not the Deepest." *Dalhousie Law Journal* 18:310–379.

Fratkin, E. (1991) *Surviving Drought and Development: Ariaal Pastoralists of Northern Kenya.* Boulder, Colo.: Westview Press.

Freud, S. (1931, 1963) *Female Sexuality: Sexuality and the Psychology of Love.* New York: Simon and Schuster.

Funder, A. (1993) "De minimus Non Curat Lex: The Clitoris, Culture and the Law." *Transnational Law and Contemporary Problems* 3:417–467.

Gallay, A., E. Huysecorn, A. Mayor, and G. de Ceunick. (1996) *Hier et aujourd'hui: des Poteries et des Femmes—Céramics Traditionelles du Mali.* Genève: Université de Genève.

Gallo (Grassivaro-Gallo), P. G. (1985) "Female Circumcision in Somalia: Some Psychological Aspects." *Genus* 41:133–147.

Gallo, P. G., and M. Abdisamed. (1985) "Female Circumcision in Somalia: Anthropological Traits." *Anthropologischer Anzeiger Jahrg* 43:311–326.

Gallo, P. G., and F. Viviani. (1992) "The Origin of Infibulation in Somalia: An Ethological Hypothesis." *Ethology and Sociobiology* 13:253–265.

GAMCOTRAP (Gambian Committee on Traditional Practices Affecting Women and Children). (1994) "Knowledge, Attitude and Practices Survey from Foni and West Kiang." Gambia Committee on Traditional Practices.

Gates, H. (1998) "Footbinding and Handspinning: Modernizing Chinese Girls." In Kenneth G. Lieberthal, Shuen-fu Lin, and Ernest P. Young (eds.), *Constructing China: The Interaction of Culture and Economics.* Ann Arbor: University of Michigan, Center for Chinese Studies.

Gifford, E. A. (1994) "'The Courage to Blaspheme': Confronting Barriers to Resisting Female Genital Mutilation." *UCLA Women's Law Journal* 4:329–364.

Gilliam, A. (1991) "Women's Equality and National Liberation." In C. T. Mohanty, A. Russo, and L. Torres (eds.), *Third World Women and the Politics of Feminism.* Indianapolis: Indiana University Press, 215–236.

Gilmore, D. D. (1990) *Manhood in the Making: Cultural Concepts of Masculinity.* New Haven: Yale University Press.

Ginsburg, F. (1991) "What Do Women Want? Feminist Anthropology Confronts Clitoridectomy." *Medical Anthropology Quarterly* 5:17–19.

Gordon, D. (1991) "Female Circumcision and Genital Operations in Egypt and the Sudan: A Dilemma for Medical Anthropology." *Medical Anthropology Quarterly* 5:3–14.

Gosselin, C. (1996) "The Politics of Doing Feminist Ethnography on Excision." Toronto: University of Toronto. Unpublished manuscript.

———. (in press) "Feminism, Anthropology and the Politics of Excision in Mali: Global and Local Debates in a Post-Colonial World." *Anthropologica.*

Griaule, M. (1965) *Conversations with Ogotenmêli: An Introduction to Dogon Religious Ideas.* London: Oxford University Press.

Grillo, R. D. (1997) "Discourses on Development: The View from Anthropology." In R. D. Grillo and R. L. Stirrat (eds.), *Discourses of Development: Anthropological Perspectives*. Oxford and New York: Berg.

Grosz-Ngaté, M. (1989) "Hidden Meanings: Explorations into a Bamanan Construction of Gender." *Ethnology* 28:167–183.

Gruenbaum, E. (1982) "The Movement Against Clitoridectomy and Infibulation in Sudan: Public Health Policy and the Women's Movement." *Medical Anthropology Newsletter* 13:4–12.

———. (1988) "Reproductive Ritual and Social Reproduction: Female Circumcision and the Subordination of Women in Sudan." In N. O'Neill and J. O'Brien (eds.), *Economy and Class in Sudan*. Aldershot, England: Avebury, 308–328.

———. (1991) "The Islamic Movement, Development, and Health Education: Recent Changes in the Health of Rural Women in Central Sudan." *Social Science and Medicine* 33:637–645.

———. (1992) "The Islamist State and Sudanese Women." *Middle East Report* 179:20–23.

———. (1996) The Cultural Debate over Female Circumcision: The Sudanese Are Arguing This One Out for Themselves. *Medical Anthropology Quarterly* 10:455–475.

Gunning, I. (1991) "Modernizing Customary International Law: The Challenge of Human Rights." *Virginia Journal of International Law* 31:211–247.

———. (1991–1992) "Arrogant Perception, World-Traveling and Multicultural Feminism: The Case of Female Genital Surgeries." *Columbia Human Rights Law Review,* 189–248.

———. (1997) "Uneasy Alliances and Solid Sisterhood: A Response to Professor Obiora's Bridges and Barricades." *Case Western Reserve Law Review* 47:445–460.

Gwako, E. L. M. (1995) "Continuity and Change in the Practice of Clitoridectomy in Kenya: A Case-Study of the Abagusii." *Journal of Modern African Studies* 33:333–337.

Hale, S. (1994) "A Question of Subjects: The 'Female Circumcision' Controversy and the Politics of Knowledge." *Ufahamu* 22:26–35.

Hansen, H. H. (1972–1973) "Clitoridectomy: Female Circumcision in Egypt." *Folk* 14–15:15–26.

Hardin, K. (1993) *The Aesthetics of Action: Continuity and Change in a West African Town*. Washington, D.C.: Smithsonian Institution Press.

Harris, J. R. (1998) *The Nurture Assumption*. London: Bloomsbury.

Hartl, D. L. (1980) *Principles of Population Genetics*. Sunderland, Mass.: Sinauer Associates.

Harvey, D. (1989) *The Urban Experience*. Baltimore: Johns Hopkins University Press.

Hayes, R. O. (1975) "Female Genital Mutilation, Fertility Control, Women's Roles, and the Patrilineage in Modern Sudan: A Functional Analysis." *American Ethnologist* 2:617–633.

Henin, R. A. (1981) *Fertility, Infertility, and Sub-fertility in Eastern Africa*. International Union for the Scientific Study of Population Conference Proceedings, Manila, 1981. Liege: Ordiah Editions, 667–697.

Herdt, G. (ed.). (1982) *Rituals of Manhood: Male Initiation in Papua New Guinea*. Berkeley: University of California Press.

Hicks, E. K. (1982, 1993, 1996) *Infibulation: Female Mutilation in Islamic Northeastern Africa*. New Brunswick: Transaction Publishers.

Hite, S. (1976) *The Hite Report: A Nationwide Study of Female Sexuality*. New York: Dell.

Holding, E. M. (1942) "Women's Institutions and the African Church." *International Review of Missions* 31:296–297.

hooks, b. (1984) *Feminist Theory from Margin to Center.* Boston: Southend Press.

Hosken, F. (1976) "Female Circumcision and Fertility in Africa." *Women and Health* 1:3–11.

———. (1978) "The Epidemiology of Female Genital Mutilations." *Tropical Doctor* 8:150–156.

———. (1981) "Female Genital Mutilation and Human Rights." *Feminist Issues* (Summer): 3–23.

———. (1982, 1993) *The Hosken Report: Genital and Sexual Mutilation of Females.* Lexington, Mass.: Women's International Network News.

Huddleston, C. E. (1949) "Female Circumcision in the Sudan." *The Lancet* 1:626.

IAC (Inter-African Committee). (1995) *Female Genital Mutilation in Nigeria.* Inter-African Committee, Nigeria.

———. (1997) *Female Genital Mutilation in Nigeria.* IAC (Nigeria) Monograph Series on Harmful and Beneficial Traditional Practices in Nigeria, No. 1. Ibadan, Nigeria: Ibadan University Press.

Ibrahim, F. A. (1972) *Hassadona khilal ishrin Amann.* (Our harvest in twenty years). Khartoum: Karmal Press.

Imathiu, I. (1990) "Wives in Circumcision Ordeal." *Daily Nation*, September 19, 3.

Inhorn, M. C., and K. A. Buss. (1993) "Infertility, Infection, and Iatrogenesis in Egypt: The Anthropological Epidemiology of Blocked Tubes." *Medical Anthropology* 15:217–244.

Jackson, M., and I. Karp (eds.). (1990) *Personhood and Agency: The Experience of Self and Other in African Cultures.* Stockholm: Almqvist and Wiksell International.

James, S. (1998) "Shades of Othering: Reflections on Female Circumcision/Genital Mutilation." *Signs* 23:1031–1048.

Jaulin, R. (1967) *Le mort Sara.* Paris: Plon.

Joseph, C. (1996) "Compassionate Accountability: An Embodied Consideration of Female Genital Mutilation." *The Journal of Psychohistory* 24:2–17.

Kameldy, R. (1964) "Le canton Maro." Unpublished manuscript.

Kamunchuluh, J. T. S. (1975) "The Meru Participation in Mau Mau." *Kenya Historical Review* 3:193–216.

Kanogo, T. (1987) *Squatters and the Roots of Mau Mau, 1905–63.* London: James Currey.

Kanté, N., with the collaboration of Pierre Erny. (1993) *Forgerons d'Afrique Noire: Transmission des savoirs traditionnels en pays malinké.* Paris: L'Harmattan.

Kashif, H. (1994) *Elharka Elnisaia fi el Sudan* (The women's movement in the Sudan). Khartoum: Khartoum University Press.

Kassindja, F., and L. M. Bashir. (1998) *Do They Hear You When You Cry?* New York: Delacorte Press.

Keesing, R. (1982) "Introduction." In G. Herdt (ed.), *Rituals of Manhood: Male Initiation in Papua New Guinea.* Berkeley: University of California Press.

Kéita, A. (1975) *La vie d'Aoua Kéita racontée par elle-même.* Paris: Présence Africaine.

Kellner, N. (1993) "Under the Knife: Female Genital Mutilations as Child Abuse." *Journal of Juvenile Law* 14:118–132.

Kelly, T. (1996) "Doctor Fights Ban on Circumcising Girls." *Seattle Times*, June 6, B3.

Kennedy, J. G. (1970) "Circumcision and Excision in Egyptian Nubia." *Man* 5:175–191.

Kenyatta, J. (1965 [1938]) *Facing Mt. Kenya: The Tribal Life of the Kikuyu.* New York: Vintage Books.

Kere, L. A., and I. Toposiba. (1994) "Charity Will Not Liberate Women: Female Genital Mutilation in Burkina Faso." In *Private Decisions, Public Debates: Women, Reproduction and Population.* London: Panos.

Khan, S. (1995) "The Veil as a Site of Struggle." *Canadian Woman Studies* 15:146–151.

Kheir, E.-H. H. M., S. Kumar, and A. R. Cross. (1991) "Female Circumcision: Attitudes and Practices in Sudan." *Demographic and Health Survey World Conference Proceedings,* vol. 3. Calverton, Md.: Macro International, 1697–1717.

Kirby, V. (1987) "On the Cutting Edge: Feminism and Clitoridectomy." *Australian Feminist Studies* 5:35–55.

Knudsen, C. O. (1994) *The Falling Dawadawa Tree: Female Circumcision in Developing Ghana.* Hojbjerg, Denmark: Intervention Press.

Kogongar, G. J. (n.d.) "Introduction a la vie et a l'histoire precoloniales des populations Sara du Tchad." These pour le doctorat, Université de Paris, Paris.

Konnor, M. (1990) "Mutilation in the Name of Tradition." Review of *Prisoners of Ritual: An Odyssey into Female Genital Circumcision in Africa,* by H. Lightfoot-Klein. *New York Times Book Review,* April 15, 5.

Kopytoff, I., and S. Miers. (1977) "African 'Slavery' and an Institution of Marginality." In S. Miers and I. Kopytoff (eds.), *Slavery in Africa.* Madison: University of Wisconsin Press.

Koso-Thomas, O. (1987) *The Circumcision of Women: A Strategy for Eradication.* London: Zed Press.

Kratz, C. (1994) *Affecting Performance: Meaning, Movement, and Experience in Okiek Women's Initiation.* Washington, D.C.: Smithsonian Institution Press.

La Violette, A. (1995) "Women Craft Specialists in Jenne: The Manipulation of Mande Social Categories." In D. C. Conrad and B. E. Frank (eds.), *Status and Identity in West Africa: Nyamakalaw of Mande.* Bloomington and Indianapolis: Indiana University Press.

Lamizana, M. (1995) Comite National de lutte contré la pratique de l'excision. *Update on female genital mutilation in Burkina Faso: Report of the Second Annual Interagency Working Group Meeting on Female Genital Mutilation.* New York: RAINBOW.

Lane, S. D., and R. A. Rubinstein. (1996) "Judging the Other: Responding to Traditional Female Genital Surgeries." *Hastings Center Report* 26:31–40.

Larsen, U. (1989) "A Comparative Study of the Levels and the Differentials of Sterility in Cameroon, Kenya, and Sudan." In R. Lesthaege (ed.), *Reproduction and Social Organization in sub-Saharan Africa.* Berkeley: University of California Press.

———. (1994) "Sterility in Sub-Saharan Africa." *Population Studies* 48:459–475.

———. (1995) "Differentials in Infertility in Cameroon and Nigeria." *Population Studies* 49:329–346.

Last, M. (1985) "The Early Kingdoms of the Nigerian Savanna." In J. F. A. Ajayi and Michael Crowder (eds.), *History of West Africa,* 3rd ed. New York: Longman.

Laughton, W. H. (1938) "An Introductory Study of the Meru People." M.A. thesis, Cambridge University.

Laycock, H. T. (1950) "Surgical Aspects of Female Circumcision in Somaliland." *East African Medical Journal* 27:445–450.

Leakey, L. S. B. (1931) "The Kikuyu Problem of the Initiation of Girls." *Journal of the Royal Anthropological Institute of Great Britain and Ireland* 61:277–285.

Leigh, J. (1997) "The Agony of Daphne Pratt." *New African* (January): 28.

Lenzi, E. (1970) "Damage Caused by Infibulation and Infertility." *Acta European Fertility* 2:47–58.

Leonard, L. (1996) "Female Circumcision in Southern Chad: Origins, Meaning and Current Practice." *Social Science and Medicine* 43:255–263.

Lerner, G. (1986) *The Creation of Patriarchy.* Oxford: Oxford University Press.

Lewis, H. (1995) "Between Irua and 'Female Genital Mutilation': Feminist Human Rights Discourse and the Cultural Divide." *Harvard Human Rights Journal* 8 (Spring): 1–55.

Lewis, J. M. (1994) *Blood and Bone: The Call of Kinship in Somali Society.* Lawrenceville, N.J.: Red Sea Press.

Lightfoot-Klein, H. (1989) *Prisoners of Ritual: An Odyssey into Female Genital Circumcision in Africa.* New York: Harrington Park Press.

Locoh, T. (1998) "Pratiques, opinions et attitudes en matière d'éxcision en Afrique." *Population* 6:1227–1240.

Lowenstein, L. F. (1978) "Attitudes and Attitude Differences to Female Genital Mutilation in the Sudan: Is There Change on the Horizon?" *Social Science and Medicine* 12:417–421.

Lutkehaus, N. C., and P. B. Roscoe. (1995) *Gender Rituals: Female Initiation in Melanesia.* New York: Routledge.

Lyons, H. (1981) "Anthropologists, Moralities, and Relativities: The Problem of Genital Mutilations." *Canadian Review of Sociology and Anthropology* 18:499–518.

MacCormack, C. (1972) "Mende and Sherbro Women in High Office." *Canadian Journal of African Studies* 6:151–164.

———. (1979) "Sande: The Public Face of Secret Society." In B. Jules-Rosette (ed.), *New Religions of Africa.* Norwood: Ablex.

———. (1980) "Proto-social to Adult: A Sherbro Transformation." In C. MacCormack and M. Strathern (eds.), *Nature, Culture and Gender.* Cambridge: Cambridge University Press.

MacCormack, C. (ed.). (1994a) *Ethnography of Fertility and Birth.* Prospect Heights, Ill.: Waveland Press.

MacCormack, C. (1994b) "Introduction: Biological, Cultural and Social Meanings of Fertility and Birth." In C. MacCormack (ed.), *Ethnography of Fertility and Birth.* Prospect Heights, Ill.: Waveland Press.

MacCormack, C., and M. Strathern (eds.). (1980) *Nature, Culture and Gender.* Cambridge: Cambridge University Press.

Mackie, G. (1996) "Ending Footbinding and Infibulation: A Convention Account." *American Sociological Review* 61:999–1017.

Macpherson, R. (1970) *The Presbyterian Church in Kenya.* Nairobi: Presbyterian Church Press.

Magnant, J. P. (1977) "Quelques grands types de systemes fonciers traditionells au Tchad." Unpublished manuscript.

Mammo, A., and P. Morgan. (1986) "Childlessness in Rural Ethiopia." *Population and Development Review* 12:533–546.

Manstead, A. R., and Miles Hewstone. (1995) *The Blackwell Encyclopedia of Social Psychology.* Oxford: Blackwell.

Maran, R. (1921) *Batouala.* Paris: Albin Michel.

Masland, T. (1999) "The Ritual of Pain." *Newsweek,* int. ed., July 5. 45–46.

Mbiti, J. (1990) *African Religions and Philosophy.* London: Heinemann Educational Books.

McElroy, A., and P. K. Townsend. (1989) *Medical Anthropology in an Ecological Perspective.* Boulder, Colo.: Westview Press.

McGarrahan, P. (1991) "The Violence in Female Circumcision." *Medical Anthropology Quarterly* 5:269–270.

McLean, S. (1980) *Female Circumcision, Excision and Infibulation: The Facts and Proposals for Change.* London: Minority Rights Group.

McNaughton, P. R. (1988) *The Mande Blacksmiths: Knowledge, Power and Art in West Africa.* Bloomington and Indianapolis: Indiana University Press.

Meek, C. K. (1925). *The Northern Tribes of Nigeria.* Oxford: Oxford University Press.

Meinardus, O. (1967) "Mythological, Historical and Sociological Aspects of the Practice of Female Circumcision Among the Egyptians." *Acta Ethnographica Academiae Scientiarum Hungaricae* 16:387–397.

Melching, M. (1999) *Breakthrough in Senegal: The Process Used to End Female Genital Cutting in 31 Villages in Senegal.* New York: Population Council.

Melly, J. M. (1935) "Infibulation." *The Lancet* 2.

Meniru, G. I. (1991) "Female Circumcision Among the Igbos of Nigeria: Trends." *Nigerian Journal of Medicine* 1:55–60.

———. (1994) "Female Genital Mutilation (female circumcision)." *British Journal of Obstetrics and Gynaecology* 101:832.

Meuwissen, J. H. J. M. (1966) "Human Infertility in West Africa." *Tropical and Geographic Medicine* 18:147–152.

Miers, S., and I. Kopytoff (eds.). (1977) *African Slavery: Historical and Anthropological Perspectives.* Madison: University of Wisconsin Press.

Miles, A. (1998) "North American Feminisms/Global Feminisms: Contradictory or Complementary?" In O. Knaemeka (ed.), *Sisterhood, Feminisms and Power: From Africa to the Diaspora.* Trenton, N.J.: Africa World Press.

Miller, K. (1998) "Circumcision Ritual Creates Cultural Conflict for Somali Women." *Minneapolis Star Tribune,* May 24, A1, A10.

Ministry of Planning, Democratic Republic of Sudan. (1979) *Sudan Fertility Survey 1978,* Standard Recode, Version 5 MROF. London: International Statistical Institute. Revised 1982.

M'Inoti, P. (c. 1930) "Asili ya Wameru na Tabia Zao" (The Origin of the Meru and their Customs). Unpublished manuscript.

Mohanty, C. (1991) "Under Western Eyes: Feminist Scholarship and Colonial Discourses." In C. Mohanty (ed.), *Third World Women and the Politics of Feminism.* Bloomington: Indiana University Press.

Moore, H. (1988) *Feminism and Anthropology.* Minneapolis: University of Minnesota Press.

Morris, R. (1996) "The Culture of Female Circumcision." *Advances in Nursing Science* 19:43–53.

Morsy, S. (1991a) "Spirit Possession in Egyptian Ethnomedicine." In I. M. Lewis, A. S. Ahmen, and S. Hurreiz (eds.), *Women's Medicine: The Zar-Bori Cult in Africa and Beyond.* Edinburgh: Edinburgh University Press for International African Institute, 189–208.

———. (1991b) "Safeguarding Women's Bodies: The White Man's Burden Medicalized." *Medical Anthropology Quarterly* 5:19–23.

Murdock, G. P. (1959) *Africa: Its Peoples and Their Cultural History.* New York: Mc-Graw-Hill.

———. (1967) "Ethnographic Atlas: A Summary." *Ethnology* 6:1–36.

Murray, J. (1974) "The Kikuyu Female Circumcision Controversy, with Special Reference to Church Missionary Society's 'Sphere of Influence.'" Ph.D. diss., University of California, Los Angeles.

Mustafa, A. Z. (1966) "Female Circumcision and Infibulation in the Sudan." *Journal of Obstetrics and Gynecology, British Commonwealth* 73:302–306.

Myers, R. A., F. I. Omorodion, A. E. Isenalumhe, and G. I. Akenzua. (1985) "Circumcision: Its Nature and Practice." *Social Science and Medicine* 21:581–588.

MYWO (Maendeleo Ya Wanawake Organization). (1991) *Harmful Traditional Practices That Affect the Health of the Women and Their Children.* Nairobi: MYWO.

Nabia, A. (1991) *L'éxcision feminine.* N'Djamena, Chad: UNICEF.

Nadel, S. F. (1942) *A Black Byzantium: The Kingdom of Nupe in Nigeria.* Oxford: Oxford University Press.

Nathan, M. A., E. M. Fratkin, and E. A. Roth. (1996) "Sedentism and Child Health Among Rendille Pastoralists of Northern Kenya." *Social Science and Medicine* 43:503–515.

N'Diaye, B. (1970) *Les Castes au Mali.* Bamako: Éditions Populaires.

Négué, F. K., and J. Kemoral. (1997) *Initiation feminine: Resultats des recherches sur les possibilites d'amelioration de l'initiation feminine dans le Moyen-Chari.* Sarh, Chad: Cellule Regional CONA-CIAF de Sarh.

Ng'ang'a, L. (1995) "Female Genital Mutilation. Activities in Africa: Focus on Kenya Using a Case Story." In *Report from the Seminar on Female Genitial Mutilation.* Arranged by KULU—Women and Development and Ministry of Foreign Affairs. Copenhagen, Denmark: DANIDA.

Ngoussou, N. (n.d.) *Les Sara-Kaba de Ngague.* Sarh, Chad: Centre d'Études Linguistiques.

NPC (National Population Commission). (1994) *Census '91: National Summary.* Lagos: National Population Commission.

Nthamburi, Z. J. (1982) *A History of the Methodist Church in Kenya.* Nairobi: Uzima Press.

Nypan, A. (1991) "Revival of Female Circumcision: A Case of Neo-traditionalism." In K. A. Stolen and M. Vaa (eds.), *Gender and Change in Developing Countries.* Oslo: Norwegian University Press, 39–65.

Obermeyer, C. M. (1999) "Female Genital Surgeries." *Medical Anthropology Quarterly* 13:79–106.

Obiora, L. A. (1997) "Bridges and Barricades: Rethinking Polemics and Intransigence in the Campaign Against Female Circumcision." *Case Western Reserve Law Review* 47:275–378.

OECD (Organization for Economic Cooperation and Development). (1996) *Geographical Distribution of Financial Flows to Aid Recipients 1992–1996.* Paris: Organization for Economic Co-operation and Development Publications.

Ogbu, M. A. (1997) "Comment on Obiora's Bridges and Barricades." *Case Western Law Review* 47:411–422.

Ogiamien, T. B. E. (1988) "A Legal Framework to Eradicate Female Circumcision." *Medicine Science and Law* 28:115–119.

Onadeko, M. O. , and L. V. Adekunle. (1985) "Female Circumcision in Nigeria: A Fact or a Farce?" *Journal of Tropical Pediatrics* 31:180–184.

Orde Browne, G. St. J. (1913) "Circumcision Ceremonies Among the Amwimbe." *Man* 79:137–140.

———. (1915) "Circumcision Ceremony in Chuka." *Man* 39:65–68.

Orubuloye, I. O. (1981) "Abstinence as a Method of Birth Control." Changing African Family Monograph no. 8, Australian National University, Canberra.

Orubuloye, I. O., J. Caldwell, and P. Caldwell. (1993) "The Role of Religious Leaders in Changing Sexual Behaviour in Southwest Nigeria in an Era of AIDS." *Health Transition Review,* supplement to vol. 3, *Sexual Networking and HIV/AIDS in West Africa,* 93–104.

Ostrom, C. (1996a) "Harborview Debates Issue of Circumcision of Muslim Girls." *Seattle Times,* December 9, 1.

———. (1996b) "Is Form of Circumcision Outlawed? Procedure at Harborview Under Review." *Seattle Times,* October 14, B3.

Ottenberg, S. (1989) *Boyhood Rituals in an African Society: An Interpretation.* Seattle: University of Washington Press.

———. (1994a) "Initiation." In P. Bock (ed.), *Handbook of Psychological Anthropology.* Westport: Praeger Publishers.

———. (1994b) "Secret Societies among the Bafodea Limba." In T. Blakely, W. van Beek, and D. Thomson (eds.), *Religion in Africa: Experience and Expression.* London: James Curry.

Page, H. J., and R. Lesthaeghe (eds.). (1981) *Child-spacing in Tropical Africa.* London: Academic Press.

Parker, M. (1995) "Rethinking Female Circumcision." *Africa* 65:506–523.

Parrinder, G. (1996) *African Mythology.* London: Chancellor Press.

Parsons, R. (1964) *Religion in an African Society.* Leiden: J. Brill.

Paul, R. A. (1992) "Bettelheim's Contribution to Anthropology." In M. Szajnberg (ed.), *Educating the Emotions: Bruno Bettelheim and Psychoanalytic Development.* New York: Plenum Press.

Paulson, T. (1996) "Harborview, Somalis Try to Compromise on Female Circumcision." *Seattle Post-Intelligencer,* September 13, 1.

Pedersen, S. (1991) "National Bodies, Unspeakable Acts: The Sexual Politics of Colonial Policymaking." *Journal of Modern History* 63:647–680.

Petchesky, R., and K. Judd (eds.). (1998) *Negotiating Reproductive Rights: Women's Perspectives Across Countries and Cultures.* New York: Zed Books.

Presley, C. A. (1992) *Kikuyu Women, the Mau Mau Rebellion, and Social Change in Kenya.* Boulder, Colo.: Westview Press.

Quammen, D. (1996) *The Song of the Dodo: Island Biogeography in an Age of Extinctions.* New York: Touchstone Books.

Rasmussen, S. J. (1997) *The Poetics and Politics of Tuareg Aging: Life Course and Personal Destiny in Niger.* DeKalb: Northern Illinois University Press.

Reissman, C. (1987) "When Gender Is Not Enough: Women Interviewing Women." *Gender and Society* 1:172–207.

Renteln, A. D. (1988) "Relativism and the Search for Human Rights." *American Anthropologist* 90:56–68.

Richards, A. (1982 [1956]) *Chisungu: A Girl's Initiation Ceremony Among the Bemba of Zambia.* London: Routledge.

Richards, P. (1996) *Fighting for the Rainforest: War, Youth and Resources in Sierra Leone.* Portsmouth: Heinemann.

Riesman, P. (1992) *First Find Yourself a Good Mother: The Construction of Self in Two African Communities.* New Brunswick: Rutgers University Press.

Robertson, C. (1996) "Grassroots in Kenya: Women, Genital Mutilation, and Collective Action, 1920–1990." *Signs* (Spring):615–642.

Ruminjo, J. (1992) "Circumcision in Women." *East African Medical Journal* (September):477–478.

Rushwan, H. (1980) "Etiological Factors in Pelvic Inflammatory Disease in Sudanese Women." *American Journal of Obstetrics and Gynecology* 138:877–879.

Rushwan, H., C. Slot, A. El Dareer, and N. Bushra. (1983) *Female Circumcision in the Sudan: Prevalence, Complications, Attitudes and Changes.* Khartoum: Faculty of Medicine, University of Khartoum.

El Saadawi, N. (1980) *The Hidden Face of Eve.* Boston: Beacon Press.

Said, E. (1989) "Representing the Colonized: Anthropology's Interlocutors." *Critical Inquiry* 15:205–227.

Sami, I. R. (1986) "Female Circumcision with Special Reference to the Sudan." *Annals of Tropical Medicine* 6:99–115.

Sanderson, L. P. (1981) *Against the Mutilation of Women: The Struggle to End Unnecessary Suffering.* London: Ithaca Press.

Sargent, C. (1989) *Maternity, Medicine, and Power: Reproductive Decisions in Urban Benin.* Berkeley: University of California Press.

———. (1991) "Confronting Patriarchy: The Potential for Advocacy in Medical Anthropology." *Medical Anthropology Quarterly* 5:24–25.

Schaffer, M., and C. Cooper. (1987 [1980]) *Mandinko: The Ethnography of a West African Holy Land.* Prospect Heights, Ill.: Waveland Press.

Scheper-Hughes, N. (1991) "Virgin Territory: The Male Discovery of the Clitoris." *Medical Anthropology Quarterly* 5:25–28.

———. (1995) "The Primacy of the Ethical: Propositions for a Militant Anthropology." *Current Anthropology* 36:409–420.

Schroeder, P. (1994) "Female Genital Mutilation: A Form of Child Abuse." *New England Journal of Medicine* 331:739–740.

Schwartz, R. L. (1994) "Multiculturalism, Medicine, and the Limits of Autonomy: The Practice of Female Circumcision." *Cambridge Quarterly of Healthcare Ethics* 3: 431–437.

SDHS. (1991) *Sudan Demographic and Health Surveys 1989/1990.* Khartoum, Sudan, and Columbia, Md.: Department of Statistics, Ministry of Economic and National Planning and Institute for Resource Development/Macro International.

Seddon, J. S. (1993) "Possible or Impossible? A Tale of Two Worlds in One Country." *Yale Journal of Law and Feminism* 5:265–287.

Sequira, J. H. (1931) "Female Circumcision and Infibulation." *The Lancet* 2:1054–1056.

Shandall, A. (1967) "Circumcision and Infibulation of Females." *Sudan Medical Journal* 5:178–212.

Shaw, C. M. (1995) *Colonial Inscriptions: Gender, Race and Class in Colonial Kenya.* Minneapolis: University of Minnesota Press.

Shell-Duncan, B. (in press) "The Medicalization of Female 'Circumcision': Harm Reduction or Promotion of a Dangerous Practice?" *Social Science and Medicine.*

Shell-Duncan, B., W. O. Obiero, and L. A. Muruli. (1996) "Health Consequences of Female Circumcision in Northern Kenya." Paper presented at the annual meeting of the American Association for the Advancement of Science.

Shweder, R. (1996) "The View from Manywheres." *Anthropology Newsletter.*

Singateh, S. (1985) *Female Circumcision: The Gambian Experience.* Banjul, the Gambia: Gambia Women's Bureau.

Singer, M. (1993) "A Rejoinder to Wiley's Critique of Critical Medical Anthropology." *Medical Anthropology Quarterly* 7:185–191.

Slack, A. T. (1988) "Female Circumcision: A Critical Appraisal." *Human Rights Quarterly* 10:437–486.

Skramstad, H. (1990) "The Fluid Meanings of Female Circumcision in a Multiethnic Context in Gambia: Distribution of Knowledge and Linkages to Sexuality." Working Paper, Development, Research and Action Programme, Chr. Michelson Institute, Bergen, Norway.

Sonko-Godwin, P. (1994) *Ethnic Groups of the Senegambia: A Brief History.* Banjul, the Gambia: Sunrise Publishers.

Stern, A. (1997) "Female Genital Mutilation: United States Asylum Laws Are in Need of Reform." *Journal of Gender and the Law* 6:89–111.

Strathern, M. (1987) "Making Incomplete." Draft paper for symposium, "Female Initiation in the Pacific."

Talbot, A. (1992) *Mali, développement, démocratie: Transition vers une démocratie conviviale.* UNESCO, Secteur des Sciences Sociales et Humaines.

Talle, A. (1993) "Transforming Women into 'Pure' Agnates: Aspects of Female Infibulation in Somalia." In V. Broch-Due, I. Rudie, and T. Bleie (eds.), *Carved Flesh, Cast Selves: Gender Symbols and Social Practices.* Oxford: Berg.

Tamari, T. (1991) "The Development of Caste Systems in West Africa." *Journal of African History* 32:221–250.

Thiam, Awa. (1986) *Black Sisters, Speak Out: Feminism and Oppression in Black Africa.* London: Pluto.

Thomas, L. M. (1996) "'*Ngaitana* (I Will Circumcise Myself)': The Gender and Generational Politics of the 1956 Ban on Clitoridectomy in Meru, Kenya." *Gender and History* 8:338–363.

———. (1998) "Imperial Concerns and 'Women's Affairs': State Efforts to Regulate Clitoridectomy and Eradicate Abortion in Meru, Kenya, c. 1910–1950." *Journal of African History* 39:121–145.

Toubia, N. (1985) "The Social and Political Implications of Female Circumcision: The Case of Sudan." In E. W. Fernea (ed.), *Women and the Family in the Middle East: New Voices of Change.* Austin: University of Texas Press.

———. (1988) *Women and Health in Sudan.* London: Zed Press.

———. (1993) "Female Genital Mutilation: A Call for Global Action." New York: Rainbow/Women Ink.

———. (1994) "Female Circumcision as a Public Health Issue." *New England Journal of Medicine* 331:712–716.

———. (1998) *Female Genital Mutilation: An Overview.* Geneva: World Health Organization.

Toubia, N., and S. Izette. (1998) *Female Genital Mutilation: An Overview.* Geneva: World Health Organization (online edition).

Touray, I. (1993) "Reconceptualising Traditional Practices in the Gambia: The Case of Female Genital Mutilation." Unpublished master's thesis. The Hague.

Touré, Y., and Y. F. Koné. (1997) *Vaincre l'excision au Mali: Quelle dynamique pour l'action dans les zones d'intervention du Center Djoliba?* Bamako: Center Djoliba.

Touré, Y., Y. F. Koné, and T. Diarra. (1997) *L'excision au Mali: Réalitiés et perspectives de lutte.* Bamako: Center Djoliba.

Traoré, M. (1980) *Atlas du Mali.* Paris: Éditions Jeune Afrique.

UN Development Programme, in collaboration with Central Statistics Department. (1997) *The Gambia: National Human Development Report.* Banjul, the Gambia.

UN Economic and Social Council. (1991) *Review of Further Developments in Fields with Which the Sub-Commission Has Been Concerned: Study on Traditional Practices Affecting the Health of Women and Children.*

UN Fourth World Conference on Women. (1995) *Report of the Fourth World Conference on Women.*

UN General Assembly. (1959) *Declaration of the Rights of the Child.* Geneva, Resolution 1386, UN GAOR.

———. (1979) *Convention on the Elimination of All Forms of Discrimination Against Women.* Geneva, Resolution 180, UN GAOR.

———. (1984) 39th Session, Supplement 51. *Convention Against Torture and Other Cruel, Inhuman or Degrading Treatment or Punishment.* Geneva, Resolution 46, UN GAOR.

UN Sub-Commission for the Prevention of Discrimination and the Protection of Minorities, Special Working Group on Traditional Practices. (1986) *Report of the Working Group on Traditional Practices Affecting the Health of Women and Children.* Geneva.

UNICEF. (1998) *The Progress of Nations.* New York: United Nations Children's Fund.

Urdang, S. (1979) *Fighting Two Colonialisms: Women in Guinea-Bissau.* New York: Monthly Review Press.

U.S. Department of State. (1994) *Country Reports on Human Rights Practices for 1993.* Committee on Foreign Affairs, U.S. House of Representatives, and the Committee on Foreign Relations, U.S. Senate, 103d Cong. 2d sess.

van der Kwaak, A. (1992) "Female Circumcision and Gender Identity: A Questionable Alliance?" *Social Science and Medicine* 35:777–787.

van Gennep, A. V. (1960) *The Rites of Passage.* Chicago: University of Chicago Press.

Verzin, J. A. (1975) "Sequelae of Female Circumcision." *Tropical Doctor* 5:163–169.

Vizedom, M. (1976) *Rites and Relationships: Rites of Passage and Contemporary Anthropology.* London: Sage Publications.

Walder, R. (1995) "Why the Problem Continues in Britain." *British Medical Journal* 310:1593.

Walker, A. (1992) *Possessing the Secret of Joy.* New York: Harcourt Brace Jovanovich.

———. (1997) "You Have All Seen." *Ms.*: 54–59.

Walker, A., and P. Pramar. (1993) *Warrior Marks: Female Genital Mutilation and the Sexual Blinding of Women.* New York: Harcourt Brace.

Walley, C. J. (1997) "Searching for 'Voices': Feminism, Anthropology, and the Global Debate over Female Genital Operations." *Cultural Anthropology* 12:405–438.

Weed, E (ed.). (1989) *Coming to Terms: Feminism, Theory, Politics.* New York and London: Routledge.

White, L. (1990) "Separating the Men from the Boys: Construction of Gender, Sexuality, and Terrorism in Central Kenya, 1939–59." *International Journal of African Historical Studies* 23:1–25.

WHO (World Health Organization). (1979) *Traditional Practices Affecting the Health of Women and Children.* Geneva: World Health Organization.

———. (1982) *Female Circumcision: Statement of WHO Position and Activities.* Geneva: World Health Organization.

———. (1992) "Female Circumcision." *European Journal of Obstetrics and Gynecology and Reproductive Biology* 45:153–154.

———. (1996) *Female Genital Mutilation: Information Kit.* Geneva: World Health Organization.

Widstrand, C. G. (1964) "Female Infibulation." Occasional Papers of *Studia Ethnographica Upsaliensia* 20:95–124.

Winkel, E. (1995) "A Muslim Perspective on Female Circumcision." *Women and Health* 23:1–7.

Wipper, A. (1975–1976) "The *Maendeleo ya Wanawake* Movement in the Colonial Period: The Canadian Connection, Mau Mau, Embroidery, and Agriculture." *Rural Africana* 29:196–214.

Women's Bureau of the Gambia. (1991) *Knowledge, Attitude and Practice Study.* Banjul, the Gambia: Monitoring and Evaluation Unit.

World Bank. (1996) *World Development Report 1996.* New York: Oxford University Press.

———. (1997) *African Development Indicators.* Washington, D.C.: International Bank for Reconstruction and Development/World Bank.

Worsley, A. (1938) "Infibulation and Female Circumcision: A Study of a Little Known Custom." *Journal of Obstetrics and Gynaecology of the British Empire* 45:686–691.

Zahan, D. (1963) *La dialectique du verbe chez les Bambara.* Paris: Mouton.

———. (1979) *The Religion, Spirituality, and Thought of Traditional Africa.* Chicago: University of Chicago Press.

The Contributors

ROGAIA MUSTAFA ABUSHARAF, Pembroke Center for Teaching and Research on Women, Brown University.

FUAMBAI AHMADU, Department of Anthropology, London School of Economics and Political Science.

DEBORAH BALK, CIESIN, Columbia University.

JOHN C. CALDWELL, Health Transition Centre, National Centre for Epidemiology and Population Health, Australian National University.

PAT CALDWELL, Health Transition Centre, National Centre for Epidemiology and Population Health, Australian National University.

CLAUDIE GOSSELIN, Department of Anthropology, University of Toronto.

ELLEN GRUENBAUM, College of Social Sciences, California State University.

YLVA HERNLUND, Department of Anthropology, University of Washington.

MICHELLE C. JOHNSON, University of Illinois at Urbana-Champaign.

LORI LEONARD, School of Public Health, University of Texas–Houston.

GERRY MACKIE, Junior Research Fellow in Politics, St. John's College, Oxford.

MAIRO USMAN MANDARA, Department of Obstetrics and Gynecology, Ahmadu Bello University Teaching Hospital, Nigeria.

LEUNITA AUKO MURULI, Institute of African Studies, University of Nairobi.

WALTER OBUNGU OBIERO, Southeast Michigan Council of Government.

I. O. ORUBULOYE, Department of Sociology, The State University, Nigeria.

BETTINA SHELL-DUNCAN, Department of Anthropology, University of Washington.

LYNN THOMAS, Department of History, University of Washington.

Index

About the Book

Though the issue of female genital cutting (FGC), or "circumcision," has become a nexus for debates on cultural relativism, human rights, patriarchal oppression, racism, and Western imperialism, the literature has been separated into diverse fields of study. In contrast, this volume brings together contributors from the fields of anthropology, public health, political science, demography, history, and epidemiology to critically examine current debates and initiatives and to explore the role that scholars can and should—or should not—play in approaching the issue.

In case studies from nine African countries where FGC is traditionally and currently performed, the contributors evaluate the impact of international efforts to eliminate the practice. A focus on local reactions to external involvement underscores that the myriad programs fashioned to effect changes in FGC ritual and procedure must be initiated and supported by indigenous communities if they are to be lasting and effective.

BETTINA SHELL-DUNCAN is assistant professor of anthropology at the University of Washington. YLVA HERNLUND is a doctoral candidate in anthropology at the University of Washington.